Between Marriage and Divorce
Who Killed Sal Mineo?
What the Movies Made Me Do
This Crazy Thing Called Love

FAMILY CIRCLE

FAMILY CIRCLE

*The Boudins
and the Aristocracy
of the Left*

SUSAN BRAUDY

 ALFRED A. KNOPF   NEW YORK   2003

THIS IS A BORZOI BOOK
PUBLISHED BY ALFRED A. KNOPF

Grateful acknowledgment is made to the following for
permission to reprint previously published material:
Michael Boudin: Excerpts from the poems "Creation,"
"Mother/Daughter," and "Thank You Papa" by Jean Boudin.
Reprinted by permission of Michael Boudin.
John Castellucci: Excerpts from *The Big Dance* by
John Castellucci. Copyright © 1986 by John Castellucci.
Reprinted by permission of the author.
Ms. Magazine: Excerpts from "Sing a Battle Song" by
Kathy Boudin from *Ms. Magazine* (August 1976).
Reprinted by permission of *Ms. Magazine*.
Jonah Raskin: Excerpts from *Out of the Whale* by
Jonah Raskin. Reprinted by permission of the author.

Library of Congress Cataloging-in-Publication Data
Braudy, Susan.
Family circle : the Boudins and the aristocracy of the
left / Susan Braudy.—1st ed.
p.   cm.
Includes bibliographical references and index.
ISBN 0-679-43294-9
1. Boudin, Kathy.   2. Boudin, Leonard, 1912–   3. Boudin,
Jean.   4. Left-wing extremists—United States—Biography.
5. Radicalism—United States.   I. Title.
HN90.R3B73 2003
322.4'2'092—dc21   [B]   2003052702

Manufactured in the United States of America
First Edition

In every government on earth there is some trace of human weakness, some germ of corruption, some degeneracy.

—THOMAS JEFFERSON

Contents

Contents

Illustrations

Preface

I first met Jean Roisman Boudin in 1974 at a crowded party for the publication of *A Book of Common Prayer*, by Joan Didion. It was the novel of the hour and loosely based on Jean's life. Jean announced to everyone that no character in Didion's book was based on Jean or on her daughter, Kathy. After all, wasn't her presence at the party proof enough of that since the book depicted a mother who, although like Jean in many ways, was utterly devastated by her daughter's radical acts. Of course by denying this bit of literary turf, Jean was actually claiming it.

Jean was still a beauty then, with the small, perfect shape of a silent movie star. Her dashing panama hat was a hand-me-down, she confided, from her brother. Although her conversation appeared to jump from subject to subject, she interrupted her flow deftly, like a jazz musician, one moment digging deep into pained truth, the next, employing stinging wit to jump away from it.

And despite the fact that Jean disparaged herself as an amateur ("I'm not a writer-writer"), I knew she had published two volumes of poems. When I told her that at Bryn Mawr College I had known her daughter, Kathy, Jean clasped my wrist with both hands and gazed at me warmly.

Kathy Boudin and I met in 1961. She was a freshman and I was a junior. Kathy's room was across a dreary Gothic hallway from mine at Rockefeller Hall. Next door to me that same year lived Diana "Das" Oughton, a debutante who poured tea from a silver pot with aplomb and who would be blown to smithereens nine years later in the town house bombing on Eleventh Street in Greenwich Village, an explosion that almost took Kathy's life as well.

I remember the way Kathy flushed beet red, as she excoriated me on that first meeting about not doing something about the sad lives of the elderly black maids in hair nets and starched gray uniforms who served meals and emptied ashtrays in our dormitory. I wilted. Kathy already possessed fully formed and condescending adult views on politics and power.

Soon afterward I was stunned when I read in the dorm sign-out book that Kathy was visiting the brilliant, scrappy journalist and government critic I. F. "Izzy" Stone, a man who apparently feared no one and who had achieved fame in the 1950s for fighting for the rights of people who were accused of having been members of the American Communist Party.

When I asked her about him, Kathy told me Stone was married to her mother's sister, Esther, and then walked away with the lowered eyes and restrained swagger of a teenager who is used to being admired. Kathy had no small talk. She dated professors. ("She loves brilliant older men and they love her," said a friend.) To someone like me, a scholarship student from Philadelphia, Kathy was far scarier than preppies like Das Oughton.

I stayed up all night on the verge of tears after learning that Kathy's good-looking, tousle-haired boyfriend, Michael, who strummed so poignantly on his guitar "This land is your land, this land is my land," was the son of Ethel and Julius Rosenberg. The couple had been executed ten years earlier by the U.S. government for spying for the Soviet Union. Michael Meeropol was a child of tragedy. How could he bear to live in the United States? What complex issues had Kathy been forced to deal with to be with him? ("Mike's more into the relationship than Kathy is," said a friend.)

Kathy continued to astound: she soon brought a second left-wing royal to the dorm. The former Socialist Party candidate for president, Norman Thomas, was bony and draped in black like a Presbyterian elder. He had, it turned out, narrowly beaten President John Kennedy in a mock presidential election at Kathy's progressive high school.

I had heard that Kathy's father was an important figure, a courageous lawyer who had won a Supreme Court battle that restored the black singer and theater star Paul Robeson's right to travel after the government accused him of being a communist and revoked his passport. Leonard Boudin and his law partner had also trooped around the country to defend scores of people accused of membership in the Communist Party by congressional subcommittees, school boards, and the U.S. Navy.

Leonard himself was soon invited by the Bryn Mawr political science department to lecture on the necessity of balancing individual freedoms against government authority. Listening to him, I resolved to become a constitutional lawyer too. As we filed out of Goodhart Hall, I was bewildered to hear that Kathy's older brother, Michael, was a conservative Republican. He was also reputed to be first in his class at Harvard Law School.

That night, just before dinner, I watched Leonard across the crowded lobby of our dorm. He resembled a pinwheel, shirttails escaping from his tailored navy suit as he spun from one adoring girl to another.

A month or so afterward, I heard Kathy arguing with her father on the telephone. She'd loathed her freshman year at Bryn Mawr and wanted to quit and go to work for her uncle Izzy's newsletter. "Izzy never graduated," she shouted.

I lost track of Kathy until 1968, when I saw her a few weeks after the Democratic national convention in Chicago, where to great effect, she had dropped a stink bomb on the carpet of the Hilton Hotel in protest of the Vietnam War. Now notorious, she didn't bother to say hello but asked me simply, "Are you with us, or are you a member of the pig press?" A watcher, not an actor, I replied.

In 1970, I cried as I read in the morning paper about Kathy fleeing naked from an exploding town house in Greenwich Village. The homemade bomb that was being made there had killed three young activists, including my former next-door neighbor at college, Diana Oughton. Das was identified only by a piece of skin from a finger. I took the subway downtown to see the sodden mess on West Eleventh Street. For me and many others, it signaled the end of something important. Our youth, our ambition to change the world for the better. The town house tragedy was the first time death brushed close.

At Swarthmore College, my brother had dated Cathlyn Wilkerson, the Quaker daughter of the town house owner. I went cold when I heard a few days later that the bomb on Eleventh Street that had exploded by accident was an antipersonnel bomb with nails in it—designed to kill people. According to the press, Kathy and Cathlyn were successfully continuing to elude police.

The "movement" was over. We were not going to be the generation that changed the world. Worse, it felt as if there was something sordid about our defeat.

During the next eleven years, I heard occasional news from mutual friends of Kathy's life as an underground radical, and the fact that she had an infant son. Then, I was horrified when in 1981, I saw a photograph of Kathy on the front page of the *New York Times*. No longer resembling the arrogant plump college girl I had known, she was too skinny, almost sick-looking, with her head down and her hands cuffed behind her back. She was wearing terry-cloth prison bedroom slippers. She had been arrested running away from a roadblock after participating in the holdup of a Brinks truck in Nyack, New York. Three people had been murdered during the course of the robbery, one of whom was a popular young black policeman named Waverly Brown.

I found I couldn't stop thinking about the strange twisting path of Kathy's life. What had been the forces driving her? A magna cum laude graduate of Bryn Mawr and a revered student leader, she was now in 1981 a bank robber and murderer.

Thinking about the possibility of writing a book, I went to see Jean Boudin in 1992 still filled with curiosity. Also visiting Jean was Bert Gross, one of her admirers since college days and a former member of President Franklin Roosevelt's brain trust on economics. We watched Jean gracefully warm her fingers around a cup of tea while talking on the telephone to her son, Michael. She was saying in a droll tone, "I'm having Thanksgiving 1992 with my daughter the prisoner, not my son the judge." Jean and Michael apparently did not see eye to eye on much of anything. Although Jean seemed all about feelings, Boudin family feuds coalesced around political issues. The previous Thanksgiving, according to Jean, she'd found it hard not to shout across the table: Okie dokie, Mr. Michael Boudin, you make a perfect stranger indeed! My son the retired litigator for AT&T! Sometimes, she said, his changeling nature frightened her, he was that alien in his beliefs and allegiances.

But Jean also liked to say that Michael was turning out to be the biggest genius in her exceptional family. "My son the rebel!" she said of him. Now teaching at Harvard Law School, Michael was also a judge of the prestigious United States Court of Appeals in Massachusetts, appointed by President George H. W. Bush. He was even described in a legal journal as a likely Supreme Court nominee—that is, if voters were to elect a conservative president.

Jean now informed Michael, "Darlingest, I'm needed elsewhere." She slammed down the phone and said in a harsh voice, "I've had enough of that."

Jean announced that Thanksgiving was special because it was the anniversary of her husband Leonard's terminal heart attack. He had died in 1989 at the age of seventy-nine, but he was still very alive to Jean. Jean explained what we already knew, that Leonard had been a sort of legal wizard. He was also, according to her, his own kind of hero, smarter than everyone else, a struggler against huge, malign forces. But Kathy had refused to admire Leonard; she wanted him to admire her. His clients had included Fidel Castro, the Socialist Workers Party, Daniel Ellsberg, Dr. Ben Spock, and finally his daughter, Kathy. (Kathy's twenty-years-to-life conviction for murder was a rare defeat for Leonard.) In fact, wherever he was, and with whomever, Leonard was always trying to win. His days had roiled with competitions. There would be that raw instant at first meeting when Leonard Boudin measured a man. Then he decided how to one-up him.

On Thanksgiving morning, 1992, Jean and I listened to the weather report on her portable radio. Jean was wearing a full painted skirt from Paris that Kathy had worn as a teenager. Jean and Kathy did not believe in "yours" or "mine," and, anyway, Kathy was never much for skirts. Jean buttoned her down coat—for her, a security blanket—and her snap-on galoshes. I helped pack her heart pills, blood pressure pills, and a turkey sandwich for the train, as well as one of her poems in progress. I was to wait outside Bedford Hills prison while Jean visited Kathy. Jean told me that Kathy had told her not to see me or to talk to me.

As we crossed St. Luke's Place, where the Boudins had lived for more than four decades, a truck braked sharply at Jean's heels. Frightened, Jean teetered on slushy ice. A second later, she told me that a tickle of electricity had just jumped from her head down to her ankles. She explained rather offhandedly that ever since her visits in 1953 to "the fancy lunatic asylum," her body sizzled unexpectedly with memory of electric shock treatments she had undergone.

The Westchester commuter train was empty. Most Thanksgiving travelers were eating turkey. Jean took a moment to admire her own breath puffs. "Eighty-one," she said, throwing her scarf round and round her neck, "and traveling light."

Soon, though, she sighed. Visiting Kathy submerged Jean in sadness, although Jean had long since gotten over her fury at Kathy. Psychiatrists had calmed her with their theories. One man described Kathy as the family's lightning rod, acting crazy to try to keep Leonard and Jean together by giving them a shared problem. He said Kathy had taken it upon herself to provide glamour and power to her mother, so she could hold Leonard's interest. "Mother's little helper," said Jean wryly.

Of course Leonard and Jean had planned a totally different life for Kathy. But Kathy'd jumped off the map. On her new map are lines Kathy can't cross. Limits and losses. Everybody warned Jean that people leave prison less than they were before they went in. But Jean was making sure that Kathy's prison story was better than most. Jean had inherited this job from Leonard, his obsession, until it just about killed him.

Jean sentimentalized Kathy's incarceration. She spoke of Kathy's years of good works in the Bedford Hills maximum-security facility the same way she alluded to Kathy's superior athletic skills as a child at camp. She chose not to mention Kathy's depression and ongoing mourning for her life. On our ride up, Jean said twice, "Kathy never shot anybody. She never even touched a gun." While the train passed houses with porches, Jean read aloud to me from a single page of Kathy's master's thesis on teaching literacy and AIDS prevention in prison: "Prisoners are viewed primarily as misfits, and the job of a prison rehabilitation program is to help them adjust to society; the notion that prisoners could make a contribution to a changing society so that it could be improved is not part of prison ideology."

After the thesis was excerpted in the *Harvard Educational Review,* Jean had mailed out six hundred copies. It was hard for Jean to believe, but before Kathy put her mind to it, the many women in Bedford Hills prison who were HIV positive had tried to hide their illness. When they woke up in the middle of the night with high fevers, they pretended it was just a cold. Suspicious fellow prisoners spat at them in the mess hall and set fire to things they touched. Now, after years of educating prisoners about AIDS, Kathy was one of many volunteers who bathed and played cards with dying patients.

Jean liked to lose the present in thoughts of Leonard: she had never been surprised at how Leonard's slight, disarming lisp had drawn women dangerously close to his sensual mouth. She knew that Leonard's energy also made men wary.

Jean began reminiscing about a night at St. Luke's Place sometime in the late 1960s when Leonard peeled and ate four nectarines and talked for hours about his litigation on behalf of Fidel Castro. He was entertaining Kathy's then best friend, the student leader Bernardine Dohrn.

Bernardine's body was reflecting Leonard's firecracker energy; she chewed on a strand of her hair, twisted in the rocking chair, tugged on her short skirt, and uncrossed her legs. Jean's chair scraped, making an unhappy noise. Leonard by now was explaining how he might put the undeclared Vietnam War on trial instead of his client, Dr. Ben Spock, the world-renowned pediatrician who had been indicted for conspiring to counsel young men to evade the draft.

The climax came when Leonard twisted away from an imaginary punch from the opposition lawyer. Despite herself, laughter exploded out of Bernardine. By now she was looking at Leonard as though he was going to stop the Vietnam War single-handedly.

That night midnight came and went. Jean wistfully recalled good times when she had been the one to provoke such displays of mental energy from her Leonard. But, nonetheless, Jean had made herself into a perfect companion for him, a delicate pillow that conformed to the shape of Leonard's soul. Little did Leonard suspect how much Jean had edited herself for his pleasure, flattering him by repeating interesting words he used and in general making sure he was always front and center. Their spare and witty dialogue was dedicated to his enhancement. How did Thoreau say it? Jean recited: ". . . my life is the poem I would have writ, / But I could not both live and utter it."

After the empty stretch of train platform in the town of Orange went by, Jean explained to me that she and Leonard had made sure that Kathy understood she couldn't win if she fought prison life. And although Jean was not allowed by prison regulations to visit Kathy's little room, she knew all about it.

Kathy's day typically started at 6 a.m., when the guard banged on the metal door of her cell. It was the first count of the day.

After she got up, Kathy heard sounds of other women's televisions. Jean was proud that Kathy had decided against owning one. Instead Kathy read books, wrote in her diary, counseled other prisoners, wrote proposals for grants for new prison programs, and looked out her small window at gray sky and wire prison wall topped by spiraling razor wire, a maximum-security precaution built especially for Kathy's arrival.

Today Kathy probably had pulled on the purple polo shirt that Jean had ordered from the L. L. Bean catalog. Jean was not allowed to order Kathy any polo shirts in blue because it is a color the guards wear, so they can spot one another—in case of a crisis. Guards confided to Kathy they felt like they were in prison too, rooted always in the same spot. You didn't have to look far to see tragedy in life in Bedford Hills prison. Small things hurt too—like the time a guard purposely dumped orange peels on a snapshot of Kathy's little boy.

By seven o'clock, Kathy would have finished mopping and cleaning her room as well as an assigned area in the kitchen that smelled day and night of curry and garlic. She went into the cafeteria with her ID badge—KATHY BOUDIN #84-G-171—pinned on her untucked T-shirt. Some women forgot the ID badge, but Kathy never took a step out of her cell without her ID, even for the count. All prisoners endured four head counts a day. Kathy listened to telephones ringing that she could never answer. No forks in cells. Scissors were also contraband. Kathy never got a decent haircut. At 7:10, the loudspeaker announced "On the chow."

But today, Jean knew, Kathy would not have gone to breakfast. Because at noon, turkey, sweet potatoes, and stuffing were brought to the honors floor. Thirty women celebrated the holiday in the communal TV room.

Daydreaming about Leonard's smiles, or so she said, Jean arrived at Bedford Hills station. She told me that she missed the times Leonard woke her before dawn, pulling at tufts of the fierce gray hair sticking up on his head. She had had to talk and talk, persuading him that he was a good man, despite his vainglorious ambition to be thought of as a great man.

He'd sounded like Kathy when he asked, "How can you still believe in anything? Is it me? Have I lost my way?" Jean had patted her husband's spikey hair. "No, dear, like me, you think people have possibilities." He'd asked why she was so blind to hard facts. "Well, you're the visionary with cataracts," said Jean.

Jean stepped out of the cab in front of the prison. The sight of it tickled depressions long banished. It was hard to believe all the torment and melodrama in the lives inside the desolate brick buildings. To Jean, the place looked like a prep school fallen on hard times. "Not as hard as the time Kathy is doing," Jean said, crossing the prison parking lot. Jean was dreading the walk under an arbor of coiled razor wire to the visitors' room. After all these years, Jean knew many prisoners and their stories. Young girls who'd smoked crack, sold sex, and slept in alleys. The schoolteacher from New Hampshire who'd gotten a boy sexed up and made him kill her husband. Over her shoulder, Jean said to me, "It's worse than Shakespeare around here." Bitter jokes were Jean's fragile bridges over abysses of pain.

The sentry recognized Jean. "God bless." Jean got in line at the metal door of the visitors' room, which reminded her of a windowless church basement. Muddy sneakers had made an art-deco pattern on the linoleum floor. Young black and Hispanic women sprawled in chairs around small metal dining tables. Many wore red nail polish for the holidays. Thanksgiving drawings by prisoners' children hung on walls. Kathy helped to supervise the visits of children who stayed in local homes. It was an irony—and Jean appreciated irony—that many of these women were fed, sheltered, and listened to here for the first time in their lives.

Jean scanned the room: no Kathy. There was a damp and churchy look in the prisoners' eyes. Jean waved at Kathy's favorite protégée, Precious Bedell, a young black woman with the manner of a celebrity. Precious was a converted Catholic; Kathy attracted Catholics! Jean felt the violence in Precious, though. She had killed her two-year-old daughter in the bathroom of a Syracuse restaurant by bashing her head seven times. Precious was teaching parenting with Kathy—now that was an irony that was hard for Jean to ignore. Actress Glenn Close, who lived near the prison, was championing Precious's lawsuit to get out of prison. Precious and Kathy and Kathy's friend (and Brinks codefendant) Judith Clark had been here longer than anybody except the elderly Italian woman who had gotten her brother to kill her battering husband.

A girl named Ruthie Rodriguez whispered in Jean's ear. "Did Kathy tell you? She sent my drawings to a *Ms.* magazine editor." Kathy had fallen in love with Ruthie. She told Jean that Ruthie helped her to find joy. Jean walked past two women kissing. Necking. Hugging. Squirming against each other's bodies. Petting—nobody used that word anymore.

A guard lolled against a wall. Jean knew he did not carry a weapon. But he was capable of grabbing tear-gas canisters and a gun in three seconds.

Jean herself had been gassed in 1939 in a picket line around a Nazi passenger ship, the *Bremen,* docked in Manhattan just before the United States entered World War II. All she'd wanted was water, but water seemed to make her eyes and skin burn worse.

The guard did not blink when Jean caught him staring at her; to him mothers of prisoners were lesser beings. Jean hated the fact that Kathy was going to have to bend over, pull down her state-issued green pants, and show her private parts to him or another guard as soon as Jean left. The guard scowled as Jean took off her coat. Jean was defiantly wearing a blue blouse, the forbidden color for prisoners. No dress rules for visitors!

Kathy soon strode in. The sight of her robust daughter had a way of evening out Jean's losses. Kathy grinned broadly at Ruthie, then made her way slowly to her mother, shaking other inmates' hands, hugging. Always a grand entrance. Kathy's public style reminded Jean of Leonard's heroic courtroom manner. Her hair was getting long again. Kathy looked blue-collar, like a waitress living at a trailer camp. Kathy clasped Jean, who repeated her Thanksgiving joke. "I'm glad I dumped my son the judge to visit my daughter the prisoner."

Jean emerged from the prison an hour later to report Kathy's two pieces of good news. A new guard was a chess player. And Judith's group was training Seeing Eye dogs. Kathy reported that she'd fallen down on the floor with one big dog, rolling around, the dog licking her. She'd told her mother, "I forgot all about dogs. He's the first dog I've seen in thirteen years." And then her smile had disappeared.

Jean had hurriedly held out a stack of color snapshots to Kathy. Kathy raised her hands like a bandit under arrest in a cowboy movie. "Leave them at the package room."

Jean felt a pang. She always forgot that Kathy was not supposed to be handed anything from visitors. Jean flipped to several photographs she had taken of Kathy's son Chesa shaking hands with the captain on the *Queen Mary*. (With his parents both in prison, he was being brought up by their friends Bernardine Dohrn and Bill Ayers.) "He's even taller now," said Kathy. "He always tilts his head to pay extra attention like Leonard." Her voice had wavered to a high note. Her blue eyes were bemused and imploring at the same time.

Peering at Jean in one photograph, Kathy wiped away her tears. "Lipstick? Pancake makeup? You look worldly." A few seconds later, Kathy said, "Ruthie's getting out. I get attached to her, and she leaves."

Jean knew exactly how Leonard might have diverted Kathy, and so she prompted, "Tell me again about this year's AIDS walk, and start from the beginning."

Kathy clasped her hands, smiling again. "I know, I know. I'm in this place for a reason. There's so much I can organize here." She told Jean once again about decorating the barbed-wire wall with ribbons and messages addressed to the prisoners who had died of AIDS. All day long, women had marched, danced, and told stories of dead friends. Guards and local people pledged money to help the sick.

Jean told me proudly what a different person Kathy was from the eerily thin, dead-eyed young woman shackled to her friends after those awful murders in the suburbs. The prison had narrowed her horizons and deflated her grandiosity. Limits and losses. But before prison Kathy had refused to deal with her sad feelings. It had been all intellection and angry politics. By now, she had not changed the world, but her teaching had broadened the horizons of other women. Many learned to take better care of babies. Many learned to read. "Kathy's fifty-one, the oldest on her floor," said Jean. "A den mother now."

In the taxicab back to the Bedford train station, Jean checked her wristwatch. It was three o'clock. Kathy was walking back to her cell for the count. Guards routinely called out her name as she passed—a security risk after all these years. Jean wished aloud that she could be walking with Kathy back down the narrow green metal corridor of open metal doors to her room. She'd even put up with the guard patting and probing.

She blinked away her fantasy as we boarded the Manhattan-bound train at the Bedford Hills station. She said she felt as if she were doing time too. But her time was almost up. Her body was betraying her. Still it was not about her. It was about Kathy. Jean forced a smile. "As I tell Kathy, I'm a celebrity because I'm her mother."

Four years later, I went to Bedford Hills prison to visit Kathy. She asked me what the point was of this book.

My struggle to be honest in my answer made me slow to respond. I knew that whatever effect my answer had, it would help me to understand Kathy. And I wanted to tell her the truth.

"I blame your father."

Kathy reacted as if I had hit her. Gone was the jocular and bossy public figure. She pulled on her bottom lip with her thumb and forefinger. In a small voice she asked, "You mean for my fate? The fact that I am here?"

I abstracted the point. "No, the fact that you felt you had to risk your life over and over again to compete with Leonard to get his attention, and at the same time keep him at arm's length."

"What about my mother?" asked Kathy quietly. "Her suicide attempts screwed everything up." I felt I had said enough. "It's worth thinking about," I answered.

Kathy nodded, still physically hunched over. But after a moment she recovered her hearty—indeed, superior—attitude. She began to interview me again. "When was the last time," she asked, "that you went back to visit Bryn Mawr College?"

I responded obliquely that thinking about why Kathy had hated Bryn Mawr had illuminated my own four campus years. Kathy corrected me. "I loved Bryn Mawr." As we said good-bye, Kathy asked nervously, "Would a book go into things that I did—happened—before I got put in here?" I nodded. I said nothing.

A few weeks after this encounter I heard from Leonard Boudin's law partner and Kathy's lawyer, Victor Rabinowitz, that Kathy felt that a book that put her father in a negative light was not in her interest to support.

FAMILY CIRCLE

1

LEONARD BOUDIN—DEEP
BACKGROUND

*The refinement of our historical past chiefly means that we keep it
properly complicated.*
— Lionel Trilling, "The Sense of the Past"

The great labor lawyer and scholar Louis B. Boudin (the initial B.
denoting Boudinovitch, the original English transliteration of the
name) cast a long shadow over his nephew Leonard B. Boudin's entire
life. While still a small child in the second decade of the twentieth century, Leonard proclaimed that he planned to learn "all the laws in the
world and be more famous than Uncle Louis."

For Louis, legal scholarship was holy; he saw the courts as a locus of
enormous powers. He wrote the weighty book *Government by Judiciary,*
attacking the Supreme Court during the Depression when the justices
were blocking President Roosevelt's economic reforms. Louis's was a
populist message; the people and their elected representatives should
make the laws.

The fact that Louis had no sons made his arm's-length relationship
with his nephew Leonard more momentous. Louis would be a prime

influence on Leonard's children, Kathy and Michael, although they remembered little of his physical presence.

Louis's belief in the greatness of his mission—an intellectual life of legal service to the underclasses—overshadowed the influence of Leonard's far more ordinary father, Joe, a coarse, bellicose man who made a living in real estate law and foreclosing mortgages.

Louis was small and plump and looked like a storekeeper until he opened his mouth often to shout an opinion. And because he was so revered in Europe and the United States as an outstanding labor lawyer, foremost interpreter of Karl Marx and historian of the Supreme Court, his temper tantrums as well as his parsimony prompted fond jokes instead of enmity. He was considered "a great man" and allowances were made.

His nephew Leonard would treasure a cartoon from 1919 of Louis, scowling disdainfully as he walked out of a socialist convention in Chicago because he scorned Lenin and his revolution. Lenin had nonetheless honored Louis with a chair at a Moscow university. Under one arm was a volume of the writings of Karl Marx. The caption of the cartoon: "Boudin walks out."

Louis B. Boudin was born in southeastern Russia in 1874, the oldest of five children. He immigrated to Manhattan in 1891 on his own, where he almost miraculously flourished in just a few years. Louis was too proud to admit that anti-Semitism had forced him to leave Russia. He earned his master's degree at New York University Law School in 1897, while shedding most traces of a Russian accent in his spoken English.

Louis's love for his new country was ever-expanding. He saw no conflict between his belief in both Marxist economics and the genius of the United States Constitution. He felt socialism was fairer than capitalism and should prevail.

Louis's mother longed to immigrate to the United States because she missed her favorite person in the world. On the rare day that a letter from Louis failed to arrive, she wept. Louis soon made arrangements for his parents, two brothers, and two sisters to flee. His brothers Joe and Samuel, and his sisters Sarah and Mary, packed handwoven linens and sateen featherbedding in preparation for their journey.

But when they reached the nearby city of Kiev, a cholera epidemic was raging. Leonard's grandmother's featherbedding was confiscated and burned. She managed to hide one little embroidered silk pillow in a brass samovar, and later bestowed it upon her favorite grandchild, Leonard.

Louis's parents never learned much English. A family story, told as a joke, illustrates that fact. Riding the subway during World War I, Louis's father misunderstood a stranger's remark about pacifists and was almost arrested as a spy. The anthropologist Margaret Mead later observed that nearly all Boudin family problems were grist for jokes.

After graduation from law school, Louis had started a general practice on the Lower East Side, but soon represented almost all of the socialist and communist unions in New York, including the furriers, restaurant workers, united office and professional workers, and the amalgamated utility workers. In the first decades of the twentieth century, emerging labor unions were on the minds of many serious thinkers, politicians, and working people.

A difficult aspect of Louis Boudin's legacy is illustrated by his obdurate attempt to join the first convention of the International Workers of the World, known as the "Wobblies," on June 27, 1905, in Chicago.

Two hundred socialists, anarchists, and union leaders gathered there to create "one big industrial union" to be "founded on the class struggle." The delegates refused to seat Louis, then thirty-one, because as a prosperous lawyer he was "a parasite on the working class." Louis shouted out for six long days his commitment to the working man. But it was no use.

The situation was complex: Louis believed himself to be morally superior to middle-class friends because of his work on behalf of the less fortunate. But Louis's life was buttressed by the objects and security of class privilege, and this anomaly led him to sometimes talk as if he were trying to destroy himself. Seventy-five years later, Kathy Boudin claimed to see her birth to a family of well-to-do whites as an agonizing defect to be obliterated by rationalization, violence, and self-deprivation. Kathy wanted above all somehow to discipline her mind and body into being a member of the black working class.

Soon after Louis's humiliation at the convention in Chicago, his brother Joe fell for fair-haired Clara Hessner at the Henry Street Settlement in Manhattan. Founded by Lillian Wald, a shrewd, generous nurse of German-Jewish descent, the center trained volunteers to teach immigrant women like Clara Hessner how to talk back to school superintendents, court clerks, police sergeants, and other public officials who condescended to them.

Louis Boudin (upper right) and David Dubinsky at a reception at the Commodore Hotel, circa 1940. Major figures in organized labor, the two men were rivals. Boudin represented the Amalgamated Clothing Workers Union and Dubinsky was the anticommunist president of the International Ladies Garment Workers Union.

Although overlooked as a role model for Leonard and his children, Louis and Joe's sister Sarah was a pioneer in the emerging field of social work. As a young woman, Sarah sewed neckties in a sweatshop, the rare Boudin to possess a legitimate if brief membership in the proletariat. Nights she took classes to qualify for law school. She organized coworkers for the International Ladies Garment Workers Union. The hours were long—the harsh cry of management was "If you don't come in on Sunday, don't come in on Monday"—and the male shop foreman had free rein to humiliate female workers.

Sarah retaliated by organizing the women to stop work as soon as he was out of sight. But she was fired after the foreman saw her picture at a strike meeting on the front page of the *Forward*, the six-page daily Yiddish-language newspaper. She then went to work as a secretary for her favorite brother, Louis, in preparation for law school. But Sarah came to realize that she'd find legal research boring, and she soon married William Edlin, an editor and drama critic at the *Forward*.

When Louis's wife, Anna, died, Sarah and William moved into Louis's

Anna Pavitt Boudin, circa 1938, wife of Louis Boudin, was one of the first women to graduate from Columbia Dental School and the first president of Women's ORT, a Jewish charity that financed education. She avoided speaking to her husband because he disliked her Russian-accented speech.

big house in Brooklyn, where Sarah tended to Louis's small children. Sarah's husband felt neglected. After a divorce, Sarah thought about going to law school again, rejected the idea, and enrolled instead at the New York School of Social Work, vowing to "make a difference."

After her graduation Sarah took over the Lakeview Home on Staten Island for unmarried mothers sponsored by the Jewish Board of Guardians. Recent immigrants from Russia, the young girls had worked as domestics and factory workers. Her duties for the next fifty years ranged from "statistics to shoveling coal." Sarah insisted the girls see themselves as worthy members of society. She canceled restrictive practices such as locking the girls' clothes in lockers in the basement to keep them from running away. Encouraged by Louis, she wrote a blunt book called *The Unmarried Mother in Our Society,* replete with common sense and affection.

Following Louis's lead, Leonard's mother, Clara, disdained Sarah's endeavors as not truly intellectual. Clara also saved all adulatory reviews of Louis Boudin's ponderous books. Presumably she knew exactly how much that practice irked her insecure husband, Joe. Joe felt more comfortable around his brother Samuel, also a City College graduate, and a highway and tunnels engineer.

Joe screamed that Louis was "selfish" and cared only about famous friends and footnotes in his books. Louis bragged of shouting at Leon Trotsky and of his correspondence with Rosa Luxemburg as well as with Jack London, who signed "Yours for the revolution." A founder of the U.S. Socialist Party, Louis was a popular speaker on socialism and democracy at college campus meetings of the LID (League for Industrial Democracy, the precursor to SDS, Students for a Democratic Society).

Leonard B. Boudin (he adopted the "B" in homage to his uncle) was born on July 20, 1912. When he was six, his father moved his family from Brooklyn to a large corner house at Eighty-fifth Avenue and 150th Street in Richmond Hill, Queens. Leonard loved rolling on the big lawns with his collie. He watered the family's acre of cornfields and helped his father grease his automobile on Sundays.

There was perhaps only one person who could have foreseen that the dazed little boy with a lisp would one day be known as "a great man" to judges and legal theorists in England, Chile, Cuba, and the United States. But that person made all the difference. She was Leonard's weepy and fine-featured mother. Throughout his life Leonard would retain the attitude of an adored boy.

Clara saw her own angelic face every time she looked at Leonard. She brushed his fair hair and whispered in his ear that despite Joe's insults, Leonard was "the smartest little boy in America." He seemed unable to stop hugging her. When he lost her full attention he pretended to duck under her skirt. As an adolescent he became sexually aroused for the first time at the sight of her underwear.

Much of Leonard's difficulty as a small child stemmed from his humiliating lisp. Joe berated Leonard for not speaking up in classrooms. Leonard's elementary-school teachers, two of whom lived next door, told Joe that Leonard daydreamed four serial fantasies at once.

In later years Leonard remembered his teachers as "mediocre and dull." But as a child he agonized with Joe over Leonard's poor performance in Latin and German. Leonard also had terrible handwriting, despite hours of practicing the Palmer method with Joe. He despaired: his father and uncle wrote beautifully. To please his mother, Leonard played the piano, but not well. Nonetheless Clara dreamed aloud that Leonard might be a concert pianist. To make her smile, Leonard danced while Clara played Chopin.

In 1920, when Leonard was eight, his brother Arthur was born. Athletic Arthur was his father's favorite.

A few years later, Clara told her husband she was leaving him. Joe threw himself on the floor and banged his head against it. Leonard welcomed the silence that followed such fights. Leonard's parents disagreed about most things—including politics. To her husband's dismay, Clara worked for the speakers' bureau of the Queens Communist Party (according to the FBI).

A legendary flirt, Clara practiced Christian Science, influenced by one of Joe's real estate clients who was smitten with her. As a result, she treated Leonard's frequent headaches only with prayer. But she did enroll Leonard in speech therapy classes for his lisp.

After school he cut out editorials for his father from the *New York Law Journal,* cross-indexing "matrimony and divorce," and pasted bookplates in Joe's law books. Clara wept because her husband "treated Leonard like an enslaved law clerk."

When Joe taught Leonard to play chess, the boy's inability to concentrate vanished. Chess can be a harsh lesson for a child: one player's gain is another player's loss. Joe was thrilled by Leonard's passion for beating him. Mortified by his lisp, Leonard had an immediate affinity for the "silent" war strategies of chess. He enjoyed "quick slaughter." Leonard read book after book about chess champions and decided that arrogance was key.

Clara soon invited Morton Gould, whose father worked with her husband, to perform at one of her musical soirees. Three years older than Leonard, Morton was a piano prodigy and the most famous boy in Richmond Hill. He had written original compositions at the kitchen table before he was five years old. By age eight he'd won one of many scholarshops to music school. Thrilled to have him in her home, Clara flirted with the boy. Sixteen-year-old Leonard was jealous of the older boy's effect on Clara. Leonard began to practice the piano more feverishly than ever. Desperate to bask in Morton's reflected glory, Leonard embarked on a brief and fumbling intimate relationship with the older boy.

In winter 1929 Joe Boudin startled neighbors walking by his home on 114th Street in Richmond Hills by yelling to one and all, "I'm a failure. I can't buy food to put on the table." Joe cursed his sweeping losses in Florida real estate. Leonard hid in his room where he read novels and daydreamed. Joe refused to listen to "pie in the sky" solutions to the vicissitudes of the Great Depression, espoused by his wife and his brother Louis. Joe jeered at reports that a million frightened Americans marched on May 1 in Manhattan to commemorate the Russian Revolution.

Joe was reduced to doing clerical work: he foreclosed mortgages for landlords. He also managed a bail bond agency.

Joe was soon dealt another blow. Leonard's application for admission to City College, Joe's alma mater, was rejected. The humiliating reason: bad grades in geometry, Latin, and German. Joe pulled strings to get Leonard an interview with the college president. Leonard was winning in the interview and was admitted. In later years, Leonard simplified his problems by claiming that he had attended Harvard, where he said that he'd been nothing special as a student.

Life on the City College campus was fervent. The all-male student body was gripped by the political crises of the Depression. Many were fanatically devoted to competing intellectual solutions. They brought lunch from home, and the select among them ate in special areas of the cafeteria. Anti-Stalinist students ate in alcove #1; these were socialists and Trotskyists and included Irving Howe, Irving Kristol, Daniel Bell, and Seymour Melman. In alcove #2 were pro-Stalin students who were at times forbidden by the party to talk to members of #1. After shouting at one another until they were hoarse about how best to save the world, the boys scurried off together to afternoon classes.

Leonard helped to run the exclusive alcove of the chess team. Pure intellection was the credo. Leonard gulped down his mother's jelly sandwiches and supervised concurrent combative games of chess. Tryouts for the chess team, advertised in the school newspaper, consisted of playing three games against Leonard.

A sly dig in his yearbook caption hinted at Leonard's lifelong fascination with famous men. "Lenny lives on the strength of his uncle's intelligence and his friends' cynicism." One friend was Paul Goodman, an older student, and a sensation of New York literary life. Leonard was Goodman's adored protégé and briefly his lover. Again, Leonard basked in another boy's glory. He loved the euphoria of sexual power. Goodman was scornful and soulful, with dark hair curling down over his eyes. He was "cynical" about most people, but was "dazzled by Leonard's ambivalent nature." Goodman wrote "nonfiction" stories that jumped from Plato and Beethoven to "Leonard my first great love."

"Leonard" is portrayed when swimming naked as "a black-blond sea

Paul Goodman, upper right, circa 1931, at the Parthenon. Goodman was a mentor to Leonard Boudin. The biographer Taylor Stoehr writes that despite Goodman's outpouring of poetry, fiction, and books that sold in the millions of copies, his greatest influence was on people who accepted him as a mentor.

lion" with his wet blond hair and brown suntan. Leonard lacked good form as a swimmer. He refused to submit to instruction, but compensated with ferocious enthusiasm.

Friends said that despite Leonard's tense and eccentric movements he looked like "one of Botticelli's cherubs." His big warming blue eyes were dreamy—but measuring—his jaw plump, his lower lip pouted. His teasing banter intensified if a pretty girl was in hearing distance. With his mussed, bright curling hair and rumpled clothing, Leonard had the air of a young man recently lounging—perhaps not alone—in bed.

In a nonfiction story, Paul Goodman wrote a romantic description of what he loved about "Leonard's" complex intellect: "Between Leonard and Johnson [Goodman] was the hard shock and somewhat hot cauterization of hyperlogical characters. They were both inveterate scholastics: ingrown, tough, frank, quick and tortured."

Goodman was dumbfounded, however, that his brilliant Leonard could not learn even rudimentary German. And in another short story Goodman describes "Leonard's" elusive quality:

"It was not that Leonard was indifferent towards [Goodman] but that he hated himself for being attracted to him."

Goodman wrote that "Leonard" was deeply ambivalent and self-absorbed. "For when Leonard thought only of himself, it was not in pride, satisfaction or even lust. But it was that he felt himself so divided, so desperately at war. He was like all who were suicidally cleft at the very bottom of their personalities. Oh, Leonard! Leonard!"

Encouraged by Goodman, Leonard published his own autobiographical short story in the City College literary magazine, the *Lavender*. The self-torturing, complex, and highly accomplished piece was titled "Meal with Illustrations," and one of its themes was Leonard's anxiety about his sexuality.

Seeking the cause for a sudden bout of nausea at family dinner, in the story Leonard contemptuously examines his father's table manners and intellectual shortcomings—as well as those of his brother and grandfather. (He sits facing an expensive, mediocre, black-and-white Diego Rivera–style etching of "poor peons eating mush.")

By the end, the narrator decides that he is disgusted by his own reflection in the glass over the etching on the wall facing him. Something about it was "obtrusively corrupt and blighting." "Perhaps it [his face] was degenerate, he wondered, something wrong with its heredity, a mental quirk or twist, a diminution of neural connections, or a low cranial capacity. Perhaps, perhaps anything."

Leonard corresponded with Paul Goodman in the summer of 1932 from Delaware Cliff Camp, in Bushkill, Pennsylvania, where Leonard was a swimming counselor. In his letters Leonard pushed Paul away by exaggerating his summer love affairs:

> *Your letter is so charming that I am quite ashamed, and almost abject. I have fallen in love not once but five times and now feel that I love everyone, even Sonia Peretz who was third on my list and has met you. But I cannot end each love affair with tact, my girls are venomous zu Ende, and I suffer endless pain from their unspoken words, even from their unarched backs and assumptions of unconcern.*

Leonard "jilted" Paul in another letter:

I am very much afraid that I am of that very ordinary stuff seen in those men who jilt poets.

Adopting Paul's condescension toward communism, a word they used to describe a fashionably bohemian attitude, Leonard wrote to Goodman:

Things have an unnatural but rather amusing simplicity here— girls are demure virgins—or they're not; men are bluff liars or married; nudism, free love or any absurd eccentricity are in the same swim: all are entitled communism. So that a girl with bare breasts flapping in the breeze will derisively (not defensively) say, "I'm going communist."

Rain, Leonard

Delaware Cliff Camp was run by a follower of socialist Jay Lovestone, who was a friend of Louis Boudin.* Unlike other campers, Leonard did not argue politics. His friend Georgette Schneer believed Leonard was "torn between his father's business point of view and his uncle's socialism." (His respect for his mother's radical stance was perhaps more relevant.) Georgette decided she had never seen a human being as beautiful as the swimming counselor. Leonard's appearance was enlivened by "the personal gleam of his nimble, impatient mind. He was filled with eccentricities and highly intrigued by the tangents of his own thoughts." She named Leonard "my juggler of thoughts." He would be the love of her life.

The adoration of a camper with Georgette's bold intelligence and leggy beauty added to Leonard's star quality. Five foot eight, she was graced with a long neck, like a girl in a Modigliani portrait. She was on a dance scholarship, and she and her mother moved every autumn to take advantage of the first month of free rent landlords were offering because of the Depression. Bert Gross considered himself blessed to have glimpsed Georgette's long naked body as she stepped from a stall in the coed shower. Georgette was as ambitious for a career as boys she knew and went on to dance with Anna Sokolov's company.

---

*Like Louis, Jay Lovestone rejected Stalin and Soviet communism, though a decade after Louis had. Lovestone went on to fight communism around the world as a CIA operative.

Meanwhile, back in Manhattan, Paul Goodman wrote daily beseech-
ing letters to Leonard. He'd written another nonfiction short story about
missing "Leonard" and falling apart at the sound of anyone with lisp-
ing speech, or at the sight of anyone with "off-color" blond hair. Goodman loved the way "Leonard" perplexed adults but delighted children
with his teasing tone signifying that anything he said could mean its
opposite.

> *So full of irony he is, yet very humble, so bitter, eager, sarcastic*
> *with himself, and full of love . . . [and also] he is not cast into*
> *confusion by his curious personality.*

In August, Leonard sent Paul a postcard inviting him to visit. Paul left
at once for the camp, where Georgette and Leonard had been building
fires and cooking hot dogs in the pine woods. Paul Goodman made a
grand entrance to Delaware Cliff Camp. Other campers envied Leonard
his connection to "famous Manhattan intellectuals like Paul and 'the great
Louis.' "

Paul and Leonard went swimming in the nude at night on the
Delaware River, and Goodman rhapsodized: "What is there in this boy
that I am so struck. First he is beautiful. Black blond . . . his eyes are blue
and clear as water and cold as glass with anxiety. [and] his body lean
moves with erratic grace. He is on edge—that is why I love him!"

Throughout Leonard's life, articulate men and women sputtered trying to describe Leonard's charisma.

"He looked like Paul Newman with a softened jawline," said Belle
Harper. "He was so impatient. You did anything to catch his attention,"
said Ruth Gilbert. "When he talked to my class [at Harvard Law School],
it was like he was talking only to me," said the esteemed Manhattan
lawyer Leon Friedman.

"He'd heat up a room, faster than a furnace," said Bert Gross.

In autumn 1932, Leonard continued to see Georgette in Manhattan. He
jumped over fire hydrants, showing off for her, and then ran back to con-
fide every new thought. At a Greenwich Village café, after they went to
see Pirandello's play *Six Characters in Search of an Author*, Leonard
beamed as the scholarly song collector Alan Lomax admired Georgette's

long fingers. Lomax and his father, John, had tracked down black singer and songwriter Leadbelly digging rocks on a Texas chain gang. Lomax liked to sing verses of "Home on the Range" that his father had learned in 1908 from a black cook whose chuck wagon trailed herds of cattle to market in Kansas. The song included the line, *"Oh, give me a jail where I can get bail,"* as well as

> *The red man was pressed from this part of the West.*
> *He's likely no more to return*
> *To the banks of Red River where seldom if ever*
> *Their flickering campfires burn.*

Georgette told her mother that she didn't need money, since she and Leonard lived on love. Leonard took Georgette to a lecture given by his uncle Louis at New York University School of Law. (Georgette found no family resemblance to "my beautiful Leonard.") Louis spoke of researching pogroms. He lectured that some Jews fleeing persecution in Europe had substituted a belief in social justice for traditional faith.

The City College newspaper was suspended during Leonard's senior year after he helped to write an April Fools' Day parody issue. A front-page story began, "Professor Gall today manifested his latest manifesto limiting the amount of urine in the pool water to 2%." A psychology professor named "Dr. Pain" reported that 90 percent of the freshman class are sexually perverted. The other 10 percent, said Dr. Pain, are perverted sexually. Interjected into a paragraph was the question: "Why wear a truss?"

Every Saturday morning Leonard got up early and drove through Queens to collect overdue rents and mortgage payments for a bank that had hired Joe. Leonard stopped at court during the week to start dispossess proceedings. Leonard claimed he suffered no pangs of Marxist guilt. He wryly called the tasks my "early connection with the working class."

He wrote to Goodman on April 19, 1933:

> *My dear Paul,*
> *   . . . too many times have I banged doors crying aloud my wares of "RENT RENT RENT." I shall explain to you my little trick for getting people to inquire about empty houses.*
> *   A sign I place which reads thus:*

*Leonard B. Boudin's picture from
the City College yearbook, 1932.*

For Rent
This Voluble Property
It
Speaks for itself.

*And the natives phone in to tell me I misspelled valuable and
now that they're so bright, how much do I want for the house—the
assumption being that we expect less rent of a bright tenant.*

*Meanwhile, Paul, send me a diagrammed illuminated brief of
some thirty-odd pages recounting your adventures and outlining
plans and specifications for our next meeting which if you act with
proper interest should be any minute.*

Leonard started St. John's Law School and clerked one summer for his
uncle Louis. While he was in his uncle's office, he published a book
review lauding Roosevelt's pro-labor reforms for the *International Juridi-
cal Association*, a left-wing law journal. He had no contact with Louis
except on those rare times he escorted his uncle—due to Louis's poor
eyesight—home to 200 West Fifty-eighth Street.

Leonard was thrilled when his famous relative appeared at Leonard's
graduation in 1935 from St. John's. Louis presented to the new graduate
an inscribed copy of his two-volume book *Government by Judiciary.* In it,

The Furriers' Union strike, 1927. The union, a client of Louis Boudin, was headed by Communist Party official Ben Gold.

Louis accused legal historians of expurgating the shameful Dred Scott decision, in which the Supreme Court held that a slave had no rights and that Congress had no right to prohibit slavery in the territories.

Leonard's first job after law school was writing appellate briefs for the New York State Mortgage Commission, created to protect home owners during the Depression, when banks holding their mortgages went bankrupt. He soon lost the job to another political appointee.

After failing to find employment with business law firms specializing in mortgage law, Leonard was finally offered $15 a week as the lowest paid lawyer in Louis's law firm. Leonard joked about his career path, "Thus after all those firms rejected me, I came to my real love, labor law."

It was an auspicious time in U.S. history to be practicing labor law. A year or so earlier, the trade union movement had sprung to life, with a new philosophy of labor relations. Legal machinery was put in place to prevent management from stamping out the new unions formed by workers, who had what Louis called revolutionary rights. (Indeed President Franklin Roosevelt had pushed through legislative reforms because, he said, he did not want to be the last president of the United States.)

One of Leonard's tasks was to interview union members with grievances against owners of businesses in fur, food, painting, and office work. If a union could prove that it represented the majority of workers at a place of business, then the newly formed Labor Relations Board certified the union. Hundreds of new unions formed, and millions of workers joined them.

Leonard noted one fascinating paradox: although Louis represented communist unions in the Congress of Industrial Organizations (CIO), he opposed the Communist Party. For starters, he was far too arrogant to tolerate being dictated to.

That summer, back again at camp, Bert Gross took photographs of Leonard in a canoe on the Delaware River. Leonard confided spasms of secret misgivings: had he ever truly perceived, let alone loved, another person? In years to come he hummed Marc Blitzstein's lyrics for a song called "What's the Matter with Me?"

> *I'm trained in all the arts,*
> *My heart's like other hearts,*
> *I've all the essential parts,*
> *Tell me, what's the matter with me?*

Bert promised a solution. "I have the perfect girl for you to marry. Every man I know is in love with her, and she has rejected all of us." Bert showed Leonard artistic photographs clothed and unclothed of Jean Roisman, the "most beautiful girl I know." Bert wrote to Jean, "Since I cannot have you, I have found the perfect man for you to marry." He enclosed a photograph of Leonard naked in summer sunlight in a canoe.

2

BEFORE ME THERE WAS NOTHING

*Before me there
was nothing*

*All have being
With my knowing*

*With my knowing
Leaves fall.*

*Green goes
with my going.*
—Jean Roisman Boudin

Jean Roisman drolly blamed her blurry sense of identity on her elusive birthday. The third child of Celia and Morris Roisman, she had been born in Philadelphia on February 29, 1912, on leap-year day. Jean's birthday parties were held either on February 28 or March 1. At four, Jean was appalled to discover that every child she knew, including her sister Esther, three years older, and her brother Charlie, seven years older, had only one birth date.

Far more seriously, Jean's birth precipitated the tragedy that shadowed her life. Her mother Celia (Cilly) Siementowsky Roisman had died at age thirty-three of heart problems brought on by childbirth, hours after she named her younger daughter. The suffering created by the desertion, however unintentional, of a child by parent would be part of Jean's legacy to her own son and daughter.

Although Jean started making up verse in elementary school, she never wrote about her mother. In later years, she blamed the loneliness of her childhood on the fact that her sister Esther and their father, Morris, held Jean's birth responsible for her mother's death. Jean was jealous of Esther, who was Morris Roisman's favorite, and more emotionally grounded. Still she was not a beauty like Jean.

When Jean was six and her brother, Charlie, thirteen, their father married again. His new wife was a plump woman, with a smooth complexion, named Jean and nicknamed "Jennie." If little Jean could not change her birthday, she would change her name. She began calling herself "Janet." When that proved unsatisfying, she became "Jeannette." Each name change was an attempt to invent a happier self.

Life in a series of working-class brick row houses in South Philadelphia, Strawberry Mansion, and West Philadelphia ground Jean down; the rooms were dark, and a small front porch would open to neighbors' porches on both sides.

Morris Roisman's new wife was not as intelligent as her stepchildren, and she was hurt by little Jean and Charlie's secret codes and jokes. Jennie particularly disliked Jean, the youngest and the one who needed the most help. According to Jean and Charlie, "stupid" more aptly described their stepmother than "wicked."

"She gets away with murdering potatoes," Jean would giggle as she described her stepmother's overworked vegetables. Jean and Charlie winced at the hard "z" and gutteral "ckha" sounds of Jennie's Yiddish-accented English. Jean's father was fat, causing his cousins to assume incorrectly that Jean's stepmother was a good cook.

Charlie Roisman was known for his nonconformity. He dated black women, smoked marijuana cigarettes, and announced that he was going to make a living as a jazz drummer. Roisman relatives crossed their fingers and hoped their children would not turn out like him. "He was bisexual and biracial, and bi-everything," said one cousin. He and his father, Morris, were short and had small noses and mouths and rounded cheeks. Father and son loved music—although Morris Roisman loved Rachmaninov and Charlie sneaked out to listen to Cab Calloway in black jazz clubs on South Street.

When she was eight, Jean announced she was lucky because she would be "young forever," since it took her four years to age one year. She decided to celebrate her birthday by herself and only on February 29. She pretended that a "perfect mother" was throwing her a party.

An early poem addressed her father's reluctance to interfere with his second wife's dismissal of Jean's needs. The poem began:

LETTER

Dear Papa:
Asleep I grind my teeth
Spike out the eyes and
Trample on
Those pogrom princes
Who taught you well to fear to be
Not well-liked.

To cheer Jean up, Charlie made up a running joke about their father's adventures as an entrepreneurial pickle maker. Morris Roisman worked six days a week, bottling and selling cured foods door to door. His white delivery van was painted ROISMAN HOME PRESERVE AND PICKLE COMPANY. He had a prized recipe for pickling half-sour tomatoes. No matter how hard Morris scoured his fingernails with yellow soap, he smelled of vinegar and spices. When business waned, Morris worked for a rival pickle maker.

Morris was head of the Roisman family. He led prayers and singing at yearly seders and made sure his brother Richard's family and his sister, Letty, lived close by in the row of small houses. He was distressed by his son Charlie's frenzied snare drum playing that made neighbors bang their walls in protest.

Like Jean, Charlie had great physical presence despite his small size. He wore white Panama hats. As time passed, many of Jean's girlfriends developed crushes on him and called him "the prince of charm" because they thought he resembled Edward, Prince of Wales.

One afternoon in spring 1924, when Jean was fourteen, she sat on a bench surrounded by yellow tulips, "a thinking place" in Rittenhouse Square. A West Philly high-school classmate stopped to introduce Jean to a jolly woman a decade older. Madeleine (Madi) Leof glanced at Jean's book of poems by Walt Whitman and recited: "I am the poet of slaves and of the masters of slaves." Jean never remembered her response, but it was precocious enough to impress Madi Leof, as did the sorrowful expression in the younger girl's lovely eyes. Madi invited Jean home to "talk of poems and morality."

The first of many women who would look after Jean, Madi was studying Elizabethan poetry at the University of Pennsylvania. A Barnard graduate, Madi was also writing "the great American novel."

Jean never forgot her initial astonishment at Madi's home. Situated in a proud row on Sixteenth Street in Philadelphia, a block from Rittenhouse Square, the Palladian-style mansion was inhabited by three generations of Leofs. The sparse furnishings of 322 Sixteenth Street reflected Dr. Morris Vladimir Leof's complex attitude toward privilege.

Students on campuses as far away as Yale jockeyed for an invitation to "322." Madi and her brothers and sister, Charlotte, invited their most brilliant and restless friends to dinner. Several of the young "regulars" at "322" had—like Jean—lost a parent.

Soon a frequent guest, Jean always stopped short in the foyer when she arrived to stare at a superb primitive painting of a snowy landscape by a local black artist named Horace Pippin. Pippin had been "cannon fodder," and was injured fighting on the front lines during World War I in an all-black regiment. Jean liked his credo: "Pictures come naturally to my mind—and I tell my heart."

Jean never knew who would appear for dinner. Emma Goldman came once. Jean liked the tale of the argument between "Poppa" Leof and Eugene V. Debs, one of the most courageous men alive, thought Jean. In 1922, Debs had run for president on the Socialist ticket, while in jail for speaking out against U.S. involvement in World War I. (He said it was not a war for democracy, but between opposing capitalists.)

Another visitor, Earl Browder, a leader of the American Communist Party, shouted at Poppa Leof, who disliked Joseph Stalin. Other guests included Franchot Tone and theater stars Luther and Stella Adler.

Within six months Jean was sleeping at "322" several times a week, doing homework with Madi's younger sister, Charlotte. Her "adoption" into the remarkable Leof family circle altered the course of her life. Dr. Leof was one of the world's generous souls. Far and away the most exhilarating part of life at "322" was arguing with him. A tall man, straight-backed, he told Jean that truth was the elusive goal. (At the age of seventy-five, he reread Freud and became a convert, saying, "I was very wrong.")

Jean modeled herself on Morris Leof's common-law wife, Jennie

Chalfin. A "spit-fire," Jennie Chalfin rarely spoke if "Poppa" was in earshot. She set Poppa's reputation by calling him a great man.

One day Jennie Chalfin impressed Jean by showing her a poem pleading for the end of World War I that her grandmother had sent to President Woodrow Wilson. Jean was also impressed by Jennie's instant scrubbing off of the "322" scrawled in scarlet paint (a lurid accusation of pro-Soviet communism) on the façade of her home.

Like Poppa Leof, Jennie spiced her conversation with warm Yiddish expressions. Neither presumed to answer the great questions, just to chip away at them. They both cited Thoreau's warning that in an ideal world a person would be respected for all the possessions he realized he no longer needed.

Tempers exploded at the Leofs' table over dreamy possibilities of democracy and socialist theory. Jean and her friends were righteous and inconsistent, each feverishly defending his or her own hopeful reading of Marx's writings. The youngsters formed a frequently pretentious intellectual elite who romanticized members of the working class, however uneducated, with one notable exception—their own tired parents. Jean once told her father that the idea of making a profit in business was somehow shameful.

At dinner, Madi laughed and advised Jean how to make boys feel important. One night Madi and her father dissected a current novel by Theodore Dreiser called *The Financier,* set in Philadelphia. The main character was no hero, although he was fine-looking and enjoyed intellectual musing. Jean soaked up the arguments: If a man is cruel to his family, and charitable to society, is he a good man? Is ambition a kind of greed? Dr. Leof fanned flames by reading aloud from Walt Whitman: "I am not asleep to the fact that among radicals as among the others there are hoggishnesses, narrownesses, inhumanities, which at times almost scare me for the future."

Dr. Leof reported at dinner one evening with Horace Pippin, his wife, Ora Jean, and his art dealer, Robert Carlen, that Pippin, "our authentic American hero," was painting a masterly series on abolitionist John Brown, the white man hanged by the U.S. government for murderous antislavery actions that helped to precipitate the Civil War. Brown led a raid in 1859 on Harper's Ferry in an attempt to liberate slaves who were treated like animals and killed on whims of owners. Many abolitionists were appalled by Brown's violence, but after Brown was hanged, Henry

Jean Roisman, West Philadelphia
High School yearbook, 1929.

Thoreau said, "He is not Old Brown any longer, he is an angel of light."
Dr. Leof was reading a new biography by a young southerner named
Robert Penn Warren, who portrayed Brown as a failed farmer and a
horse thief. Leof dismissed Warren's book as *narishkeit,* a Yiddish word
meaning "nonsense."

Dr. Leof asked Jean and the other youngsters to consider questions
such as: Was Brown crazy to say men were nothing, principles everything? When is it okay to make war on the government? Brown was
white, not black; did that make him a meddler?

By the year 1927, Jean was a high-school sophomore and considered the
most beautiful girl at the Leofs'. In fact, men and women alike pronounced her the most beautiful girl in Philadelphia. Her heart-shaped
face reminded boys of Lillian Gish. Jean's dentist and her high-school
Latin teacher sent her valentines. Clifford Odets sent her mash notes.
(Odets was a favorite of Dr. Leof's, and was already writing plays about
workers fighting bosses that soon made him famous. At this point, Odets
was still living with his parents in Oak Lane, a neighborhood in North
Philadelphia.)

Although she occupied a small space, Jean was magnified by exaggerated grace. She looked ready to flirt. Her personal style would have been grandiose if not for her "tear-stained" quality—sadness lingered in her eyes even when she smiled. At dinner Jean did not simply put a hunk of cheese on a piece of bread. She carved a piece of cheese to match the bread, and added a leaf of lettuce as if completing a sculpture.

Harry Kurnitz (who later wrote for Groucho Marx and the Broadway stage) loved matching wits with Jean during dinner at "322." Laughter was relief from all the talk of human suffering and philosophy. Together they created doggerel such as the lines treasured by their friend Alice Serber, working as a lab technician:

> *Alice is such a dainty miss*
> *Who would dream she handles piss*
> *And why do the doctors grow romantic durin'*
> *her analysis of urine?*

Harry Kurnitz raged with jealousy when Jean made a foray to Manhattan to date Clifford Odets. Harry called Jean an "artsy-fartsy pickle heiress" when she confided worries that Odets was suicidal. He had escaped Philadelphia to live on Fifty-ninth Street in Manhattan with members of the innovative Group Theater. When Kurnitz gave up on Jean, he became engaged to the daughter of orchestra conductor Leopold Stokowski.

Bert Gross was jealous of the way Jean and her brother, Charlie, slow-danced to Bessie Smith recordings. He accused them of being lovers; he knew they were not. Jean did not fall in love with Bert Gross, despite his muscles and blond hair. After they had slept together, he bored her by declaring his great love until dawn.

Although Jean terrorized her father by advocating "free love," there was nothing free about the way she fell in love. It was about being gripped by miserable yearnings for perfect love. When she sighed about her unrequited love for older boys like the music prodigy Marc Blitzstein, Harry Kurnitz whispered "poor half-Orphan Annie" and made her smile.

Marc Blitzstein's impatient blue-gray eyes did not alight on Jean, no matter how raptly she stared at him.

A star in serious music circles, Marc displayed all aspects—including self-absorption and agony—of an artistic nature. He dressed like a romantic poet, in starched white shirts. Marc was setting Walt Whitman's scandalous sexual lines to music—in experimental pieces such as "O Hymen! O Hymenee."

Marc Blitzstein thrilled Jean by performing an original piece at her sixteenth birthday party at the Leofs'. He crouched with his back to the piano, reaching his hands over his shoulders to the keyboard. Laughing, he warned Jean that artists in Paris gave him a rectal pain because they took themselves too seriously. It was Madi Leof who took Jean aside to explain that Marc was not a romantic prospect. He had sought Madi's counsel about his homosexual longings.

Madi dragged Jean through a posthumous exhibit of the work of Philadelphia painter Mary Cassatt at the Philadelphia Museum of Art. Cassatt had caused a scandal by painting human anatomy from a live model, side by side with male students, at the nearby Pennsylvania Academy of Fine Arts.

Nothing prepared Jean for the terrible impact of Cassatt's paintings on her feelings. She'd tried not to blame her moodiness on the fact that she'd lost her mother. But happiness, as defined by Cassatt, was the absorption of mother and child in each other. In *The Kiss*, mother and baby lock almost like lovers.

In 1929, Jean's father was flabbergasted when his difficult and delicate younger daughter announced she was applying to Bryn Mawr, the bluestocking college for rich young women, fifteen miles away from their home. Like many men of his time, Morris Roisman saw the education of women as perverse. He had not sent Jean's older sister, Esther, to college. Morris had, however, insisted that his son, Charlie, get a law degree, rather than rely on playing snare drums for his livelihood.

When Jean's father refused to send her to college, she locked herself in the family bathroom and had a tantrum. She vowed to run away to Paris, as Mary Cassatt had done at age twenty-one. Jean was not daunted by the factor of Mary Cassatt's father's vast fortune.

Morris Roisman was cowed by Jean's sudden rages at real or imagined betrayals or if she sensed injustice. He was soon insulted by a visit from Poppa Leof, who offered to pay Jean's college tuition at the University of Pennsylvania, located ten blocks south of the Roisman home. At that, Jean's father capitulated and agreed to pay the tuition there himself.

Jean Roisman and Madi's sister, Charlotte Leof, entered the University of Pennsylvania in 1929, at the height of the Depression. For the next four years, Jean drifted "semi-homeless," living mostly in a small bedroom at "322." Her college classes were no match for the raucous and hilarious arguments fueled by Poppa Leof at the dinner table. It did not embarrass Jean that as a woman, she was permitted only to enroll in the school of education. She knew that her grades were not expected to be as good as those of boys.

Jean had a superb ear for languages and loved Latin and French. She spoke English in formal, whole sentences, unconsciously rounding the nasal, middle-class Philadelphia vowels.

She dressed like most rich Penn girls, in long navy or gray "Ivy League" tailored skirts and matching sweater sets. But when she was invited to a dance at the Philmont Country Club by Ben Snellenberg, whose family were rich German Jews known for charitable works, she had nothing appropriate to wear. She had never been initiated into the pleasures of shopping by a doting mother. She borrowed a tight-fitting, gold wool dress with real leopard cuffs from Alice Serber. Throughout her life Jean borrowed dresses and blouses from women friends, and she loved to recite the provenance of each article of clothing. Jean soon decided she was not attracted to Ben Snellenberg. What mattered to her was brainpower.

Jean worked as a waitress to buy textbooks and concert tickets to the Academy of Music. She and her brother, Charlie, also modeled nude for human anatomy classes at the Pennsylvania Academy of Fine Arts. Jean loved the fact that Cassatt had studied here, and proclaimed that as a modern woman she took pride in shedding her clothes while her body was still young and beautiful.

Lila Roisman was horrified to see a series of nude photographs of her beautiful cousin Jean in the window of Burison's downtown framing shop. Lila dared not tell Jean's father. Jean's sister, Esther, cited the photographs as "one more appalling symptom of poor Jean's need for male admiration."

Even though Jean was not religious, she was steeped in Jewish culture. In the past that had taken the form of the continual study—by men only—of moral arguments in the Talmud. Jean, however, saw no reason why she could not argue moral issues.

Jean's romantic appeal to the boys in her crowd was heightened when she quietly joined a student Communist Party group called the Benjamin Franklin Society. She joined in large part to impress Marc Blitzstein and Bert Gross, but was proud to be part of a great force fighting the evils of poverty.

Jean was in good company. Socialist theoreticians were dreaming of

*Esther Roisman, West
Philadelphia High School
yearbook, 1926.*

economic plans to end the horrific poverty of the Depression. Many intellectuals had hopes for the socialist experiments happening in the Soviet Union.

Dr. Leof urged Jean not to derive political beliefs from self-interest. For example, when Jean agreed to picket the navy ROTC at the University of Pennsylvania, it should be because of a commitment to peace, rather than the worry that a relative or future husband might die in war.

During Jean's junior year at Penn, her sister, Esther, fell in love "after one glimpse of his dimples" with Izzy Feinstein, an aggressive, bespectacled, bantamweight young journalist from Haddonfield, New Jersey. (Esther and Izzy were on blind dates with two other people.) Izzy, who soon changed his name to I. F. Stone, was a leader.

He became a regular at "322," having disdained his father's prosperous chain of dry goods stores and his world "of bourgeois capitalism." He saw conversation as a duel for expressing his moral superiority. Izzy would one day be a beloved American original. He never hesitated to criticize his government or his own beliefs. Using his pen like a sword, he would be the country's foremost intellectual essayist and gadfly. Above all, Izzy believed in his own ability to discern the moral truth in any complex set of circumstances.

In 1922, at the age of fourteen, Izzy had started his own small newspa-

I. F. "Izzy" Stone, graduated from Haddonfield High School, New Jersey, in 1924. The son of a well-to-do merchant, Izzy had already published his own radical newspaper called the Progress, *in which he criticized William Randolph Hearst and praised Gandhi. He would marry Esther Roisman and would become brother-in-law to Leonard and Jean.*

per: the *Progress.* In it he supported humanitarian causes such as the League of Nations and Gandhi's first efforts for freedom in India.

The newspaper foreshadowed the independent, frequently contrarian *I. F. Stone's Weekly,* his fiery, acute, antigovernment newsletter that would be studied closely by government leaders and critics.

A high-school member of the Communist Party, Izzy was elected to the New Jersey State Committee of the Socialist Party before he was old enough to vote. He was a teenage reporter for the Camden *Courier-Post.* Like left-wing intellectuals as far away as Europe, Izzy had been enraged by the case of two Italian immigrant anarchists, Nicola Sacco and Bartolomeo Vanzetti, living near Boston, who were sentenced in 1921 to be executed for the murder and robbery of two employees at a shoe factory in South Braintree, Massachusetts. Izzy saw the evidence against the men as only circumstantial and the death penalty harsh.

Izzy ran away to Boston from his parents' home in New Jersey to protest the execution. He quit the University of Pennsylvania before graduating in order to be a full-time newspaper reporter. Izzy wrote publicity for Norman Thomas's presidential campaign in 1928, but soon gave up on party affiliations. He vowed "to be free to help the unjustly treated without concern for leftist infighting." He was a cocky young man and firmly believed in his own destiny. As Esther's husband, Izzy became the leader of the Boudin family circle. He won all arguments.

Jean graduated from Penn in 1933, frightened about her future. She worked as a secretary to an assistant mayor in City Hall and was active in the State, County, and Seaway Municipal Workers Union. Jean called herself an American radical—but embedded deep in her was the desire to be a good girl. She saw her poetry as mainly ornamental, part of what drew men to her.

Leonard Boudin instantly impressed Jean and everyone else in the Leof circle despite the way he loftily removed himself from arguments such as how many Jews Lenin had butchered. Madi Leof and her parents congratulated Bert Gross: he had found the perfect man for Jean. Leonard was flattered. Bert never told Jean that Leonard tried to kiss him while the two were sleeping in Bert's bed at his parents' house. Leonard said, "It's no big deal. You like me, don't you? Paul Goodman and I do it." Leonard was thrilled to be playing Prince Charming for the whole illustrious circle at "322."

Jean told Bert that at the first sight of Leonard, she knew "this was it." There were dark contradictions in Jean's plan. How would she obtain and then keep Leonard's unconditional love? With tricks? Yes. How else to hide her glaring imperfections? Leonard must never see her do anything unattractive.

Jean's adoration induced in Leonard a flurry of political feelings. He squeezed himself into her romantic fantasies. He never got as far as his brother, Arthur, who actually sold the *Daily Worker* newspaper on street corners. Nonetheless, throughout most of his life Leonard strained to be the hero Jean envisioned.

He wrote to Paul Goodman:

> *My heart is delighted and I am prepared to enjoy myself in life and law.*
>
> *Tiny (but enough) barbs and lancets of Communist propaganda have so lacerated me that I'm going to subscribe to the* Daily Worker, *write some book reviews for the* New Masses, *and possibly work the soap box game. Nothing persuasive, of course, but my emotions have always been dilute and high, and now they're overbrimming, and the surplusage may as well go to the Party.*

Clifford Odets (left), Stella Adler, and Luther Adler, circa 1935. Odets, who wrote about working people, was part of the Philadelphia circle that included Jean Roisman Boudin.

Leonard was thrilled to accept the invitation from Bert Gross and Jean to hear Cliff Odets read an early draft of a play to his spiritual father. At "322" Dr. Leof worried about Odets's mood swings from worthlessness to grandiosity, little dreaming that Odets would in two years be hailed as the spokesman of his generation and the country's foremost writer of social protest.

Jean had told Leonard that Jacob, the protagonist of the play that would be produced in 1935 under the title *Awake and Sing*, was modeled on Poppa Leof. Odets describes "Jacob" as "a sentimental idealist with no power to turn ideals to action. He is an old Jew with living eyes in his tired face." Jacob believes that "slavery . . . begins where success begins, in a competitive system." He says, "If this life leads to a revolution, it's a good life. Otherwise it's for nothing."

During the reading, Jean fondly watched Leonard lying on a worn Turkish mat. He was ostentatiously playing a game of chess against himself. "This way I always win," he whispered.

Perhaps Leonard was so tantalizing to women because, despite his seductive ways, he was primarily interested in challenges created by his own brilliant mind. Recalled Ruth Gilbert, "Lying there and playing his solitary chess game, Leonard made it clear he felt superior to all of us."

After the reading, Leonard formally proposed to Jean, promising to carry her off to Greenwich Village. For Jean, and others of her generation, Greenwich Village had an "immense beckoning sweetness." It looked like London and was filled with outrageous, unconventional people. It was as "arty" as Paris, only better, since it was American.

Announcing her engagement at the Leofs', Jean toasted Leonard with champagne: "I promise you, this man . . . my Leonard, this lawyer . . . is going to be a great man."

3

THE MOST GORGEOUS COUPLE
OF THE LEFT

On February 20, 1937, in early afternoon, Leonard and Jean were married in Manhattan at City Hall. For the party held in the railroad apartment on Gansevoort Street in the West Village, Jean pushed real daisies into the wedding cake. Charlie Roisman provided a saxophonist who got drunk on the train ride up from Philadelphia.

But Jean's new marital state did not negate her desire to affect old beaux. When she bent low to cut a slice of wedding cake for Bert Gross, the sweetheart neckline of her dress opened to reveal that she was not wearing a brassiere.

Jean's father and stepmother were not invited. Louis Boudin was the "great man" in attendance. Izzy was thrilled to argue with him and Dr. Leof about who had done more to precipitate the Civil War: the Supreme Court with its "bad" Dred Scott decision or John Brown with his murderous moral sense. Leonard scowled when Izzy grew emotional and pronounced Louis his spiritual father.

*Marc Blitzstein and his wife,
Eva, Provincetown, 1935.
A musical prodigy, Blitzstein
was, like Jean Roisman
Boudin, a protégé of Dr.
Morris Leof.*

Jean cried with happiness when Dr. Leof boisterously raised a glass to toast "dear Jean" and "our Leonard" as "the most gorgeous couple of the American left."

In two short months, Jean's bliss was history. She found that she had no one to have dinner with except Marc Blitzstein and his gloomy wife, Eva, living in separate white lofts on nearby Jane Street. Jean frequently watched the sun slip down behind the Hudson River by herself. She missed the rest of her Philadelphia family and had plenty of time in which to do so as her new husband seemed to be hiding at his uncle's labor firm fourteen hours a day, seven days a week.

The problem was that Leonard saw himself as a suitor and not as a husband. Somehow before he could take charge of it, the momentum for marriage was set up by Jean's clamoring suitors and friends at "322." Bert Gross was one of several who had enthusiastically filled in the blanks between Jean and Leonard.

Jean had no idea that Leonard had told Georgette Schneer that his

Earl Browder, an official in the American Communist Party, visited the Leof home.

marital vows would not significantly alter their relationship. Georgette told him, "Watch out. Jean is sharp as a tack and just as stinging."

And indeed, Jean's "demandingness" quickly became distasteful to her husband once they were living on their own. By her own admission, Jean was "overly self-critical, overly emotional, overly moralistic, and overly curious."

Leonard had married Jean to win a prize. He had not realized that playing Prince Charming for the applauding "322" crowd was more fun than playing it only for Jean.

One afternoon in the summer of 1936, an acquaintance from Philadelphia recognized Jean on Eighth Street. Leon Berkowitz had sketched Jean in human anatomy classes at the Pennsylvania Academy of Fine Arts. Walking with her in the Village, he was soon urging Jean to make use of her lonely feelings in a poem.

Leon was a wiry young painter with strong eyebrows and tense, unblinking eyes. Jean found him compelling even though his hair was thinning and his nose sometimes ran. She'd recently read a review of his painting.

Though an abstract "color field" artist, he described himself playfully as a "landscape" painter, because he literally set up his easel in meadows

Leon Berkowitz, a color field painter and friend of Jean Boudin.

to paint invisible grassy hollows, for example, where sunlight made the greens jump with clarity.

Jean and Leon had both lost a parent early in life; in Leon's case, it was his father. Leon had showed artistic precocity as a small child. His mother told him that with his manual dexterity, he might become a carpenter. At school, however, his teachers saw that he was extraordinary and put him in a corner to make art.

Jean responded sharply when Leon asked to see her again, but he answered sweetly and she was ashamed.

That summer Leon was teaching at the Art Students League on Fifty-seventh Street in Manhattan, having studied art in Mexico City and Florence. He loved teaching. His students swore he jumped inside their skin and in his low, compelling voice channeled their artistic dreams while staring at their paintings. The love in his classroom, recalled a student, was palpable.

Jean and Leon were soul mates: Leon craved dialogue, while Leonard required Jean just to listen to him. Jean had the best ear for language of any woman Leon knew. In the Manhattan loft he shared with the painter Kenneth Noland, Leon and Jean spoke as if they held nothing back that was true. There was, however, much art and deft ellipse to their pronouncements. The friendship deepened into a love affair.

Some people found Leon too intense: he recited the Kabbalah and mused about scientific findings about light. "Einstein is right," he said. "Light is the only constant in nature. All forms change." Jean and he embarked on a dual project, a poem about light and emotions having physical weight. Jean referred to Leon so frequently and fondly that her friend Ruth Gilbert wondered about the third person in the Boudin marriage.

Jean strolled to Eva's bare loft at dusk. Marc appeared moments later with Turkish coffee and perfumed candles. Jean felt hopelessly bourgeois when she compared her own marital problems to those of Marc and Eva Blitzstein. The Blitzsteins' experiment in free love was a mess. Marc made no secret of his brief sexual encounters with sailors and construction workers in bars in Paris, Marseilles, and Berlin—a passion, said Jean, that dovetailed with his politics of solidarity with workingmen. Eva castigated herself for failing to maintain a physical union with her husband.

The dark miracle was how much the Blitzsteins loved each other. Madi had at one point surprised Marc on his knees declaring to Eva that he was unworthy of her.

The young people did not light candles until night blanketed the loft. Marc drank Scotch, a workingman brand he had bought in Wales. Eva made up inscriptions for plaques to be placed at dwellings where Marc composed his works.

Like Marc and Eva, Jean was puzzled by her romantic passions: despite the joyous moments she enjoyed with Leon, she pined for Leonard. She recited one of Marc's couplets: "I am building a fence / Against feeling intense."

Before departing for a hospital in Boston to be treated with forced feedings for dangerous weight loss, Eva told Jean that permanent separation from Marc was inevitable, and without him, her life was pointless. A few days later, on May 3, 1936, Madi telephoned Jean to tell her that Eva had died of starvation in her hospital bed at age thirty-four.

Leonard shivered when Jean alluded to Eva's death. Eva's love was, according to Leonard and Jean, the height of romantic attachment. Leonard understood something of Marc Blitzstein's problem. His mind wandered away during Jean's responses to his questions. He grew angry when she complimented him: Why was she buttering him up?

Jean dragged the unshaven and jittery Marc on "forced marches" through Washington Square Park. She heated milk and honey to help him sleep. She packed his suitcase when he went to Connecticut to stay on a farm with a patron of artists named Bess Eitingon and her husband, Motty—socialists, despite the millions of dollars Motty had made in Russia exchanging U.S. currency for furs. After big dinners cooked by servants, Motty read *Das Kapital* aloud in German, translating as he went along.

Marc used his time there to pour himself into the major work of his life—a "proletarian opera." *The Cradle Will Rock* is a fable based on daily newspaper headlines of steelworkers who organize for higher wages. The villain is named Mister Mister and owns a steel mill in Steeltown USA. Leonard was soon flattered to be questioned by Marc on labor law and to escort Marc to night-court sessions. Marc set a scene in night court where steel mill foreman "Larry Foreman" sings a song comparing the inevitability of workingmen forming unions to nature, using the upbeat tempo of the communist May Day march.

> *You can't stop the weather, not with all your dough!*
> *For when the wind blows, oh, when the wind blows,*
> *The cradle will rock!*

It took Marc months to find money for a Broadway production. His benefactor was the theater division of the Works Progress Administration (WPA), a New Deal agency created by President Roosevelt to support artists.

Jean and Madi organized an opening-night benefit for early June 1937. The proceeds were to fund a new educational institution where Marc taught—the Downtown Music School located on East Twelfth Street and under the influence of the Communist Party. They sold tickets months in advance.

On June 6, 1937, the morning of the big opening, Jean and Madi woke up to terrible news. The WPA officials had "temporarily" closed the production, blaming "financial cutbacks." Jean was ready to fight. She had marched six weeks earlier, on May 1, with members of the American Communist Party: May Day issues included more unions and no WPA cuts.

Now the two women telephoned ticket holders, friends, and members of the press to ask them to show up at the Maxine Elliot Theatre. (As a result Jean was instantly hired by the Federated Press, a left-wing news agency. She worked part-time as a photo editor.) Meanwhile Leonard huddled inside the theater with Marc and the play's young director, Orson Welles.

An hour before curtain time Jean joined hundreds of people milling in front of the locked theater on Thirty-ninth Street and Sixth Avenue. One union local threatened to break down the theater's doors. The crowd shouted, "Government censorship."

Leonard was instrumental in devising an audacious solution: cast members could perform a "rehearsal" somewhere else. This was the sort of fight Leonard would enthusiastically be drawn into again and again. He loved to dash to the rescue of illustrious intellectuals and artists being bullied by government bureaucrats.

Orson Welles agreed to keep the ticket holders from dispersing. John Houseman, the sympathetic WPA producer, was dispatched to find a neutral "rehearsal" space. A government representative begged the angry crowd to disperse quietly. But then Will Geer, the play's star, jumped up on the hood of a parked car and sang two numbers from the show. Meanwhile John Houseman located an empty space, the Venice Theatre, at Fifty-ninth Street and Seventh Avenue. He personally posted $100 in rent.

The ticket holders and cast surged twenty blocks north to the Venice Theatre. Jean stood in the back of the packed theater, since all seats were filled. The president of Actors' Equity jumped onstage to forbid cast members to perform.

But following Leonard's advice, the actors spoke lines from seats in the audience. The next day, newspapers hailed *The Cradle Will Rock* as an urbane and devastating attack against economic royalists.

4

A REVOLUTIONARY
CHILDHOOD

I can hire one half of the working class to kill the other half.
—Jay Gould

Jean was twenty-eight when her son, Michael, came into the world on December 8, 1939, at the progressive French Hospital in midtown Manhattan. Jean kept dreaming that her mother, Cilly, had not died in childbirth. She was flooded with feelings about how much she had been denied. She confided all this to a new friend, the world-famous anthropologist Margaret Mead, who was also having a baby. Mead's room was across the hall of the sixth-floor maternity pavilion. In addition, Jean was in a panic about her son's paternity. The relationship with Leon Berkowitz had gone on and on.

Mead was a sweet-faced dynamo, ten years Jean's senior. A fount of nonconformist strategies, Mead had made international headlines after sailing to Samoa in the South Seas on her own at the age of twenty-three to study adolescent girls and their relaxed sexual mores.

In French Hospital, Mead did not seem disturbed by the absence of her third husband, anthropology professor Gregory Bateson, who was in England working in the war effort.

Lacking a mother or grandmother to tie her to family tradition, Jean took many of the anthropologist's innovative practices to heart. For example, Jean started a log of observations of Michael Boudin's long attention span and eyebrow wiggles, all of which suggested to her prodigious intelligence.

Like Mead, Jean would begin looking for a Village brownstone to share with another family with young children; she and Leonard were currently living in a basement apartment on Jane Street.

Jean also copied Margaret Mead's revolutionary approach to breastfeeding, called feeding on self-demand. Michael's feedings were scheduled to coincide with his internal hunger rhythm. (The practice would be popularized by Mead's pediatrician, Dr. Benjamin Spock, without crediting Mead. Spock factored in the mother's comfort as well.)

Michael was a baby who cried a lot. Jean cried too as she heated baby bottles. "I'm so tired, I don't know if I even like him," she confessed to Ruth Gilbert. "I wanted a little girl." Jean was joking and not joking.

Leonard reluctantly accompanied Jean to a meeting organized by Margaret Mead, who had decided to found a "revolutionary" parent-run elementary school. Michael would be one of the first students. Jean nominated Leonard as the school's first president, extolling him. Leonard was an intellectual, whereas she was, she said, merely intuitive.

Leonard helped Margaret Mead establish the Downtown Community School. He raised money, and found and bought the old Fleischmann's Yeast factory building on Eleventh Street and Third Avenue. Leonard also planned budgets, hired teachers, and calmed fights between parents and teachers over salary and curriculum.

Under Mead's supervision, the factory was rebuilt with cramped observation booths for parents to watch children through a white screen. Jean painted chairs and filled in as a teachers' aide. Pete Seeger taught folk songs. At that time Third Avenue was wall-to-wall bars, and in the morning Michael and his mother walked around drunks lying on the street to get to school.

Leonard and Mead were exasperated by the blowout fights among parents: Trotskyites denounced Stalinists, and Stalinists denounced liberals. After one particularly acrid meeting, the highly esteemed intellectual

Dwight MacDonald indignantly withdrew his son, Michael, from the school.

A liberal, MacDonald noted that four of the twelve parents running the school were high-handed and highly sympathetic to the totalitarian ways of Soviet communism. He noted the absence of anticommunists on the board and said furthermore that the "Stalinoids" were in principle opposed to the freewheeling ways of progressive education.

He singled out Leonard: "For years, he [Leonard Boudin] has acted as a lawyer for pro-commie unions in the CIO, and has been active always on the commie side in the recent struggle between commies and anti-commies in the CIO."

Meanwhile, Leonard's blood boiled at the "bossy behaviors" of Margaret Mead. He said, "She takes over any committee she joins."

When Mead suggested assembly programs combining Hanukkah and Christmas rituals, Leonard interjected, "What about children from nonobserving homes? Let's provide nonsecular holiday interpretations too." But Mead said, "You first-generation atheists make me sick." Another time Mead silenced arguments, saying, "Hurry up. I've got to get back to the national scene."

Progressive education, as defined by John Dewey, was "teaching by doing" and meant in no small part confronting students with the nitty-gritty of reality. For example, when school maintenance workers held an election about joining a union, Leonard asked teachers to use the election as a way of studying unions. Or later, students visited coal mines in Pennsylvania to see how poor people lived and worked there.

As a small child, Michael showed artistic promise. His paintings were later confused by an aesthetics professor with those of Paul Klee. But he was a formal child who gave few clues that he was capable of artistic feelings.

He did, however, have an extravagant secret life, a little of which he shared with Margaret Mead's daughter, Cathy Bateson. The two children listened to the radio and made up serial stories about Michael's brown box turtle, named "the Great God Geyser." It was Michael and Cathy's favorite game. They created narrative fantasies in which the "Great Geyser" warred against his mortal enemies—a large kingdom of imaginary white mice. Geyser was the hero holding back the mice invasion. The two children surrendered up their own paintings as "sacrifices to the great tortoise."

Differentiating racial minorities was considered prejudice at Down-

Jean Boudin (left), age thirty-one, and her son, Michael, age three, with her girlhood friend Alice Carlen (right) and her daughter, Susan, in Atlantic City, circa 1942.

town Community School. It was confusing. Most black classmates were forbidden to curse by their middle-class parents. Thus white students such as Michael initially assumed blacks scorned tough language.

Michael absorbed the school's etiquette, which forbade displays of wealth. The children wore unpressed shirts and were embarrassed to be seen in swanky cars or with mothers who wore mink coats. One former student, Fred Gardner, joked that the school was a "real classy place," meaning that offspring of successful parents were looked up to. He remembers his mother's pride that he was attending school with Michael Boudin, who had a famous uncle.

Meanwhile luck and circumstance soon set Leonard's professional life firmly on course. Victor Rabinowitz, a twenty-nine-year-old lawyer and heir to a family fortune, left corporate law and burst into the Boudin firm, bristling with revolutionary moxie.

Leonard instantly was drawn to Victor, whom he declared "tough." Victor resonated commitment. He dreamed of sweeping revolutionary solutions to the ills of poverty in the United States and all over the world. Victor was stable and unemotional.

Leonard liked to be "jazzed" by strong personalities. Mutual friends say that Leonard virtually appropriated Victor's credo: Leonard vowed that he too would take cases only to fight social injustice.

Victor Rabinowitz, age sixteen, taken in Prospect Park, Brooklyn, 1927. Rabino-
witz, the son of immigrants, came from a long line of rabbis. His father, Louis,
made a fortune—he invented the machine that made the hook and eye—and was
also an anarchist. After law school, Victor joined the Louis Boudin labor law
office in 1937 and became Leonard Boudin's partner.

To Victor, Joe Boudin, a lawyer for hire by anyone with a real estate
problem, was just plain ridiculous. Indeed Victor looked down on all people (with the singular exception of Leonard) whose politics were less radical than his own. He did not smile, however, when Leonard joked,
"When I die and go to hell, it will be one long political meeting."

Victor later defended controversial clients like Alger Hiss, who was
convicted of spying for the Soviets. Victor spoke of violent revolution,
but shot a gun only once out of politeness to a host. Aiming at a crow, he
was happy to have missed it. He fought the evils of capitalism only in
court. "The only revolution I ever took part in is in my head," he said
apologetically in later years. He joined the Communist Party in 1940,
after most intellectuals here had quit. His reasoning: the Soviet Union
was our new ally in the war against Germany. Izzy Stone tried to dissuade
him: "Facts, facts, facts, Victor, we need more facts about the Russian
experiment." But Victor had no desire to visit Russia. Although he

Leonard, age twenty-six (center), and his partner Victor Rabinowitz, age twenty-seven (right), in 1939 at an annual banquet of the National Lawyers' Guild at the Hotel Woodstock in Manhattan.

dreaded his wife Marcia's relatives because they were "too religious," Victor's own ironclad belief system contained a great deal of wistful faith.

Victor's lack of interest in material possessions gave little indication (at least superficially) that his father was rich. Louis Rabinowitz commissioned formal portraits of himself on horseback, and was driven in a limousine. Renowned in the ladies' garment business for his reliable ways, Victor's father had been an anarchist in his youth. Like Victor he was antireligion, despite his ancestry of generations of rabbis in a small community in western Russia. It seemed to Victor that there was no problem that "Pop" could not solve or transcend. (In contrast, Victor's mother was timid.)

The legal secretaries called Victor an intellectual snob. But if ever one of them had a legal problem, he instantly took the case—and refused fees. (In later years Leonard said he set his own famously low fees by multiplying Victor's scale by four.) Victor was, said one legal secretary, "objective to a fault." When Victor's first children, a set of twins, were stillborn, he investigated and decided not to sue, because he was convinced the doctor would never make that mistake again.

Victor rarely swerved from a commitment to a person or an ideal. Leonard, on the other hand, called himself a "wobbly agnostic" unable to commit to atheism. He was obsessed with his own death and commented on it matter-of-factly.

Leonard and Victor loved thinking together—even on Saturdays and Sundays. They prepared arguments to be delivered in front of Roosevelt's new Labor Relations Board on behalf of their client, the United Office and Professional Workers Union.

Belle Harper, an associate, recalled, "Victor and Leonard were an incredible team, two great-looking young guys fighting for a better world." She added acerbically, "Victor is overly modest, and back in those days of course Leonard wanted to be adored, but he kept his ego more under wraps." The relationship was surprisingly impersonal,

Striking employees of the American Communications Union picketing the main office of Western Union in Manhattan, 1946. Louis Boudin and Victor Rabinowitz were their lawyers.

although Lucille Perlman, Victor's sister, said, years later, "Leonard was a brother to Victor. Victor never had a closer friend."

Victor believed personal problems had few solutions and were the province of women and Shakespeare. "You can't expect people to be consistent," he said. He tried not to notice that Leonard chased women, bragged a lot, and suffered from moods, colds, headaches, stress, and insomnia.

Leonard continued to seduce men and women, but by now he was limiting his conquests of men to the sphere of the intellect.

The two young lawyers vanquished company practices of firing pro-union employees and organizing company-controlled unions. Leonard and Victor also defended picketing workers accused of beating up scabs. "We were only thirty years old and we were playing a wonderful new game," said Victor. "We enjoyed watching corporate lawyers approach the [National Labor Relations] Board with foreboding. They knew the deck had been stacked against them by Roosevelt's New Deal legislation. They saw the Board as a sign that the old order of capitalism was crumbling. We had at our feet some of the biggest corporations and highly paid gray-haired corporate lawyers in the country. We could strut—it was a great joy. It was fun and games."

Victor and Leonard spent hours at night court getting picketing workers out of jail. The Depression was a fact of life. Every night, around midnight, twenty homeless people were herded into the unheated courtroom. At first, Victor and Leonard tried to ignore "the human wrecks" by reading books, but the lighting was dim. Leonard and Victor debated the problem abstractly: What did the spectacle say about the ineffectual role of law in society? It did not occur to the two lawyers to attempt to alleviate the vagrants' suffering.

As time passed, Leonard saw encounters, friendships, love affairs—indeed most of the world—in terms of win-lose and as adversarial. The law, he decided, was superior to life, since legal victories were more easily and precisely measured. Al Socolow recalls, "Leonard was always three feet off the ground. He was as foreign to stare decisis [arguing from past legal decisions] as anyone could be. He took nothing for granted."

As long as Leonard was winning cases he was a hero. He glossed over the oversimplifications and potential heartbreak such a belief entails.

At the office, however, Leonard was losing the competition to inherit the Boudin firm. Sidney Cohn was earning a partner's salary even though he was only three years older than Leonard. Leonard's rival was married to the boss's (Louis's) daughter Vera. Leonard called Cohn an operator and accused him of not bothering with legal research.

On January 31, 1940, Leonard and Jean (who was wearing short gloves and a panama hat) traveled to Washington to witness Louis Boudin defend a brief before the Supreme Court. Louis spoke without notes; he was too blind to see them. Louis's client was the Amalgamated Utility Workers Union. They were fighting Con Edison in New York. The National Labor Relations Board had ordered Con Edison to stop firing employees for trying to form a branch of the Amalgamated Utility Workers Union. Con Edison ignored the order.

Chief Justice Hughes rejected Louis's petition, saying it was up to the National Labor Relations Board—and not the unions—to make sure Con Edison did the right thing.

Michael was a wiry, scowling three-year-old in the summer of 1942 when he and Jean "went down the shore," as Philadelphians say. Leonard did not join Jean and Michael in Ventnor, New Jersey, a hot seaside suburb of Atlantic City. Jean and friends from "322" were renting a Victorian mansion with huge curving porches. Jean explained her husband's absence: "My Leonard is busy changing the world with his famous uncle Louis."

She had a short visit from Leon Berkowitz, who detoured from a family reunion in North Philadelphia. Days passed as Jean sunbathed on a blue-and-gray-striped beach chair resting on scorching sand. One day Bert Gross's small son, David (who would grow up to be a theoretical physicist), sat down next to Michael, who was dripping wet sand through his clenched fist to construct a castle. Unprovoked, Michael hit David with his red metal shovel. In later years, Bert joked that the "shovel event" foreshadowed Michael's cold, pro-corporate politics.

When Leonard learned in 1942 that Jean was pregnant again, he and Victor lobbied for raises. They earned $100 a week, the lowest-paid lawyers in the firm. Louis turned them down, saying that they brought in no clients and what's more, the firm could always buy brains.

At this point, a lawyer named Sam Neuburger invited Victor to be partner at a small firm that litigated for the Communist Party and for left-wing unions at department stores such as Macy's, Bloomingdale's, Gimbel's, and Stern's. But because Victor had grown used to reading, arguing, consulting, and pacing himself with Leonard, he agreed to join the firm only if Leonard was invited too. Leonard initially consented but pulled back, fearing his uncle would see him as the "family traitor." In reality, Leonard's ambition was fixed on his aged and fading uncle: he desperately wanted to inherit the Boudin firm. He wanted to surpass Louis.

So Victor left the Boudin firm without Leonard, taking with him the American Communications Union and a local chapter of the Furniture Workers. He kept pressing Leonard, who was still ambivalent. At one point Victor even had stationery printed up: "Neuburger, Shapiro, Rabinowitz, and Boudin." But Leonard again backed away, saying, "The only reason you want me is because a labor law firm without the name 'Boudin' on the letterhead seems minor."

5

SWORD AND FIRE

The children born of thee are sword and fire,
Red ruin, and the breaking up of laws.

—Tennyson, Idylls of the King

The arrival of an adored little sister on May 19, 1943, sent the introspective four-year-old Michael Boudin further inside himself. Jean explained to friends in her most droll tone that it was her fault that Michael was too inward. Michael was in fact already steeling himself to Jean's inconsistencies. He grew to resent Jean's ready sympathy for each passing underdog, since she seemed to have so little for him. He became an autodidact. Angered by Jean's emotionality—particularly about politics—he decided early on to map out a secret path of such worldly power and intellectual purity that it would checkmate Jean, Leonard, Kathy, and even Izzy.

Kathy was a good baby who seemed to smile even when she was hungry. She slept peacefully through the night and was fed and cuddled on demand as per Margaret Mead. Kathy was extroverted and cheery, particularly when compared to Michael, perhaps because Jean was more consistent in her affection and in the application of progressive child-care methods to Kathy.

Jean wrote of her delight in the birth of her daughter:

MOTHER/DAUGHTER

And yet as though it were now, she remembers . . .
how you howled your first cry
. . . It's a girl, the doctor said.
Nothing was ever so right . . .

It was Jean who would joke about Kathy's "revolutionary" birthday. The date—May 19—is also the birthday of black power activist Malcolm X and of North Vietnam communist leader Ho Chi Minh. Later on the coincidence weighed on Kathy—particularly when she needed something beyond rational thought to help her commit to a path of action.

No one except perhaps Michael could resist Kathy. She was blessed with a combination of Leonard's seductiveness and Jean's flirty charisma—and she seemed endearingly vulnerable. "She was a stunning presence," said a neighbor. "I swear she did not pose or try to get attention." Even as a preschooler, she kept an entire family entranced by describing a film of the birth of a calf.

Uncharacteristically reserved with Michael, Leonard gave his ebullient attention to his daughter, a gift that enlivened her entire being. Leonard had a wild sense of play. Kathy shrieked and laughed in his presence. When her father's eyes flashed in her direction, Kathy flushed and her words tumbled out in a happy, spirited rush, her voice cracking and rising. A shriek of laughter from him elicited shrieks from her, and suddenly they were crawling around on all fours. Or sometimes their voices sank melodramatically as Leonard hid behind a small chair in a game of hide-and-seek. Georgette Schneer observed, "Leonard loved Kathy best of anyone in the world." He began addressing women he liked as "little girl." He flinched, however, when one woman addressed him in response as "little boy."

Leonard had enormous antic energy and loved the company of women, yet no woman was able to command his respect. "He sparkled at pretty young women he wanted to seduce," said Edith Tiger, who worked for Leonard for thirty-five years. "Others were invisible."

Jean took pride in Kathy's physical confidence: she was the only little girl who walked unaided on parallel bars in the playground. But Leonard said that no child of his could possibly use athletic prowess to make her mark. He despised all sports except swimming, at which he believed he excelled. Friends remember that Kathy was a great swimmer. Leonard swam the way he played tennis: with fierce, uncoordinated movements. Also like her mother before her, Kathy was "something of a genius" at picking up foreign languages, which irritated Leonard—since this was one of his intellectual weaknesses.

A father who spoiled his daughter, Leonard was paradoxically unable to focus his dazzling attention on her for very long. Said Random House editor John Simon, "Leonard was easily distracted—by women and by tangents of thoughts."

In 1945, when Kathy was two years old, and Michael was six, Leonard and Jean moved a few blocks to the upper two floors of a shabby-gracious house at 12½ St. Luke's Place. The town house was part of a row built in the mid-nineteenth century, and had been owned by a Village landlady. The exterior was festooned with disheveled hanging vines, iron latticework, and wood trim weathered in the European manner of unabashedly showing the age on heirlooms. The house implied success. It could have been the Beacon Hill home of a Harvard professor with a trust fund.

Inside, rooms were small, cozy. Leonard's law journals and tan law books covered walls. They spilled off a side table in the upstairs bathroom and were stacked under Leonard's side of the bed. Before sitting on the couch, guests pushed aside clumps of journals.

In the spring Jean threw open windows and breathed in the sour odors of ginkgo trees. She listened to children shrieking in the city playground and outdoor swimming pool across the street. Summers, when Leonard made a rare appearance before sundown, he, Jean, and Kathy put on bathing suits and ran hand in hand across the street to join the splashing youngsters.

The writer Sherwood Anderson had lived next door decades earlier. Jean recited dryly: "Even in Winesburg, Ohio, people live and die alone."

Despite lofty aspirations for communal living, relations between the Boudins and the Riley family downstairs became distant over the next forty years. "We agreed not to socialize by mutual consent," said Bob Riley.

Jean hung beach photographs of the family on the walls of the curving entrance staircase. Her squinting children leaned against the bare legs of their gloriously handsome parents. Leonard and Jean were better-looking than nearly everyone, including their own children.

Jean also pinned handwritten notices of poetry readings on the kitchen door, urging others to go with her to hear Frank O'Hara and William Carlos Williams.

Leonard stole time from law books to teach Kathy and Michael chess. (Jean diplomatically declared herself "the chess illiterate.") Michael was a far better player than Kathy, although Leonard defeated both children over and over. Michael struggled to grasp shards of paternal love in the power lessons.

President Harry Truman suddenly declared a "cold war." Most Americans were terrified and revolted by the monster of insidiously organized communism. The new enemy had underground tentacles all over the world. Worse yet, the Soviet Union might soon have the atomic bomb. Soviet communism inspired almost as much dread as the polio virus. Joseph Stalin was perceived as someone who was out to destroy the United States and all it stood for. Socialists were lumped with communists and no longer viewed as charming intellectuals with naïve dreams of a better world. They were satanic, hairy, atheists, Jewish, antidemocratic. Children were warned by parents to shun playmates whose parents were rumored "sympathizers." Red-hunting became savage sport. Walter Winchell warned his radio audiences, "Wake up America or you and your children will die in your sleep."

What Red-haters did not understand was that American communist sympathizers were mostly theorizers—not doers—and most had left the party because they balked at being told what to think. And although some people had been recruited by the Soviets to spy—none of these was discovered by Senator Joe McCarthy or any other congressional investigators.

Jean was a self-described parlor revolutionary. Her faith was loosely analogous to that of people who believe in distant biblical miracles, but who dismiss contemporary wonders as craziness. Jean joked at such contradibions in her life. "I'll pay you come the revolution," she would say, hanging up on a bill collector.

Ambition suddenly ignited Leonard. Giving up on inheriting his uncle Louis's firm, he hurriedly joined Victor's firm when he learned that at the young age of forty, Victor was to argue before the U.S. Supreme Court. Leonard brought with him his client, the United Office and Professional Workers Union. Leonard helped to research Victor's brief condemning the Taft-Hartley Act, whose section 9(h) required union officers to disavow Communist Party membership. Leonard was quoted in the *New York Times* on March 16, 1949: "The non-Communist affidavit insults American workers."

The defendants were leaders of the Radio and Telegraph Union. Government lawyers postulated ominous ties between steel strikes and Communist Party orders. It was a hard case to win, and although Victor lost, he made his mark.

Kathy was the most popular child at her elementary school. She played on both the boys' and girls' sports teams. Despite the fact that he practiced long hours in the playground across from their house, Michael was not the least bit athletic. Kathy would develop into a great basketball player armed with what was later described as "a deadly accurate corner jump shot." After lunch, the nursery-school director, Eleanor Brussel, sat on the little girl's cot, patting her, sometimes singing to her, to help her fall asleep for her nap.

Michael was the best student his teachers had ever seen. He seemed older than his years, clearly focused on what he wanted and how he could win it. He analyzed situations with keen logic that seemed to be formulated at a distance. The children rarely had homework, but when given it, they cheered. Michael is remembered by a chorus of admiring classmates: "Oh, he was—a genius, but I barely knew him."

Sitting behind Michael at a party, Edith Tiger was appalled to hear him lecturing a little girl. "I couldn't believe my ears—he was reciting some of Leonard's research about rape statutes." Michael had adopted Leonard's almost fey way of speaking tentatively, as if he were thinking hard as he went along. It was more tough-minded than it sounded.

"Mike talked like a prissy intellectual," said Jennie Simon, Kathy's inseparable best friend, who rarely spoke negatively of anyone. Her parents were divorced, and her father was the owner of the large publishing firm Crown Books. He lived next door to the Boudins on St. Luke's Place. Jennie spent many nights sleeping over with Kathy. She lived a few blocks away with her mother in a small apartment. "There was the fastidious way Michael selected his verbs and adjectives. Kathy did not talk like that, and she was smart. Michael made it clear he had no time for his sister and her little friends."

Michael could be darkly mischievous. Margaret Ullman, a friend of Margaret Mead, sometimes walked Michael and Mead's daughter, Cathy Bateson, home from school. Michael knew that this temporary guardian had lost her peripheral vision due to a brain operation. He made a game of confusing her by running along the curb where she could not see him.

In school, Michael's art teacher, Alan Ullman, the husband of Margaret Ullman and a pacifist, asked the class to draw the atomic explosion over Hiroshima, calling it the most lethal weapon ever used. The class created frightening drawings—Michael's one of the most powerful. Jean's joy at the exploding of the atomic bombs over two cities in Japan in August 1945 had confused Michael, who was nine years old. Although Jean spoke out angrily against wars in general, she supported World War II as "the war against fascism." When Japan finally accepted the Allies' terms for surrender, cheers filled the house. Jean and Leonard were elated for a second reason, having just learned of the pivotal role played by Bob Serber, Jean's "322" friend, in the creation of the atomic bomb at Los Alamos, New Mexico, whose explosions had caused Japan's surrender. He had also witnessed the bombing of Nagasaki from one of the airplanes. (Bob Serber had married Charlotte Leof.)*

Several months later, Michael decided to test his father on the complicated morality of the use of the bomb. One afternoon he inquired, "Leonard, do you believe dropping the atom bomb was good or bad?" (Both children called Leonard and Jean by their first names.)

Leonard believed the issue impossibly complex. But perhaps, because he was sitting in his living room with Al Socolow, whom he considered "tough"—very radical—Leonard answered, "Dropping the bomb was bad."

---

*Bob Serber staunchly believed that the bombing of the two Japanese cities had saved at least 500,000 lives of U.S. soldiers. It ended the war and it was, he said, "a good clean ending."

After Michael skipped upstairs to his bedroom, Leonard had second thoughts. He asked Al, "Do you think it was wrong of me to impose my own views of the atom bomb on Michael? I usually encourage him to adopt his own views." He told his friend that above all he wanted Michael to come to issues with an open mind.

Michael also received confusing messages at school. There was a reluctance to teach children that some human behavior was unequivocally bad—or dangerous. Teachers hesitated to set limits on tolerance. For example, Michael's class went out daily for fresh air to Tompkins Square Park, where one morning they were admonished for staring at a disabled man. Soon afterward, while the teacher was absent, a man exposed his genitals. The little children discussed moral imperatives: they must not stare, but above all they must not hurt the man's feelings. When he heard about the incident, Leonard laughed and said, "A liberal is a man too broadminded to take his own side in an argument."

Leonard was depressed at the Roisman family's seder in April 1946. He disliked the overheated West Philly row house of Jean's father and stepmother. The smell of Jennie Roisman's burnt noodle pudding made him sick. Leonard tried his best to tune out Izzy's bombast. But the real problem was his guilt at not spending Passover with his mother, Clara, who was terminally ill with cancer.

Izzy suddenly declared himself heartbroken that the "bullies of the world" had not been stopped by the Allied victory of World War II. He was trying to force Leonard to commiserate over the fact that the British had refused entry to Palestine to pitiful Jewish refugees from Hitler's concentration camps.

"Face it, Leonard," Izzy shouted up the table, "you're nothing but an apolitical SOB!" No one was shocked. Izzy picked fights for entertainment and even his jokes menaced. He translated everything into political terms. He once shouted at his daughter about a typographical error in her poem: "Typos are worse than fascism."

Instead of answering Izzy, Leonard massaged his spikey hair, knocking a knife to the floor. Ironically, Leonard longed to merge with higher truths. He passionately envied Izzy's capacity for arriving at new righteous analyses of such political complexities as Tito's socialist experiment in Yugoslavia.

Nonetheless Leonard complained in private to Jean that Izzy acted like he had died and was running socialist heaven. Leonard was also threatened by Izzy's ability to maintain a solid marriage. Esther apparently filled all of Izzy's needs. Their son Marc noted, "Whatever Izzy wanted, that's what was done. His life was charmed that way. Like very few men." Esther polished and even wrote parts of Izzy's essays without credit.

Jean scooped up Leonard's knife from the floor and shouted hoarsely at Izzy, "Leonard's activism is in his goddamn law books."

"Good lord—" blurted Jean's stepmother.

"If anything, not good but neutral," interjected Jean sweetly.

Staring intently at her father, Kathy registered his relief and grinned. "My activism is in my goddamn law books" would be Leonard's anthem.

Most members of the circle argued and argued—and argued. "As satisfying as mothers' milk," said Bert Gross. If Izzy was bored, he could always take sides on goodies such as: Did President Roosevelt save capitalism for rich people and ruin chances for serious revolution in the United States?

Soon after the raucous Roisman seder, Izzy followed his moral compass to Palestine. There he joined the underground warriors in the militant Haganah. Izzy was the first journalist to evade the British blockades against refugees and to report the building of a Jewish state through armed rebellion. The book he wrote about it would be used by Menachem Begin, leader of the militant Irgun, as a military training manual.

Nonetheless, the moment Izzy heard that Israelis were shunting Palestine Arabs to settlement camps, he incurred the wrath of many Jews by declaring himself in favor of a binational state.

Leonard jockeyed with Izzy in vain. As the "anti-ideologue" of the circle, Leonard loftily declared himself "in favor of justice and human rights as guaranteed by the United States Constitution—period." He claimed that "the law" was the best pursuit. He was, he said, still modeling himself on his uncle Louis, the "great man" of the circle.

6

THERE IS NO PROOF

And again it is stated that there is no proof that the appellant hated the United States.

—Leonard Boudin in defense of Judith Coplon, convicted Soviet spy, 1949

In the winter of 1950, the cold war was gaining momentum. During the rare times Leonard was home, six-year-old Kathy noted fresh hurt in her mother's silences. Leonard had told Eleanor Brussel, his close friend and Kathy's former kindergarten teacher, that his newest client, Judith Coplon, was the "great love of my life." A lowly clerk in the Justice Department whose job had been to clip articles from such newspapers as the *Daily Worker,* Coplon had been convicted in Washington of stealing government documents. At Coplon's personal request, Leonard was appointed by the court in the middle of her second trial, which was held in New York, on separate charges of having passed the stolen documents in Manhattan to a Soviet agent. She'd fired her first lawyer, Archibald Palmer, claiming he had struck her.

During her two trials, newspapers were filled with details about the beautiful Barnard graduate with the high forehead and sullen mouth. Judith Coplon looked much younger than her twenty-seven years and dressed in the career-girl uniform, tight suits with big shoulders. Tabloid headlines denounced the "outlaw girl" with a penchant for lurid sex and spying. Photographs emphasized her mysterious dark eyes. While at Barnard, she had lived with her parents in Brooklyn, had been managing editor of the school newspaper, and briefly joined the Young Communist League.

News of Coplon's spying for the Soviets fed the primal fears of the American public; her guilt was assumed. Graffiti in New York subways read: GET JUDY COPLON, MOCKIE, COMMIE SPY. Coplon later wrote of her first visit in jail from Leonard, remembering his intense reaction to her distress.

> I remember the first time Leonard visited me in jail. He was in one of these small tiled prison conference cells at the Women's House of Detention. I entered and I could see him gasp at the sight of me in my faded jail dress and slippers. I don't remember what he said or any special gesture he made. But what I do remember so vividly that I can still see it now was his look of anguish. It was as though the responsibility he felt toward me, toward my case, made him ache physically. Somehow this very tortured compassion in Leonard was more reassuring to me than any words of encouragement could have been.

Many men, including lawyers in Leonard's firm, fell in love with Coplon and were disappointed when Leonard's young associate Al Socolow, considered a bit dull, married the flamboyant young woman. One lawyer, Belle Harper, figured Judith wanted a family to come home to if she had to go to prison. Bright and fiery, Judith Coplon was doing her best to mask her daily terrors. She fooled at least one FBI agent who angrily watched her "laughing and skipping" through corridors of court buildings.

Judith Coplon's legal troubles had started when Special Agent Robert Lamphere pounced on a few pages of the top-secret government papers called the Venona communiqués, in which one Soviet spy based in the United States claimed he'd recruited an anonymous woman working in the Justice Department. The spy promised to send information the woman was stealing to the Soviet Union.*

---

*In 1998, the government revealed that it had deciphered (by 1949) fourteen messages about the anonymous woman's zealous work. She was learning Russian to discover identities of moles reporting to the FBI about Soviet activities.

Judith Coplon, Foley Square, Manhattan, 1949.

These top-secret Venona communiqués were only partially decoded and were not made public for another forty-five years. The documents could not be used in court as evidence for many reasons. First, Director Hoover had not wanted to alert the Soviets that cryptographers were slowly decoding the Venona communiqués. The documents were also, of course, communications between anonymous foreign spies and thus not reliable. They might be boasts or outright lies. For example, the communiqués contain an alleged attempt to recruit Izzy Stone, code-named "Blini" or "Pancake," as a Soviet spy. Izzy's response was said to be no, but only because he was worried about the safety of his family. This incident is unlikely to have happened as the Soviet spy described it.

Nonetheless, according to the Venona communiqués, the anonymous woman spy had moved from Manhattan to Washington at the precise time Judith Coplon herself was transferred.

Special Agent Robert Lamphere was thrilled: instead of "the usual spy trails that led nowhere," he finally had indication, although not strong enough for conviction or use in court, of a real spy.

But Director J. Edgar Hoover told Lamphere to have Judith Coplon

J. Edgar Hoover (right) with Clyde Tolson, Miami Beach, 1939. Leonard consistently fought the tactics that Director Hoover set up in the FBI.

fired. She was "small potatoes." Hoover was having problems enough putting together the far more important espionage case against Alger Hiss.*

Lamphere disagreed. He convinced Hoover to allow Lamphere to "bait a hook" and see if Coplon bit and revealed her espionage contacts. So Lamphere created a fake FBI file, a decoy, and had Coplon's supervisor in the Justice Department pass it to her saying that it was "hot."†

Lamphere's subsequent telephone taps revealed that on her next trip to

---

*Hoover's chief witness against Hiss, Whitaker Chambers, was waffling about how much he was prepared to testify. And to make matters worse, Chambers now admitted he had been a practicing homosexual.

†The decoy file "faked" the information that the American lawyer for Amtorg (the official Russian purchasing agency in the United States) was disloyal to Russia and secretly reporting to the FBI. "Pinning a snitch jacket" on the Amtorg attorney would make the decoy file important to the Soviets and would also cause distrust and chaos inside Amtorg. Some scholars, such as Harvey Klehr, the expert on the Venona papers, believe that Coplon had already alerted the Soviets about their agent Elizabeth Bentley, who had changed allegiance and was now tattling to the FBI about Soviet spies in the United States.

Manhattan Coplon was planning to pass the "decoy file" and other secret documents to Valentin Gubitchev, a Russian KGB agent stationed at the United Nations.

But Hoover firmly rejected Lamphere's request for a warrant for Coplon's arrest. Hoover still thought she was small potatoes. Nonetheless the zealous Lamphere continued to supervise thirty FBI agents who watched Coplon night and day. They tapped her parents' phone in Brooklyn as well as her office and home telephones. Agents named the surveillance the "Punch and Judy Show"; Coplon neglected to close her living-room curtains while entertaining men.

Shortly thereafter, the thirty FBI agents followed Coplon from Washington to Penn Station. She limped off the train, a shoe strap torn, and panicked Lamphere by asking one of the agents trailing her for directions to the Independent subway line.

Twenty-four agents on foot and seven in two-way-radio cars watched Judith Coplon stroll with the handsome Valentin Gubitchev near Fort Tryon Park. The couple suddenly separated, looking over their shoulders, and then ambled back together again. Typical spy behavior.*

When Gubitchev and Coplon arrived at Luchow's Restaurant, Lamphere panicked. He disobeyed Hoover's orders. Despite a lack of warrant, Lamphere impulsively ordered the couple's arrest. Agents seized Coplon's purse, which indeed contained Lamphere's "decoy file." The FBI also found a letter of apology for not having one FBI document, "data slips" containing extracts from FBI reports, written sketches of fellow employees that the FBI suspected were recruiting material for the Soviets, notes about illegal FBI raids of suspected Soviet spies, as well as a tube of Irresistible pink lipstick and a safety pin.

The effect of the publicized arrest on Coplon's private life seems to have been catastrophic. Details of her romances were splashed across tabloids, and her father died soon after her arrest. Until Leonard entered the Coplon case, it had pivoted on a lurid question. Was Judith Coplon a spy or had she been carrying on a love affair with a married Russian working at the United Nations?

Her first trial lawyer had audaciously argued that Coplon's arrest was a misunderstanding. She was merely an author carrying three chapters of an incomplete autobiographical novel titled *Government Girl,* about

*Coplon's first lawyer, Archibald Palmer, claimed the "spy behavior" was a ruse meant only to deter detectives hired by Gubitchev's jealous wife.

changes in Washington during the cold-war period. Valentin Gubitchev and she were having lovers' trysts and were "crazy, crazy in love." The couple had met, said her first lawyer, at the Museum of Modern Art on Labor Day weekend in 1948, in front of a cubist painting. Valentin had asked a crowd of people including Coplon what the painting meant.

In cross-examination during her first trial held in Washington before Leonard entered the case, a government lawyer asked Coplon if Valentin Gubitchev was the only man in her life. "Yes and I love him," she said. The lawyer raised his voice. "If Gubitchev was the only man in your life, how is it that on January 7, 1949, you registered in a hotel in Baltimore as the wife of Mr. Harold Shapiro [another Justice Department employee], and the following night in another hotel in Philadelphia?"

Coplon screamed at her lawyer. "You son of a bitch! I told you this would happen. How could you let it happen with my mother in the court-room?" Mrs. Coplon wept. Pandemonium ensued.

Although Coplon went on to insist she had kept her clothes on all night in both hotels, and had only discussed philosophy until it became too late to go home, in effect the Washington trial was over. She was sentenced to forty months to ten years, and this was just trial number one.

Leonard was hired in the middle of Coplon's second trial (this one for *passing* the stolen documents), which took place in New York. He changed the course of the defense: he dropped the subject of Coplon's romantic life and attacked FBI tactics. Although he lost the second trial, he won appeals of both of Coplon's convictions using this defense.

Leonard seized upon the raw, secret internal FBI reports that were mistakenly released by a lower-echelon agent of the FBI during Coplon's Washington trial after Coplon's previous lawyer had asked to see evidence against her.

The FBI pages were purported to be admissible evidence against Coplon from a source code-named "Tiger." Among other things, "Tiger" reported a disagreement between Judith Coplon and someone about if "we should ask for an adjournment next Wednesday." Unlike Coplon's first lawyer, Leonard realized the disagreement was in fact a piece of a telephone conversation between Coplon and that lawyer.

Leonard knew the only way the government could have gotten wind of conversations between Coplon and her lawyer was through illegal wire-taps of Coplon's telephone. Such wiretaps violated the lawyer-client relationship.

Thus, during the New York trial, Leonard made a thundering accusation of government misconduct after reading into the record the few pages of the raw FBI internal files about Coplon.

The words *government misconduct* would hereafter be a courtroom refrain throughout Leonard's courageous and successful legal career.

This time Leonard noted that, after the raw FBI files had been introduced in court in Washington, J. Edgar Hoover moved to drop the case. President Harry Truman blocked Hoover, but Leonard intuited that Hoover was trying to hide something.

Leonard asked one FBI agent about the person code-named "Tiger." The agent swore that "Tiger" was a single anonymous, real person. Other agents took the stand, however, and refused to back him under oath. The first agent had clearly perjured himself.

Leonard stunned the New York courtroom when he asserted that "Tiger," described by the FBI as "a confidential informant of known reliability," was a fraud. "Tiger" was a construct, a catchall of assorted government evidence against Coplon including illegal wiretaps.*

Leonard raised his voice and accused the FBI of "rankest perjury." He also pressed to see all of "Tiger"'s reports. Hoover lied and claimed all other "Tiger" files had been routinely burned.

Leonard then asserted that the trial was illegal; Coplon had been deprived of the right to see evidence against her and to have confidential conversations with her lawyer. (Leonard would also argue in his successful appeal of the Washington trial—which was for stealing the documents—that Coplon had been arrested without a warrant and thus the contents of her handbag should not be used against her.)

Leonard's public accusation of fraud infuriated Hoover and frightened Lamphere. This was an early legal attack on Hoover, venerated by nearly all Americans until then as a hero. Leonard smirched Hoover's reputation for integrity. Reprimands, transfers, censures, and demotions would be given to the agents who had been assigned to the Coplon case.

Years after Hoover and Leonard died, it was revealed that Hoover possessed three kinds of evidence against Coplon, none of which could stand up in court. First were illicit phone taps and second were government documents seized from Coplon's purse when she was arrested without a

---

*Leonard did not know, of course, about the partially decoded top-secret Venona communiqués, the inadmissible source that had led the FBI to Coplon. When some of the Venona papers were made public forty-five years later, some historians took liberals to task for having underestimated the seriousness of Soviet recruitment of people working in the U.S. government.

Judge Learned Hand, perhaps the greatest living judge, was a revered figure in the Boudin household, having sided with Leonard's appeal in the Judith Coplon espionage case.

warrant. Third, although Leonard did not know it, Hoover possessed an indication of Coplon's espionage activities in the fascinating and confusing Venona papers, top-secret Soviet spy communications that were slowly being decoded when Coplon was arrested.

Leonard showed that Hoover's FBI had framed Coplon because they believed very strongly in her guilt on the basis of inadmissible evidence against her. Leonard succeeded in getting both of Coplon's convictions reversed on appeal. In New York, Judge Learned Hand wrote a famous ruling that stated that the government had violated Coplon's right to a fair trial by refusing to produce evidence against her. Hand wrote: "Few weapons in the arsenal of freedom are more useful than the power to compel a government to disclose the evidence on which it seeks to forfeit the liberty of its citizens."

Thus Leonard defeated the FBI and came astonishingly close to toppling Hoover himself, the most ruthless and powerful government official in U.S. history. And this was despite the fact that Hoover knew his case against Judith Coplon was stronger than cases he was preparing against Alger Hiss and Julius and Ethel Rosenberg.

Leonard would also, unbeknownst to himself, Victor, or Izzy, throw Hoover into a tizzy of reorganization. Hoover privately called Leonard's Coplon victory "one of the worst disasters I personally suffered." He was forced to go to enormous lengths to hide FBI files containing illicit information. He hid files in the headquarters basement under twenty-four-hour armed guard, keeping them off-limits to most agents. Hoover also made illegal wiretapping so confidential that it was frequently done without the knowledge of the agent in charge of a case. Files were passed around with "cover letters" containing illicit information. The cover letters were destroyed.

Hoover's secret files contained a list of such secret enemies as Leonard Boudin, with potential blackmail information gleaned from privileged medical records; sealed court documents; illegally obtained bank, telephone, or credit company records; IRS data; as well as results of surveillance—including mail openings, break-ins, wiretaps, microphone installations, and theft and deciphered codes. Also in secret files were informants' identities, lies in testimonies of government witnesses, and incriminating personal information about government witnesses and officials. Hoover was determined to hide his records from court-ordered discovery motions, congressional subpoenas, and requests from the Justice Department. It would thus be virtually impossible to ferret out illicit origins of evidence.

Hoover also invented a category of top-secret surveillance files known as June Mail, which later the FBI collected on Kathy Boudin and the Black Panthers, among others. June Mail would first be sealed in an envelope marked JUNE, and then placed in a second sealed envelope, marked PERSONAL AND CONFIDENTIAL and addressed to Hoover himself.

As a result of the Coplon case, President Truman decided to fire Hoover for fraudulent methods. Unlike other presidents, Truman did not personally fear Hoover. The man from Independence was straitlaced; the constantly maneuvering Hoover could dig up no blackmail material on him.

Documents released after Hoover's death show Hoover scrambling to save his career. Behind the scenes, the most powerful secret policeman in the world commanded partisans in Congress to draft laws to make his FBI independent of the president. Hoover failed to achieve the audacious goal, but Truman did back off. Firing the FBI director would bring too many repercussions from right-wing Democrats. (Firing Hoover was more than Truman or the next three presidents of the United States were able to do with all the power of their office.)

Soon after the Coplon case revelations, on December 27, 1950, Hoover did rally Congress to pass laws allowing FBI agents to make warrantless arrests in cases involving espionage.

At the heart of Leonard's major, tumultuous, even dangerous legal career of the next forty years was the battle against government pressures on many left-wing dissenters. Thus Leonard gained the enmity of a disciplined group of armed men often operating above the law. As in many feuds, Hoover and Leonard were as alike in drive as they were opposed in ideology. In the pitch of battle, each man was convinced of the justice of his cause and of his own formidable powers and destiny. Both were workaholics who loved a fight. Hoover was far more ruthless, his power based on raw muscle. But when pitted against Leonard, Hoover would lose again and again.

Leonard broke away from Coplon appeals to accompany Jean to what was to be Paul Robeson's last Carnegie Hall concert. Jean had front-row seats. Robeson had invited Communist Party leader Eugene Dennis and his family to sit near the stage, too. Having been convicted of sedition, Dennis was about to go to prison. Robeson sang "The Purest Kind of Guy," written by Jean's old friend Marc Blitzstein, while a small spotlight lit Eugene Dennis and his wife, Peggy, holding their son, Gene Jr., a classmate of Michael and Kathy at Downtown Community School. It was a surprisingly festive evening.

Jean was lonely. She packed satchels of clothing and books and took Kathy and Michael to Fire Island for the summer. Esther and Izzy were also renting a small cedar bungalow on the thirty-two-mile ribbon of sand in the Atlantic Ocean. It was a relief to flee St. Luke's Place, where hundreds of phone calls, postcards, and letters had arrived attacking Leonard as a traitor. Death threats and anti-Semitic slurs accompanied accusations of cash payoffs by the Soviets.

On Fire Island, Jean's porch was the setting for debates about Judith Coplon. Izzy and Jean saw Coplon as somehow "one of our own," although they assumed her guilt.

For Izzy, the Soviet Union was not simply the new cold-war enemy of the United States. It was still a place where socialism was being attempted on a huge scale.

Victor Rabinowitz, who visited Fire Island with his wife and two children, still had what Leonard called a "tough" (radical) perspective. Victor argued that Coplon's actions were above the law. "If Judy was guilty, she was acting out of her loyalty to an idea [socialism] she believed in, not loyalty to a particular country. She was not turning over documents for money, as would a traditional spy."

As time passed, the reality of Hoover's stealth confirmed Jean's worst fears. Hoover's agents opened her mail, entered her home, and rifled through her dresser drawers on St. Luke's Place. They monitored her bank accounts. Leonard was followed, sometimes in a threatening fashion, by the FBI in the United States and by the CIA abroad. (His CIA tails included E. Howard Hunt, the Watergate plumber chieftain attached to U.S. embassies in places such as Mexico City.) The FBI spent hundreds of hours amassing more than three thousand pages of repetitive, frequently inaccurate reports, searching in vain for proof that Leonard was destroying the American way of life.

And although the U.S. government went on to win espionage cases against Alger Hiss and Julius Rosenberg, the prosecution would look weak, in no small part because Leonard had made Hoover fearful about introducing top-secret and illegally obtained material.

After a few years, Leonard ceased to mention the Coplon case. When asked directly about it, he said disingenuously in the 1980s, "I've never asked Judith about the facts at all, and when I wrote the appeal brief, of course I didn't have to. I never felt it was my business. I know it must show a lack of curiosity on my part. Maybe it's a feeling that everybody has a right to his own life or her own life. Why should I know?"

By then, Leonard doggedly refused to admit his emotional attachment to one side or the other. He excelled, as do many lawyers, at self-justification. He wanted to be a hero to the legal establishment as well as to his radical friends and relatives.

Interestingly, in the long aftermath of the Coplon appeals, Judge Hand made sure that Judith Coplon did not breathe freely. He ruled that the evidence against her was overwhelming, and that the government could bring another case against her; she was out on bail, and could not leave Manhattan. The threat of a new trial would hang over Coplon's head for the next seventeen years.

Judith Coplon responded years later to accusations that she had left the country illicitly. She wrote:

> In the thirty-four years since my trials, I have lived in New York city continuously, raised a family of four, worked and been active in my community. For seventeen of those years, until my case was dismissed in 1967, I remained on $40,000 no interest cash bail, raised by my family (a considerable amount in those days). During those years, I was not permitted to vote, drive a car, or leave the Southern or Eastern districts of New York. Flee the country indeed! I couldn't cross the Hudson River to attend the unveiling of my father's gravestone.

But members of the Boudin family circle believed that, in fact, Judith Coplon had illegally visited Mexico with Leonard's help—he'd arranged matters with Mexican officials. Had he been discovered, the story went, Leonard might have lost his license to practice law. True or not, it became part of Leonard's myth, and was one factor people cited to illustrate Leonard's extraordinary emotional involvement with his clients.

Such feelings would be sorely tested when Leonard faced far riskier challenges from his daughter, Kathy.

The Judith Coplon case provided Kathy with knowledge of a path to her father's heart. Another of its results was that Leonard and Kathy became the rare father and daughter with membership on Hoover's secret enemies list.

7

ARE COMMUNISTS PART
OF AN INTERNATIONAL
MOVEMENT?

The question is not whether Communists are part of an international movement; of course they are. The question is not whether these organizations named by the Attorney General are "fronts"; let it be assumed that they are. The question is whether we are to abandon the standards and habits of a free society, fleeing the risks of freedom for the deadlier risks of oppression. The question is whether we are to relinquish the standards of Jefferson for those of Torquemada.

—Izzy Stone, 1953

It was not apparent even to Leonard, during the second decade of his marriage, that Jean was slowly losing her sanity. She blamed herself for the fact that Leonard found her invisible. As days passed, Jean felt more and more instantaneous hurt, subjective blame, and impatience. She was numbed by homesick dreams of Philadelphia. Her moods would tumble "down down and low," providing Leonard with new excuses to avoid her company.

There was the summer morning when Kathy was away at Belgian Village overnight camp and Jean turned up her portable radio while showering. Bert Gross, who was a houseguest at the time, rapped on the bathroom door and asked Jean to turn down the radio. Jean shouted back in an agonized tone, "Go to a hotel." Later she cheerily confessed to Bert that she was losing her mind.

By way of response, Bert asked, "How're things with our Leonard?"

He had seen Leonard lingering over late suppers with a succession of pretty women at a nearby restaurant.

"Just great," said Jean.

"Tell me the truth."

"What will that accomplish?" asked Jean in a humorous tone of voice.

Esther Stone, Jean's sister, noted that when Jean met new people, she was too open, making euphoric and hopeful assumptions about kinship. Then all too soon the new person disappointed her by an act as small as not telephoning the day after borrowing three of Jean's poems. Esther rather cruelly dismissed Jean's loneliness by telling her she had had too much attention from boys as a teenager. Jean was now carrying a small FM radio ("my paramour," she dubbed it) around the house. One day Jean listened proudly to her former lover Leon Berkowitz broadcast news of an exhibit of work he had mounted by a new painter named Willem de Kooning.

Leonard's professional triumphs had abruptly ceased. Indeed, his life had been reduced to a hunt for sexual conquest in large part because he had virtually no work. He fretted as soon as he woke up about his dwindling law practice. The problem was that all the union leaders who had been his clients were now out of jobs, having been removed from union ballots after refusing to sign loyalty oaths. Newly elected union leaders wanted no association with a firm that had been litigating for the Communist Party.

Payment for what work he did do was practically nonexistent: he had not been paid for the Coplon case because he was appointed by the court.

Leonard mocked his own righteous adherence to the American Bar Association's maxim: "No fear of judicial disfavor or public unpopularity should restrain [a lawyer] from the full discharge of his duty." It was not easy to walk into his offices on Beaver Street now that it was filled with silent typewriters. Leonard found it difficult to fire junior lawyers, who were good friends, yet there was no money to pay them.

To help matters, Victor found tenants for the empty offices. He told his wife, Marcia, that there are consequences when cases are chosen for political reasons. In Leonard's family circle, no one was as "pissed off" as Izzy Stone about the disintegration of his brother-in-law's firm. Izzy was still raising his voice against injustice, and he particularly enjoyed revising an opinion when it cost him friends.

In 1950, Izzy and his family had moved to Paris where, as foreign correspondent, he wrote six columns a week for the progressive *Compass* newspaper. Izzy was galvanized by articles in the French and English press contradicting U.S. news reports on the Korean War. The European view was that the Soviets had been as stunned as the United States by communist North Korea's initial attack on South Korea.

Izzy sounded a bit like a street tough when he attacked Secretary of State John Foster Dulles as "a hateful person, a real phoney," for spouting frightening propaganda exaggerating the power of the Soviet Union over North Korea.

Izzy wrote that in fact North Korea was "a pain in the ass to Moscow and Peking because it acted independently of them." Always ready to assume that nothing he read in the American establishment press was necessarily true, Izzy was the only journalist in the United States to discern the enormous gulfs between the three communist countries. Izzy said that North Korea was not a puppet of the Soviet Union.

In Paris, Izzy commandeered a committee of illustrious people including Albert Camus and Jean-Paul Sartre to try to stop the United States's involvement in the Korean War. (Later, well-known and respected names would be collected in a similar fashion in the United States to oppose the Vietnam War.)

On February 22, 1952, Leonard sat with his partner, Victor Rabinowitz, and his family in the front row of an auditorium in New Haven. Yale University president Chauncey Brewster Tinker (an outspoken anti-Semite) was forced to present a Yale medal to Victor's father, Louis Rabinowitz. Louis had contributed several million dollars to Yale in funds, rare books, and important Italian paintings.

Three months later, on May 23, Leonard received a phone call from his uncle's secretary telling him that Louis had fallen on the subway tracks. Despite his blindness, Louis Boudin rode the subways. When his uncle died a week later, Leonard panicked. Louis's arrogance and success had made him seem invulnerable to one and all, and yet now he was dead.

Jean taped Louis Boudin's *New York Times* obituary to the kitchen door. The man's independent nature was evident in the columns of formal prose. Jean underlined phrases: "the noted labor lawyer and authority on Constitutional Law whose numerous charitable endeavors included serving as chairman of the American ORT unit." The obituary confirmed Louis's membership in colliding establishments.

When Leonard's mother died at Christmas, he virtually collapsed. In a poem, he compared his mother to the moon and himself to the sun, and noted that the sun had gone down.

In his mourning, Leonard sought solace from women as if he were single. Always on the prowl, he perked up his ears at any mention of a pretty girl he had not yet met. He lit up "like a Christmas tree" when a pretty girl passed him on a street or entered a room. Just forty-one years old, he felt "diminished by inexorable history and mortality," as he told Jean when he came home late one night.

Meanwhile, having returned to the United States from Paris, Izzy was springing into action again. Disgusted by the reluctance of liberals to defend the free speech of people accused by congressional committees of Communist Party memberships, some of which dated back to the 1920s and 1930s, Izzy decided to found his own independent newsletter: *I. F. Stone's Weekly,* "radical in content, but conservative in format."

Known by now as a "Red," Izzy had been banned by President Harry Truman from government press conferences. He turned this to his advantage by simply digging deeper than reporters who had access—reading endless government transcripts. He searched for what John Galsworthy called "the significant trifle"—the overlooked fact that illuminated the entire situation.*

Still, Izzy was pleased to be invited to the White House once again for President Dwight D. Eisenhower's press conferences. Irrepressible as always, on his first day back Izzy stood up and ceremoniously loosened his tie. Smiling broadly and blinking with glee behind his thick eyeglasses, he bowed and unbuttoned his shirt to reveal a bright red undershirt.

Jean took great pride in Izzy's growing prominence and, despite Leonard's grumbling, she made a point of mailing to friends the copy of Izzy's new journal dated May 2, 1953. The cover story, "Making America a Police State," was a polemic against the first order by the Subversive Activities Control Board directing that "Communist action and Commu-

---

*I scrolled through Izzy's newsletters on New York Public Library microfilm some forty-plus years after he wrote them. Time has thus far confirmed so many of Izzy's hunches and research. I admired the clarity of the prose, his analysis spiced with colorful literary and street language. In the preface to one anthology of pieces, Izzy later proclaimed his identity as an independent capitalist—beholden to no mortgager, patron, party backer, or big-news organization; just to his good readers. He added, "I am even one-up on Benjamin Franklin. I have never accepted advertising."

nist front groups register." The penalty for not doing so was five years in jail or a $10,000 fine or both.

Izzy Stone had found a new enemy. Joseph McCarthy, the junior senator from Wisconsin, was a jocular ex-marine who had transformed himself overnight into a rousing, red-faced, hard-nosed media star by raising anticommunist paranoia of the cold war to a fever pitch.

Speaking to a women's Republican club in Wheeling, West Virginia, Senator McCarthy launched his famous cold-war hunt. He declared that he had in his hand a list of 205 "known communists" who were actively shaping State Department policies. The press trumpeted his grandiose claims.

McCarthy continued to attack government agencies for lax screening policies when hiring new employees. On the basis of a few facts amid inflammatory rhetoric and broad accusations, he manipulated coverage in newspapers and the new medium of television to convince the public that communists had orchestrated a conspiracy so immense that only he, Joe McCarthy, could be trusted to extricate the U.S. government from the clutches of Soviet totalitarianism.

Although McCarthy and other congressional investigators actually discovered no new communists, Izzy and the rest of the country did not yet know all the facts behind the bombast.

Hoover had in fact learned of a communist cell in Monmouth, New Jersey, that had once included Julius Rosenberg. The FBI had indications that Rosenberg had passed military information to the Soviet Union. He had been identified by the same secret Venona espionage communiqués that had been used to "make" Judith Coplon. (In the documents, Rosenberg appeared to be code-named "Liberal"; his wife was referred to as Ethel.) But the FBI still wanted to keep secret the fact that it was slowly decoding the Russian spy communiqués.

Izzy Stone astutely accused McCarthy and his ally, Hoover, of trying to extend their kingdoms. According to Izzy, Hoover wanted to take over all government intelligence operations including the Secret Service, OSS, CIA, and the intelligence branches of the military.

Izzy discerned that Senator McCarthy welcomed complaints "from assorted crackpots and malcontents" who worked in the government. The senator, Izzy said, was trying to forge a secret ring of informers who would give him information for Hoover's smear campaigns. Izzy said that the goal was to make government employees fear Hoover and McCarthy more than their own bosses.

Senator Joseph R. McCarthy (left) and Roy M. Cohn, counsel to McCarthy's Senate Investigating Subcommittee, at the Army-McCarthy hearings, 1954. Leonard and his partner, Victor Rabinowitz, courageously defended many hostile witnesses summoned by McCarthy in his controversial investigation of American communism.

Unlike Senator McCarthy's panic-inducing attacks on communists, Izzy's prose went unread by the majority of Americans.

Stone wrote of one Washington hearing:

> The cast assembled slowly. That swarthy urchin Roy Cohn was one of the first to arrive. . . . The TV machines were up and the bright camera lights on when McCarthy made his entrance alone, 15 minutes late. He had his left hand in his pocket and walked with what is meant to be a modest slouch, a self-conscious grin on his face. The gray jailbird complexion, the covert look of a smart fox, were unchanged. In that gravelly voice, bored, impersonal and inexorable, like the detective hero in a soap opera, McCarthy called the meeting to order.
>
> The scene was a familiar one—the caucus room of the Senate office building, on a Monday morning in late September. The Fall hunting season, Red Hunting, that is, had begun.

Izzy Stone decided that the situation required more of him than the role of press watchdog. He audaciously decided to form an activist com-

The Leof Christmas party, Philadelphia, 1949. Seated on floor, front row, Leonard Boudin, Kathy Boudin, Madi Leof. Jean Boudin sits on a chair next to Madi. Above Leonard is Marc Blitzstein, Morris "Poppa" Leof, and his common-law wife, Jennie Chalfin.

mittee designed to be a "prodder" to the American Civil Liberties Union, whose liberal lawyers were pretty much ducking legal crises of people accused of past or present communist affiliation.

Although he needed at least one lawyer as staff, Izzy did not initially hire his brother-in-law, Leonard Boudin. Nonetheless Leonard later took credit for forming "the prodder" activist group. He said, "Remember some leaders of the American Civil Liberties Union were actually collaborating with J. Edgar Hoover."

Albert Einstein himself helped Izzy recruit an esteemed board of directors—only one of whom had probably joined the Communist Party. Izzy named the group the Emergency Civil Liberties Committee—called ECLC by insiders.

Izzy's board members were mostly illustrious southerners from

Alabama, Virginia, and Kentucky, who had at least one foot in academia. Except for Izzy, they were Christian, and the racial issue was central to their lives. They had toiled for unpopular measures—such as the repeal of the poll tax. Like Izzy's newsletter, board members were radical, but highly conservative in appearance. They included Paul Lehmann, a minister and professor of religion at Princeton Theological Seminary. Hugh Wilson was also a Princeton professor whose field was American history. The family of Clark Foreman owned the *Atlanta Constitution* newspaper. Paine Webber was a stockbroker from Virginia and on the board of the NAACP. James Imbrie was a retired banker. The board's only black member was E. Franklin Frazier, a Howard College professor of sociology. Thomas Thackeray was Izzy's publisher at the *New York Post* and later at the *Compass*.

Many board members had worked in New Deal programs for rural improvement like the Tennessee Valley Authority with the then agriculture secretary and later vice president Henry Wallace. Five years later, all were still reeling from the "losing battle" that had been the 1948 presidential campaign defeat of Henry Wallace.

Izzy astutely picked the courts as his battlefield. Following Louis Boudin's analysis, Izzy targeted the U.S. Supreme Court as the pivotal source of power. He wanted his staff lawyer to "test" laws that denied rights of alleged communists. (That there was initially no money to pay a lawyer was of little consequence to Izzy.) ECLC was instantly attacked as a communist front by many, including Irving Kristol of the American Committee for Cultural Freedom.

Izzy's board members met in Corliss Lamont's stately Ossining "farmhouse," with its long lawns, swimming pool, and tennis courts. Lamont was a major source of funds and would later become Leonard's closest friend on the board. He possessed a patrician manner, a desire for social justice, and a great fortune; his father had been a close associate of J. P. Morgan. He was a philosophy professor at Columbia and a philanthropist.

After visiting Russia in the 1930s, Lamont had exulted: "The Russian people are better dressed [than before], food is good and plentiful, everyone seems confident and happy."

Most recently, he had shouted at friends in a Moscow restaurant, "I have been a socialist my entire adult life. But damn it, nobody tells me what to believe or to think."

The Boudin family home was the two upper floors of 12½ St. Luke's Place. The mid-nineteenth-century exterior appeared frequently during each episode of The Cosby Show. *It was meant to be the residence of Bill Cosby's well-to-do television family.*

Izzy offered the position of staff lawyer to Harvard labor law professor Victor Brudney. But Brudney quickly declined, not relishing the prospect of the uphill fight to the Supreme Court for Paul Robeson's passport—the first test case Izzy was planning. (Restricting travel was one way that the United States government was making war on prominent members of the left, calling them potential spies.)

After two more lawyers turned him down, Izzy turned to his brother-in-law. Leonard accepted the unpaid position as staff lawyer: he had little other work.

Soon Michael Boudin was impressing classmates at the Downtown Community School with news that his father and Albert Einstein were going to fight the State Department all the way up to the Supreme Court to get the great Paul Robeson's passport back.

Apart from the ECLC passport cases, Leonard and Victor Rabinowitz—who quickly signed on without pay—were instantly sucked into crises suffered by scores of people labeled as Reds by congressional investigators who called them to testify as witnesses. Victor and Leonard represented only "hostile witnesses," those who refused to reveal past or present membership in the dwindling Communist Party.

Leonard recalled, "There was no legal reason to suspend civil liberties. We had not declared war on Russia; debating the cold war was an important part of public discourse; the Communist Party was not illegal, and present or former membership was protected by freedoms of speech and belief."

Leonard's legal strategy was the same one used by other lawyers. The client was to tell the committee only his name, address, and education, and to cite the Fifth Amendment instead of answering questions about attending Communist Party meetings or actual membership. His clients took the Fifth Amendment privilege even though the question did not call for an incriminating answer. The problem was that if a client admitted membership or just having attended meetings, the next question would have been a request to name names of people he saw there. And Leonard's clients did not want to be informers. Leonard advised them against citing the First Amendment right to belief, since a client who did so would have been held in contempt of Congress and possibly jailed. Nonetheless his clients were demonized and lost jobs, and one committed suicide.

The roller-coaster aspects of the rescue operations appealed to Leonard. It was a high-risk, high-pressure ride. Leonard said with ironic understatement: "It was no way to make a living."

Soon, however, Leonard observed another irony: most clients were no longer pro-Soviet.

"There were so many political events that resulted in people leaving the Communist Party. There were the purges in the Soviet Union before 1935. There was the Nazi-Soviet pact in 1939. People change. [Young] people [grew up], getting jobs and moving into different cultures and different occupations. Military service changed people's ideas. There were a hundred different things, each representing a break with the Communist Party. Philosophically and practically."

Leonard condescended to Joe McCarthy and called him "a smiling fool, a publicity hound who did not believe in his cause." After facing Leonard in city after city, McCarthy actually began to check legal points with him in sessions.

If Leonard, Izzy, Edith Tiger, and Victor thought a case looked "good" (meaning an impoverished person was in terrible crisis), ECLC paid Leonard and Victor's travel expenses. The two lawyers clumped clients' hearings together to economize on travel fares. Some clients— fired from jobs—had no money for food and rent. Victor invited impoverished civil rights activist Carl Braden to submit a book proposal to the Rabinowitz Foundation in order to be awarded a small amount of money. In Gary, Indiana, Victor defended terrified steelworkers. He and Leonard took the train to Philadelphia to represent high-school teachers. They faced investigators in a hotel room in Buffalo with a table dragged in. Leonard also represented United Nations officials subpoenaed by the McCarran Committee. Other clients included a radio station announcer, a *New York Times* employee, many civil servants, an orchestra conductor—all fired from jobs and blacklisted for refusing to answer the question: "Are you now or have you ever been a member of the Communist Party?"

Leonard spoke to investigators outside of sessions only once. In Atlanta, an air-raid siren went off while Leonard was standing in the courthouse next to Senator William Jenner. Holding the door open, Leonard said, "Come on out," to the senator. For three minutes, the two adversaries compared prices of airplane fares to sessions.

Ann Braden never forgot her gratitude upon reading Leonard's written offer to appeal her husband's case after Carl Braden was convicted of sedition for refusing to testify before a congressional committee.*

She wrote: "I've never forgotten the gloomy day in Dec. 1954 just after my husband Carl had been sentenced to 15 years in prison and was being held under 40 thousand dollars bond. Louisville was in hysteria . . . old friends were afraid to speak to me and I felt almost totally alone. I went to our post office box that day and found a note from Leonard, a man who hardly knew us.

" 'Tell Carl,' he wrote, 'that I am proud to know him. I stand ready to do whatever you want me to do on an appeal. Money is not a consideration. I will be glad to do this without a fee if need be.' "

---

*Carl Braden had probably been a communist at some point. Braden and his wife, Ann, had raised neighbors' hackles by buying a small house in an all-white Louisville suburb and then selling it to the Wades, a black family. The Wades moved into their new home a few days before the Supreme Court outlawed school segregation. Their home was immediately bombed, but miraculously no one was killed. Local authorities refused to arrest a white segregationist known to have planted the dynamite. Police made other local whites angry by accusing Carl Braden and a group of Reds of secretly bombing the Wade home to foment unrest among blacks.

Mrs. Braden recalled: "Suddenly the day was not so gloomy, and I knew with people like that in the world I could go on fighting.

"After that we fought many battles together. . . . We sometimes disagreed. We often engaged in verbal battles. But just knowing Leonard gave wings to our struggles through the years."

Leonard was particularly thrilled to represent famous clients, and disappointed when recurring pneumonia, brought on by stress, forced him to turn down writer Dorothy Parker, who had been subpoenaed by a congressional subcommittee. He claimed in later years that Parker had been a client.

On May 6, 1953, Leonard and the movie actor Lionel Stander marched into the U.S. Courthouse in Manhattan in Foley Square to face the House Committee on Un-American Activities.

Like Leonard, Lionel Stander had stopped short of joining the party in the 1930s. In fact, he'd already sworn an oath to the committee in 1941 that he had not been a communist. But now he had been summoned again, no doubt simply because he was well known. Stander had built a movie career playing the somewhat disreputable pal who comes to the rescue of the hero in such films as *A Star Is Born* and *Mr. Deeds Goes to Town.*

Per Leonard's instructions, at the start of his second hearing Stander instantly seized the upper hand. He ordered the committee to shut down television cameras whose function, he said, was to smear witnesses and help congressmen get reelected. Stander declared he was a professional who appeared on TV only for entertainment or philanthropic organizations. "This committee has a far more serious purpose," he thundered.

The committee refused his request. In a voice quivering with righteous indignation, Leonard said slowly, "It's been done for other witnesses." Television lights faded.

On the other hand, witnesses who cooperated with the investigating committees by admitting party membership and naming names of friends were flattered by congressmen. In 1952, Congressman Clyde Doyle told Jerome Robbins, "Again I want to compliment you, you are in a wonderful place, through your art, your music, your talent which God blessed you with, to perhaps be very vigorous and positive in promoting Americanism in contrast to Communism."

Surprisingly, in order to expand his influence, Leonard himself "cooperated" to some degree. He swore on two separate occasions to U.S. government officials that he had never been a Communist Party member

Leonard Boudin (at table, second from right) and other members of the Lawyers Guild representing U.S. citizens employed by the United Nations who were charged by their government with having ties to the Communist Party, circa 1952.

instead of refusing to answer the question. (Unlike nearly all his clients, Leonard had never actually joined the party.) A less confident man would have worried that breaking ranks would anger clients.

Leonard's gesture was analogous to a good chess move: it ensured greater power for him by giving him mobility among his clients' government adversaries. And as far as the government was concerned, it appeared to distance Leonard from his clients. As Leonard told Jean, he could be a better advocate for clients if perceived to be a member of the Establishment.

Leonard's first surprising cooperation occurred after he'd applied for a passport to visit clients stuck in Prague. When passport officials asked Leonard to sign a noncommunist affidavit, they figured that they had him cornered. But he signed it.

Later, on June 12, 1956, Leonard would be called before the House Un-American Activities Committee, where he swore he had never been a member of the Communist Party.

Rockwell Kent, circa 1950.
Leonard won Kent's right to
travel at the Supreme Court.

J. Edgar Hoover instantly sent a flurry of memos to local FBI bureaus and to Senator McCarthy preparing to arrest Leonard and try him for perjury. Unfortunately for Hoover, the evidence boiled down to a report by an unreliable informant named Maurice Malkin who was on the FBI payroll. Leonard boldly sued the U.S. government for his passport. It was issued.

Despite Paul Robeson's prominence, Leonard and Izzy cannily attached the "famous but less threatening" name of Rockwell Kent to the right-to-travel fight against the government. As was often the case with his clients, Leonard became a close friend of Rockwell Kent, who was soon a beloved guest at Sunday brunches on St. Luke's Place and a member of the family circle. The talented seventy-five-year-old book illustrator was a fearless explorer and adventurer, a self-styled socialist, and a sensualist. He and Leonard loved to speed up Madison Avenue in Kent's pink Cadillac convertible with the top down, joking with one pretty New York pedestrian after another. With Kent as mentor, Leonard developed a passion for carefully reading wine menus, much to Jean's amusement.

Kent invited Kathy, then about eight years old, to visit him and his young wife, Sally, at his rustic kingdom, a dairy farm high in the Adirondack Mountains at Ausable, New York. He wrote:

> *Dear Kathy,*
> *I am feeling better*
> *Now that I have your lovely letter*
> *Not that I've been exactly ill.*
> *Nor sick enough to take a pill;*
> *I guess I've just felt kind of sad:*
> *I've wanted to see you so bad . . .*
> *So, Kathy, come along please do*
> *And meanwhile I'll keep loving you.*

Adults noted that while Kathy was poised and extroverted with adults and children, Michael appeared almost furtive. One rainy afternoon, when he was about twelve, he was studying at the home of a girl in his

Maurice Malkin's membership card in the American Communist Party. Malkin, a paid FBI informer, accused Leonard Boudin of having been a communist. After Leonard swore an anticommunist loyalty oath, J. Edgar Hoover reluctantly dropped his plan to arrest him for perjury. Malkin was an unreliable witness.

*Paul Robeson flanked
by attorneys Boudin
and Conrad Lynn,
1954.*

class who lived eight blocks away on Horatio Street. When Rose Rubin, the girl's mother, saw how hard it was raining, she invited Michael to stay overnight and telephoned Jean, who gave permission.

But Michael soon slipped out of the Rubin home, bareheaded, and ran eight blocks to St. Luke's Place. He was soaked but did not stop to change his clothing. He quickly scooped up his pajamas, his toothbrush, and an umbrella, without knocking on his mother's bedroom door. He raced back to his friend's house.

Michael had taken charge of his own sleepover arrangements. Relying on his mother was too risky, and he understood this at an early age.

His parents did not ask Michael why he ran home and back in the rain. He did not welcome inquiries. Telling the story to friends, Leonard joked that Michael was unaccustomed to overnight visits with girls.

Late one afternoon during this period, two FBI agents rang the doorbell at St. Luke's Place. One man asked Jean what she knew of Leonard's "secret life" with other women. Jean pushed him out the front door with a broom. Peering down the stairwell, Kathy was mortified by the rude spectacle. Jean sat down on a step and explained to Kathy that the men were trying to punish people who criticized the government.

Sometime in 1952, Leonard had indeed fallen deeply in love with a young woman named Doriane Kurtz who worked for the United Nations. FBI agents followed Leonard thousands of miles to whirlwind romantic trysts in Belize and Mexico City. Doriane was a beauty with an exotic accent, having been born in Italy of Jewish parents. When she met Leonard, she was working as a secretary in the Administrative Tribunal, a group hurriedly set up by the United Nations to determine whether they should fire employees from the United States suspected of communist affiliations.

Leonard began hinting to Doriane of marriage. The fact that Doriane was already married to a man she characterized as "extremely caring" was no deterrent. In first drafts of Leonard's love letters to Doriane written in a gray ledger book, many sentences began, "If only." He wrote whole paragraphs expressing his desire to spend the rest of his life with her. After proposing marriage, Leonard reluctantly retracted the offer. Unable to solve his romantic problem, Leonard begged Doriane to give him time, calling her "the great love of his life."

Leonard was more attached to Jean than he knew. Although he spoke disparagingly to her privately and in public, nonetheless, she balanced his world. It was her admiration on which he had based so much of his professional life.

Soon the situation was so fraught that Jean heard Leonard whispering desperately into the telephone one morning that the separation caused by the miles between him and the person at the other end of the line made his days empty. Vowing to change his life, he swore he was counting the hours until he held the other person in his arms.

Hearing this pushed Jean over the edge. She was plunged into a feeling of time suspended. She stopped sleeping. She forgot to pay the housekeeper, hose down the back deck, or even return phone calls. She mocked herself for having been foolish enough to expect to pull the wool over Leonard's eyes forever. She believed that she had had only a fleeting sex appeal to offer and no other virtue. Jean told herself that Leonard had ceased to love her because she was "a hollow nothing."

Jean examined her face in a pocket mirror. Something was wrong with her, something broken under the skin, she decided. Her love must be poisonous. Or else why did people back away?

Jean knew her husband was running away from her, but she did not then realize that there were several women in Leonard's life. Georgette Schneer, for example, remained close to Leonard. No matter what else she was doing, she would pause on July 20, Leonard's birthday, for a private champagne toast "to my loving friend."

Early in 1953, Jean awoke from a midday nap and decided that, after all, she might be the sort of person who commits suicide. She was a poet, wasn't she, and part of that job description was to flirt with death. She tried to picture Leonard's response to news of her suicide; feeling sorry for him made her weep. She listened to her heartbeat thump, and it seemed to say, "Do it, do it."

Jean dressed slowly on the day of her attempted suicide, choosing from her jewelry an antique blue-enamel bar pin that matched her eyes. Putting on a freshly ironed blue blouse, Jean felt overcome by a vision of her corpse in the ground, feeding tulips. As she remembered it: "Then I made the children jelly sandwiches, wrapped them in waxed paper, set them on the table with glasses of milk, took pills, and stuck my head in the oven."

The oven grate scratched her cheek so she stood, folded a dish towel, put it in the oven, rested her cheek on it, and breathed in the fumes. When Jonie Robinson, the Boudins' part-time housekeeper, unlocked the downstairs door, Jean was unconscious. Moments later, Michael and Kathy arrived. Frightened, Michael pulled his mother away from the oven. Kathy ran downstairs to get help from the Rileys and then across the street to the public library.

There a librarian noted Kathy's unnatural composure. Moments later sirens blared. Back at the house, firemen carrying axes clambered upstairs and opened windows. Marin Riley called her husband, Bob, back at Lord & Taylor's department store, to tell him he was not needed. Jean was taken to St. Vincent's Hospital in an ambulance.

Jean's suicide attempt rocked Leonard as hard as she had hoped. He was on a train with Victor Rabinowitz to Washington, D.C., preparing for a meeting with Izzy Stone in which he intended to elaborate his legal argument that travel was a human right, not a privilege. Suddenly Leonard heard his name called by the conductor.

When told that Jean had tried to kill herself, Leonard raked his hair with his fingers until tufts stood all over his head. He kneaded the flesh of his scalp, perhaps an unconscious attempt to stimulate his brain. He disembarked at Baltimore, boarded a train back to New York, and went directly to St. Vincent's Hospital.

Jean regained consciousness and was transported from the hospital three days later, with Leonard at her side, to Silver Hill, a rest home and clinic in New Canaan, Connecticut. Madi Leof rushed up to see Jean. Madi scolded her friend: had Jean really expected Michael and Kathy to enter a house filled with gas, unwrap jelly sandwiches, and eat them with their mother sprawled on the kitchen floor, dying?

At Silver Hill, electroshock treatments sent Jean into a near-fatal coma. One jolt caused her to bite down so hard on the tongue protector in her mouth that she broke a molar, whole sections of her memory were erased, and those that remained were peculiarly fragmented. The left side of her tongue became numb. The 400 volts she received added up to more than if she had been struck by lightning and less than the Rosenbergs got in the electric chair.

Jean believed that her body had been permanently disrupted by the electric current. For the rest of her life, she was afflicted by sudden shakes and a sensation of being jolted, particularly in her ears and chest.

Yet sometimes at Silver Hill she felt more alive than ever and, in fact, superior to other people. She had dared to throw herself at death in order to try and claim the life she wanted. Novel ways to commit suicide were added to a long secret list. The idea of suicide would remain on her mind for as long as Leonard was alive.

Leonard wrote Doriane a letter proposing that they marry "and not look back."

> *Dearest Doriane,*
>   *I know how late likely too late this, so I write not call. If you can, want to, and will, let us marry as quickly as we can, and certainly live together immediately with few backward looks and much to the future . . . If it is not to be, there remains regret and love.*
>
>   *Yours, Leonard*

Doriane rejected Leonard's proposal by return letter. She began: "Dearest Leonard, my Leonard." She wrote that she could still feel the touch of his hand in her hand and his skin under her lips. But Jean's suicide attempt had made a permanent step toward Leonard too agonizing. Doriane concluded by hoping for an eventual happy adjustment for herself and for something happy to happen to Leonard.

Leonard's proposal was too late. Nonetheless the relationship continued until 1961.

Leonard wrote another note and locked it in his desk drawer with Doriane's letters and his drafts. He requested that in the event of his death, her letters be returned to her. He wrote: ". . . and probably the stuff should be destroyed, but she can have it if she wishes. Assure her that I did not commit suicide. Too painful and would prevent my seeing how her life worked out which is important to me. She won't believe it, but . . ."

Jean's suicide attempt had the effect of tying Leonard to her with a bond that was often stretched but never broken, despite his scores and scores of passing attractions to other women. Leonard admired people who dared to go to the edge—and Jean had done precisely that. On the one hand, Leonard was furious with Jean, and at the same time he was afraid he might send her careering toward death at any moment. He did not yet grasp the calculated flattery of her gesture.

Jean almost never spoke of her suicide attempt. It was Leonard who told friends and acquaintances, while failing to mention that his romance with Doriane had precipitated it. Jean had attempted to desert him, he said, by trying to kill herself. Thus he did not owe her faithfulness. He used Jean's fragility as a reason to end love affairs. Her obsessive romantic attachment to Leonard soon became part of his legend.

Six weeks after Jean had been admitted to Silver Hill, Marcia Rabinowitz, Victor's wife, drove to the sanitarium to take her out to lunch. Marcia and Jean had gotten to know each other in their husbands' long shadows, but Marcia genuinely loved Jean. She was one of many kind women who did. The visit was Leonard's idea. "Tell her to come home," he said. He was unable to run his household and do his work. The kitchen on St. Luke's Place smelled of failure.

After tea sandwiches and coffee at a country inn (where Jean politely refrained from mentioning she could not, temporarily, taste food), Marcia and Jean made a quick stop at a department store to buy stockings. Marcia knew that Jean was an indifferent shopper. The last time Jean and Leonard had visited the Rabinowitz family in New Rochelle, Marcia had searched storage boxes to find a beige knit dress of hers that was ideal for Jean's small, perfect figure. Jean still treasured hand-me-down blouses and dresses, viewing them as proof she was cared for. That day with Marcia, Jean was still confused from shock treatments. She remembered the address of her home, but not the names of Kathy's friends. Her nerves were "like slushy carrots."

While at Silver Hill, Jean modeled many clay pieces of a mother and child. Bert Gross thought that her images were similar to those of painter Mary Cassatt.

Leonard visited on Sundays, standing stiffly in Jean's room in a tie and jacket. She presented herself with composed affection. The telephone conversation that she had overheard between Leonard and his mistress was mentioned only once and in the presence of a psychiatrist. Jean smiled at Leonard's tale of little Izzy raising his fists and daring a brawny teamster to step outside to settle a dispute in Buffalo.

Leonard reported that domestic routine on St. Luke's Place was being maintained by three Yale law students who also worked for Leonard at the office. They read their law books at night curled up under one of Jean's afghans, while Leonard read at the library of the New York Bar Association. In Jean's absence, Leonard found himself unable to devote any more time than usual to Kathy and Michael. He made sure that the law students were available during the day to take Kathy or Michael to visit other children or to a doctor. Other baby-sitters included a young woman who told Kathy exciting stories of union brawls. During a strike she and other union women dropped open pocketbooks to distract police, while union men beat up scabs on their way to work.

Jean's suicide attempt was experienced by her small children as terrifying desertion. They masked their terrors with contempt for her weakness, seeing her—above all—as an example of what not to be.

During this time, Leonard's approval became all that Kathy desired from a parent. He was both father and mother and made it clear that in his view he was a better parent than Jean. Begging Kathy to be a good girl, Leonard tapped the corners of his mouth with his thumb and forefinger if her grin sagged.

Although in his careful, orderly way, Michael avoided Leonard's forced exuberance, Kathy did not. She understood that he wanted to see her happy and coping well, and if necessary she put on an act. Any hint of loss of her father's love pushed her close to pure terror.

To please Leonard, Kathy immersed herself in Girl Scout activities, managing to earn several social service badges. She also took a commuter train to Connecticut every weekend for many months to live with the

Willcoxes, passport clients of Leonard, and began thinking of their big golden retriever as her own dog.

By pretending to take her mother's desertion in stride, Kathy trapped herself into a pose of invulnerability and became, as Jean later said, emotionally "dumb," refusing to acknowledge her misery.

At school, Kathy's hearty grin, her physical skills, her forthright gaze, and her courage made her a student leader. She was, said classmate Susan Kapit, "the in-est of the in-group and always teacher's pet." (Her teachers had been advised by Leonard of Jean's hospitalization.) "If I happened to be talking to another girl like Jennie Simon, she was perfectly friendly until Kathy came by. But if Kathy wanted to talk to Jennie, she would dump me. I understood. My feelings were not hurt. Amazing isn't it, that the same person in the class could be smartest and most popular—I believe that only a really decent person could balance those two qualities gracefully in one personality." Susan added, "I swear girls weren't even jealous of the fact that Kathy had her pick of boys in our class."

Kathy flattered classmate Josh White Jr., the son of the eponymous folk singer, by inviting him to take her to annual Pete Seeger concerts at Carnegie Hall. As a matter of course, he bought balcony tickets to avoid rich people in the orchestra pit. He recalls, "Kathy was the prettiest, smartest girl. It was an honor to be asked by her."

Mike Meeropol, the younger son of the late Julius and Ethel Rosenberg, was one of many boys who had a crush on Kathy. With rumpled hair and shy, vivid eyes, he was very attractive despite mild acne. Mike taught Kathy guitar licks and rousing songs about injustice with lyrics written by his adoptive father, Abel Meeropol, a white schoolteacher, poet, and dues-paying member of the Communist Party. Abel Meeropol had written lyrics and music for the amazing song "Strange Fruit," sung by Billie Holiday. The title refers to the horrific sight of lynched blacks hanging from trees in the South. It includes the lines: "The scent of magnolia sweet and fresh / And the sudden scent of burning flesh." The song was, decades later, voted best song of the twentieth century by editors of *Time* magazine.

During Jean's absence from home, a teacher tried to discourage Kathy from playing with the boys' baseball and basketball teams. Kathy patiently explained why the restriction made no sense. But the teacher forbade it. He told her that it was inappropriate since Kathy had developed breasts. She wrote an essay entitled, "Why Can't I Play Football

*Michael Meeropol, the son of
Ethel and Julius Rosenberg,
age fifteen (1958). He was a suitor
of Kathy Boudin at Elisabeth
Irwin High School and Bryn
Mawr College.*

with the Boys?" She won a baseball-throwing contest at the playground
across St. Luke's Place from her house, but still wasn't allowed to play on
the team.

Ruth Meyer, a psychologist, counseled Kathy and Michael and moved
into the Boudin home to care for them. Leonard, desperate for reas-
surance, began an affair with the young woman. Friends visiting the
household were embarrassed by the obvious sexual tension and
Leonard's showing off for the counselor. Making no secret of the affair,
Leonard said that this was no ordinary time—ordinary rules did not
obtain.

Barely back home for a week, Jean found Kathy changed from an easygo-
ing child to one with taunting demands for orange juice or for help finding a book. Jean tried to kill herself again. This had the effect of making
her children's need for her flow back upon itself again and churn subterranean tides inside them. She was hospitalized and given more electroshock treatment.

Jean was, nonetheless, determined to get well. When she returned
home from the hospital for the second time, she was crushed by Kathy's

Kathy Boudin introduced Pete Seeger during a fund-raising assembly at Elisabeth Irwin for the American Friends Service Committee on February 13, 1960.

uneasy stares and by her insistence on continuing to visit the Willcoxes on weekends. Kathy acted as if Jean's nearly fatal vulnerability was contagious.

Easily overwhelmed, Jean wept over a squashed pigeon in the gutter. When Geyser, the brown box turtle, died, Jean placed his empty shell on the dining room mantel.

Michael's abusiveness toward Jean at this time was noted by Kathy's best friend, Jennie Simon. "It was an adolescent thing, but incredibly magnified. He really acted as if Jean were the most stupid, annoying person that he had ever dreamed of. He often would not answer her at all. He sometimes treated Kathy the same way."

Jennie marveled at Jean's composure during these encounters. Jean was following the progressive teachings of Dr. Ben Spock and John Dewey by assuming that in nearly all instances, the child was right. Jean's friends wondered if Kathy and Michael were ever categorically refused anything.

His parents' tense relationship created the equivalent of a household war zone for Michael. He could not bear his mother's fawning desire to please his father. He embraced a credo that virtually ruled out a personal life.

During the next months Jean "pulled up her socks" and gamely competed for her husband. With the help of a psychotherapist, she trained herself to be "practical." Jean later told fellow poet Frances Waldman that difficulties with Leonard were compensated for by her pride in his altruistic legal work. Jean sensed that "the other woman" was still hovering.

Said Victor Rabinowitz, "The problems in the relationship between Leonard and Jean were not concealed particularly. I mean, Leonard's mistresses were part of the social scene. I don't mean that they were publicly acknowledged as mistresses, but all of their friends and even the children knew that there were—you know—problems. Jean got along even worse with Michael than she did with Leonard. That relationship was absolutely dreadful. He had contempt for her emotionalism and her belief that the practice of law was a way of making things better for poor people or dissenters."

Jean spoke to psychiatrists and to her old school friend Bert Gross of her daily struggle to keep the marriage together. She sensed sexual rivals everywhere. "I showed them," she said under her breath to her old friend Ruth Gilbert, referring to Leonard and Doriane. But a week later, when Ruth asked if the marriage was worth risking her life, Jean claimed not to know what Ruth was talking about.

Leonard was the subject, Jean believed, of her life. Her poems encouraged Leonard to stay by her side, weaving what she hoped was a spell of words. The best parts of their lifelong drama were when she sensed his return to her side after having rejected the possibility of linking his life to another woman. These reunions were marked not by explanations, but by a renewed, if temporary, focus on Jean.

8

LEONARD WINS THE LEGAL
FIGHT OF HIS LIFE

In the first week of June 1958, Jean finally had reason for public celebration. She invited "nearly everyone" to Sunday brunch to commemorate the surrender of the U.S. government to Leonard, and, "of course," she said, "you must personally congratulate Leonard's magnificent and dear friends Mr. Rockwell Kent and Mr. Paul Robeson." After six years of writing and filing appeals, Leonard had won the right-to-travel case. Jean confided to one and all: "Izzy says Ike and [Secretary of State] John Foster Dulles are pressing Congress for a bill to get back what our Leonard took away. Izzy says it'll never happen." She did not mention it had been Izzy's master plan to fight the right-to-travel issue through the courts all the way to the Supreme Court. Nonetheless it was Leonard who had achieved the landmark Supreme Court victory.

The *New York Times* headlined on page 1: "Passports May No Longer Be Denied Because of the Beliefs and Associations of Applicants." The legal reversal established the right to travel as "a human right, an inno-cent right that no government can steal."

It was, in Leonard's estimation, the most important case of his life. (It is cited as precedent at the time of this writing.)

On Sunday morning, at 11:30, guests were arriving. The weekly brunch at the Boudins was much more festive than usual. Jean pulled a hot tin from the oven and elbowed the oven door closed. Marcia Rabin-owitz peered in anxiously as Jean dropped a large knife in the small kitchen. Was she prepared for guests?

Still tacked to the inside of Jean's swinging kitchen door were yel-lowed news clippings from March 1954 extolling Leonard's adroit han-dling of Albert Einstein's seventy-fifth birthday party that had been the occasion for an ECLC seminar on "the meaning of academic freedom." When Princeton University banned the birthday celebration, after protests launched by the professor of physics and principal inventor of the atomic bomb, J. Robert Oppenheimer, Leonard cannily switched the party to the Nassau Tavern, a privately owned restaurant near the cam-pus, where it was deemed a great success.

Throughout the Sunday victory brunch, Jean kept up a witty hum of approbation about Leonard. There was strain in Jean's enjoyment of her husband; she knew that in order to keep him, she must work hard. Together she and Leonard had a self-conscious exquisiteness, a deep appreciation of their own ambience. Jean quoted "our brilliant Leonard Boudin" and then asked him, "Won't you please tell the story Justice Frankfurter told you?" Leonard demurred, "No, no. It's his story. Let him tell it." When Bert Gross interrupted Leonard a moment later, Jean shushed him with a smile. Bert understood that Leonard craved Jean's attentions, despite his apparent condescension. "In fact, Jean's public flat-tery," noted Bert silently, "is making Leonard's dreams a reality. She insists that he is spoken of as a great man. These Sunday brunches broaden and deepen Leonard's power."

Leonard hosted past and present lovers at the brunch. Jean invited Doriane and Georgette Schneer. He patted and kissed hands. Leonard's conversations with pretty women were monologues delivered in an extravagant manner, interspersed with his self-mocking asides and smiles. As Marcia Rabinowitz said after Leonard's death, "That dear self-deprecating smile, I will keep it with me until the day I die."

Jean also went out of her way to invite beautiful new acquaintances who fascinated Leonard, like Joan Baez, as well as the family's pretty au pair, a native Inuit studying anthropology at NYU.

First-time brunch guests exclaimed at the austere New England–style furnishings of the Boudin home. Setting a tone of upper-class simplicity, they were similar to those in Corliss Lamont's old farmhouse in Ossining. In pride of place was a maple rocking chair rubbed with beeswax, which was found in a church thrift shop.

At the brunch, Leonard explained the importance of common law to a group that included Joan Baez. He then began to muse aloud about an old newspaper column by Eleanor Roosevelt, who'd asked why the hostile witnesses summoned by McCarthy did not just say, Well, look, this is why we were communists, and then describe the high hopes they had once placed in the party to bring about world peace and an end to poverty. Leonard acknowledged that the drawback was the possibility of going to jail for contempt, because clients would refuse to answer the next demand: "Tell us the names of other former communists." "But," asked Leonard, "would the government really jail hundreds of these people?" Leonard sighed. "Public opinion was the problem. Nothing could be done in the courts [because] there was no public opinion sympathetic to communist radicals or anybody else who might have a nuclear bomb."

When Leonard then confided his "compassion for poor Joe McCarthy, who never disguised the fact that he was a ham and made no pretext of ideology," the insider's view elicited a gasp from Joan Baez.

Baez had become a client, but she soon told friends that Leonard touched her frequently and inappropriately when they were alone or walking down the street, and she fired him.

Rockwell and Sally Kent arrived midway through the victory brunch, in an explosion of congratulatory hugs. Kent had driven his pink Cadillac from their dairy farm. Although close to eighty, Kent vibrated adolescent energy. Hugging Kathy, he read aloud the inscription to Leonard that he'd painstakingly written across white snow in an Alaskan landscape painting of his hanging in the Boudin dining room: TO MY DEAREST FRIEND. The elderly illustrator added, "and God's only honest man."

As Jean rinsed forks, she watched Leonard spin from guest to guest, ebulliently describing plans to use his own passport to make an unusual trip "penetrating the Iron Curtain to Prague, Czechoslovakia" in order to console his "expat" clients there. These clients included Albert and Martha Dodd Stern, pro-communist intellectual adventurers (they preferred to be called "activists") who fled the United States one step ahead of government accusations of passing secrets to Russian employees at the United Nations during parties at their sprawling Central Park West apartment.

Leonard was one of a handful of Americans permitted by Soviets to glimpse life behind the Iron Curtain. Izzy Stone, whose ability to admit mistakes continued to be heroic, had been horrified during a recent visit to the Soviet Union, declaring afterward, "These are not men of honor."

At Jean's side, Marcia Rabinowitz folded napkins. A giant coffee urn steamed on Jean's child-size desk wedged in a corner between the mantel and an open front window. Theater critic Kenneth Tynan sipped hot milk and honey—Jean's remedy for Leonard's sleeplessness. A British subject, Tynan proudly declared himself an official un-American, having recently been mysteriously subpoenaed by Senator McCarthy.

Corliss Lamont stood at the top of the stairs, a one-man receiving line to Dwight MacDonald, his handsome son, Michael, and a contingent of Princeton professors and their wives. Lamont bowed almost imperceptibly to each person, saying: "At your service, and a pale substitute for Leonard Boudin, our hero."

Lamont also reminded Kathy, now almost fifteen, that his tennis pro was still begging to train her without fee. The man had been enthralled by Kathy's skills while watching her play against Leonard on Lamont's outdoor clay courts. Leonard had scoffed, "No child of mine is going to be a professional athlete."

Lamont laughed. "I can't even teach Leonard how to swing a croquet mallet. He digs holes in the lawn."

"At least he doesn't cheat," said Jean, who made other players giggle by ostentatiously nudging her croquet ball.

Kathy and Jennie Simon were enthralled by Lamont's sermonizing (he intoned his stories like an Episcopal preacher) about his righteous fight for minimum wages for maids and porters while he was a Harvard student. Lamont maintained: "I do not believe in Christian service to an improbable God but in service here and now to our fellow human beings."

Leonard was exclaiming to guest after guest, "Isn't the United States a rare and wonderful country. The law can be used to curb government improprieties against individuals. Any one of us can now travel anyplace."

"You wouldn't let Mike travel to China. It's too dangerous," said Marcia Rabinowitz.

Said Leonard, "I'd let Mike make up his own mind. He's a big-deal Harvard student now."

"But, Leonard, your parental duty—" asked Marcia.

"—is to tell him that as a student he has a moral duty only to his conscience."

Izzy and Esther and their family arrived late that afternoon from Washington and Cambridge. As usual, Leonard did his best to tune out the rise and fall of Izzy's vehement declamations. But Kathy and Jennie Simon were totally impressed by Izzy's certainty that he could make government bureaucrats fairer. He began making fun of someone who'd insisted that American democracy was "joined at the hip" with unbridled capitalism. In great form, Izzy jumped from raw insults and bitter Yiddish sayings to quotes from Plato and Mae West.

Leonard interrupted Izzy to tell a story about buttonholing two FBI agents who followed him home nightly from the law library of the New York Bar Association. But Izzy accused Leonard of having "enjoyed the honor too much."

Leonard bummed a cigarette and lit it, holding it in his thumb and forefinger. His smoking was a sign he was feeling beaten up by Izzy. The two brothers-in-law competed for admiring glances from the "Roisman sisters," as well as from their sharp-eyed children. Izzy's sister, Judy, would soon decline a summer invitation to accompany the two men and their wives to Europe on the *Queen Mary,* saying she disliked "fights to the death."

The family circle hummed with conflict. Esther asked Jean why Bert Gross was still in the picture. "You flirt too much," said Esther. Esther's daughter, Celia, had married her childhood boyfriend, Walter Gilbert, a star on the Harvard science faculty who had switched from physics to new fields concerning DNA and gene research. Jean introduced "Wally" as "my nephew, the shoo-in for the Nobel Prize." "What's he doing about world hunger?" asked Leonard under his breath. He found Wally's silences condescending and fearsome.

It was dusk when famed actor Paul Robeson climbed the stairs. The air was swirling with cigarette smoke. At six feet four inches, Robeson towered over other guests. When he called out to Leonard in his rumbling voice, all other sounds in the room diminished. Robeson was not a regular at Leonard's brunches, despite heartfelt invitations. He feared being "collected" by white friends as "the exceptional Negro."

Joe Boudin suddenly appeared, holding a scrapbook of Leonard's press clippings and a big ear horn. He screamed hellos. Leonard was embarrassed by Joe's manners. Victor Rabinowitz saw Joe as "a cranky son-of-a-bitch, five foot five inches of bristling eyebrows and big ears. He had none of Leonard's graces. He did not give a damn what anyone else thought." Joe no longer berated Leonard for his inability with foreign languages, but railed against his son Arthur, absent today, who had lost three retail businesses.

By seven o'clock, guests were luxuriating in the sensation of having been adopted by a dazzling family. They sipped tea, unwilling to leave the charmed circle. A few snuggled into the sofa under shelves and shelves of tan law books.

Down at the front door, Izzy kissed Leonard good-bye. Then Izzy wagged a finger and proclaimed himself the sole heir of Louis B. Boudin. "Remember Louis and I—we studied Marx like the Talmud. Your law books are hammers and nails."

Hurt, Leonard raced back upstairs. Other guests took Jean's cue and smiled indulgently as Leonard began to dance by himself, kicking his legs, throwing his arms up, and twirling in an ungaited frenzy. He was an amazing and preposterous dancer; big floppy gestures seemed to throw him in several directions at once.

Corliss Lamont was soon singing "Daisy, Daisy, give me your answer true," as his host kicked, twirled, lost his balance, and flung his arms this way and that, his movements unrelated to the rhythm of Lamont's singing. Social dancing in the late 1950s was about having a partner, and holding that partner's hand. No one danced like Leonard.

That autumn, Kathy and her tenth-grade classmates sat in a beat-up yellow school bus headed north to Walden Pond in Concord, Massachusetts. The teacher told them that Henry Thoreau's essays were not literally true; he spent weeks here, not the years he described. The children strolled the banks of the small brown pond, rereading his essays aloud and peering into the small house that was a shrine to conscience. They liked the story of Thoreau's night in jail for refusing to pay poll tax (he paid other taxes) to a government that condoned slavery. Apparently Ralph Waldo Emerson (who derided Henry Thoreau as "the captain of the huckleberries") visited Thoreau in jail and asked him, "Henry, why are you there?"

Thoreau drew himself up and asked: "Why are you not here?"

Later, back at Elisabeth Irwin, Kathy led classmates in a protest of the regular air-raid drill, encouraging fellow students to refuse to crawl under their desks. They sang, "Gonna lay down my sword and shield . . . ain't gonna study war no more."

In addition, Kathy crusaded against "conspicuous consumption" and "vanity." She and her friends made fun of kids with unlimited use of their parents' department store charge cards. As the most popular leader, she set the standard of dress: her slip hung below skirt hems. Like Leonard, during intense conversation her shirt tended to become untucked. Her long hair was thick, lustrous, and uncombed.

She deliberately avoided any hint of bragging when classmates wanted to know all about Leonard's important new client, the handsome young revolutionary Fidel Castro, hero of the Cuban Revolution. Her friends also knew that Leonard's clients included the Rosenberg boys' grandparents. (Representing them, Leonard lost a custody suit for their grandsons, Mike and Robby Meeropol, in 1955.)

When she ran for school president in her junior year, Kathy won, surprising no one. (Her successor would work in the Clinton White House.) "If Kathy hadn't done . . . you know, I . . . we . . . kids in our class all pretty much assumed she'd be president of the United States. What else could she be?" said classmate Susan Kapit.

Meanwhile Michael was hiding behind thick eyeglasses at Harvard. He seemed not to inhabit his body and conveyed little grace when he walked or gestured. He was leading a monkish life. Milton and Judy Viorst visited him. Milton recalled, "Mike looked the same as he would in middle age, only slightly less wrinkled. He was hardly a happy-go-lucky undergraduate who went on dates and had a Harvard banner on his wall. On his furrowed brow were the cares of the world." Viorst added, "His mind worked on an abstract legal plane just like Leonard's." Viorst omitted vital distinctions: unlike Leonard, Michael never spoke of himself or his work, and perhaps more intriguing, he hated left-wing politics. He was a young Republican, very conservative, a believer in big corporations, which he said made the world go 'round.

Michael had found his groove. During his sophomore year at Harvard, Learned Hand, of the U.S. Court of Appeals—perhaps the greatest living judge—lectured to a packed auditorium at Harvard Law School.

Michael Boudin's yearbook picture, Harvard, 1961. A young conservative, he wrote his senior honors thesis on religious freedom.

Hand was a revered figure in the Boudin circle, having sided with Leonard's appeal in the Coplon case.

Michael warmed to the elderly man's example of a highly intellectual and conservative life. Judge Hand abhorred advocacy lawyering and activism—as was practiced by Leonard. According to Hand, courts should restrict their scope. He declared that changing the law was what state legislators and congressmen did. Hand lived a life of balancing precedent on both sides of an argument.

Both Learned Hand and Michael were wary bachelors for many years. The two men were gloomy, introverted, anxious, and self-blaming. The image of Hand's father, a highly successful lawyer, daunted him, and, like Michael, Hand was disturbed by feelings of personal failure, even though he was first in his class at Harvard College and made law review.

Kathy was the best student in the Elisabeth Irwin senior honors French course, taught by a formidable woman named Mlle Francine Fontaine. Kathy soaked up the language better than any student Mlle Fontaine had ever encountered. And Kathy was the only senior who did not stop working hard once her transcripts and recommendations had been sent to colleges.

Francine was taken aback by a confrontation with Kathy's father on

Kathy Boudin's graduating class from Elisabeth Irwin High School, 1961. Kathy, bottom row, second from right, and note Angela Davis, bottom row, third from left.

parents' night, 1961. Catching sight of her, Leonard shouted angrily, "So you're the 'genius' French teacher I keep hearing about."

"Well, perhaps you mean Madeleine who teaches next door," said Mlle Fontaine.

"No," said Leonard in a belligerent tone that Francine found mystifying. "You're the one Kathy claims is a damn genius."

Leonard's frustration at his own inability to learn languages also prompted Jean to fib. She proclaimed that she too was hopeless at new languages. Leonard would spend a decade trying to absorb conversational Spanish from tutors.

The only field that mattered, Leonard insisted, was "the law." It was in the Boudin genes. In the right hands, the law could be used to create a better world.

Francine Fontaine was tutoring an unusual student in Kathy's class: Angela Davis was an intensely timid black girl from Birmingham, Alabama, who'd won a scholarship from a Quaker group to study at Elisabeth Irwin.

In 1959, a few years after black hero Rosa Parks refused to move to the back of a segregated bus in Montgomery, Alabama, the frightened

Angela Davis had traveled north for the first time in the "For Colored" section of a train. Her mother worried that Greenwich Village was "a haven for weird beatniks."

Angela moved in with the family of the Reverend William Howard Melish, a white minister in Brooklyn who'd had a high position in the Communist Party. She found it difficult to make friends with classmates, geographically and culturally "foreign," whose own friendships had ten-year-old roots. As liberals, they made a point of not noticing her skin color. Angela Davis was unnerved by their relaxed attitudes, finding it strange that the principal was introduced to her by his nickname, "Rank."

Angela Davis, the outsider, and Kathy Boudin, the quintessential insider, were rivals, not friends: both were competitive, studious, and accustomed to getting top grades.

At Elisabeth Irwin, Angela Davis began to reinterpret painful aspects of her life and the lives of other blacks in America from a Marxist point of view—discarding views shaped by white media. She began to hope that blacks might make a revolution.

Later she wrote, "When I learned about socialism in my history classes [at Elisabeth Irwin], a whole new world opened up before my eyes. I became acquainted with the notion that every person could give to society according to his ability and his talents, and that in turn he could receive material and spiritual aid in accordance with his needs."

Karl Marx's writings hit Angela as hard as they had hit Paul Robeson, "like an expert surgeon . . . cut[ting] cataracts from my eyes." She was moved by Marx's vision of a new society—where no one person could own so much that he used his possessions to exploit other human beings. She decided that racial hatred was part of the inevitable consequence of one group oppressing the other for the sake of profit. "Profit was the word: the cold and constant motive for the behavior, the contempt and the despair that I had seen."

Kathy, Michael Meeropol, Jennie Simon, and other classmates picketed Woolworth's as part of the "civil rights movement" to protest the store's policy of segregated lunch counters in the south.

By mistake, Kathy and Jennie Simon carried handmade signs on the subway to an untargeted Woolworth's store. Kathy decided to march there anyway. They chanted, "Two-four-six-eight, Woolworth's doesn't integrate." Kathy politely asked customers not to cross the picket line. Most agreed.

The two protesters waved painted signs, chanting, "One, two, three, four, don't go to Woolworth's store."

They sang, "Mary had a little lamb, its fleece was white as snow. Now Mary had another lamb, its fleece was very black, and everywhere that Mary went, that lamb was turned right back."

At the end of the day, they ritually clasped arms, singing in high notes: ". . . deep in my heart, I do believe, we shall overcome someday."

During a larger rally in Times Square, the students had a scare when one boy from Elisabeth Irwin was dragged by a mounted policeman.

As years passed, both Angela Davis and Kathy Boudin would be enraged by what seemed to be lackluster results of nonviolent protests against racial inequities. Both went on to perform grandiose and self-sacrificing gestures to create a better world. Angela became a notorious Black Panther freedom fighter, a fugitive, a communist, and—finally—a professor at the University of California at Santa Cruz.

In little more than a decade, President Richard Nixon would sign an anticrime bill, proclaiming, "Let this be a warning to Angela Davis and to all other terrorists—"

In the winter of 1960, Kathy was quoted prominently in the *New York Times* about "contributing to a social struggle." The article described a weekend she and her classmates spent in East Harlem under the auspices of the Quakers. A classmate said later, "We were painting and plastering to help black people live better."

Another headline appeared in the London *Daily Mail* in late August 1960: "U.S. Girl Joins 'Ban Bomb' March." Below a photograph of Kathy's plumpish face, the article detailed her participation in a 150-person peace walk from Edinburgh to London.

Kathy was the first girl in her class to "go all the way" in senior year. Nearly all the boys had crushes on her. The other girls admired her vanguard action. Kathy did not join other seniors who smoked cigarettes at lunch.

If Kathy was the most popular person in her high-school class, she was fearful of losing her place as Leonard's most cherished offspring. Leonard's increasing surges of affection for Michael were based on his son's extraordinary academic accomplishments, which included virtually perfect College Board and law aptitude scores. Teachers said that Michael was "a budding genius" with a photographic memory. Leonard soon announced happily that Michael was writing an honors thesis at Harvard on the historic role of the Supreme Court in preserving free exercise of religion. Leonard was thrilled to have a hand in steering his son's research. It was a clever choice of subject, for Michael could affirm views of his father and Louis Boudin, without compromising his own conservative leanings.

The thesis was unsurprising. Michael wrote: "The state is supreme in the temporal realm and may not intrude into strictly spiritual matters."

Kathy began wishing she were a different person. She had failed to earn Leonard's respect for her formidable skills in foreign languages or tennis and basketball—or in handling people.

The problem was that Leonard insisted women admire him. For Kathy, it was a no-win situation. Following in her father's footsteps was not the answer. Leonard disparaged female lawyers.

Only once did Mlle Fontaine catch a glimpse of Kathy Boudin's hidden turmoil. It was during a lively recital at the Elisabeth Irwin school. Each senior honor student had memorized a favorite French poem. Jean was among proud parents seated in the back rows of the auditorium. Students occupied front rows.

On a signal, Kathy walked purposefully to the stage. She began to recite *"Le Dormeur du Valle"* by Arthur Rimbaud. She spoke in tight French vowels and flourishing Parisian singsong, ending one sentence on a high pitch, the next sentence low.

When she got to the second verse, Kathy's eyes suddenly filled with tears. In a tremulous voice, Kathy recited the lines about a young soldier stretched out in a lovely, serene green grassy field, his temporary bed, sweetly sleeping with his mouth open, his head bare under the sun.

> *Un soldat jeune, bouche ouverte, tête nue,*
> *Et la nuque bagnant dans le frais cresson bleu,*
> *Dort; il est étendu dans l'herbe, sous la nue,*
> *Pâle dans son lit vert où la lumière pleut.*
>
> *Les pieds dans les glaïeuls, il dort. Souriant comme*
> *Souririait un enfant malade, il fait un somme:*
> *Nature, berce-le chaudement: il a froid.*

Kathy was openly weeping as she recited the last verse in a low sad voice. In it the poet discovers, on close examination, that the young soldier is not sleeping: there are two red holes in his right side—he is dead.

Jean got it. Kathy was crying in front of a hundred people about an event from her own past: the shock of finding her mother not really "sleeping" but lying close to death on the kitchen floor, eight years earlier. Mlle Fontaine never forgot this display by the student she usually found "surprisingly cold, so remote you could never reach her, [as if] she had decided not to live in the world of feelings with all of the rest of us."

That spring, Kathy lost a major round in the competition for "favored heir" when, in May, her application for admission to Oberlin College was rejected. Jean blamed Kathy's College Board test scores.

Leonard complained about Kathy's bad news to Robert Johnson, his professional adversary and the government's chief passport lawyer. Leonard had decided to make Johnson a friend. At dinner in Washington at the Hilton Hotel, Leonard said, mournfully, that to make things worse, Kathy was even ambivalent about studying the law. She was taking premed courses.

Changing the subject, Leonard began to ruminate about his recent trip to Prague. He was indirectly bragging about his unusual trip behind the Iron Curtain. He'd come back, he said, with depressing news of life under Soviet communism. Capital punishment was meted out for critics of the government, priests, artists, intellectuals, Jews, and embezzlers of "socialist property." It made U.S. congressional investigations, blacklists, and passport suspensions look, said Leonard, "like flea bites."

What Leonard didn't know was that Robert Johnson was writing top-secret reports of his conversations with Leonard and mailing them to Director J. Edgar Hoover.

Leonard said that his career had been shaped by a social preference for mingling with idealists, even oddballs with critiques of society. "I've preferred the company of lefties." Thus, said Leonard, it was only natural that when such friends got in legal trouble with the government, they turned to him.

Memories of what he had seen in Prague depressed Leonard. "How is it that this evening I'm once again depressed over totalitarian socialism?" he said, mocking his grandiosity.

At another dinner meeting, Leonard told Robert Johnson how melancholy he had been walking on deserted Jew Street in Prague's ghetto. The Czechs had scapegoated, massacred, run out of town, and conscripted Jews for a thousand years. As a result, the Catholic country now had a Jewish population of less than 3 percent. He said that his expat clients from the United States did not greet each other in the street. They were scared to call attention to themselves by acting like a clique.

Leonard spoke of Soviet blunders. Although Czechloslovakia was one of the richest manufacturing countries of Europe, few married people had food or living space for children.

In a conversation with Johnson about the Soviet bloc ban of Boris Pasternak's acclaimed novel *Dr. Zhivago,* Leonard indignantly described the ban in Prague of another superb novel, called *The Cowards,* written by Josef Skvorecky. Leonard's client Martha Stern had laughingly told Leonard he "just might" identify with the young narrator. "Danny" makes up his mind to shoot a gun in the revolution to win a girl's admiration and love. Although Irena loves another boy, she is Danny's constant imaginary audience. At the end of the novel, Danny sees crushing reality in the foul-smelling, greasy, and drunk Russian "liberators" who tower over the rumps of their flea-bitten ponies. Leonard had in his wallet a folded, handwritten translation of the last page of *The Cowards:*

> I didn't have anything against communism [and Marxist study groups and people's hunger for knowledge and comforts]. . . . I didn't have anything against anything, just as long as I could play jazz on my saxophone, because that was something I loved to do. . . . And as long as I could watch the girls, because that meant being alive for me.
>
> . . . But finally, ultimately, nothing mattered. . . . There was only the animal fear of death, because that's the only thing nobody knows anything about, and that fear alone was enough to keep a person going in this nothingness. I wondered whether some day this fear, too, would lose its importance for me.

Robert Johnson wrote excitedly to J. Edgar Hoover that as a result of visiting Prague, Leonard had become disenchanted with Soviet communism. Director Hoover seized upon the news as proof that his formidable adversary was ready to alter his life course. Hoover wanted to enlist Leonard Boudin. In a memo dated June 25, 1959, Hoover alerted all New York agents to "give particular attention to the investigation of Leonard Boudin and be alert for any other occurrences which might indicate that Boudin is becoming disillusioned with Communism . . . and how [Boudin's change of attitude] can be utilized to the Bureau's advantage."

Irony was not Hoover's strong point. Nor was complexity. Leonard had been trying to bond with Johnson. And as a liberal, when asked what he believed in, Leonard declared: "As de Tocqueville wrote, in the United States all political issues are Constitutional issues."

9

KATHY WAS SOMEBODY
SERIOUS

I always thought Kathy was living a larger life than the rest of the students at Bryn Mawr College. . . . She was somebody serious—you sort of know in your mind who the great souls are or who you think they are.

—Liz Bogen, 1998

For god's sake Kathy, for once in your life, rebel.

—Fred Gardner to Kathy Boudin, 1962

On September 19, 1961, Kathy warily pulled her khaki duffel bag under a splendid Gothic arch on the Bryn Mawr College campus. Hurricane winds lifted her long hair. She hugged a guitar case to her chest. Confrontation, or at least heightened tension, was in the humid air as Kathy surveyed rain-drenched flower beds and low beige stone buildings.*

Kathy and Jean had winced at news that Kathy's assigned dormitory at Bryn Mawr was named after John D. Rockefeller. Initially, there were no

---

*Katharine Hepburn was the college's most admired former student. Graduate Marianne Moore was another rare woman who was allowed by society, because of the sheer force of her will and her talents, to live life by her rules. Marianne Moore's mother's modest inheritance and the support of rich friends freed Moore to move to Greenwich Village to write poetry. In 1968, Kathy would be voted by the graduating class as the most admired graduate. (I missed the decorously unstated point entirely—until long after my own graduation—that family money usually lubricates the paths of such unusual lives.)

classmates in Rockefeller Hall with whom Kathy could commiserate about the building's inappropriateness for its new tenant. Rockefeller was one of several American heroes perceived by Kathy to be in illegal possession of a fortune that was rightfully the property of the thousands of workingmen whose labors had built that fortune. The Boudins saw Bryn Mawr as Kathy's failure, so much so that Jean faltered at making it a joke.

But Kathy's moralistic scoldings would bruise or help to transform lives of scores of Bryn Mawr students. These girls included me and Mary Thom, who became a feminist activist and author. Liz Schneider, who wanted to teach law, applied to Bryn Mawr because it had been "good enough for Kathy Boudin."

There was also, of course, Diana "Das" Oughton, my next-door neighbor in Rockefeller Hall who less than ten years later would be blown to bits in the explosion of the Wilkerson town house in Greenwich Village, from which Kathy barely escaped with her life. Das was a sweet-faced girl with a triumphant laugh. Her delicate upper body was set on chunky hips and wide legs. She had graduated with highest marks from Madeira, an elite boarding school in Virginia, and lived in her green Bryn Mawr gym tunic.* She walked in an unfeminine, rolling way.

A descendant of the founder of the Boy Scouts, she had grown up on a vast estate in Illinois. At home she drove a pickup truck and hunted pheasants and ducks. Her father owned factories as well as tenant farms in Alabama. Her laughter in the dorm was sometimes at the expense of a classmate who "goofed" in choice of words or clothing.

Upon returning from her junior year of study in Germany, Das said German students had convinced her that the "so-called Holocaust" in Germany had not really happened. I wondered if that made her anti-Semitic, but looking back, it was probably evidence of her gullibility.

Kathy's moral lessons hit each of us harder than anything in classrooms. They resembled hostile first dates and required soul-searching and promises of transformation in order to qualify to be in Kathy's life. Kathy's own disappearance from campus after her junior year added to her legend: she was such a genius at languages and so "in" on the left, it was said, that she breezed through her senior year at the University of Leningrad and graduated as a Russian-language major, in absentia, at the top of her Bryn Mawr class.

---

*In view of Das's short life, the Madeira boarding school motto is tragic: "Function in disaster, finish in style."

Diana Oughton, Bryn Mawr, 1963. Oughton lived across the hall from Kathy Boudin at Rockefeller Hall. "Das" was killed in the 1970 Wilkerson town house bombing in Greenwich Village, from which Kathy narrowly escaped.

The rebellions of the sixties would likely have passed Bryn Mawr by, if not for Kathy. Students at nearby Swarthmore College—half of whom were male and many of whose parents were intellectuals and big-city liberals—had been in an uproar over anticommunist investigations of the 1950s. But Bryn Mawr students had ignored the hysteria in favor of Princeton football weekends and nights in the library researching such subjects as Emmanuel Kant's moral imperative and John Ruskin's study of the waterlogged stones of Venice.

In fact, when Kathy entered college, Bryn Mawr was in a placid phase. A student leader wrote contentedly that the only campus controversy was over the maypole, stolen by Haverford College boys after a decoy display of fireworks.*

The college's Quaker heritage was evident: liquor was banned; students were devoted to the social and academic honor system.

Nonetheless there were also indications of the aristocratic Quaker habit of mostly talking a good game of societal responsibility. There was only one black student in the class of 1962 and two black young women in my class, the class of 1963. Jewish scholarship students, like myself and several classmates from the public school I attended—Girls High in Philadelphia—felt uneasy about feeling uneasy.

---

*A number of freshmen from places such as Greenwich, Connecticut, and Grosse Point, Michigan, had already met at boarding schools or at coming-out parties. They set the tone, as they checked new acquaintances in the Social Register and dreamed of big church weddings.

Kathy was smarting over her rejection for admission to Oberlin. "I was a grind," she said later. "I worked hard for grades."*

Michael had by now been admitted to Harvard Law School. To Leonard, Kathy shouted that she would help more people after medical school than Leonard and Michael combined.

Kathy was also openly envious of tense dispatches about Joni Rabinowitz, Victor's daughter, who was courageously working in the South to encourage blacks to register to vote. Joni was a student at Antioch, a college whose activist atmosphere was the antithesis of Bryn Mawr. Jean Bouldin consoled her daughter: "You are far too young to pick up and move to the Deep South for civil rights work."

Two years older than Kathy, Joni was soon arrested in Albany, Georgia, as part of the new radical group of blacks and whites called SNCC (the Student Nonviolent Coordinating Committee).

Joni never panicked in jail: she had faith "in the legal system because of Victor." But nonetheless, when Joni was interrogated by a grand jury, she defiantly wore a black armband, mourning the death of justice.

As Joni's lawyers, Leonard and Victor worked out of a motel in Macon, Georgia. They took turns cross-examining witnesses. Leonard worried that the ordeal of representing his own daughter would be too great for Victor.

Leonard fought hard to help his partner's family. On the last day of the trial a juror inadvertently revealed she did not hear the judge call her name. Leonard jumped to his feet. "She's deaf," said Leonard. "Mistrial." The judge ignored him.

Leonard and Victor won Joni's case on appeal, using a favorite issue: the jury pool had almost no black members in a district in which half the population was black.

Joni was a hero. Victor carried around an article about her arrest from the black separatist newspaper *Muhammad Speaks*.

But as the sixties progressed, more and more young people would grow frustrated about the possibility of peaceful social change. Joni Rabinowitz bitterly observed that only "violence would make changes in the segregated South," although in the end just a small number of radical stu-

---

*Years later, in an interview in 1984 for the Oral Archive at Columbia University, Leonard tried to shift blame for Kathy's fate by bringing up the rejection by Oberlin. He was implying a fundamental lack of some kind, perhaps even intelligence. And on the only day when Jean was absent from the interview, he introduced the subject of Jean's suicide attempts to explain Kathy's problems.

Joni Rabinowitz, November 1963, during her trial in Macon, Georgia. Her father, Victor Rabinowitz, and Boudin defended her for charges stemming from her attempts to help black voters to register.

dents, such as Kathy, would actually cross the line between protest and violence.

Upon settling into her assigned room at Rockefeller Hall, Kathy unpacked blue jeans, denim work shirts, and a poster of Ernesto "Che" Guevara, the gloriously handsome young Cuban revolutionary and poet with the glossy black beard. Kathy had a proprietary interest in Che. She knew that quite apart from the fact of Leonard's legal work on behalf of the Cuban government, her father had vanquished the legendary Che Guevara at several games of chess.

As a result of Victor Rabinowitz's successful campaign in Cuba for the job of counsel for the revolutionary Cuban government in U.S. courts, he and Leonard were suddenly litigating dozens of groundbreaking cases and almost routinely making headlines in newspapers.

It was exhilarating, said Leonard, to fight on U.S. judicial turf for a small impoverished country that had been traditionally exploited economically by U.S. corporations and by tourists seeking prostitutes and Mafia-run gambling. Tourists and rich businessmen had ignored the grim spectacle of the Cuban people, few of whom had running water and many of whom were starving. Leonard and Victor were litigating for Fidel Castro's right to nationalize (or seize, depending on one's point of view) a billion dollars' worth of factories, banks, sugar mills, farms, and other assets owned by huge U.S. corporations such as United Fruit and Chase Bank. They were trying to work out a way for Cuba to compensate foreign property owners, along the lines established by Mexico in 1938, when that country seized oil wells owned by U.S. citizens.

Presumably the presence of two distinguished U.S. lawyers arguing property disputes for Cuba in U.S. courts was a factor in helping to stall U.S. military retaliation.

"Leonard is fighting the real war with Cuba," said Jean with a proud nod.

One morning, Jean woke her fitfully sleeping husband with bad news: Fidel Castro had just been grossly insulted by the U.S. government. It seems Fidel had landed at La Guardia Airport with fifty-one young soldiers in army uniforms and had driven to a meeting at the United Nations. Meanwhile his airplane had been seized by the U.S. government. Not only was Castro insulted as a Cuban, a man, and a visiting head of state, but he had no way of getting home.

The U.S. government, it seems, was feeling inhospitable, since its cold-war enemy and Castro's ally, Nikita Khrushchev, was also in Manhattan to urge the U.N. to adopt a Soviet Union demand for disarmament and ban on nuclear testing. Leonard immediately demanded and received a State Department order granting Fidel Castro and his airplane diplomatic immunity under international law.

Besides litigating on Fidel Castro's behalf, Leonard was sharing a twenty-year-old mistress with him. Kassana Worszeck was a Cuban dancer, a muscular girl, with a thin face and long neck with feathery black curls. She possessed the physical arrogance of a flamenco dancer. Born in Queens, she had become a favorite protégée of the blind choreographer Alicia Alonzo, who ran the national dance troupe of Cuba. People remarked on the crazed look in Kassana's dark eyes; disconcertingly, they appeared to be on different planes when she faced a person straight on. Old friends of Leonard remarked on her resemblance to the young Georgette Schneer, also a dancer. Kassana was seen as one of Leonard's acolytes, not terribly brilliant, but kind.

Leonard told his friends that Kassana and other women who knew Fidel Castro well referred to him as "Him" (making a small motion at

Victor Rabinowitz with his and Leonard Boudin's client Fidel Castro and an interpreter.

their chins to indicate a beard) and nicknamed him "the horse" because of his sexual endowments.

Kassana Worszeck was a presence at St. Luke's Place. Jean took her shopping for books on dance. Friends marveled: Was neither Jean nor Kathy jarred by yet another of Leonard's public love affairs? It seemed not.

Meanwhile, at Bryn Mawr, Kathy did as little as possible to comply with dress requirements for dinner under Rockefeller Hall's chandeliers. She merely pulled a skirt over her jeans. Like Leonard, part of Kathy's appeal was the impression she gave of having just tumbled out of bed. Kathy's face reddened with anger and she mouthed "oh shit" as she watched white-haired black maids in gray hair nets, gray uniforms, and short white aprons bend to present a silver platter of green beans and sliced almonds to student after student.

There was something utterly compelling about Kathy. A sturdy figure, she was also radiant, and the combination gave her a no-bullshit, confident charisma. Her manner was enhanced by her apparent desire to listen and think and speak better than anyone. She expressed herself in restless, rushing sentences. Sometimes when excited about an idea, she swallowed her words, seeming almost to gurgle.

She amazed us with her well-researched views about subjects that other students had not questioned, such as the morality of U.S. corporations making profits at the expense of Cuba's natural assets and underfed workers and children.

Kathy also impressed us with her inside track to Fidel Castro. One night she read aloud from her mother's letter. "Leonard does not mind that Fidel Castro's message is extremist," wrote Jean. "Fidel is good for Cubans. When it comes to his clients, Leonard minds almost nothing."*

On superficial observation, Kathy seemed informal and the opposite of rigid—particularly if compared to prep-school graduates like Das Oughton, who at this stage of her political evolution refused to tolerate disagreement even about her conviction that Barry Goldwater was a voice of reason.

In an early letter home to St. Luke's Place, Kathy expressed dismay at her surroundings, and outlined her mission: "I was surprised by three things which should be changed. The maids, all black, are underpaid and not organized; no one reads the *New York Times;* and there is not enough awareness of the civil rights movement."

One night Kathy had the first of two public temper tantrums during formal dinner in Rockefeller Hall. She recalled, "There was a picket line that afternoon at Woolworth's protesting segregated lunch counters in the South and I was the only undergraduate there. No one would join me. I stood up at dinner trying to speak about the picket line. No one stopped talking. I lifted my plate and smashed it against the wall. No one looked up from their plates." (The facts are slightly different: at least fifteen undergraduates picketed, although perhaps not on Kathy's shift. I marched on an afternoon shift with several other students, including Anna Kimbrough, the sole black student in the class ahead of mine.)

---

*Fidel had also said, "All my military science can be summed up by the game of Ping-Pong. Return the ball where your enemy least expects it." After learning about it, Leonard invented "the Boudin knifing technique" to use in chess and the law. "I come up with an attack where my enemy, believing himself to have won, least expects it."

Kathy was soon spending hours between classes interviewing each maid in Rockefeller Hall. Several had come from a tiny farming town in Virginia called Cheriton. Besides preparing, serving, and clearing meals, the elderly women dusted and vacuumed student bedrooms, washed bathrooms, ironed sheets, and made beds once a week. They answered student telephone calls on an ancient plug-in switchboard.

Kathy was outraged to discover that the maids earned less than $2.00 an hour and that they lived in cubicles in the basement of Rockefeller Hall that were smaller than bathrooms in homes near campus.

Maids were also required to go caroling from dorm to dorm on Christmas Eve. The carolers ended the night outside the president's stately home, where college president Katharine McBride presented each servant with a miniature Whitman sampler box of candy.

Under Kathy's guidance, Mary Thom and a score of other Bryn Mawr students sat down with pen and paper to ask maids in every dormitory about job problems and to define "their issues." It was "organizing," and Kathy's role model was Corliss Lamont, her father's friend and the ECLC financial sponsor who had done similar work as a student at Harvard in the 1920s. Leonard and Victor, too, had represented hundreds of labor union workers. Nonetheless, to her classmates it was a totally original gesture.

Mary Thom, the valedictorian of her high-school class in Minnesota, credits Kathy for teaching her more than any professor. "Radicalizing"— an exciting change of perspective—was what young people called it, and Kathy inspiringly led the way. (She herself had never gone through such a transformation, having believed as long as she could remember that life was about doing socially responsible intellectual work.)

Mary Thom was shaken as maid after maid told her of her struggle to make her life work. "The older women worked until they died, because there was no pension plan. It was a real eye-opener and was probably more valuable to us than to them." Mary worried because she was only a transient participant in the harsh life of each of the maids and did not want to make things worse for them.

Kathy's social work made her feel cockily superior to the rest of her classmates—and in many ways she was. Her moral perspective was more important to her than sports, possessions, impressing boys, or being a Bryn Mawr student. It was as important as academic achievement and was somehow key to obtaining her father's respect.

Das Oughton squirmed in the face of Kathy's scolding. Yes, she had read textbooks citing President Andrew Johnson's Reconstruction and the abolishing of racial inequities after slavery was abolished. But, no, she had not questioned those textbooks. What was racism? Was it the curse of anyone who was white in the United States?

Those life-changing confrontations between Kathy and other students such as Das lasted through the night. Kathy questioned Das closely about her career ambitions and romantic hopes, and then critiqued them. Das was shamed by Kathy's contempt for indifferent rich people like Das's parents. It was difficult to counter Kathy's passionate premise that any decent citizen could not enjoy luxuries, liberties, or even the necessities of life while others were starving.

Newly enlightened, Das rejected an offer of marriage from a Princeton college quarterback named Johnny Hendriks. She began tutoring black students in Philadelphia. She was, as Bill Ayers later wrote, a gifted teacher who taught "by example and by illustration," by observing a student and helping him or her in a way that was "indirect, muted, or enigmatic, its shape and substance apparent only slowly."

After graduation, Das signed up with the international VISTA program for two years. She taught the poor children of Chichicastenango in rural Guatemala, where she started living like a native, patching her worn-out clothes and eating only corn and coffee instead of meat, fruit, and tins of pâté mailed by her mother. When her parents visited, she admonished them to "stop acting rich." She hated to see so many tiny coffins sold at the weekly market; half the deaths in Guatemala were the result of little children starving.

But as Thomas Powers, who wrote a poignant book about Diana Oughton, has said, "Willfulness and frustrated idealism alone cannot explain Diana's and Kathy's ambition to be among this country's executioners."

What no one at Bryn Mawr suspected was that Kathy's stance was not as secure as it looked. Her equilibrium depended on Leonard's intoxicating approval, and this was not a sure thing. It was, in fact, a tragic paradox of Kathy's life that Leonard's competitive, ambitious spirit clashed with the egalitarian philosophy he espoused.

Decades later, Kathy's Bryn Mawr classmate Liz Bogen spoke perceptively and sadly as she struggled to make sense of Kathy's complex nature.

President Katharine McBride, Bryn Mawr College, 1961. Kathy courageously argued with McBride while attempting to organize the college's maids and porters.

Liz said that at school she'd seen Kathy as a superior person—but not in any way cold or predictable. Liz remembered Kathy as being totally enviable. Liz was not the only one who was awed by what she saw as Kathy's ideological passion and intellectual rigor. In addition, classmates remember Kathy as a little stocky, a little messy, and a little boyish. Liz used to watch Kathy heat up milk and drink it with honey when she had insomnia. Liz also remembered wistfully the sound of Kathy's lovely speaking voice, so round and resonant that she'd assumed Kathy was a singer. Her dorm mates at Coop House loved Kathy's chocolate chip cookies—and she baked them frequently. Liz also noted that Kathy liked older men—and they liked her back.

Ever her father's daughter, Kathy could never resist a kind of flirting or teasing—with just about everybody. It started with a little toss of her head, a cocking of her chin, a huge grin—and then a savvy challenge. She won virtually every competition she embarked on (setting the terms herself) and exuded superiority. She pulled men and women toward her and pushed them away at the same time, seeming to say "refute me if you can but of course you can't."

The little swagger in Kathy's self-presentation was one of many unusual things about her that was a direct imitation of her father.

Looking back, it seems inevitable that Kathy would clash with Katharine McBride, Bryn Mawr college president. President McBride (as she was referred to and addressed) was a handsome woman of military posture, who dragged one leg made of wood. Her graying hair was pulled back over a high, bony forehead and into a knot. Her transatlantic vowels were like those of Katharine Hepburn, "her dearest friend."

After meeting with Kathy and Mary Thom about the plight of the maids, President McBride delivered her formal response to a packed auditorium. She assured her listeners that no racial discrimination was involved. Salaries might be low, but employees received a room and meals in the dorms. The reason for maid service, she explained, was to give students more time to study. Furthermore, she said, "the constant improvement of employee living conditions, especially in view of fire precaution, has been the objective of the administration in providing space for the staff."

President McBride concluded with a declaration: "I want to advise you that working conditions of the maids are of no concern to students." In her view, this was the truth and a warning as well.

But Kathy Boudin immediately jumped up to reply: "Funny that you say that, because I am very concerned about their working conditions." She added, "The maids are grotesquely underpaid and are an extension of the slavery system." No other human being dared to speak to President McBride this way. Kathy's friends smiled with awed disbelief—and pride—at her courage. But Kathy had learned early on from Leonard that the social order was flawed at the top, that no government or president was holy. Rules were invented by people whose motives were all too often neither clear nor unselfish.

In an abrupt turnabout, the Bryn Mawr administration stopped fighting Kathy. Instead the college announced plans to phase out the maid system altogether. It was "economically unfeasible." The administration did concede that maids could, for the first time, entertain friends and family members in their basement bedrooms.

To Kathy's dismay, at Thanksgiving dinner that year, Leonard barely acknowledged her lively account of how she'd championed the maids. What was on his mind was Michael's reaction to whatever was being said, and Leonard frequently asked, "Okay, what does my son the Harvard lawyer think?" He let Michael win an argument about whether or not only harmless religious practices were constitutionally protected. "You can't be wrong," he teased. "You're going to have two degrees from Harvard and if you're wrong the world seems smaller." Kathy denounced Michael's undergraduate honors thesis on the Supreme Court and religious freedom as reactionary. To her horror, Leonard continued to praise Michael's conclusion that "freedom of belief is absolute, freedom to act cannot be."

Father and son sat in a corner that night until 11:30, planning a summer trip to England to observe court proceedings, browse bookstores, and attend Shakespeare productions (the vacation would become an annual tradition).

Kathy's unathletic and withdrawn older brother soon zoomed to the top of his class at Harvard Law School. "He's better than Louis, even," said Leonard, who was beginning to tell people that Michael was going to ensure a Boudin legal dynasty.

At age fifty, Leonard was ready to stretch his beliefs to include Michael's reactionary leanings. He startled people by saying, "I was apolitical all my life."

Edith Tiger sputtered, "But you've defended lefties all your life."

Leonard smiled. "That's only because the right wing has been in power."

Leonard kept on proclaiming Michael's triumphs, and new friends were led to believe that Michael was following in Leonard's footsteps at Harvard Law School. Upset and angry, Kathy continually railed at her father, unwilling to see him abandon the moral certainties of progressive politics, which she had so embraced. From Bryn Mawr, she would scream long arguments at him into the phone, startling passing students.

Mutual friends soon decided that Constancia "Dinky" Romilly would be an ideal mate for Michael, who at this point in his life seemed to have only distant relationships to women. Dinky, the daughter of author and British aristocrat Jessica Mitford, was studying at Sarah Lawrence. Tickets were purchased, and it was arranged for Michael and Dinky to attend a concert together. Hopes ran high.

Afterward, however, Dinky offered her verdict: Michael was dull. And in any case, her interests centered on psychological theories of health with an emphasis on the emotions far from Michael's purview. What few friends knew was that Leonard quickly took action. Including Michael at first, Leonard pursued Dinky for tennis double dates and soon was having a brief affair with her.

Kathy flew to Havana with Leonard on her Christmas break. In the Havana airport, Kathy turned down her father's entreaties that she keep him company at the Habana Libre Hotel. "Too bourgeois," said Kathy, almost bantering. But she was soon shouting at Leonard, causing embarking Cubans to stare. Kathy loudly accused Leonard of playing it safe. He was all talk, a parlor progressive, just one more snobby privileged liberal. And what's more, his legal victories put no food on the table for poor people.

In a household where Leonard's legal stratagems were served up to oppose government authority, it was inevitable that Kathy and her brother, Michael, would take on Leonard himself. In the Havana airport, Kathy angrily accused Leonard of caring only about winning his famous legal cases.

Leonard, who did not raise his voice in public, listed the "revolutionary possibilities" of his litigation for Cuba. His daughter withheld admiration. He then pronounced himself a good—even great—lawyer who stood up for clients' dissenting beliefs, even though he did not necessarily agree with them. Fine, but Kathy then accused her father of not having the guts to do what the clients did. And what about blacks, who were not protected by white men's laws? How much had the Supreme Court ruling—*Brown v. Board of Education*—really accomplished?

Leonard wilted, just as he had years earlier when his father had shouted. The argument ended when Leonard fled to the Habana Libre Hotel. Kathy traveled alone out to the sugarcane fields where she helped to bring in the harvest as a member of the Venceremos Brigade, made up of students from Cuba and the United States with stars in their eyes about Fidel Castro's plans for the future.

On January 2, Kathy was close to hysteria as she stood pressed into a surging crowd of nearly a million cheering Cubans—Criolla, Negra, and mulatta—dancing skin to skin in Havana. They were celebrating the anniversary of the revolution. Her father had already flown home, exhausted from dealing with difficulties Fidel Castro was creating for him and Victor by proclaiming himself a Marxist-Leninist "until the day I die."

That day in Havana, Kathy was holding hands with a Cuban boy with whom she was having a love affair. For seven hours, she drank in the euphoria of the people around her who shouted their high hopes for socialism. She was also exhilarated by the riot of color and pounding conga drums and by mouthwatering smells of roasting garlic, yucca, and pork. Shouts, laughter, drumbeats, and clicking maracas grew louder. The three-day street fair was in full blast. As she had been doing while working in the sugarcane fields, Kathy was trying to act Cuban: cheering, waving a flag, dancing, drinking rum, hugging strangers, eating pork and pepper sandwiches.

Then, finally, hundreds of sweating Cuban boys in battle fatigues marched by carrying big Russian guns, riding in tanks, and proudly displaying rocket launchers. Kathy was shocked into silence. Frightened by the sight of lethal weapons and unhinged by the unbridled emotions of the crowd, Kathy burst into tears.

What Kathy was witnessing was the anniversary tumult of the first mobilization of 1961. Fidel Castro was trying to cheer up his deprived people by showing off armaments supplied by his new Soviet allies.

Kathy attributed her tears to the fact that the guns and armaments on parade went against her belief from childhood that positive social change had to be effected by nonviolent means. Her Cuban boyfriend tried to comfort her, embracing her and shouting over the uproar, "We don't like guns and weapons either, but your country makes us do this."

Fidel Castro himself soon addressed his countrymen from a raised wooden platform. Kathy witnessed what few Americans had seen: the passionate bond between Castro and the Cuban people. His spontaneous speeches were one reason Cubans loved him and, in fact, he liked to make major policy decisions on the spot in response to crowds' reactions.

During the first hour of Castro's speech, the Cuban people packed around Kathy were restless. It was only in the second hour, as Castro attacked *gusanos* (counterrevolutionary Cubans who planted bombs where people shopped for Christmas toys), that Cubans again became impassioned. Castro then denounced CIA agents in Havana who were, he said, pretending to be diplomats but were actually directing terrorist campaigns against Cuba. The crowd roared in Spanish, "Kick them out, kick them out."

Within hours, Castro ordered all U.S. embassy and consular officials to leave Cuba. This made Kathy's own presence in Cuba illegal, and excitingly dangerous.

Kathy was eager to make friends with Karen Burstein, another Bryn Mawr student from Manhattan. The slight, highly charged young woman with cropped curly hair and freckles was a star from the moment she arrived on campus in a large black limousine. She was the oracular member of a round-the-clock bridge game in her dorm, Rhodes Hall, and was famous for her pronouncements on novels, art, politics, and life, interspersing them with pithy jokes offered in a gravelly voice between puffs on a cigarette. One evening, she collected money to send a telegram to Vice President Nixon condemning his belief in military solutions.

Karen's father, Herbert Burstein, had worked in Louis Boudin's office several years earlier than Leonard and had also attended St. John's Law School. He too was an affluent progressive Manhattan lawyer.

Like Kathy, Karen was not crazy about Bryn Mawr. Unlike Kathy, however, Karen read novels, got poor grades, and cut dull classes.

Karen was sorry that Kathy Boudin was depressed at being stuck among young women whom she disliked because they seemed unlikely ever to act or even reflect upon political truths. But the future New York State senator also resented Kathy's holier-than-thou attitude and hated the way Kathy pretended not to get Karen's self-mocking jokes about such problems as the conflict between her left-wing politics and her "arrival in state at Bryn Mawr in a limousine."

Karen was also annoyed by Kathy's habit of waiting in Karen's room late at night, fully dressed and asleep in Karen's bed. "Kathy was not exactly fastidious about cleanliness. She never washed her hair." Karen attributed this to depression. "She struck me as somebody who understood the point of manners, even if she did not always use them."

Karen confronted Kathy in response to one of Kathy's scolding lectures. "I am sick and tired of your sanctimony," Karen told her. "It's impossible to know everything better than everybody—and it's not smart to think you do." She added, "My pleasures in life are reading novels and talking to friends about novels and about our perceptions about the human condition. And—I like to make jokes."

Kathy said, "I don't entirely approve of your great love of novels and jokes. Novels are a luxury and less important than making sure people are not starving."

Karen stood her ground. "You are incredibly rigid. You have no belief in irony or gray areas and, what's more, there's no romance in your soul." She said, "I consider myself pretty left, but individual people are more important to me than abstract ideas."

In the spring of 1962, Kathy strolled hand in hand with a pale young man down the dark first-floor corridor of Rockefeller Hall. Michael Meeropol wore a khaki army jacket and was now a student at Swarthmore College. Kathy curled up on her side on a window seat in Rockefeller Hall and twisted strands of her hair while Michael played on his guitar and sang "This land is your land, this land is my land."

A classmate of Michael's from Swarthmore College waved to him and told me that Michael Meeropol was one of two sons of the late Ethel and Julius Rosenberg, electrocuted eight years earlier at Sing Sing prison by the U.S. government for treason. The crime: stealing secrets about the atom bomb and passing them to the Soviet Union.

That night I relayed the terrible news about Michael's identity to friends in the small smoker at the end of our corridor. We stayed up all night in our bathrobes discussing it. Kathy's friendship with Michael added layers to her mystique. Did Michael Meeropol know how frequently people whispered his real identity? Did he cry a lot? What I did not know until researching this book was that Leonard had turned down Julius Rosenberg as a client. Jean Boudin believed that if Leonard and Victor had taken on the Rosenberg case, the trial would not have resulted in their execution—and she was not the only one.

Kathy frequently accused her father: "You took Judy Coplon instead of the Rosenbergs because she was so pretty and so famous."

Kathy's father was the next fascinating man in her life to appear at Rockefeller Hall. Professor Peter Bachrach invited Leonard to give an afternoon lecture in the spring of 1962, at cavernous Goodhart Hall. The subject was civil liberties. We were dazzled: Kathy had recently escorted the historic Norman Thomas to lunch.

Leonard drew a large crowd of girls and appeared prosperous and handsome with his graying flyaway hair. Despite all the sleepless nights and head colds after flights from Havana, he was in his prime. Fighting for the exhilarating revolution in Cuba on the side of a ragged army that had vanquished a corrupt government imbued Leonard with renewed vitality and a sense of "possibilities in life."

Norman Thomas addressing a group from the Fair Play for Cuba Committee, in Philadelphia, on October 6, 1962. The former Socialist candidate for president had lunch that day with Kathy Boudin at Rockefeller Hall.

He delivered an uplifting, uncondescending lecture, punctuated by references to his passport victory at the Supreme Court. His message was simple: governments are the enemy of individual rights. He warned that individual rights should not be balanced against the government, but against the rights of other individuals. He said that it is in courts that civil liberties were getting due consideration. "The whole thing boils down to," Leonard said, "determining who is the master of this house that is called democracy." We did not know that he was echoing sentiments of Tom Hayden and other friends of Kathy who were taking steps to found a "student movement."

That night after his lecture, Leonard came to Rockefeller Hall. Before dinner, Kathy's father was gesturing wildly and laughing in the center of the circle of girls, including Karen Burstein and Das Oughton.

Leonard was describing exotic weekly flights to Cuba by way of Mexico City, Guadalupe, Bermuda, Madrid, Montreal, or Toronto: travel to Cuba was forbidden by the United States, and the State Department had canceled all flights. Leonard told Kathy's friends that he minded the Bermuda stopover the least, because he and Victor walked on the beaches. Since the government had banned Cuban travel, U.S. dollars could not be spent in Cuba. But Victor and Leonard were "hosted," meaning that all their expenses were paid for by their client, the Castro regime.

Officials in Mexico had been instructed by the FBI to waylay Leonard on his way home by "forgetting" to issue his and Victor's reentry permits. As yet unaware of this ploy, Leonard did know that "embassy attachés" who were working for the CIA trailed him in Mexico, Bermuda, and Spain.

Speaking to the admiring circle of college girls, Leonard skillfully combined braggadocio and self-deprecation. He modestly shrugged off his litigation on behalf of poor people in Cuba, explaining nonetheless that he was litigating for Fidel's right to nationalize sugarcane factories owned by huge U.S. corporations. Leonard said, with an ironic smile, that he was an enemy general in the real war (a pacifist war) with Cuba. Previously such conflicts, he said, had been decided by guns on battlefields. The more powerful country had prevailed.

"But will anything I do matter in a hundred years?" he asked, flashing a self-deprecating smile at each girl. "No, I suspect not. I suspect not." Leonard bowed and then twirled in a self-mocking pirouette. The girls disagreed with his disclaimer in a clamor of applause.

Without prompting, he began to describe how he had challenged Che Guevara to several games of chess in a café in Cuba. Victor Rabinowitz had warned, "He's a client. Let him win." But Leonard had been unable to hold back. "I won all four games despite the fact I do not speak a word of Spanish," he sighed.

I was not the only one who brushed close enough to feel there was much to learn from Leonard. I remember all of Kathy's friends doubling over with laughter. That night several girls asked if they could intern at Leonard's office for a summer. They were inspired by his good works and his contempt for second-rate thinkers. Leonard was thrilled. When one girl began her internship, he seduced her.

Although Kathy was elected school president in spring 1963, defeating a Goldwater Republican, she decided she could not live two more years at Rockefeller Hall.

She arranged a whirlwind week of meetings with deans. She petitioned to set up a new kind of place to live—a "coop dorm" run by students. Triumphant, she seized upon a shabby antique house at the far end of the campus that had been recently vacated by a professor of German. The third floor was structurally unsound, but all the rooms had working fire-places. For Kathy, this "coop house" was a "mini-utopia" away from Rockefeller Hall's phony niceties.

Plans for it were, of course, structured by Kathy. She and her eight recruits negotiated parietal rules with the Bryn Mawr administration. The nine students were obligated only to eat lunch at a bigger dormitory and agreed to share cooking, cleaning, and food shopping. Such rules as dressing for dinner were done away with.

Life at Coop House was largely seen as a series of desirable negatives. It was "unlike a Bryn Mawr dorm," having "no scary authority figures," "no bullshit," and "no maids." It was a retreat. Many of its residents, including Kathy herself, would move farther away at the end of the year by transferring to other colleges.

Despite the absence of adult supervision, students at Coop House pretty much followed the college honor system. (When Kathy's mother's friend, the poet Kenneth Koch, visited, however, his conversation was so exciting that nobody objected when he broke the rules and stayed into the night.)

Kathy's predilections had a way of becoming Coop House rules. An exception was her attitude toward private property. Liz Bogen admitted that she'd loathed Kathy's lack of respect for other people's things. Liz mused that perhaps Kathy's attitude prefigured "the atrocities of which she later became a part. She borrowed all sorts of things without asking and she showed no remorse if people complained." She thought friends were silly for caring. "To be fair, she didn't mind in the least," said Liz, "if you used her stuff as well."

Kathy protested vigorously when the Bryn Mawr College newspaper quoted Coop House residents as saying that the dorm had disadvantages, such as a two-hour wait for meals. A letter signed by all Coop House residents accused the reporter of misrepresenting them and stated that in the future they wanted to preapprove anything written about them.

Kathy's next big project was a conference she named the "Second American Revolution." She invited prominent friends of her parents to give "seminars on current race relations in the United States," including civil rights leaders James Forman, national director of SNCC, and James Farmer, director of CORE (Congress of Racial Equality).* The unprece-

---

*Forman had married Dinky Romilly, the daughter of Jessica Mitford.

dented campus event was scheduled for the first weekend of February 1964.

Two months before "The Second American Revolution" conference was to take place, President John F. Kennedy was assassinated. Leonard canceled his flight to Cuba scheduled for that day. Rumors flew that Cubans might even have been responsible for the assassination. Jean observed that if he had flown to Cuba via Mexico as planned, a newspaper article might have appeared saying, "Cuba's Lawyers Flee to Mexico as Inquiry in Kennedy Assassination Continues."

At Bryn Mawr, after news of the president's death was announced, Kathy wandered the campus lawns. Her classmates sat under trees, stunned or weeping. Kathy soon bumped into Paul Mattick, a tall, thin Haverford College student whose modesty belied his superior intellect. Paul began to help Kathy grapple with her intellectual response to the assassination. Paul had known exactly whose daughter—and whose niece—Kathy was the moment he saw her "apple cheeked" picture in the 1961 Bryn Mawr freshman handbook. He and his father had read her great-uncle's criticisms of Karl Marx. Paul's infatuation with Kathy had grown after her forthright rejection of his attentions.

On the day of President Kennedy's assassination, Kathy's questions to Paul about Kennedy's death were about power politics. She was not grieving. After a while Kathy and Paul walked into the village of Bryn Mawr and impulsively bought tickets to see *The Sound of Music* at the local movie theater.

Kathy's conference, "The Second American Revolution," was held two months later, as scheduled. It was her attempt to force students and professors to face the horrors of being black in the United States. Victor Rabinowitz was among a handful of the financial supporters of the weekend conference; his foundation contributed $100.

Although Malcolm X had agreed to speak and was to be the controversial highlight, he was forced to withdraw at the last minute. His mentor, Elijah Muhammad, forbade Malcolm to appear in public: Malcolm had expressed satisfaction over the assassination of President Kennedy. "The chickens have come home to roost," he said.

James Farmer of CORE opened the conference in a debate with segregationist James J. Kilpatrick, editor of the *Richmond News Leader*. The all-black Freedom Singers sang beautifully, but afterward male members accused Bryn Mawr students of rejecting their blunt sexual invitations because of racism.

The next week, Kathy accosted a popular political science professor who had not attended "The Second American Revolution." "How dare you teach that stuff in class and, when it comes to doing something, go out partying in New York."

On several mornings in autumn 1963, Kathy picketed the entrance of an elementary school in Chester, Pennsylvania, some twenty miles from Bryn Mawr. She joined hundreds of Swarthmore students and black members of the Chester branch of the NAACP. The goal was to improve the wretched conditions in Franklin Elementary School. One of the poorest cities, Chester had a Republican boss who was seen by Swarthmore students as the embodiment of bigotry. Franklin School had been built in 1912, to house five hundred students. Kathy wrote in the Bryn Mawr College newspaper: "Twelve hundred Negro children crowd through [Franklin's] entrance doors every morning. There are no fire escapes, two toilets, and a basement coal bin is the gymnasium. Three classes are held in the boiler room of a housing project."

Kathy, Cathlyn Wilkerson, Connie Brown, and local blacks picketed and urged youngsters to attend a temporary "freedom school" on Swarthmore's campus. On Tuesday morning, November 12, Kathy was arrested with a score of other protesters. Fifty more shouting protesters trailed police and prisoners to the front door of the police station. Kathy and her fellow activists were charged with "unlawful assembly and affray" for blocking the entrance to a public school.

Kathy led the cheers and whistles as each new woman was ushered into the cell block at Broadmeadows jail. The prisoners eagerly watched TV news broadcasts of their arrests. When she called collect to St. Luke's Place, Kathy was stunned and hurt. Her mother angrily told Kathy she should be studying, not endangering her life. "You'll never get into law school if you're convicted." Unlike Victor who, however self-consciously, worked at being supportive of his daughter Joni in similar circumstances, Jean and Leonard were wildly unpredictable. Jean also scolded her daughter for distracting Leonard from more important legal matters in order to post Kathy's bail.

That night Kathy and others insisted on sleeping on the jail's dining-room floor, refusing to go back into their cells. Kathy exhorted her coprisoners to "keep the spirit," while prison officials ordered them to behave or else. The officials called it "a near riot."

During dinner a few days later at Rockefeller Hall, Kathy suddenly became hysterical. She was exhausted after attending a late-night meeting with Swarthmore students about Governor Scranton's refusal to meet with them. Kathy wanted to tell Bryn Mawr classmates the unhappy news of a second mass arrest in Chester. One hundred blacks with no money for bail had been badly beaten. They were eating and sleeping on the floor of a Chester County garage. After shouting above the dinner chatter, Kathy suddenly found herself sobbing. She sagged to the floor, cursing the "self-indulgent rich-bitch" girls who were ignoring her. Although she blamed her outburst on the indifference of other students, Kathy was no doubt still reacting to Jean and Leonard's lack of support. Her father, frightened by a newspaper account of bloodied protesters, was pressuring her to abandon the whole enterprise.

After finishing her junior year at Bryn Mawr, Kathy told Leonard she was quitting school and he could not stop her. She had not swerved in her desire to work on Izzy's newsletter, which was gaining circulation and influence. He was making his mark by exposing government lies about scores of projects he considered immoral or reactionary.

But her father regarded Kathy's decision to quit college as an act of "disloyalty" against him. What about law school? "Izzy is utterly independent of 'the system,' " Kathy said. She knew her unblinking respect for Izzy galled Leonard.

Leonard fought back with a tantalizing offer: the chance of a senior year of study at the University of Leningrad—a first for an American undergraduate. His friend Rockwell Kent, with ties to the Soviet Union, could arrange it.

Leonard had ulterior motives. He was sick of Kathy's increasingly harsh attacks on his "upper-class privilege" and civil liberties work that did not put food in poor people's mouths. He wanted Kathy to see for herself the wretched conditions of life under Soviet communism. Leonard placed a call to President McBride to make sure that Kathy would nonetheless receive a Bryn Mawr degree. As expected, President McBride welcomed the early departure of her severest student critic. Kathy agreed to go to the Soviet Union but refused to commit to law school. She was, she wrote to Rockwell Kent, taking science courses to prepare for medical school.

During the fifteen months she spent in the Soviet Union, Kathy was not obliged to attend classes, although she was as always a good student. She also filled spiral notebooks with statistics about crops and rainfall. Leonard read her letters aloud at brunches with unabashed pride. Several guests found his attitude unsettling. Recalled Michael Standard, "Leonard would declaim from them with a kind of pleasure which bespoke 'that's my girl.' He acted as if they were terribly clever. But they were terribly unclever, if well organized. There was always paragraph one, sub A, sub B; of dull production statistics. It was as if she was shaping everything to be who Leonard expected her to be."

Kathy did indeed find herself shaken by the poverty and apathy of her own generation of Russians. Born twenty years after the revolution, the young people were utterly disillusioned about socialism.

No matter whom she met—teachers, painters, scientists, filmmakers, and students—all envied the U.S. government commitment to civil liberties. Kathy argued with Russian students who were nonetheless totally impressed when she said that protesters in the United States decided whether or not they wanted to ignore police barricades and get arrested. In Russia, demonstrators were automatically arrested, and often expelled to Siberia.

Her acquaintances asked, "How many of your friends, for all their protests, are in jail now?" And her answer had to be—none.

On winter break, Kathy sampled harsh peasant life on a collective farm at Knyazheve, not far from the birthplace of Joe Boudin and "the great Louis." The family she lived with ate mostly potatoes and drank tea and had no indoor toilets or refrigeration. Like them, Kathy spent a lot of time chewing sunflower seeds and spitting them on the floor. Rockwell Kent had written to Kathy that Russian peasants sang in the fields and he wished American farmers did the same. She slept with the family wrapped in sheepskins on different floors around a tall wide stove (a *pech*) that threw off incredible heat. The family also cooked on it and heated the house with it; it was the center of their lives. No one seemed to be singing; it was too cold.

While in Leningrad, Kathy received a letter from her father pleading with her to apply to Yale Law School and "to join Michael in the family tradition." Since the prospect of medical school had begun to seem less and less appealing, Kathy took the road of least resistance and applied to Yale Law School.

Although the correspondence between Leonard and Kathy was clumsily opened and resealed by the CIA, Leonard, surprisingly, lodged no legal protest. He told acquaintances somewhat disingenuously, "I'm a litigator, but I'm not litigious."

Esther Roisman Stone, Jean's sister, hides behind her husband, Izzy, and Joanne Grant Rabinowitz, at a party given by The Nation *magazine, circa 1964. Izzy was by now a venerated, highly visible government critic and the leader of the Boudin family circle. His newsletter,* I. F. Stone's Weekly, *had eloquently criticized tactics of Senator McCarthy as well the war in Vietnam. His wife, Esther, wrote unsigned editorials.*

· · ·

Leonard underwent a cataract operation just before Christmas. Bad eyesight had plagued his father and his uncle Louis. Meanwhile, Victor had divorced and was planning to marry a second time, to Joanne Grant, a civil rights activist and reporter for the *National Guardian*.

The new Mrs. Rabinowitz was a sharp-tongued woman with radical opinions and considerable charm. She had been a secretary to W. E. B. Du Bois, and, like Kathy, had almost gone to work at the I. F. Stone newsletter. The fact that her ancestry was partly black was undoubtedly a plus in Victor's eyes.

Because Leonard pleaded poor health, Victor volunteered to bring the wedding ceremony to St. Luke's Place. Leonard murmured apologies for Jean, saying she would not be up to handling the details of such an event. Victor's sister, Lucille Perlman, took charge, ordering champagne and glasses. Lucille and Victor assumed erroneously that Jean had attempted to kill herself again.

The bride, despite her unequivocal charm and place in the spotlight, didn't stand a chance. It was Leonard who commanded everyone's attention. He sat in the middle of the living room wearing a black eyepatch and a double-breasted suit. He stole the show, looking for all the world like a prosperous pirate. (He would have been best man if, as Victor put it, "more attention had been paid to such details.")

The ceremony was quick, but not quick enough for the putative host, who unbuttoned the top button of his dress shirt, shed his jacket, and unbuttoned his shirt cuffs. Despite the offbeat social dynamic, the event was considered a success.

Three months later, Leonard flew to the Soviet Union as the bearer of unhappy news: Yale Law School had rejected Kathy's application. Kathy was devastated: this had the effect of proclaiming to the world, yet again, that she was not as bright or worthy as Michael. She blamed her law aptitude test scores, which were damagingly average. At a rural train station, Kathy found herself shouting at her father, who had purchased first-class tickets for the trip back to Leningrad. Kathy wanted to ride with ordinary people. Neither would give in, and so they traveled in separate cars.

Back home again, Kathy was faced with the issue of whether to attend her Bryn Mawr graduation. Her decision to boycott followed the example of her father, who had not taken part in his City College graduation. Unlike Leonard, however, Kathy was one of the top five students in her class.

A long interview with Kathy describing her unusual year in Russia appeared in the *New York Times*. Her friends and acquaintances took her celebrity in stride. "She's a girl who makes headlines," they all agreed.

10

A REPUBLICAN JUST WANTS
TO GET RICH

The thing I like about Republicans is that they're no damn good at all. I know, I'm one of them. A Republican just wants to get rich, buy oceanfront property, dump the old wife and get a new blond one who'll listen attentively while the Republican talks about unfunded mandates over the arugula salad.

—P. J. O'Rourke, *Age and Guile Beat Youth, Innocence, and a Bad Haircut*

. . . our treasonable, reasonable taunts to save the country . . .
—Robert Lowell, "The Spock etc, Sentences," *Notebook 1967–68*

The 1970's promises to become the decade when youth becomes a state of mind and overflows all traditional age boundaries. . . . Businessmen find the prospects exhilarating.
—*Business Week* magazine, 1970

The spring of 1965 found Kathy living on St. Luke's Place and facing purposeless months. Despite her fluency in Russian, Leonard and she disdained translating jobs; who wanted to be a "passive technician"?

Kathy decided to write a book about her trip to the Soviet Union. She wrote to Rockwell Kent that it was going to be as serious as Oscar Lewis's prizewinning *La Vida*. One morning in May, Kathy escaped her silent electric typewriter and Jean's worried countenance to take a subway to an impoverished black neighborhood in Newark. There Connie Brown, a soothing and perceptive friend from Swarthmore who'd picketed Franklin Elementary School with Kathy in Chester, was living "purely" in a communal house furnished with torn mattresses purchased from the Salvation Army. More impressive, perhaps, Connie was romantically involved with Tom Hayden, the rising star of the student movement. Hayden had an immodest aura. He wore unbuttoned shirts exposing his hairless chest. Despite his unconvincing avowals against "bullshit celebrity trips," Tom Hayden and his fellow movement leaders (an exclusive and all-male group) were also superconscious of their growing fame and superior status.

Tom was making headlines with the Newark SDS neighborhood project (called ERAP, the Economic Research and Action Project) whose ambitious goal was to forge an interracial movement of poor people and students in northern cities.

Kathy scoffed at Connie's hope that she could improve lives of poor blacks in Newark. Connie did admit that nothing had changed in Chester; once out of the glare of national publicity the town's Republican boss had reneged on all his promises to improve Franklin School.

Nonetheless it was not difficult for Connie and Tom and thousands of other "movement people" to get the feeling that wherever they led, "sparks from their fiery swords would fly throughout the world." It seemed as if the entire country was poised to follow their hypnotic and righteous example.

Tom Hayden spoke contemptuously of President Lyndon Johnson and his domestic War on Poverty. That night in Newark in the bleak movement house Connie called home, Kathy hugged old friends and people who had only heard about her. The young movement people considered her a figure to reckon with because she was related to two important adults on the left. Leonard Boudin was respected and the I. F. Stone newsletter was "the Bible."

Kathy and Connie Brown whispered far into the night. Kathy was still reeling over rejection by Yale Law School. Could it really be that she wasn't "good enough" to do legal work like Leonard and her brother? By now, Kathy had given in to the family speak and was referring to her brother Michael as "the bright one." The conversation kept returning to Leonard so frequently that Connie put her troubled friend on notice: Leonard's presence in her life was overwhelming.

On her second day in Newark, Kathy accompanied Connie to knock on doors. Connie invited her black neighbors to a night meeting with a city councilman about getting CHILDREN PLAYING signs put up around a playground where a car had recently hit a child.

Connie noted Kathy's warm and reasonable way of talking to local blacks and gaining their trust. She was skilled at drawing people out to discuss their problems, and also at convincing them to join together in order to get things done.

When Kathy told her father about Connie and Tom and their organizing efforts in Newark, Leonard's response was to warn her about "frittering away her life by holding other people's hands."

Meanwhile Leonard kept Kathy posted on Michael's triumphs, ignoring the fact that Michael rarely returned Leonard's phone calls. Leonard was elated when Michael was elected president of the Harvard law journal. Leonard was soon pleased to hear that his brilliant offspring was "a very formal and disciplined" president who "did not chitchat." Leonard grinned and grinned when, during lunch with his elusive son at the Harvard Club in Manhattan, a law student timidly approached and addressed Michael as "Mr. Boudin." The editors working under Michael were awed by the meticulous way he turned out each volume at precisely the same length.

In Jean's words, Leonard was "mentally clicking his heels" all during Michael's graduation ceremony from Harvard Law School. First in his class, Michael won a coveted clerkship with the well-regarded and very intellectual Henry J. Friendly of the Court of Appeals in New York. Leonard did not mind in the least that Henry Friendly was a right-leaning centrist—a term of approbation in judicial circles that meant Judge Friendly had declared himself "above politics." His conservatism, in fact, ran deep.

Leonard was still refining his self-definition to include his son's successes. "I believe only in the law," he told Michael's startled friends.

For his part, Michael found life very satisfying indeed in Judge Friendly's mostly silent chambers. The only disruption was the arrival of a fake copy of the Harvard law journal. To shock Michael's conservative beliefs, it was bound in outrageous pink.

The job was the young law clerk's life. Michael loved chasing legal doctrine through history, trying not to take sides until he found precedents or common law or constitutional guideposts. Week after week of research fed his passion. As Friendly's clerk, Michael was an apprentice in a line of judges that went back to Supreme Court Justice Louis Brandeis himself, for whom Henry Friendly had clerked.

Judge Friendly's plain, sober face lifted with happiness, his hand reaching to the shelf each time his clerk cited a conflicting precedent. Empathizing, Michael wrote, "It was, I think, the happiness of a man who has found his perfect calling."

Kathy, still at home, had—in sharp contrast to her brother—no career path. Angus Cameron, an influential editor at Alfred A. Knopf, politely rejected her proposal to write a biography of Dostoyevsky. He urged her to develop better understanding of human nature. "Start by trying to understand your own motives," he advised.

Her family connections worked against her when she applied for a job as a junior editor at Random House. The editor to whom she was applying found himself resenting Kathy's "red diaper" heritage. John Simon thought to himself, "She never had to struggle to get her views; she just took received information."

Watching her sit dejectedly at home, Leonard pressed Kathy to apply to law schools less prestigious than Yale. Kathy said no. She told Leonard he was obviously ashamed of his own alma mater; he never mentioned St. John's.

Finally Kathy did apply to join an SDS neighborhood project similar to the one she'd visited in Newark. The Cleveland Project was devoted to helping unemployed white teenagers. It was led by Charlotte and Ollie Fein, two married Swarthmore graduates. The Feins were trying to figure out a way to unite outspokenly racist white people with blacks in similar economic straits. The goal was familiar to Kathy: her parents and indeed her uncle Louis had chewed over the difficulties of making alliances between intellectuals and members—both black and white—of the working classes.

On her application to the Cleveland Project, Kathy debated a problem she somewhat pretentiously dubbed "flammability": she wondered if the whole process of organizing young white men without jobs might be about to go down in flames. Her essay was mimeographed and mailed to young people throughout the country.

"A few questions," she wrote, "if we will be organizing unemployed youth, what is the purpose? Is it to get them to discuss the problems of unemployment? Is it to help them to find jobs? Is it to give them something to do and thus prevent formulation of gangs? I imagine that some goals would have to be formulated so as to give some direction to the process of organizing."

Kathy arrived in Cleveland on a Saturday morning in June 1965. She greeted nine other breathless young activists. Kathy eagerly settled into the women's communal living space, an old run-down house on 3128 Woodbine Avenue. Kathy helped Ollie Fein paint three of the women's rooms Saturday night and all day Sunday. The rent was only $100 a month, because the house needed so much work and because it was located on the near North Side, a neighborhood of impoverished white people from Appalachia, many of whom were unemployed.

Charlotte and Ollie Fein were modest, "earnest"—even dour. They were also full-time medical students at Case Western Reserve. To make friends with unemployed neighbors, Ollie helped them to avoid paying rent. He dragged their cardboard boxes into his station wagon to move them out of their houses in the middle of the night. He also jumped out of bed to drive small children to the emergency room.

Three young women, including Kathy and Charlotte, were "potato keepers," which meant they planned menus and bought food. Ollie was the "broom keeper": he did repairs and painting in both houses. (Daily records of goals and achievements were kept; the young people were confident that they were making history.) The Feins were usually exhausted from their double obligations of medical studies and neighborhood services, but their presence lent an air of earnest goodwill. The atmosphere was not as competitive as it was in Newark where pulses raced in the presence of the famed Tom Hayden.

As they grew more familiar with one another and their tasks, and as the group dynamic became clear, Kathy and the other women began to sow seeds of the second wave of feminism by trying to define themselves as separate from and in opposition to their domineering, superintellectual male counterparts.

Among the young men in Cleveland was a lanky, self-searching, and almost monklike graduate of Oberlin College, Paul Potter. Like her father, Kathy reeled in admirers—both male and female—and kept them in her orbit. Paul Potter would write in his memoir, *A Name for Ourselves*, about his dreams of Kathy, in which she'd brush him with her long, tangled hair as she hovered tantalizingly over him.

Months passed, and as the snow became slushy and gray, Kathy's initial euphoria vanished. The drafty houses on treeless streets continued to be filled with bitter, suffering human beings with no job prospects.

Kathy knocked on door after door, confronting suspicious men and women who had little food or furniture. After convincing a frightened householder to let her in, Kathy tried to draw the woman out about her worst practical problems. Kathy then attempted to convince the woman that her toothache, her hungry children, and her unheated rooms could be ameliorated if she came to a neighborhood meeting. But people rejected Kathy's entreaties, insisting that their main "issue" was their desire to "get the hell out of the near North Side."

Jean visited Kathy in Cleveland and screamed at the sight of a rat in the bathroom. The fact that the humble standard of living was being maintained in order to show solidarity with neighbors did not impress Jean. Kathy countered, "Roaches and rats are easy. The hard thing is knocking on doors and having people slam them in your face."

Jean demanded, "Why not go to medical school and raise standards of health for everyone, instead of just lowering your own?" Kathy airily assured Jean she was still corresponding with Rockwell Kent about writing a book about her experiences in Russia.

In long telephone conversations, Leonard brought his authority to bear by convincing Kathy to apply to Case Western Reserve Law School, also located in Cleveland. That way, he argued, she could combine law classes and her neighborhood work.

Unable to start writing the book, Kathy turned her attentions to reviving an organization of black mothers on welfare. She wrote defensively to Rockwell Kent that she was very fulfilled indeed, trying to get Ohio laws changed on behalf of women receiving welfare. Kathy was good at approaching women on welfare lines. She asked questions from one time to the next showing that she remembered details about their lives.

Many welfare employees resented dispensing money to women on relief. Kathy cited their own rules back at them. She painstakingly framed legal questions to officials who claimed that appeal procedures did not exist. One woman at age fifty-two was earning $20 a week as a baby-sitter because she was too old to be hired for factory work. Nonetheless welfare officials claimed that she must wait until age fifty-five for financial help. They never told her they were obligated to line up job interviews for her in the meantime.

To help the women, Kathy discovered a rule guaranteeing the right to appeal in the huge manual of Ohio Public Assistance of February 1, 1964, sections 170–177. Kathy was proud. The word *appeal* had magic resonance at the Boudin dinner table, where Leonard described victory after victory at courts of appeals.

Early on the morning of March 2, 1966, in a basement waiting room, an older official named Blanche admitted to Kathy that she could contact a public relations official. But the PR official was out. After days of persistent questions, Kathy was told by the PR official that the appeal process did exist, but that Kathy would have to fill out forms.

"Where can we get the forms?" asked Kathy.

"Unavailable," he said.

Kathy finally elicited six forms. The PR official refused to surrender more despite the fact that he had a huge stack on a shelf.

Kathy was soon helping women mimeograph forms, then write, file, and refile appeals to the State Welfare Commission. Using legal terms to show that local laws contradicted national rules for welfare, Kathy kept trying to force bureaucrats to work the system in favor of the women it was supposed to benefit.

Obstacles kept cropping up. Many young women activists, like Connie Brown and Leni Wildflower, quit the neighborhood projects, heartbroken. Connie picked up her life to become a psychologist. Others attended social work school.

But Kathy's ambitions were bigger. She wrote Rockwell Kent that she was taking notes for a major book on the struggles of welfare women. And yet Kathy was flagging. For every small measure of progress there were big setbacks. In one instance, after Kathy gained a woman's trust, she kicked Kathy out of her house. The woman's husband, an unemployed father of two, accused Kathy of being a communist. He told her he would come to a meeting only if she bought him a working toilet. A discouraged Kathy told a friend, "Getting out of bed every morning to organize is like making yourself jump into a pool of freezing water."

Suddenly, in Cleveland and other cities across the country, angry young black men wearing black leather jackets and berets were proselytizing on street corners, their rhetoric fiery and militant. The Black Panthers were taking up Malcolm X's cry for armed self-defense, if necessary.

Could the Panthers be the true voice of black oppression? Kathy and her friends wondered.

In August 1966, after fourteen uninspiring months in Cleveland, Kathy and the other women of the Welfare Grievance Committee helped fifty black women stage a "buy-in" at May's, the local department store. They announced in advance that each woman was going to "take" children's clothes from racks at the May Company, charge the clothes to the Welfare Department, and then leave the piles of small shirts and dungarees by the cash register.

The protest was legal and only hinted at lawbreaking. It was a bid for publicity—to back up their request to raise the clothing allowances for children of welfare mothers from $5 per child.

Kathy was terrified as they walked into May's. But there were no policemen or angry salesclerks. "As long as there is no disturbance," said a spokesman for May's, "it's all right with us."

"My teenagers have only one pair of pants each without a hole in them," said Mrs. Bertha Rice to a newspaper reporter. "There's plenty of money in this land. People shouldn't live like this."

By autumn 1966, Kathy knew better than to turn to her mother for praise or guidance. A distraught Jean was making frequent visits to her brother, Charlie Roisman, who was drinking himself to death in Philadelphia. As if alcoholism wasn't enough, he had a heart condition. Charlie no longer played drums with jazz greats, and friends made sure his two showy white Afghan hounds were walked.

Jean was drawing closer to her niece Celia Stone Gilbert, who was writing good poems and was poetry editor of the *Boston Phoenix*. Jean was still vowing that it was just a matter of time until Celia's husband, Wally Gilbert, won the Nobel Prize for defining genes, whose structure might reveal mysteries about the origins of life.

Leonard was excited to hear that the world-famous author and pediatrician, Dr. Benjamin Spock, a good friend of Jean's friend Roz Baxandall, was going to be teaching in Cleveland. Leonard decided that Dr. Spock was the perfect person to talk sense into Kathy. He told Jean to invite Spock to dinner.

Jean ordered couscous and vegetables from a nearby Middle Eastern restaurant for Spock and his wife, Jane. Though his specialty was pediatrics, Spock was a good choice to counsel a rebellious and idealistic daughter. His manual for parents, *The Commonsense Book of Baby and Childcare,* with its reassuring tone and emphasis on permissiveness, was selling a million copies a year, second only to the Bible.

In the course of dinner, Spock, a tall patrician New Englander, revealed he had been psychoanalyzed. Jean teased him for encouraging parents to trust their instincts, while dispensing hundreds of pages of specific advice on topics ranging from colic to idealism.

At the end of the congenial evening, Leonard asked Ben Spock to look up Kathy in Cleveland. Putting his arm around his wife, Leonard said, "I am absolutely sure you will be a great and good influence on our daughter."

But before Dr. Spock had the opportunity to telephone Kathy, he

Diane Schulder, a colleague of
Leonard Boudin.

bumped into her. She was on her knees, washing the front steps of the Cleveland opera house in exchange for a concert ticket. Her hair was cropped, her nose running in the cold, her gloves and sweater torn, and yet she enchanted her new acquaintance.

Here, Ben Spock felt, was "no parlor liberal." Leonard and Jean's daughter was a saint or a madwoman. Jane Spock invited Kathy to dinner, and the three became friends.

Ben Spock was stirred by Kathy's wholehearted commitment to improve the lives of the struggling black women in Cleveland. When he later protested against the Vietnam War and the draft, he cited the arguments of "my friend Kathy Boudin."

Meanwhile Leonard liked to hang out at Jimmy's, a dim, all-night Greenwich Village bar two blocks from his home. There, in a red leather booth in the back, he ate scrambled eggs and drank wine into the small hours of morning, accompanied by one of several young pretty women.

However, it was at the more formal setting of a dinner party in the spring of 1967 that Leonard, with Jean stoically looking on, was whispering into the ear of Diane Blossom Schulder, a young legal associate at his firm. Pulling Diane to her feet, he announced gaily, "We're going back to work." Someone giggled. John Simon, the Random House editor, avoided looking at Jean's sweetly composed face.

Friends mused endlessly about Leonard's sex life. They repeated Kathy's statements about how cool it was that her father was still attractive to women. Kathy said, "My mother's just too neurotic." They wondered why Kathy wasn't more angry.

In any case, Leonard showed off his young lovers even to Jean and Kathy. The Boudin circle never seemed to tire of trying to get a fix on Jean's reality quotient. Did she actually admit to herself that Leonard was cheating and couldn't stop? But the truth was emotional, not epistemological. Jean loved Leonard, a habit of heart she had no intention of abandoning. "So he has a sweet tooth for women," she once said in her droll tone.

An intelligent and strong-minded young woman, twenty-seven-year-old Diane Schulder became another in the succession of girls who fell in love with Leonard. She and Leonard counseled young men who wanted to avoid being sent off to fight what they considered to be the illegal war in Vietnam. And later the two worked on the conspiracy trial of antiwar radical priest Father Philip Berrigan. To serve Leonard and his causes was a kind of mission for his associates. Thus it is not surprising that Diane Schulder's mother said to her daughter, "If only you'd use some of the energy you put into your idealistic projects to find a husband, I'm sure you'd do very well."

In the summer of 1967, Victor Rabinowitz and his second wife, Joanne Grant, rented a large and sunny cedar-shingled house near the white sand beach in Amagansett, Long Island. They shared it with Diane Schulder.

On a gray Thursday, Leonard and Jean took a train to Long Island to spend the July Fourth weekend with Victor. Leonard believed that he and Jean were going to Amagansett for an early celebration of Leonard's birthday, which fell two and a half weeks later, on July 20. However, Victor, Joanne, and John and Janet Simon were under the impression that they were gathering to celebrate Victor's birthday, which fell on July 2.

As the train sped through suburban Long Island hamlets, Leonard was feeling pleased: he had come up with a stratagem to extricate Kathy from the slums of Cleveland. Rockwell Kent had again pulled strings, and

Kathy possessed a six-month visa that would allow her to go back to the Soviet Union to do further research on her memoir. Her plan was to leave on September 15.

Jean and Leonard discussed the fact that Kathy's book about her work in Cleveland had never jelled. Jean said that whatever Kathy might say, the work had been "too depressing" to turn into a book.

In Amagansett, rain beat down on the beach house. Diane Schulder and Jean sat in the kitchen, watching Joanne Grant cook a large blanquette de veau. Being in such close quarters with her lover's wife was difficult for Diane. Jean seemed unruffled. Leonard, playing chess with Victor, was in his own world.

The next day it poured again. For Victor's birthday dinner, the group drove in blinding rain to Harbor Cove, a candlelit seafood restaurant with a view of the bay in Sag Harbor.

Leonard drank several glasses of wine and danced with each of the women in the party except Jean: Janet Simon, Joanne Grant, and Diane Schulder. He circled the dance floor like a spinning top, kicking out his legs in big improvised gestures. He seemed to be working too hard at having fun.

Suddenly Leonard sank to his knees and fell over on his right side. The orchestra stopped. The room was silent. A doctor put his head to Leonard's chest and pronounced him dead. But Janet Simon grabbed Leonard's wrist and detected a pulse. She put a spoon in his mouth to stop him from biting his tongue.

An ambulance quickly arrived from Southampton Hospital. John Simon recalled, "I remember how frightened we were because Leonard was still unconscious." Diane Schulder fell apart weeping. But when she started to follow firemen carrying Leonard on a stretcher into the ambulance, she found her way blocked by a formidable obstacle. Jean elbowed Diane aside, climbed into the ambulance, and pulled the doors closed. Victor Rabinowitz was amazed at Jean's forthrightness.

The frightened group waited for an hour in the Southampton Hospital emergency room until Leonard was admitted. Victor was hoping his partner had not suffered a stroke that would affect Leonard's brain. There were conflicting reports from physicians. A neurologist said that Leonard had suffered a heart attack, while the staff cardiologist diagnosed a stroke.

Victor drove Joanne and Jean to the nearby Southampton home of his sister, Lucille Perlman. Diane kept vigil at the hospital. Sitting on a deck facing the dark ocean, Victor tried to divert Jean. They were tense; the longer Leonard remained unconscious, the more likely there was to be brain damage.

The next day, still unconscious, and now accompanied only by his wife, Leonard was driven in an ambulance to Beth Israel Hospital in Manhattan. He stayed there for eleven days. When he came out of his coma on the second day, his first words were passed around as proof he was still his charming self. (There is, of course, the possibility that Jean spruced up the story.) A pretty young nurse apparently watched Leonard open his eyes and asked him, "What is your name?"

"Leonard B. Boudin," he answered.

"What do you do?"

"I am a lawyer."

"What kind of lawyer?"

"A lawyer who does his best to help good working people like you, my dear," said Leonard, eliciting a broad smile from his nurse. He explained that he represented the United Hospital Workers Union.

During his recovery, Leonard began to rely on Jean—as he'd relied upon his mother. She confounded their friends by competently assuming responsibility for him.

Madi Leof visited Leonard in the hospital and told Jean that Leonard was obnoxious and preening. Madi said that when he called himself "a man of the world," he was referring to his mistresses. Jean shouted at Madi to hold her tongue. The two old friends stopped speaking to each other.

A pacemaker—the first of three—was installed in Leonard's chest, and Jean teased her husband. "You are now technologically immortal." Leonard appropriated the joke. He also spoke frequently and dispassionately of his own impending death and of his heart attack, which had happened—in his version—simply because he had eaten too much that night at his birthday dinner in Amagansett.

11

REPENTING GOOD
BEHAVIOR

If I repent anything, it's good behavior.
> —Henry David Thoreau

S oon after a hospital stay in which he received another pacemaker, Leonard made a serious error. He seduced Jennie Simon, Kathy's old friend, who was pregnant and staying, without her husband, Fred Gardner, in Kathy's bedroom on St. Luke's Place. When Fred learned about the incident, he railed to friends and acquaintances that Jean was "a pimp for Leonard." After all, hadn't she continued to welcome Jennie as a house guest?

Leonard piled mistake upon mistake by insisting that Jennie, a kindhearted and passive young woman, accept a gift of clothing along with a ring belonging to Kathy. He confided to Jennie that famous spy Judith Coplon had been the great love of his life and, referring to the jagged scar on his chest where the pacemaker had been inserted, he said almost jocularly that he did not expect to live much longer.

Leonard loved to compete against friends and family members for first place in a pretty woman's heart. And the competitions, which did not necessarily include sex, might last several seconds—or a lifetime.

Kathy, informed of her father's behavior by Gardner, sought revenge by commencing a love affair with Leonard's favorite junior partner, Michael Standard. ("There is no word in English for my place in Leonard's life," said Standard. "I was more than a protégé and only slightly less than a son.") Extremely handsome, darkly smoldering, with a self-torturing macho streak, Michael had stood in the shadow of his father, William Standard, a distinguished Maritime Union lawyer and friend of Louis Boudin.

Kathy soon attended a convention of the National Lawyers Guild in Detroit, Michigan. She, Leonard, and Michael Standard were assigned rooms on the second floor of the Cadillac Hotel located in the city's black ghetto. At some point late that night, Sanford Katz, another lawyer, left his hotel room. He heard noises ahead. What he soon realized was that the sounds he heard were being made by Michael Standard and Kathy, who were making love in the dark hallway next to the closed door of Leonard's room.

Leonard was disturbed by news of the sexual relationship between his protégé and Kathy. Back in New York, he invited Michael to go swimming in the city pool across St. Luke's Place. Leonard stared fixedly at Michael's genitals as they donned their swimming trunks. To Michael, it seemed as if Leonard were checking him out. Worse, Leonard began to reject all of Michael's contributions in Wednesday lunch meetings at the firm.

During this period, the poet and Village figure Frances Waldman was thrilled to be invited to dinner at St. Luke's Place. She and Jean had chatted at poetry readings, but the evening was the start of an important friendship. Leonard dominated. Frances was impressed to hear Leonard speak with great compassion about Julian Bond, a prospective client. The young man had made headlines as the first black person elected to the Georgia State Legislature. Yet Bond had been denied entrance to the State Building by his white peers. The stated reason: a strong antiwar statement he had signed.

At dinner that night, Jean remarked to her husband that Frances's daughter, Ann, who was Kathy's age, was gorgeous. "She has the hair of a Christmas tree angel," Jean told him, causing Leonard to ask excitedly, "Where does one find your angel?"

"Leonard and I are trying to find our son, Michael, a bride," said Jean, smiling at her guests.

Frances wrote to her daughter:

> *Sunday evening, Leonard Boudin [did not go on to the theater with us after dinner but] stayed at home to work on the Julian Bond case—he has some 25 books of background reading, legal and historical to get through fairly soon. Naturally he was interested in talking to Daddy about speed reading and what it can do.*
>
> *He's an interesting man, obviously brilliant. He was intrigued by hearing from Jean that we have such a beautiful daughter. Jean said he immediately thinks of any beautiful girl he hears about as a possible bride for their son Michael.*

Frances also described Jean.

> *Jean's very interesting herself—seems like a lost child with those big eyes and apparent confusion, yet she's terribly sharp and perceptive with an amazing memory—amazing because she doesn't remember things on the surface too well. She seems to operate on [emotional] intuition rather than rational thought.*

Although Leonard had not met Julian Bond, he put long hours of research into the suit Bond was bringing against the Georgia State Legislature. This was despite the fact that Bond was already being represented in his quest for justice by a capable team of ACLU lawyers.

At the point at which the case made its way to the Supreme Court, Leonard jumped into action. He asked Victor Rabinowitz and his wife, Joanne Grant, who was a good friend of Bond's from her days in the civil rights movement, to arrange a dinner party so that he could get to know Bond. It was highly improper for Julian Bond even to consider dismissing his distinguished lawyers just before the case was to be appealed at the Supreme Court. But even more wrong perhaps was Leonard's pursuit. Leonard wanted the case badly; it would be the first Supreme Court case to challenge the right to criticize the war in Vietnam. It also reeked of racism.

The dinner with Julian Bond took place in Greenwich Village in the Rabinowitz living room, whose walls were insulated by a thousand hardbound books on politics, history, and law. (Fiction was admitted only if its reputation had lasted at least fifty years.) Two photographs sat on the breakfront—each of Joanne Grant with a hero of the left. One was a beaming bespectacled Izzy Stone, his wife, Esther, in the background; the other was of Joanne and W. E. B. Du Bois.

Leonard Boudin sat close to Julian Bond, who with his high forehead and wide sensitive eyes looked the part of a young hero. His flesh tones glinted gold. He was soft-voiced, with manners so good they seemed a reproach. At one point, in the midst of thought, Leonard grabbed a left-over piece of flourless cake and ate it, licking crumbs off his fingers. He then inserted his hand into the back pocket of his trousers, using his pocket lining as a napkin. Nonetheless Bond was not put off by Leonard's eccentricities.

Weeks later, Leonard was triumphant. He telephoned Kathy, his words tumbling out. Julian Bond had fired his ACLU lawyers and hired Leonard. Leonard planned to cite James Madison, who'd declared it dangerous to allow congressmen to bar a new member whose views they disliked.

"Big deal," scoffed Kathy. "Even if you win, those racist jerks in Georgia won't see the light. It takes rougher stuff than that."

Jean, however, was bursting with pride, even though Leonard had suddenly moved his eye patch, reading glasses, sleeping pills, and the unruly piles of yellow legal tablets and paperback mystery books into Michael's old bedroom. He blamed his chronic insomnia. Jean's feelings remained unconditional: she took what little Leonard gave and transmuted it into the amount she needed to survive.

Upon learning of the unanimous Supreme Court decision favoring Leonard's arguments in the Julian Bond case, Jean wept with delight. She told Leonard that she had a dream in which his uncle Louis was laughing about his legal dynasty. "The Boudins will have more Supreme Court victories than any other family," she said.

Izzy Stone wrote jubilantly: "In a world where the European Soviet states are beginning to allow a little feeble disagreement, this is a decision to make Americans proud. Thomas Jefferson isn't dead yet, despite our dirty little war [Vietnam] and our huge military bureaucracy. We can still spit in its [the Soviet Union's] eye."

Meanwhile Kathy was twenty-six years old and her life was stagnant. Living "temporarily" at home, she abruptly crossed a Village street to avoid greeting a Bryn Mawr college acquaintance pushing a baby carriage. It seemed obvious to her that, despite her examples of leadership

Julian Bond, the first African American member of the Georgia House of Representatives, seated in the hall, circa 1960. In a Supreme Court decision, Leonard won Bond's right to take his elected place, despite opposition from his fellow legislators.

and scholarship in high school and college, she was failing at young adulthood.

It is telling that Bert Gross, Jean's admirer from college days, underlined a passage in *The Devils,* the novel by Dostoyevsky, because it reminded him of Kathy's increasingly unsettling presence. "There was a tremendous power in the burning look of her dark eyes; she came 'conquering and to conquer.' She seemed proud and occasionally even arrogant. . . . There were, of course, many fine impulses to her nature; but everything in her seemed to be perpetually seeking its equilibrium. . . . Perhaps the demands she made upon herself were too severe."

Making matters worse for Kathy was having to witness her father's glee over each new addition to Michael's "A plus" résumé. "Whatever the perfect legal résumé is," Leonard said, "Michael's is better." Michael had won a second coveted clerkship, this one to the ultraconservative, intel-

Supreme Court Justice John Marshall Harlan, circa 1960. For his second prestigious clerkship, Michael Boudin drafted opinions for Harlan, a conservative judge who opposed using the law for activist purposes.

lectual Supreme Court Justice John Marshall Harlan (referred to even by critics as "the great Judge John Harlan"). "Fucking boring life, fucking bad values," said Kathy.

Michael had absorbed from his first clerkship to Judge Henry Friendly, of the Court of Appeals, Second Circuit, a narrow "centrist" view of what federal courts could do. Both Harlan and Friendly were part of a small elite group of "centrists." They were conservative jurists who viewed legal precedent as more important than nearly all human pain.

Justice Harlan—and Michael Boudin—believed that legal precedent was a better safeguard for society than the Bill of Rights, compassion, or the golden rule. Justice Harlan was vehemently opposed to the work of activist lawyers like Michael's father who worked the law to override state legislators, congressmen, juries, and lower-court judges to effect social change for beleaguered citizens.

The great divide between brother and sister was stretching wider. Kathy was livid to hear about opinions Michael was drafting. Harlan accused his colleagues on the liberal Warren court of being too far ahead of citizens on many issues. For example, Justice Harlan believed that the

federal courts did not have jurisdiction over white southerners who preferred not to associate with blacks.

Michael searched for precedents for poll taxes in a small town in Virginia (the case is *Harper v. Virginia Board of Elections*), one way of pre-
venting poor blacks from registering to vote. Michael also hunted down
historic cases to support city fathers in the South who took a public park
private to keep out blacks (*Aarons v. Newton*), since Justice Harlan
believed such local behavior was not the business of the judiciary.

Harlan accused his judicial colleagues of pushing the law too far into
people's lives by applying the Fifth and Fourteen Amendments indis-
criminately. He accurately predicted a judicial backlash to the Warren
court's liberal decisions.

Day after day, Michael typed memos in a room with fellow clerk Matt
Nimetz, who had been his successor at the *Harvard Law Review*. The two
rarely spoke.

To write an opinion, Justice Harlan called in Matt or Michael and laid
out his ideas. The clerk wrote a first draft and read it aloud to the justice.
Harlan took it home and marked it up—even though he was practically
blind—holding a magnifying glass up to one eye. Michael studied Harlan's shaky handwriting and wrote and rewrote draft after draft. He
found the justice a pleasure.

Two Saturdays a month, Michael was privileged to read his opinions
and memos aloud to Harlan at the justice's brick home in Georgetown.
Justice Harlan loved a good discussion of points. He was delighted to
change his mind if Matt or Michael's arguments persuaded him. Matt
Nimetz recalled, "He was not doctrinaire, like some judges who would
say, 'This is how I'm going to decide it and I don't give a damn about how
you read it.' " Even when Justice Harlan agreed with the majority on the
liberal Warren court, he frequently disagreed with how they arrived at
their conclusions. (Twenty-five years later, Michael would, as a sitting
judge on the prestigious Second Circuit, adopt the great justice's assidu-
ous habit of adding his judicial opinions to the record, whether concur-
ring or dissenting.)

On days court was not in session, Harlan would poke his head in, asking, "You boys want to have lunch?" Since lunch with Harlan was an
honor for the clerks, they answered, "Yes, sir." The only drawback was
Harlan's constant cigarette smoking. He told lively anecdotes about his
days as a corporate lawyer in Manhattan, before President Dwight Eisenhower appointed him to the Supreme Court. He never discussed current

cases, fearful tourists might overhear. Michael was amazed tourists failed to recognize the great justice.

Although many young people would have been exasperated by Justice Harlan's old-fashioned formality and innate conservatism—Matt Nimetz called Harlan "a throwback on relations between the races"—Michael revered the elderly justice for his integrity, his meticulous research, and his reverence for legal process.

What Kathy did not hear from her father were bulletins on Michael's state of mind—which was gloomy. He lived in a rarified atmosphere, like a prince of the church; the law was his religion. He occasionally rode his horse in a pasture in Virginia on a quiet Sunday or visited his uncle Izzy. Rarely a protagonist in conversation, Michael did not try to persuade Izzy to change his views. He listened to Izzy, fascinated by his brilliant and aggressively independent view.

Matt Nimetz noted that Michael got along with people of almost every political view because he presented himself as a sounding board. He was full of polite questions that tested people's honesty and logic.

It was while clerking for Justice Harlan that Michael witnessed Hugh Baker Cox argue before the justices of the Supreme Court on behalf of railroads in the Pennsylvania and Grand Central merger case. Hugh Cox was the star of the top-notch, white-shoe firm Covington and Burling.

Ordinarily Justice Harlan considered it a waste of a clerk's time to listen to oral argument. Reading briefs was sufficient. But the elderly justice summoned Michael and Matt to hear Hugh Cox, "not only the best Supreme Court lawyer I ever heard, but the world's most perfect advocate." Michael had also heard a great deal about Hugh Cox from Judge Friendly, who said, "Except for John Harlan, [Cox is] the finest lawyer I have ever known."

Michael watched Cox answer questions from the justices without a note in front of him. Recalled Matt Nimetz, "Cox stood up and said this is it. He was careful not to overstate his claims. He sounded utterly fair. He just brought you into it. As crazy as it sounds, he made a merger of the Grand Central and Pennsylvania Railroad exciting."

Michael was soon honored by an invitation to join Covington and Burling. So far his legal career consisted of being nurtured and recommended by a succession of "the country's best legal centrists." They knew one of their own when they saw him, and it was not Leonard Boudin's heir whom they were welcoming into their ranks.

Yet Michael's triumphant march into the belly of corporate America swept Leonard along with him, despite countervailing efforts by Kathy. Leonard was bored by Kathy's scoldings, and she knew it. To attempt to get her father to take her seriously, she was forced to fall back on the if-you-can't beat-'em-join-'em principle. She applied to several law schools, including Case Western Reserve.

At the same time Kathy was also participating in "heavy" meetings with Das Oughton, Ollie and Charlotte Fein (now both doctors), Tom Hayden, and Connie Brown. They were convinced that they were perched on the knife edge of history. Now they were concocting an audacious plan—to protest the Democratic Party's "illegitimacy and criminality" at the national convention to be held in Chicago that summer. There, in front of TV cameras, the goal was to "bring the Vietnam War home."

Das Oughton had returned from volunteer service with the VISTA organization in Guatemala, frustrated and sorely stressed. The people she'd lived among had farmed bits of arid land for corn, while a few rich families owned giant ranches of fertile land. For years afterward, Das suffered from bad dreams—*quetzales*—about dead children in the barren local market. Unable to help the children who were dying of malnutrition and a lack of medical care, she longed to make a difference somewhere.

Kathy had been impressed by Das during the previous year in Washington during an antiwar demonstration at the Pentagon. While Das's boyfriend, Bill Ayers, taunted several National Guardsmen from a distance, Das spoke quietly to one young man on her own. "My name is Diana," she said to him. "I'm from Ann Arbor, and I know you can't talk to me. I'm not asking you to say anything. Just listen. I want to tell you why I'm here." She then explained why she was upset by the war in Vietnam and what it was doing to the Vietnamese people. The soldier began to cry.

Kathy went to a meeting with Tom Hayden a few weeks before the convention. Hayden beseeched a group that included Das and the Feins to come to Chicago prepared to shed blood. When a friend warned that as many as twenty-five people could be killed in the struggle for the right to assemble in the streets of Chicago, Hayden dismissed this prediction as cowardice.

But once again, Leonard seemed effortlessly to outdo Kathy. One night Ben Spock telephoned Leonard. "I'd like you to represent me," he said, "particularly because of my friendship with Kathy."

Leonard Boudin (right) and Victor Rabinowitz (left) flank their client, Dr. Benjamin Spock, in 1968 outside Federal Court in Boston, during a noon recess of the trial of the famed pediatrician for conspiracy to counsel young men to evade the draft.

"I was expecting a call from one of you," said Leonard. The pediatrician and four others were accused of conspiring to counsel young men to resist the draft.

Leonard grabbed his coat and walked up and down St. Luke's Place formulating a defense strategy. Leonard knew that the so-called conspiracy was made up of relative strangers whose activities had been peaceful, protected by the First Amendment, and most important—utterly public.

Two nights later, the conspirators, including Yale chaplain Reverend William Sloane Coffin Jr., filed into the Boudin living room. Jean served mugs of tea laced with bourbon.

Dr. Spock's sunny personality set the tone of the meeting. He was unruffled by the prospect of jail. The attitude of the eminent and much-loved physician apparently was: Oh wouldn't that be something. I'm curious about what goes on there.

Leonard couldn't resist a note of playfulness. "The first thing I must do is introduce you conspirators to each other." He recalled facing similar difficulties when Senator Joe McCarthy accused clients of "having conspired in secret to advocate the overthrow of our government." He added a dark note: conspiracy accusations were nearly impossible to counter. Leonard promised his listeners that he did not intend to turn the trial into a political forum. But, in fact, how could he do otherwise?

At pretrial hearings in the Boston courthouse Jean stared proudly at Leonard, her hands clasped to her heart. She sat on "the family bench" next to Reverend Coffin's regal mother, who gave off the clean scent of English violet soap every time she stood proudly to greet a niece or nephew. Reverend Coffin's sister, Mary Lindsay, the wife of New York's Mayor John Lindsay, had brought long pew cushions from her church.

The courthouse was overflowing with ebullient people wearing anti-war buttons. In contrast, jurors were tense and short-haired. Seated behind Jean was Leonard's college friend Paul Goodman, an unindicted coconspirator. His recent successful book, *Growing Up Absurd*, encouraged young people to act on their own moral intuitions, no matter what society demanded.

Things started poorly. Leonard infuriated the elderly judge, Frances J. W. Ford, by moving to dismiss the entire indictment. He argued that surrendering draft cards was a kind of symbolic speech, and as such, protected by the First Amendment. Since participants had acted in public, there had been no secrecy; so there could be no conspiracy. For Leonard, such pretrial motions were always critical, similar in intention to the opening moves of a chess game. They provided the groundwork for appeals.

The judge angrily rejected the motion.

Judge Ford grimaced every time Leonard spoke. The judge instructed the jury that conscience was no excuse for breaking laws. The only question was whether or not the defendants broke the law. (These instructions made a guilty verdict inevitable and were the basis for Leonard's successful appeal.)

Since Leonard stated the issues more articulately than other lawyers representing Spock's coconspirators, he was quoted in newspapers around the world.

Jessica Mitford, in the courtroom to write a book about the case, saw Judge Ford as an abusive primitive. She wrote about Leonard Boudin: "[He] bobs about the courtroom in an elegant sort of waltz step like an untidy Christmas tree ornament loose from its mooring. He seems to have about four pairs of spectacles, which he keeps changing like a conjurer with rabbits in a hat."

Leonard argued: How can it be a crime to oppose the Vietnam War and conscription if the war itself is illegal, if the war violates the UN Charter and international law, if crimes against humanity and war crimes are being committed in the course of the war?

He asserted that the U.S. presence in Vietnam did not bring about democracy, peace, and stability, but rather a deterioration of human values and economic chaos. He cited experts who said the United States had bombed civilians, destroyed their homes, and used torture to question prisoners.

When an FBI agent described a "crime scene" at a press conference held by Paul Goodman and four others at the New York Hilton, Leonard reprimanded the man for mispronouncing a complex phrase spoken by Paul Goodman.

Leonard called Kathy in Chicago during breaks in the trial. Already the FBI was amassing reels of tape with an illegal tap on phones at the SDS office. The agents noted that Kathy had become a kind of beacon for antiwar activities. Reporters added color to reports of upcoming Democratic convention protests by mentioning Kathy Boudin and identifying her in terms of her famous father.

On the FBI tapes, when Leonard recited to Kathy the dramatic tale of his struggle for justice in Boston, he made sure she understood that the central story line was his own heroism. For example, he boasted that he had not flinched when the judge threatened to send him to jail for contempt of court. The gist of what he kept saying over and over was this: I'm part of the cause too. Listen to me, I'm doing serious work, really more serious than yours. I'm on your side, the good side.

Years later a colleague of Leonard's listened to the tapes and was startled by his intensity. "Leonard was begging Kathy to admire him. Leonard was trying harder with Kathy than he ever tried with anyone else. It was what he demanded from all women, but not so ardently. Listening, I heard Leonard at his most adorable and lovable."

But Kathy was pretending to have none of it. Jockeying for the upper hand, she told her father: "Either admire me or get the fuck out of my way. I'm the one doing serious work, manning the barricades in Chicago. I'm not interested in admiring your hijinks right now."

A student movement had sparked campus activities in Germany. Something historic happened in France, as student unrest jumped across the

Atlantic to land in Paris in May and June of 1968. In France, the whole nation—factories, hospitals, theaters, trade unions—stopped and joined the student protest against the establishment, right and left. Although the French government did not fall, Kathy took courage from the Gallic example. She and her friends, she vowed, were going to ignite a real revolution in the United States.

The jury in Boston found Spock and three of his codefendants guilty. Jean resisted her first impulse, which was to run to Leonard and throw her arms around him. She knew he would just wriggle uncomfortably and break into a sweat. Eventually, he would come to her when he needed her, like a willful, wandering male cat. Her comforting speech was already prepared: dissenters are important because their original ideas and criticisms would ensure progress as well as the health of a free society.

Meanwhile Kathy was at her post in Chicago, waiting for the opening of the Democratic national convention.* Her mother had deep misgivings about her safety. And no wonder: Kathy had four bottles of foul-smelling butyric acid in her knapsack, to make stink bombs. She and Connie Brown and Das Oughton were planning a protest that was a lot more exciting than law school classes. Nonetheless, Kathy was officially enrolled at Case Western Reserve Law School in Cleveland for the next semester.

Ben Spock and Kathy and her parents were among the millions of American citizens anguished by their government's "half-truths" about waging "undeclared" war in Vietnam. By 1968, the Pentagon had dropped more tons of bombs in Southeast Asia than had been dropped by both sides combined during World War II. Kathy raged about "suppressed government lists of atrocities" committed by the 500,000 U.S. troops.

And the outrage of the American public grew when Martin Luther King Jr. was murdered on April 4, 1968. Robert Kennedy was assassinated in June, right after he won the California primary. The assassinations were a frightening indication to movement people that any prospect of peaceful change might be just an illusion.

---

*In 1968, Chicago was home to Mayor Richard Daley's tough political machine, as well as to the national headquarters of the SDS. Tom Hayden said that Daley's police had planted drugs and hypodermic needles before raiding the SDS neighborhood project. Martin Luther King Jr. had rallied fifty thousand protesters in Chicago in 1966 in an attempt to break down segregation. Mayor Daley denounced King for "creating trouble in every city he visited."

At the same time, the rioting and looting in impoverished black neighborhoods in Atlanta, Newark, Detroit, and Chicago deepened the sense of a revolution being sparked across the land, an impression intensified when police and the National Guardsmen marched in.

To make matters worse, despite polls revealing that 53 percent of American voters did not support the Vietnam War, neither the Republicans or the Democrats seemed likely to select a peace candidate as their presidential nominee.

It was the hope of Kathy Boudin, Bernardine Dohrn, Das Oughton, and Connie Brown to "radicalize" women delegates pledged to nominate Vice President Hubert Humphrey at the Democratic convention. Kathy ignored the fact that the delegates had been chosen by party bosses to nominate Humphrey, President Johnson's handpicked successor.

Kathy's optimism was fueled by her sense of her own righteousness. She and her friends also hoped to radicalize delegates supporting the peace candidate Senator Eugene McCarthy, many of whom were young people who occasionally smoked grass and distrusted the Establishment.

Two days before the convention, tension in Chicago was heightened when a seventeen-year-old Native American boy was killed by police in Lincoln Park. Jerome Johnson was said to have "threatened" arresting police officers.

The police followed Tom Hayden and other antiwar leaders everywhere, taunting them with the prospect of prison terms and death. At the last minute, Chicago mayor Richard Daley refused to grant permits for protesters to march, permitting them only to rally. At this point, thousands of adults and young people hastily canceled plans to travel to Chicago, fearing a violent clash.

Armed soldiers and law enforcement officials began methodically to prepare for war. Seventy-five hundred U.S. Army soldiers marched into Chicago. Eleven thousand Chicago police in baby-blue helmets were poised for action, as were a thousand intelligence agents from the FBI, CIA, the army and the navy. Eleven thousand National Guardsmen with M-1 rifles, tear-gas canisters, and shotguns stationed themselves at fifteen sites. Roadblocks were set up on all entries to Chicago. Low-flying airplanes were banned.

The FBI had planted electronic surveillance devices in the headquarters of Senator Eugene McCarthy and the Yippies—the group led by Abbie Hoffman and Jerry Rubin—as well as in the SDS offices. Nonetheless ten thousand adults and young people descended on Chicago as the

Protesters face troops during the Democratic national convention in 1968. Kathy was arrested for putting stink bombs on the carpet of the lobby of the Hilton Hotel.

Democratic convention got under way—"to confront the war makers" and to protest President Johnson's request for a large war budget for Vietnam. Among the protesters poet Allen Ginsberg chanted the Buddist *om* to keep peace, and Jerry Rubin nominated a live pig representing the police as the Yippies' presidential candidate.

At SDS headquarters Das, Kathy, Bernardine, and Connie Brown were among those who stayed up through the night thinking of ways to provoke police into beating them up in front of television cameras. The young people were determined to show the world press how undemocratically the president of the United States was chosen. Shaming the U.S. government was the goal. They planned to chant, "The whole world's watching."

The fact is that Kathy and her friends had a legitimate case. Powerful political bosses like Mayor Richard Daley and Governor John Connally of Texas had handpicked delegates who promised to ignore votes cast in the Democratic primaries for antiwar candidates.

Norm Fruchter, a charismatic, intellectual young man, had also traveled to Chicago. He was the unofficial leader of "the Newsreel," a group of documentary filmmakers whose stated goal was to film "clashes between the revolutionaries and the pigs." A new chapter of the revolution was unfolding and it was his mission to film it. The fact that Kathy had started an affair with Norm two weeks before the convention (he was separated from his wife at that point) gave him a heroine for his documentary film.

Soon after arriving in Chicago, Fruchter and a film crew trailed Kathy down a hallway in a building to an unmarked door, which was a temporary headquarters of the CIA, set up to battle the convention protestors. This was a breach of law, since the CIA had been formed to fight foreign enemies on foreign soil. "This is the CIA's clandestine headquarters in Chicago," Kathy announced to the camera. She knocked and knocked. No one answered. She took a can of paint out of her knapsack, stepped back from the locked door, and solemnly spray-painted CIA in big red letters. She had learned about the existence of the office from her uncle Izzy Stone.

Kathy and her friends Das and Connie formed a "guerrilla" group. On the first night of the convention they marched with thousands of protesters to a rally in Chicago's Bryant Park. The young women wore red headbands and carried backpacks crammed with vaseline, gloves, goggles, and marbles to scatter in front of charging policemen (a tactic Kathy borrowed from the labor protesters who'd been Leonard's clients of the previous generation).

In Bryant Park, Kathy bumped into David Gilbert, yet another charismatic, superintellectual young man, and instantly began to scold him. In the midst of the angry surging crowd, David Gilbert was an island of calm. "Too calm," said Kathy. "Why the hell are you here? Are you just one more liberal playing it safe? Are you part of the problem or are you with us?"

Kathy was to share many years of her life with David Gilbert and would in ten years pick him to father a child with her. Known as a theorizer who frequently argued against radical actions, David had led the Columbia University antiwar protests while a student there. He'd been a committed pacifist, and he'd tutored graduate students, who then knocked on doors to persuade freshmen and sophomores to protest the war. When David chaired Columbia SDS meetings, the usual disputatious screaming did not occur, because he so clearly tried to be fair.

Kathy was far more hard-edged than David, although he took things hard. For example, he was still bitter about having been turned down by Harvard. His high-school guidance counselor in Brookline, Massachu-

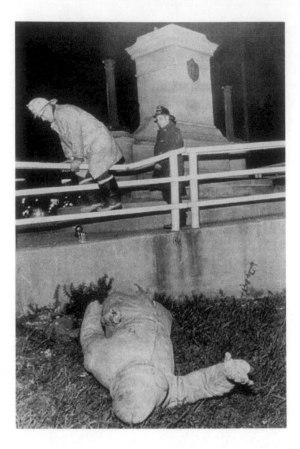

A fireman checks dynamite damage by Kathy and her group to the historic statue of a policeman in Chicago's Haymarket Square on October 6, 1970. They bombed the statue twice, first to threaten police on October 6, 1969, just before her Days of Rage demonstration. The statue commemorates a riot in 1880 between police and anarchists that left seven policemen dead and sixty-seven wounded.

setts, had warned the dean of admissions that David was a born trouble-maker; he'd raised hackles locally by asking white ministers in Boston to host job-skills classes for blacks.

David Gilbert was known to be writing a manifesto, "The Port Authority Statement" (the title a takeoff on Tom Hayden's Port Huron Statement), that targeted unbridled consumption as a key problem in the United States.

His SDS group, called the Praxis Axis, was very "touchy-feely" and in the vanguard of the women's movement. They talked about men not meeting women's erotic needs, and at one meeting debated "toe-sucking."

David was also one of the very few young men in the movement who took seriously the ban against allowing themselves to be made into media "stars." He refused to speak to reporters and was trying to act like "one of the people."

David answered Kathy meekly, explaining that he was trying to avoid coasting through life on his male, white-skin privileges. Kathy corrected him—"white cock skin privileges."

Kathy said, "I bet you fail every day of your life."

David responded indirectly that he tried not to justify bad attitudes by saying, "At least I'm being honest."

Patiently he went on to explain to Kathy that before making up his mind to come to Chicago with his best friend, Ted Gold, he'd reread books analyzing the causes of the French Revolution.

Kathy knew how David and Teddy Gold had embarrassed Columbia University by finding proof in its own library that the institution had received government defense funds to finance "impartial" Vietnam War research. Nonetheless Kathy told David she was not interested in David's or even in her own personal history. It was now only about revolutionary morality.

David did not say so, but his disillusionment with his government had a lot to do with his Eagle Scout training; indeed he took the egalitarian Boy Scout messages far more to heart than its white male founders had ever intended. Like many young people of his generation, he'd grown up expecting a government that would solve all problems and be fair in doing so. But he was slowly acquiring a set of principles that transformed his own government into the enemy. It was the only way he could make sense of events in Vietnam and in the scary streets of Chicago.

David was smarter than Kathy; he was smarter than nearly everyone. Nearly all his professors aroused his condescension. At Columbia, Professor Stanley Aronowitz described David as "a luminous intellect, one of the best I ever encountered."

David told Kathy he was trying to overcome his "tendency to exploit women by scoring sexually without feeling love." Worse yet, after he slept with a woman, he admitted that he stopped taking her intellectual opinions as seriously.

Kathy raised the ante: Was David ready to risk his life for his right to march? She commanded him to put aside hopes for a big academic career and step-by-step reform. "Get ready to put your body on the gears of the war machine. We have to burn all our bridges to move ahead."

Kathy found David's studied meekness and modesty a welcome antidote to Leonard's arrogance. Nevertheless Kathy ended their Bryant Park conversation scornfully. "If you're not working on the solution," she said, "then you're the motherfucker Malcolm says is the problem."

In Chicago, the protesters were sleeping on floors and friends' couches, and even in parks. Kathy slept with the elite group at SDS headquarters, despite not being one of the elected leaders. In fact, in the same way that Leonard had never joined the Communist Party, Kathy was not a member of Students for a Democratic Society.

Ignoring police warnings, Kathy and the others marched in the streets before rallying in Grant Park, and—as the mood of the crowd turned to screaming hysteria—large numbers of the marchers were beaten by army reserve troops and by Mayor Daley's cops.

Wrote Norman Mailer:

> Children and youths and middle-aged men were being pounded and gassed and beaten, hunted and driven by teams of policemen who had broken out of their restraints like the bursting of a boil. It was as if war had finally begun, as if the gods of history had come together before the television cameras of the world and the eyes of the campaign workers and the delegates' wives and half the principals at the convention—as if the Democratic Party had broken in two before the eyes of the nation.

As the convention went into high gear at the International Amphitheater, party bosses blocked attempts by pro-peace delegates to pass a platform plank that would support negotiations to end the war.

Meanwhile Black Panther leader Bobby Seale flew to Chicago to address the demonstrators in Grant Park. In his "war uniform" of boots, beret, and black leather jacket, Seale urged "picking up the gun" and "roasting pigs." At his side in almost ludicrous contrast, long-haired and bearded Jerry Rubin sang of peace, strumming a plastic bandolier.

Seale's presence was seen as a victory by SDS protest leaders, who felt that it legitimized their program. For their part, the arrogant Panthers were not ready to regard these overprivileged albeit rebellious young white people as real revolutionaries. Still, they were willing to keep the channels open. As he listened to Bobby Seale speak, Tom Hayden was thrilled. He recognized the tentative coming together of Panthers and protesters as "members of the black underclass connecting with overprivileged whites in a strange and explosive alliance of resentment and guilt."

Bored with chanting "Join us, join us" to disdainful women delegates leaving the Hilton Hotel, Kathy, Das, Connie, and Corinne Fales "disguised" themselves in skirts, stockings, and lipstick in order to slip past police guarding the Hilton entrances. (When Bill Ayers told Kathy she looked like a "convention hooker," she rubbed off the lipstick.)

Once inside the Hilton ladies' room, she wrote VIETNAMESE ARE DYING in red lipstick on the mirrors. Das added, MURDERER. The gesture may have alleviated Kathy's rage, but it had the effect of making delegates more hostile to Kathy's views.

In the streets again, Kathy prepared for the possibility of tear-gas attacks by smearing vaseline on her face and wetting a T-shirt to hold to her nose and eyes. Like many of her fellow protesters, she had made the decision not to attempt to flee police hurling tear-gas canisters.

At 3 a.m. soldiers drove jeeps with mounted machine guns and barbed wire–wrapped bumpers into a crowd in Grant Park who had gained permission to sleep there.

By the third day of the convention, Kathy, Das, Corinne, and Cathy Wilkerson were telephoning bomb threats to hotels housing Democratic delegates. They also placed two homemade stink bombs on the carpet in the Go-Go lounge of the Hilton in an attempt to force delegates to come outside to listen to demonstrators argue against the war.

The stink bombs consisted of wads of tissues dipped in butyric acid. When Connie Brown was caught dropping one by a Hilton Hotel security guard, she could not hide the terrible odor of rotten eggs emanating from her purse. Grabbing her pocketbook, the security guard arrested her. Kathy and Corinne could see that Connie was terrified. They ran after her and insisted to the guard that they be arrested, too. When Connie bravely reprimanded Kathy for not behaving like a truly dispassionate revolutionary, Kathy replied, "I'm coming with you to make sure that you're okay."

Kathy and her friends found themselves in Cook County jail, sharing cells with black lesbians. When angry policemen told Kathy she was facing felony convictions that could keep her in jail for twenty years, Kathy in fact panicked. She kept saying, "I hope I can still go to law school."

Connie envied Kathy for what she assumed was Leonard's wholehearted support. But when Kathy called him in New York, Leonard dismissed the goings-on as "unserious pranks."

"I have serious things to do with my time," he commented coldly, assuring her that a jail sentence would indeed ruin any plans she might have for law school. Yet, although he was enraged at what he saw as the self-indulgence of her behavior, he privately vowed to do everything in his power to help his daughter. Within hours he arrived in Chicago, his briefcase stocked with clean socks and shirts. He was ready to act as Kathy's official lawyer.

On the morning of Vice President Hubert Humphrey's acceptance speech, thousands of protesters assembled again in Grant Park and marched ten miles to the convention to condemn Humphrey's prowar stance. Some penetrated the convention hall. Dan Rather, the television newsman, found himself being beaten accidentally by a security officer who was attacking a small crowd of protesters. Rather shouted to television cameras, "This is the kind of thing going on outside. This is the first time we've had it happen inside the hall. I'm sorry to be out of breath, but somebody belted me in the stomach." Said Walter Cronkite, his familiar, jovial voice tinged with rage, "I think we've got a bunch of thugs here, Dan."

That day, hundreds of thousands of people throughout the country decided the choice between Richard Nixon and Hubert Humphrey (neither of whom publicly advocated a cease-fire) was a Tweedledum Tweedledee situation; the election was, they said, a kind of fraud.

Meanwhile Leonard persuaded authorities to reduce the charges against Kathy and her friends. The young women pleaded guilty to malicious destruction of property. The judge ordered them to pay for cleaning the hotel carpet. They served no further jail time, and Leonard picked up the cleaning bill.

Although impressed with Leonard's intelligence and aware of his charisma, Connie Brown still saw dangers inherent in Kathy's relationship with her father. It disturbed her that Kathy seemed always to be wondering if her father would approve or disapprove of what she was doing. To Connie, it was also reprehensible that this man could have had affairs with his daughter's close friends. For her it tarnished his crusader's reputation.

Nonetheless the events of the summer of 1968 marked a new state of Kathy's relationship with Leonard—that of client and lawyer. Despite the disdain he'd voiced for her protest methods, she knew she had his undivided attention—for the moment.

The Chicago police might have won battles, but from the point of view of Kathy and her peers, they lost the war. Millions of people throughout the world had seen the authorities beating idealistic young citizens exercising their First Amendment rights. And in fact, 1968 would turn out to be the last year that party bosses were permitted to choose convention delegates who ignored votes in primary elections.

Soon afterward, at a meeting of Norm Fruchter's film group, Kathy greeted me: "Are you with us or are you a member of the pig press?"

That autumn Kathy sat in the front row of a class in contracts at Case Western Reserve listening to Professor Arthur Austin. He observed that Kathy was "pumped for intellectual interaction" and had the knack of asking the right kind of focused questions. He felt she would one day become a great lawyer—as great as her famous father.

The second weekend in October, Kathy and Das made their way to the national SDS convention in Boulder, Colorado. The two young women stayed an extra day in order to hear speeches by members of a new group called the Motherfuckers. They called for small groups to train together to fight cops. Kathy and Das also wanted to discipline themselves "to get over bourgeois hangups about doing violence." The Motherfuckers— whose name came from a poem by black writer LeRoi Jones called "Up Against the Wall Motherfuckers"—argued that the new militancy would attract thousands of college dropouts and working-class people turned off by "intellectual bullshit."

Kathy quit law school. Instead of slinking away, however, she said good-bye to her teachers. At cross purposes in a conversation with Professor Austin, she spoke about "maybe going underground rather than show up in court for some trouble she had gotten into in Chicago." He thought her reference to "underground" meant taking the rapid transit train to the Cleveland airport, so he gallantly offered to provide any assistance he could. Kathy thanked him effusively; she assumed he was offering to harbor her from police and the FBI, when all he was doing was offering a ride to the airport to catch her plane.

It was a critical moment; Kathy and her friends were talking themselves into a more radical stance. The romantic notion of going underground as fugitives from the law appealed—and the fact that they were not yet fugitives did not bother them in the least. What was important was to ignite revolution as anonymous soldiers. Role models were convicted communist leaders like Steve Nelson, who'd jumped bail in the early 1950s. And there were also the violent anti-French revolutionaries depicted in their favorite film, *The Battle of Algiers*.

Kathy and Das visited an old Bryn Mawr friend, Karen Carlson, who lived with her husband, Merrill Rosenberg, in a comfortable apartment filled with books and contemporary furniture off Lake Shore Drive in Chicago. Merrill, who taught French literature at the University of Chicago, loved good wine. Kathy and Das did not hide their contempt for the Rosenberg apartment as "the height of middle-class pretension."

"The only people I know who live like this are friends of my parents," Kathy said disgustedly.

Karen and Merrill agreed that racial inequities were an outrage.

"How can you do nothing?" asked Das.

"That's just not the sort of person I am," said Merrill Rosenberg.

Das said revolution was the only way to make changes in America and that she and Kathy were revolutionaries. Merrill Rosenberg pointed out, "If you're serious, you'll have to throw bombs." His tone implied that Kathy and Das would never work up the nerve.

12

IT WAS ABSOLUTELY UP TO US

It's hard to believe looking back, but we convinced ourselves it was absolutely up to us to stop the Vietnam War.

—Bill Ayers

Kathy was serious to the point of grimness. She acted as if she literally believed that a world conflagration was coming and she wanted to be part of it.

—Stanley Aronowitz, Columbia University

Ten years ago it would have been very hard for anyone in education to prophesy that our campuses would become arenas for students shouting defiance at authority.

—Margaret Mead, *Redbook*, April 1969

Look at it, America 1969: the war goes on despite the jive double talk about troop withdrawls and peace talks. Black people continue to be murdered by agents of the fat cats who run this country, by the pigs or the courts, by the boss or the welfare department. What's new is today a lot more people are angry.

—Weatherman, August 1969

The year 1969, the twenty-sixth of Kathy's life, found her loudly threatening to transform the fantasies of Jean, Leonard, Izzy, and Victor about societal change through revolution into street violence. What had been the background noise of her childhood now sounded loudly all around her.

It was, of course, an amazing time in history to be young. Angry and gleeful street protesting was just part of it; there was also "sex, drugs, and rock and roll."

As an ardent, if oft-disdained, follower of Kathy's named Susan Stern wrote in a memoir of the period:

You could travel almost anywhere, and you would have an enclave of friends who would welcome you. You always had a place to crash, some food, some dope and some sex. You visited and exchanged all kinds of news; number of busts in your SDS chapter or among your friends . . . growth of chapters, number of demonstrations. . . . You got to know your family from coast to coast. Your collections of buttons and banners grew with your war scars. . . . And so did your faith in the viability of the revolution—and one was rewarded by a sense of belonging. One knew one's place in life, whom to depend on, and that no matter where you were, you would be taken care of.

By the middle of March 1969, however, a dozen universities had refused to host the annual SDS convention. The problem was the student leaders. They seemed at the breaking point. "Revolution now, muthafuckers," Kathy and others shouted in people's faces.

But despite loud proclamations of the righteousness of the cause and her commitment, Kathy was seriously depressed. She blamed it on her failures in Chester and Cleveland. Moreover, the convention protests had been noisy but ineffective in the main and, obviously, the war was still being waged in Vietnam.

With Michael still the absolute pride of his father's every waking moment, anyone could see that the path to her father's deepest affection was still the one her brother had taken. But in those moments when she was not contemplating going back to law school, her most passionate desire was to sit, like Joan of Arc, at the head of the army that would install the utopian future that she awaited.

The student movement was splintering, its leaders quarreling about everything—including where to hold their upcoming annual meeting. The sexy Bernardine Dohrn was living with her boyfriend, John Gregory "J.J." Jacobs. Domineering and wildly sexy, he was a street fighter and self-styled Maoist-Leninist intellectual. In his seedy "crash pad" in Chicago, J.J. was the undisputed leader of a small group of friends that included Kathy and Das, who stayed there from time to time.* Since J.J. ran the show, Bernardine gained reflected power as his live-in girlfriend, and adroitly used it.

---

*Other future Weathermen who visited J.J. and Bernardine in Chicago included Mark Rudd, the hero of the Columbia uprising. There was also Das Oughton's current boyfriend, Bill Ayers. Like Das, Bill had rich parents; his father was president of Consolidated Edison

It was J.J. who convinced rivals in the student movement to convene near his apartment on the south side of Chicago, in an old gray building called the Coliseum.

J.J. dressed like a cool working-class "greaser," his black hair slicked back in a style of the day called the "D.A." (it looked like a duck's ass when viewed from the back). In 1968, J.J. had been the important strategist behind the Columbia student uprising and had advised Mark Rudd, a young man who loved the limelight. J.J.'s power lay in his charisma and in his fervent belief that the student uprising was part of an apocalypse that included LBJ's decision not to run for reelection, and revolutionary protests in France that nearly toppled de Gaulle's government.

J.J. proclaimed that the corrupt capitalist world, led by the U.S. government, was already crumbling, and needed only a strategically applied push to send it crashing.

Bernardine had joined J.J. on the barricades, sleeping with him first on the floor of a friend's Manhattan apartment during the Columbia uprising. The friend described the event as "an animal mating." J.J. was revered for his uninhibited frenzy in sexual encounters as well as in street fights with police. When J.J. and his followers had occupied Mathematics Hall at Columbia, it was affectionately called "the hall of crazies." He led an invasion of the president's office, and when a police bust was imminent, J.J. wanted to put the college's rare Ming dynasty vases on windowsills to prevent attacks through them. That was vetoed. Instead he suggested pushing cops out windows "nonviolently."

J.J. sneered, strutted, and pushed through police lines at antiwar protests like an authentic street tough. Most important, Jacobs was able to win almost any argument by wearing his opponent down with brilliant, turgid rants. He was brutally honest, apparently fearless, a speed freak who popped black beauties and LSD. Women saw J.J. as "a diabolical beauty": full of high-energy seductive and solicitous blandishments one minute, a dangerous panther in pants the next. Dohrn and later Kathy were just two of the women he seduced. They copied J.J.'s aggressive verbal and sartorial style.

J.J. and Bernardine's palpable sexual heat (and belligerent non-monogamy) set a standard in uninhibited sexual hostility: competition for

---

in Illinois. There was also Terry Robbins, who'd committed every line of Dylan to memory. Terry Robbins and Bill had formed a tiny group who called themselves "the Jesse James gang" at the University of Michigan and had forced the other "less revolutionary" students out. Like Das and Teddy Gold, Terry Robbins would die in the town house explosion.

Bernardine led to fights at the dinner table in their apartment in Chicago. J.J. stabbed one of Bernardine's passing lovers in the hand with a fork.

Bill Ayers disliked J.J.; friends suspected he'd fallen for Bernardine. When a male dinner guest told Bernardine to button up her blouse, Bernardine pulled her breast out of her shirt and brandished it. Kathy roared with laughter and did the same. It became a kind of reflexive joke to be performed when men tried to insult them by implying they were sexually wanton.

The Chicago crash pad was furnished with old mattresses and not much else. Jacobs had destroyed the few tables and chairs during an earlier LSD-fueled evening with the nihilistic Motherfuckers, also revving themselves up to fight police during protests. After one rampage in his apartment, J.J. wandered around asking, "Whose little boy am I?"

J.J.'s violence was often laced with humor. One night he drank all the milk in a friend's refrigerator. When confronted the next morning, J.J. said, "I ain't no liberal."

"J.J. was frighteningly sane," recalled Lewis Cole, a Columbia professor of film studies. Said Coles, a fellow leader of the Columbia student protest, "J.J. was the most honest person I have ever known."

After fleeing police during an antiwar protest in Chicago, while Kathy and Das dazedly washed cuts and bruises, grateful to have survived, J.J. demanded, "What's next?" What could they do to fight back even harder?

Bernardine Dohrn, for her part, soon became one of the most dominant figures in Kathy's life. She would be protector, mother figure, lover, rival, sister. Most primal, perhaps, Bernardine would fight and overpower Leonard and Kathy as "the other mother" of Kathy's son. The daughter of a Christian Scientist Irish mother and a Jewish father, "Bernie" had grown up in the town of Whitefish Bay, Wisconsin, a suburb just north of Milwaukee. She had been an awkward kid, thin and one of the good students, who was dying to be accepted by cool boys and girls.

During her junior year of high school, Bernardine found her world transformed by two events. First, her father changed his name from Ohrnstein to Dohrn, tired of being accused by customers at the furniture store he managed of "Jewing" them out of money. Second, Bernie experienced a miraculous physical bloom, and she gloried in her new sexual powers.

Her appeal was based on attitude, but there were of course her big, dark eyes, a strong jawbone, luminescent skin, and voluptuous breasts. Boys who had previously scorned her now flocked.

Bernardine transferred from the Miami University of Ohio to the University of Chicago for her junior year, wanting "something more serious." As Kathy had in Cleveland, Bernardine worked in an SDS neighborhood project, organizing poor whites and trying to help them find jobs. She also joined a group led by Martin Luther King Jr., fighting segregation in white suburbs.

Bernardine cried when King was assassinated in 1968. She told a friend that while his politics may have been passé, she'd admired the man.

Bernardine then studied law at the University of Chicago, but instead of hanging around to pass the bar exams, she dashed to Manhattan to run the junior division of the National Lawyers Guild.

Her job was to travel from campus to campus counseling young men about the nuts and bolts of draft resisting. Not surprisingly, she proved a beacon to male students who found her message even more compelling in combination with her tight, very short purple miniskirts and her nurturing, sexual glow. It was the era of the sexual revolution for women, and Bernardine was not above using physical seduction to win converts. While other draft counselors wore buttons that said STOP THE WAR, Bernardine's read CUNNILINGUS IS COOL. FELLATIO IS FUN.

In the weeks preceding the June 1969 SDS convention, Kathy, Das, Terry Robbins, and Bill Ayers plotted with Bernardine and J.J. The young people were facing a frustrating reality: their protests and appeals to conscience had failed. Using J.J.'s oft-cited phrase, they did not have a "what's next." The Vietnam War blazed on; and despite Lyndon Johnson's War on Poverty, they believed that poor people were no better off than they'd ever been. They assured one another that they did not want to waste their whole lives like old lefties, fantasizing about better times and revolution. Their task was to keep the hundreds of thousands of movement youngsters committed, but how? And what did they need to do to cement their leadership? Trying to convince themselves that a revolution in the United States would come from black ghettoes—"slave colonies in enemy territory"—they shouted encouragement as J.J. feverishly typed his abstruse call to arms.

"You Don't Need a Weatherman to Know Which Way the Wind Is Blowing" was the title of J.J.'s thirty-thousand-word "recruiting tool" for the student convention. Terry Robbins named it after the cautionary line in Bob Dylan's song "Subterranean Homesick Blues." Kathy's contribution drew upon her knowledge of Marxist analysis, folksongs, myths, Russian novels, and historic facts about organized labor.

The manifesto prophesized a mystical worldwide political Armageddon led by the Black Panthers, who were "genuine native revolutionaries."

Jacobs and his friends chanted: "John Brown, live like him." But in fact it was a kind of in joke: they were daring each other to die like John Brown.

The SDS convention was shaping up to be a big fight for leadership between Kathy's small group and a larger organized radical group called Progressive Labor. PL members idealized white factory workers and tried to act like them. They wore inexpensive suits and short hair. (Some, like Noel Ignatiev, had left brilliant student lives to work in steel mills, with a modest financial boost from Leonard's expat clients the Sterns.) Like Kathy's group, the PL youngsters revered the memory of abolitionist John Brown. The hostility between the PL youngsters and Kathy's group was virulent, in large part because the PL group believed that revolution in the United States would be ignited not by blacks, such as the Panthers, but by mostly white factory workers. Also, unlike Kathy's group, the PL students (in imitation of factory workers) were prudes in matters of sex and cleanliness. At bedtime, Kathy kicked off sneakers and dungarees, pulled a T-shirt over her head, and—naked—climbed into a communal heap.

The rival PL students worshiped Chairman Mao Tse-tung of China and recited Mao's revolutionary sayings as distilled into a tiny volume called *The Little Red Book*, a huge seller on college campuses.

On the first day of the national SDS conference, David Gilbert and his best friend, Teddy Gold, were among thousands of long-haired students lined up impatiently outside the Coliseum in Chicago. Leaders frisked them each time they entered the building. Anyone caught with a tape recorder or camera was turned away.

Because it was an open meeting, however, FBI agents and plainclothes police walked right in. Scores of Chicago policemen hid in a building across the street and photographed David, Teddy, Das, Kathy, and Bernardine. Police broke windows of the young people's parked cars. Among the SDS factions ready to fight each other were Mad Dogs, Motherfuckers, White Panthers, Running Dogs, Progressive Labor, and, of course, the group to which Kathy belonged, soon to be named the Weathermen.

David Gilbert and Teddy Gold sat down with the Manhattan delegation. David had been thinking more and more about violent protest since his confrontation with Kathy six months earlier. He was tired of being derided as too intellectual and not action-oriented.

By June 1969, it actually looked to many serious people as if the campus and ghetto uprisings across the country might coalesce into national upheaval. There had been riots in big cities such as Newark and Detroit. The National Guard had been called during student protests at Berkeley, Duke, and the University of Wisconsin. In May, black students had shut down City College in Manhattan. At a Berkeley uprising, police fired buckshot at demonstrators and killed one of them.

Now, at the SDS convention, J.J. bent into the microphone and shouted denunciations of moderate protests. SDS founders Tom Hayden and Rennie Davis listened with horror. Student security guards in yellow armbands patrolled the aisles to make sure no fistfights broke out. Leni Wildflower wept when J.J. yelled that violence was the only way to reach the goals they sought. Leni thought it suicidal to follow the Black Panthers, whose clearest intention now seemed to be to use guns.

As J.J. finished reading his diatribe, delegates named Kathy's group Weatherman. David Gilbert was "blown away." He'd been coming to similar conclusions about racism breeding international revolution.

By the end of the first night, a speaker from Progressive Labor was lulling David and everyone else to sleep. Suddenly Kathy, Bernardine, Das, and a small group of other women stood and chanted in unison "Ho! Ho! Ho Chi Minh," cheering the North Vietnamese leader who was leading the fight against American troops. They all banged their chairs and threw copies of Chairman Mao's little red book at the speaker, mocking the PL's uncritical admiration of Chinese communism. David Gilbert was one of many delegates who burst out laughing. The Weatherman women won the moment with bravado.

Kathy and her friends demanded that a Black Panther leader named

Chaka Walls take over the microphone. A moment later Chaka Walls exhaled threateningly into the microphone and stared at the sea of white faces.

He suddenly yelled, "Pussy power." Hundreds of women cursed. Male students groaned and smiled. Chaka Walls ordered white girls to have sex with anybody if it helped revolution. Angry shouts bounced off the walls.

Progressive Labor members jumped to their feet screaming, "Fight male chauvinism!" The convention erupted in shouts of "Fight male chauvinism." The Weatherman group was defeated by their Black Panther allies.

Chaka Walls boomed into the microphone, "Superman was a punk because he never even tried to fuck Lois Lane." At that point, angry women delegates forced him to relinquish the podium. Next Jewell Cook, a Panther woman, grabbed the microphone. "He was only trying to say that you sisters have a strategic position for the revolution—prone." Boos silenced her.

It was ten o'clock at night, and someone declared a half-hour recess. Meeting secretly, Kathy, Bernardine, and Das needed to demonstrate to other delegates that the women of Weatherman were ready to fight the condescending display by Panthers toward women.

Moments later, Kathy, Das, Bernardine, Cathy Wilkerson, and fifty more women marched to the podium and formed three rows around it, backs arched, legs spread, arms crossed, in imitation of Cuban male revolutionary soldiers. Bernardine Dohrn shouted to assembled delegates, "Follow me."

Bernardine's command and the military display were impossible to resist. After shouts and hesitation, five hundred young people, including David Gilbert and Teddy Gold, exuberantly marched out into the street after Bernardine, Das, and Kathy.

Tears streaming down her cheeks, delegate Susan Stern was flying on LSD. This is better, Susan thought, than falling in love with a man. She said to herself: "I am falling in love with international liberation." But as Kathy and her friends watched the delegates disperse into the night, they realized with hearts sinking that they still had no "what's next."

The following day the convention droned on. But at 11:30 p.m., Kathy and the army of women marched in. They formed a ring around the room. The men of Weatherman obediently chanted: "Long live the people's war" while Bernardine Dohrn, who was perfecting her sexy stage routine, strutted. She euphorically expelled the Progressive Labor group from the student movement. This time she again led some five hundred mesmerized delegates—including David Gilbert and Teddy Gold—out of the convention, never to return.

Bernardine, Kathy, and Das ran in front, leading the high-spirited young people through streets of Chicago's ghetto to West Madison Street. Police made no effort to stop them. It was victory. It actually felt like revolution. On Madison Street, the women broke down the door of the national SDS offices. Amid cheers and threatening shouts, they took possession of the prized printing press. They posted armed guards at the building's entrance.

At the captured SDS offices, people sat until dawn listening to Kathy, Das, and Bernardine's hypnotic entreaties. They all pledged to "take the next step." Yet something big collapsed that night in Chicago: the hundreds of thousands of young people in the protest movement throughout the country hated the idea of violence as the "what's next."

A week later, Kathy drove to Manhattan and honored Eleanor Stein and Jonah Raskin, a young married couple that she knew from protest demonstrations, by "crashing" in the guest bedroom of their luxury Riverside Drive apartment with views of the Hudson River. She arrived with two avocado plants, a bag of T-shirts, and a guitar. Jonah was a young academic and Eleanor was the daughter of a rich ex-communist who had given her daughter a lavish wedding party at the Tavern on the Green, a restaurant in Central Park.

As Kathy's hosts, Jonah and his wife, Eleanor, were propelled to the center of current events. Friends dropped by just to stare at Kathy, who implied that she might at any moment disappear to take part in risky and violent but highly righteous adventures. She was an increasingly romantic figure.

Soon Kathy began seeing a handsome blond boy named David Palmer. He moved in with her. He was planning to go to Cuba to help the government build new houses. Kathy was torn about accompanying him.

Every Sunday, Eleanor and Jonah gave a brunch fitted out with Irish linen napkins and Spode china. Kathy's presence made a strong impact on visiting professors and graduate students. Her idea of social interaction was to poke ruthlessly at their feelings of self-worth. The message was, "Do as I do, and you will be a better human being." Among her opening gambits to women was: "Aren't you humiliated about relying on your looks to get through life?"

One Sunday afternoon, Kathy announced, "Marriage puts women in prison." She then said, "This whole brunch is bourgeois." Her boyfriend, David Palmer, picked up a pumpernickel bagel and asked her, "How could a bagel be bourgeois? And you're eating it too, so you've got the bourgeoisie inside you. You just hate yourself."

Kathy had kept a key to her parents' house, and Jean occasionally found her daughter leaning into the open refrigerator, eating strawberries. Visits terminated abruptly, since Kathy could not be in the same room with Leonard without screaming at him. Yet she could not help worrying that Leonard was recuperating too slowly from a second heart attack.

During one raid on "the white settlement," Kathy frightened Jean with news that she was working on a Weatherman plan to break ties to bourgeois parents. She would "disappear," go underground using a fake identity to fight the government. This was precisely what Jean and Leonard feared. Next Kathy criticized her mother for living in Leonard's shadow. Jean said Kathy was too involved in "self-purification and trying to scour off white-skin privilege." Kathy retorted, "Leonard is too powerful."

However, when a sore throat worsened, Kathy came home to sleep in her own bed, and for several weeks Jean nursed Kathy. Jean and Leonard soon invited friends to a special Sunday afternoon brunch at which Kathy made a ceremonial speech, explaining that she was now devoting her life to the underground struggle for black liberation.

Kathy was making notes for *The Bust Book*, a primer on how to behave when arrested. She and Eleanor Raskin declared themselves a law commune, and spread documents and yellow legal pads on the Raskin living-room floor. Kathy subtitled the book: *What to Do Until the Lawyer Comes.* One chapter was "If You Can't Make Bail"; another was "What Happens to You at the Police Station."*

Jonah Raskin became jealous as his wife and Kathy grew inseparable. When not working on the legal handbook or playing guitar duets, they were flying to distant campuses to speak and recruit students and lawyers

---

The Bust Book admonishes: "Trying to talk yourself out of an arrest is fruitless. A cop does not have to tell you what you are arrested for nor does he have to say 'you are under arrest.' "

Kathy advises: Give police your correct name and do not resist arrest (p. 40). The reason: "A cop almost never releases you once he has taken you into custody. You might say, 'I wasn't doing anything, I was just standing over there with Bill . . .' [You] may find that your statement has incriminated both yourself and your friend Bill" (p. 41). "After arresting a person . . . they may ask you political questions to try to bait you."

for the movement. *The Bust Book* was published by the Lawyers Guild under the watchful eye of Victor Rabinowitz, then revised a year later and issued in paperback by Grove Press. It sold well over fifty thousand copies.

The revised edition was angrier than the original text. The message was "Don't trust, talk to, or cooperate with the police any more than necessary." A frontispiece was a drawing of justice being gang-raped. There were photographs of black protesters and police in plain clothing. Legal instructions included: "Whatever you do, don't drop the dope on the ground." (Translation: if police find a shred of marijuana under protesters' feet, they will arrest everyone.)

Kathy's increasingly mistrustful worldview showed up in the revised edition: "The cop and the judge wear different uniforms, but they both serve the same System we seek to destroy."

Silence was "the best weapon for handling the police, . . . and do not joke around with the cops, because you risk making admissions and mentioning names of friends. . . . The best rule is not to talk at all. . . . Don't talk [heavy letters] don't talk don't talk don't talk don't talk don't talk don't talk."

She recommended plastic goggles for demonstrations. "Do not rub your eyes after being gassed or Maced . . . this can aggravate irritation," and "Carry a copy of the *New York Times,*" which "although not useful for any other purpose" made a nice weapon when "rolled up lengthwise and folded in half."

Leonard took *The Bust Book* as a personal attack: it declared the law insufficient. One paragraph read: "To rely on 'legal rights' is to ignore entirely the fundamental reality of a class society, that when those 'rights' have been granted by a ruling elite, those same 'rights' can and will be ignored when their use threatens the power of those who granted them." That his own daughter had written these words was betrayal and the betrayal hurt.

Later, reviewing the revised *Bust Book* respectfully, the *New York Times* alluded to Kathy's escape from the exploding brownstone on Eleventh Street by noting that "one of the authors—Kathy Boudin—has achieved a separate notoriety."

Like most young women still committed to the movement, Susan Stern yearned to be friends with Kathy. Susan collated *Bust Book* pages and distributed thousands of copies to college campuses.

Wrote Susan:

> The few times I had to approach Kathy concerning the distrib-
> ution of *The Bust Book,* she had such an air of authority about
> her that I quivered inside. Women like Kathy could do things
> like write Bust Books; I could only distribute their work. They
> made up the theories and I followed them. . . . [Kathy] fright-
> ened me to death. She stirred the deepest of my insecurities by
> her aloof demeanor. How humiliated I always felt in her pres-
> ence because I was so inarticulate, my thoughts were so scat-
> tered, and I was prey to the demons of my body rather than
> the cool detachment of my intellect. Kathy seemed above sex-
> ual need, beyond the petty and childish fantasies I still had in
> secret, about falling in love and being loved . . . [her] commit-
> ment to the revolution seemed to grow from more profound
> and enduring roots than mine.

During a hot spell, Kathy invited Susan Stern's roommate for dinner
and a midnight swim at the city pool across St. Luke's Place from the
Boudin house. Susan was devastated to realize that Kathy had no intention of inviting her. Kathy made it clear she thought her too ordinary.
Susan was embarrassed because she was "poorly educated"; she knew no
history of progressive politics. She worried that she had not committed to
revolutionary violence and dressed too coquettishly. She had done
striptease work when her father stopped supporting her.

Susan would have been stunned to learn how much Kathy herself suffered for failing to measure up to Leonard's standards. She would also
have been astonished by Jonah Raskin's view of Kathy. Underneath
Kathy's bravado, Jonah saw uncertainty. She was talking about applying
to law school yet again. Jonah felt that Kathy had many contradictory
sides. He knew that people behaved differently in different contexts, but
Kathy's mood swings from depression to arrogance worried him.

Jonah noted that "Kathy was too self-doubting, she was a dark person,
unhappy, troubled. . . ." She had "a sort of poor me . . . half here, half-
there, between everything . . . undecided, and not sure what to do, wanting me to feel sorry for her . . . she'd get involved with someone, then
ask herself if she should really be doing this . . . so much self-doubt."

Indeed, Kathy was agonizing over her short-lived affair with Norman Fruchter. It had been difficult to find herself at several women's consciousness-raising meetings attended by his wife, from whom he was still separated. At one meeting, she heard Fruchter's wife say, "I'd kill any woman who was sleeping with my husband."

Kathy also missed David Palmer. She wanted to join him in Cuba. She was working with members of her father's law firm to cut through red tape so Bernardine, Das, and she could go to Cuba to meet a Vietcong delegation.

At the last minute, however, Kathy relinquished her place on the Cuban trip to Eleanor Raskin, having decided that she did not want to look like she was trailing, lovelorn, after David Palmer. Her public version: someone else deserved the opportunity. (The FBI wrote internal memos for decades that mistakenly assumed she had in fact made the trip.)

In Havana, Das, Eleanor, Bernardine, and Kit Bakke listened raptly to Vietcong leaders who urged them to recruit those who fought hardest against the police. The young Americans promised increasingly violent protests, in order to show privileged Americans the horrors of war.

Das felt herself transformed by this encounter with members of the Third World, just as she had been in rural Guatemala. The women accepted metal friendship rings from the Vietcong, purported to have been crafted from downed U.S. fighter planes.

The Havana meeting alarmed FBI director J. Edgar Hoover, who had been ignoring reports that the student movement might have international communist connections. But now he alerted his bureaus: the young leaders were indeed dangerous.

While Eleanor was still off in Cuba, Kathy invited Jonah Raskin to drive with her in her old Chevy to Chicago—to do important work with the "Weather Bureau"—the new nickname of Weatherman leaders. Kathy's mission was to recruit people and organize a demonstration called the Days of Rage.

It promised to be, Kathy said, far superior to the protests at the 1968 Democratic convention. "The Days of Rage will be an offensive, not defensive action," she told friends. The protesters were teaching themselves a new, scary tactic: they were going to attack the Chicago police if police blocked the way to the city's largest army induction center—which they planned to attack as well. The "offensive action" was also a protest of the ongoing trial in Chicago of leaders of the previous year's protests at the Democratic national convention.

Kathy asked Jonah Raskin to help to write recruiting leaflets for the Days of Rage. She called them "shotguns," and it thrilled Jonah to boast that he was "working on a shotgun."

They made it to Chicago with their friendship intact. It stands to reason that they sexualized the relationship.

Kathy parked the Chevy on Madison Street a few doors away from the barricaded SDS national office. She and Jonah suddenly spotted a robbery in progress a hundred feet away: five armed black teenagers were stealing the wallet of Jeff Jones, a fellow Weatherman.

Kathy ran after the robbers but lost them. Out of breath, she pounded the locked steel door to the office building until the armed Weatherman "officer of the day" peered through a keyhole and let them in. Kathy explained to Jonah that the guard was posted to dispel attacks from defeated SDS factions, the FBI, and the police. She did not mention that local black kids had also been breaking in and stealing typewriters and money.

Kathy and Jonah found other Weather Bureau leaders arguing heatedly on the second floor. Mark Rudd, Martin Kenner, and a few others were highly agitated about the robbery. Workmen were installing steel bars and reinforcements around windows. It was difficult to argue over the sounds of hammering. According to FBI reports, Kathy began living in the office. By this time, many young people were sleeping on the office floor.

"If a kid tries to rob me, I don't care if he's black or white, I'm going to belt him," shouted Martin Kenner, a Columbia grad student in economics. Terry Robbins was taking notes. He said, "You belt the kid who did the robbery and [then his] older brothers in the B. Stone Rangers will vamp on us."

"They're potential black guerrillas," said Kathy, going for the "heavy" stance.

"Taking a wallet from me isn't revolutionary," said Martin Kenner. "The Mafia are thieves too."

"And we can learn from them," said Terry Robbins, disagreeing.

"Can't we talk to the Panthers?" asked Martin Kenner.

"The chairman's in jail," said Terry, "and besides, we're not getting along with them. They've been intimidating our printer to do their leaflets before he does ours."

Kathy and Bernardine Dohrn hold a press conference August 19, 1969, after Bernardine's return from Cuba, where she and Das and other student leaders had a warm meeting with members of the Vietcong.

Kathy added an admonishing feminist note. "The Panther men keep hassling women in our office."

"Smash monogamy," mocked Mark Rudd.

"Smash monogamy" referred to the program instituted by the Weather women, who believed that if they slept with only one man they were forced to agree with him in political arguments and were also seen as his property. Therefore each member of a cadre had to sleep with all the others—including men with men and women with women—in an attempt to "smash sick bourgeois habits."

Mark was saying, So what's the big deal—since you don't believe in monogamy, why not sleep with the Panthers? Weather members never took a vote. At some point, dissenters fell silent and they all moved forward as a group. Martin Kenner finally began nodding agreement with Kathy on the political nature of the robberies.

An hour later, Kathy dragged Jonah to lunch at a Mexican restaurant to discuss a "shotgun" she wanted him to write about political prisoners in the United States. After talking to the chef in Spanish and ordering tacos, they argued over the definition of political prisoners.

"If the black kids who steal from us are caught and sent to jail, are they political prisoners?" asked Jonah.

"Yes," said Kathy. "Every black person in jail in the United States is a political prisoner." She meant that the politics and laws of the government worked unfairly against them.

"They steal because they have to survive, and survival is political," continued Kathy. "Take Fred's case."

"Who's Fred?" asked Jonah.

"He's the chairman of the Illinois Black Panther Party, a great orator, in jail for stealing seventy dollars' worth of ice-cream bars from a Good Humor man." The Panthers were favorites of members of the white intelligentsia. Colorful, posturing, and "heavy," their black leather jackets and sunglasses were copied as a fashion statement. Their analysis rang true—the United States was riddled with racism. Their program of armed struggle seemed at first to intellectuals to be merely provocative metaphor.

Jonah later remembered with romantic awe that this was the first time he heard the name of the legendary Fred Hampton, who was later killed by police.

Days passed and Jonah never wrote the "shotgun." He and Kathy could not agree who qualified as a genuine political prisoner.

When Das, Eleanor, Ted Gold, and Bernardine returned from Cuba, Kathy sat with them at a press conference. Her arms crossed, Kathy stared at Bernardine with envy and admiration. Bernardine interrupted Kathy several times and skillfully dominated the conference; she was brilliant at public speaking. Bernardine told reporters that Vietcong generals contradicted the government's claim that U.S. troops were withdrawing from the war.

Das and Kathy secretly named themselves the Americong, seeking a name as hostile and "heavy" as "Black Panthers." Nicknames, slogans, and songs made them feel important and spurred them on. Humor was part of the group's subversive appeal. It was also used to lubricate their way in and out of contradictions and mistakes.

Leonard called Kathy frequently that summer (as revealed by FBI phone taps on the SDS office installed four years earlier). He left many messages for his daughter before he succeeded in reaching her.

Kathy was caught up in telephoning and visiting young people all over the United States. She was "head-counting" and trying to enlist "thousands and thousands" of high-school students. What she needed to find out was how many young people were coming to the Weathermen's Days of Rage demonstration, scheduled for early October. Kathy made sure thousands of Days of Rage "shotguns" were distributed.

On August 11, Kathy flew to visit a Weather collective in Seattle. Kathy impressed upon them the importance of night-and-day physical exercise and military maneuvers (practicing with clubs and slingshots and hurling Molotov cocktails).

Kathy scornfully ordered the Seattle cadre to "dump" Susan Stern, her adoring assistant on *The Bust Book*. Susan was just a hippie who did drugs and was "too individualistic." Worse, she was in love and wasn't obeying rules such as "smash monogamy." She'd refused to live with the Seattle collective. Heartbroken, Susan cried and resolved to try harder to measure up to Kathy.

Kathy was also in attack training. Jean and many others worried that the plan to assault Chicago police was a suicide mission.

Among students inspired by one of Kathy's hundreds of recruiting speeches was Judith Alice Clark, a small, wildly expressive young woman who was a sophomore at the University of Chicago. Judith quit school to join Weatherman.

Judith, who grinned if nervous or frightened, had grown up on the Upper West Side of Manhattan; her father had been Moscow correspondent for the Communist Party newspaper the *Daily Worker*. Her mother was a senior vice president at the Madison Avenue polling company Yankelovich, Skelly, and White. Later, Judith and Kathy would be imprisoned together at Bedford Hills Correctional Facility for Women.

Suddenly police raided the Chicago Panther headquarters, shooting and wounding three Panthers. As a result, Kathy toiled without sleep to recruit doctors and lawyers and reporters. It was her idea to dedicate the upcoming Days of Rage protest to the Panthers.

The Panthers refused to reciprocate, even going so far as to threaten violence against Kathy and her group. Fred Hampton said it was suicidal to announce a violent protest before doing it. "We oppose the anarchistic, adventuristic, chauvinistic, individualistic, masochistic, Custeristic Weathermen."

Abbie Hoffman disagreed: "You Weather guys perform a kind of Gandhian violence."

In September, Kathy, Das, Eleanor, Bernardine, and twenty-four other women—using fake student IDs to buy discounted tickets—flew to Pittsburgh for a Days of Rage recruiting action at South Hills High School, where students were primarily black. When a Quaker group declined to let the women use a mimeograph machine, the Weather women shoved the Quakers aside and printed leaflets anyway, just like Panthers.

The goal in Pittsburgh was to channel rebellious adolescent energy into revolution. High schools in black communities were, Kathy, Das, and Bernardine reasoned, analogous to prisons. Columbia professor Stanley Aronowitz later agreed with the analogy. "With guards at doors, the issue was law and order. Nobody cared if the kids learn anything so long as they didn't roam the halls."

On the night of September 3, the young women painted slogans on a wall of South Hills High: FREE HUEY NEWTON and HO LIVES. The next day the women barged inside the school waving huge Vietcong flags. Running through hallways, they shouted, "Jailbreak!" "Shut down the school!" and "Ho! Ho! Ho Chi Minh."

Bernardine, Das, and Kathy took off their shirts and waved them. The South Hills students were stunned by the sight of the shouting, half-naked white women. The strangers pushed leaflets into students' hands, inviting them to the upcoming Days of Rage rally in Chicago. They said it was in honor of Che Guevara, but the high-school kids had no idea who he was.

Although Kathy eluded police, twenty-six women were arrested; Eleanor Raskin was sentenced to three months in the local jail. A newspaper reporter called SDS headquarters two days later in Chicago to ask, "Why did you pick South Hills?"

"No specific reason at all," said Kathy.

When asked, she claimed success in Pittsburgh. She predicted half the students in the United States would storm Chicago for the Days of Rage.

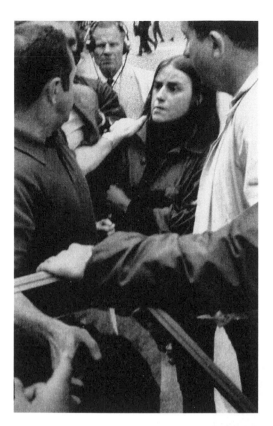

Bernardine Dohrn, October 11, 1969, national officer of the Students for a Democratic Society, confronts police at the Days of Rage demonstration, Chicago.

BRING
THE
WAR
HOME!

CHICAGO-OCT. 11

SDS

A Days of Rage recruiting leaflet code-named "a shotgun" by Kathy Boudin and her fellow organizers, autumn 1969.

Soon afterward, some of the same women got into a fistfight with kids at English High School in Boston. This time they ran to avoid arrest.

On September 25, Kathy and a small group invaded the Harvard Center for International Affairs: it contained the office of Vietnam War architect McGeorge Bundy. "We are liberating this building," they shouted. "Get the fuck out." They broke windows and kicked secretaries and professors. They spray-painted antiwar slogans on walls. They dashed down hallways shouting "Ho! Ho! Ho Chi Minh."

Although Kathy was not named in newspaper accounts, her parents and brother were furious. Her physical assault on Harvard upset Michael: it seemed a direct attack and an attempt to humiliate him. Although frightened for Kathy's sanity and safety, Jean joked about Kathy's lifelong desire to make a big impression at Harvard.

Meanwhile, David Gilbert was dispatched by Kathy and members of the Weather Bureau to live in a cadre in a working-class Brooklyn neighborhood. His job was to recruit poor black kids. Arguing with Kathy by phone, David was beginning to agree that protesters must stop waiting to be beaten by battalions of cops. But David was quickly rebuffed by the Brooklyn teenagers. He and his friends looked like college kids on a panty raid. David's instructions were, however, clear: to gain the respect of black students, he must transform himself into street tough.

So David and his Brooklyn collective invaded a high school and took over the auditorium by chaining the door. He tried to open the students' minds to analyses of working-class oppression. But he fled to avoid police, without converting anyone.

In fact, David and his Brooklyn collective were readying themselves to die for their beliefs. At the same time, they were scared to death. But their slogans and chants were saying, in effect, that it was okay if whites got killed because they had been born cursed with white privilege.

Six weeks before the Days of Rage "went down," Eleanor Raskin was released from jail in Pittsburgh. Her husband, Jonah, told her by telephone that if she brought Kathy home, he would kill her. He'd had enough. But he woke up the next morning to find his wife in her nightgown and Kathy, naked, sleeping on either side of him. Stirring, Kathy said with a grin, "So muthafuckah, I hear you want to kill me."

Kathy and Das decided to name their Weather cadre the Fork, in honor of Charles Manson's expressed desire to kill his victims and eat in the room with their bodies. It was hard for outsiders to spend time with members of Kathy's cadre. Visitors experienced hate, depression, doom, and even suicidal feelings—sensations very similar to those felt by visitors to prisons. Cadre members were deprived of simple things like fresh coffee, private space, baths, even telephone calls. They reveled in tough exercises and deprivations to make themselves "strong."

Their conversation excluded outsiders: they punned derisively about patriotism and added to nearly all comments the word *fuck*, aggressive black street slang, and harsh code words for police and other middle-class villains. They invented nicknames and pseudonyms daily, and found it less and less desirable to speak to outsiders who, upon hearing about "smash monogamy" or another tenet of the rigidly intellectualized Weather program, would show disdain or disgust by some small gesture or change of expression.

Kathy and her friends were trying desperately to make themselves into warriors. This they hoped to accomplish by rooting out of their personalities any feelings that smacked of attachment to "the sick bourgeois society." They were trying to replace old habits with programmed anger.

Moreover, they were now strictly enforcing group sex as well as homosexuality to "smash monogamy." They used LSD to force any potential FBI infiltrators to confess. They went without food or sleep for two or three days in a row. Rigid rules were meant to force each person to discard much of his individual will, his personality.

Nobody had his or her own bed or possessions, and no one cleaned up. (No sheets on communal mattresses meant less laundry.) No pets were allowed; they elicited affection, which led to vulnerability. Dishes piled up, caked with food.

Das cooked and ate an alley cat to prove she was overcoming bourgeois ways. She led a group to a cemetery and smashed gravestones. But she was also using these challenges as a way to get over losing her boyfriend, Bill Ayers, to the alluring Bernardine. Das had spent years trying to adjust to or overlook the hundreds of movement girls Bill bragged about having sex with in his role as "radical recruiter."

Kathy, meanwhile, had taken to wolfing down raw hot dogs "like a poor person." But her old friend Fred Gardner found the action "a condescending parody of poverty." To him, whose parents were genuinely working class, "it felt like Kathy was making fun of me and them."

One outsider was made "antsy" by a protracted debate about whether to ban cigarette smoking indoors. The debate about the dangers of secondhand smoke would, of course, be a mainstream concern in the future.

Because of relentless, round-the-clock "criticism–self-criticism" sessions—a diabolic use of what psychologists call group therapy—cadre members lived in fear of one another. During criticism–self-criticism sessions, each member revealed his own bourgeois inadequacies and accused others. They were terrified of harboring a fear of violence or feelings of loyalty or love for a mate. Kathy was "smashed" to sobs after being accused of ambivalence and "people pleasing." She promised to feel and act "less like Leonard."

David Gilbert was repeatedly criticized. "Smash monogamy" had yielded damaging evidence. When women compared notes about sleeping with him, they found—as had his girlfriend Naomi Jaffe from his graduate student days—that after sex David became unwilling to take a woman's opinions seriously in any argument or conversation. The women accused him of using the act of sex as a kind of intellectual "scoring."

"Smash monogamy" was seized upon by the press, eager to titillate readers with the "bohemian and free sexuality" of Weatherman. But the "smash monogamy" rule actually resulted in less and less sex—and finally in grim celibacy. This was claimed as a victory by Das and Kathy. Nonetheless Das, at least, missed the companionship of a beloved mate.

Kathy was transforming herself into someone spare, dry, and hard, without curls, curves, or earnest good manners. Her jawbone and cheekbones protruded. She ate yogurt and built up her leg muscles.

After days and nights of exhausting argument, Kathy and the others decided to try a new tactic to recruit poor white teenage boys. To gain respect, they would beat up gang members. The cadre members were tired of being punched and chased by teenagers. Respectful visitors were startled to find Kathy and the others in public parks training for gang fights by slapping, punching, and kicking one another.

"We'll prove we are not hippie faggots associated with SDS. First we show them we can fight, then we show them what we are fighting for," said David.

Kathy bragged to Leonard that at least twenty-five thousand young people would descend on Chicago for the Days of Rage. On October 2, a week before the march, she and several others dressed up in "night street-fighting clothes"—sneakers, jeans, dark long-sleeved shirts, and gloves. They eluded hundreds of helmeted Chicago police to plant a dynamite bomb at the foot of the historic statue of a policeman in Chicago's Haymarket Square. The bombing was meant to cement the link between the upcoming Days of Rage and the tragic nineteenth-century fight between anarchists and police that took place in Haymarket Square. Unlike the anarchists who battled policemen at the end of a rally, the Weathermen were ostentatiously announcing that they planned to fight the police.

Kathy was arrested moments after the explosion. Her plans for the Days of Rage were, nonetheless, undeterred. The Chicago police called the destruction of the Haymarket statue "a declaration of war," and a police spokesman told reporters, "It's kill or be killed." Leonard angrily wired Kathy $1,000 for bail.

When Kathy got out of jail, she welcomed three hundred terrified women to the Days of Rage. In criticism–self-criticism sessions they admonished one another for doubting the word of their leaders that thousands more women were going to arrive momentarily. A rumor circulated that a train was coming to Chicago from Michigan filled with young people who wanted to hit the streets and fight the "pigs."

The young revolutionaries dressed for street fights. Kathy and Das chose sneakers over boots, because "only when flat on our backs can we kick anything important to a policeman." Army surplus helmets were distributed.

In war councils, the young women crashed at the gym of the McCormick Theological Seminary tensed for battle, and many solemnly prepared to die. They memorized the route for the march: the drill was to march two by two to the rally at Lincoln Park. At that point, they were to run aggressively through police lines to the Drake Hotel on Michigan Avenue, where Judge Julius Hoffman, who had presided over the conspiracy trial of the Chicago 7, was staying.

On the first day of the protest, at 7 a.m., Kathy, Bernardine, and Das marched troops wearing helmets out of the seminary gymnasium, two by two. They carried clubs made from banisters broken off from stairwells at McCormick. They grouped in Lincoln Park around a bonfire made of park benches. They counted heads. Four hundred young men and women so far. A hundred new people marched in.

Many women wept. How could five hundred people make a revolution? Where were the thousands of troops? How could this poor showing be the result of all their recruiting, self-discipline, and drudgery? Said Susan Stern, "All that work . . . our lives almost destroyed and nothing . . . nothing." (Susan's disappointment was somewhat mitigated by the promise of a blazing sexual encounter with J.J.)

Kathy circled the frightened people in Grant Park, passionately addressing individuals as "the revolutionary vanguard of America." Bernardine Dohrn began to shout: "You are five hundred people out of a whole country who were good, strong, and brilliant enough to come to Chicago to make a revolution." Of course the number was less than expected, but "we are the people with courage, the only white people in America who realize what it takes to make a revolution."

Despite Bernardine's exhortations, the crowd believed they were going to die as soon as they hit the streets. Kathy kept moving among them, hugging and congratulating her troops for being brave and lovely, the Americong, the only nonracists in America.

At ten-thirty at night, Kathy, Bernardine, David, J.J., Das, Susan, and the others ran out of the park into the street. Teeth clenched, sweating and panting, they threw stones at glass windows in rich people's houses and at bewildered Chicagoans eating steak in restaurants. They ran right into an army of policemen kneeling, standing—and then shooting.

"Hit the ground," shouted Kathy. Some of the protesters were shot, many beaten; 90 percent were arrested. Those who could, ran.

An hour later, back at the seminary, thirty women survivors examined bruised limbs and told war stories. Kathy dispatched couriers to hospitals and jails for news of missing friends.

At 2 a.m., at a mass self-criticism session, Kathy and Bernardine denounced the rank and file for retreating from the pigs; they should have attacked. Flying on J.J.'s speed pills and adrenaline, Kathy argued until just before dawn. Incredibly the beaten and exhausted survivors finally agreed to try again.

The next day's battle was the women's militia march: one mile from Grant Park to the armed forces induction center. Many of the thirty women slept. But Kathy circulated among those still awake, buoying spirits. At 7 a.m., she leaned over each woman. "Time to get up. Women's Action. Gather in that corner. Hurry—we have to move out."

Susan Stern opened her eyes and thought, How come I'm falling apart, and Kathy looks like she's on vacation? I guess she must want to win much more than I do.

The women sat in one corner of the gymnasium, iodine and bandages on their wounds. Their eyes were red. Meanwhile Kathy left to do a field check, running quickly along the route from Grant Park to the induction center.

When she returned she led the women on a subway bound for Grant Park, where they stood under a statue of a horse and rider, still hoping for the arrival of hundreds of supporters from Michigan. Suddenly there was a loud cry. Nine women from Michigan marched into the park.

Kathy carried a large red Vietcong flag. She, Das, and Bernardine led the column of helmeted women. They marched three by three toward the edge of the park. Suddenly they faced rows of policemen. Each policeman waved a black club. One of them ordered the women to disperse. Kathy stepped forward.

"Hold it. Hold it right here," shouted Deputy Superintendent of Police James J. Riordan. "If you set foot on the sidewalk, you'll be arrested."

Kathy lunged directly into the police lines. She swung her flagpole, banging a policeman. She and women behind her were quickly wrestled to the ground. Cops pushed them headfirst into squad cars.

Most of the other women surrendered. But Deputy Superintendent Riordan refused to let them go. "You are armed, you are carrying clubs; and you can't pass unless you give them up." He added, "Please take off your helmets." They did, and policemen escorted them to the subway.

Several women, however, refused to submit. One shouted, "The sidewalks belong to the people."

"You are young, you are women . . . please stop," said Riordan. Four women lunged at him, shrilling a loud imitation of the war yodel of revolutionary Algerian women as portrayed in the film *The Battle of Algiers*.

The police beat them and broke several pairs of eyeglasses.

Inside the paddy wagon, police wrapped a chain around a group of women that included Kathy, Bernardine, Das, Susan Stern, Cathy Wilkerson, and Judith Clark. At Cook County jail, each woman was put in a small cold cell and given a bologna sandwich and lukewarm coffee in a tin cup.

Kathy raised a clenched fist to every woman who was led by to be fingerprinted. The women were touched. Kathy had anticipated massive arrests and had laid the groundwork by contacting lawyers from the People's Law Office.

Kathy, Das, and Bernardine immediately began hours of intense self-criticism about the Days of Rage. No one said the word *failure*. In fact, they declared it a success. The women did push-ups and watched TV. Black women in nearby cells were incredulous to learn that Kathy had attacked police. "That takes balls, it sure does."

Leonard again refused to come to Chicago when Kathy telephoned. And again his disdain pulled the rug out from under her. "I have more important things to tend to," he said. Although relieved that Kathy was all right, Leonard believed that his daughter's public failure sullied his reputation as a lawyer who always won.

Victor posted Kathy's $10,000 bail, chiding her immature behavior. "Do you agree," she asked in response, "that black people are in a terrible plight in this country?"

"Yes," said Victor.

"Well, do you have a better way of trying to fight injustice?"

Victor said in a low, surprised tone, "No, no, I guess I don't."

Several weeks later, Kathy, Das, David, J.J., and Bernardine again dressed in helmets. This time they joined a protest in Washington, D.C., against the Vietnam War. Kathy and her friends sang (to the tune of the Beatles' "Yellow Submarine"), "We all live in a Weatherman machine, a Weatherman machine."

A "revolutionary" contingent of several hundred led by Kathy, J.J., Das, and Bernardine broke away and marched up to the Justice Department and threw stones at it. Kathy kept up the cry: "Revolution is possible."

U.S. Attorney General John Mitchell and his wife, Martha, stared fearfully out of one window of the Justice Department Building. They flinched as stones banged the walls. "It looks like Russia in 1919," Mitchell said to his wife.

David Gilbert threw bottles and stones at the South Vietnamese embassy. Most young people scattered as police released clouds of tear gas. A Columbia friend of David's, Jonathon Shils, was shocked to see the sensitive, soft-spoken David Gilbert ignore the tear gas, grab a trash can, and heave it through the embassy window.

David was soon assigned by Kathy and the other Weatherman leaders to organize poor people in Denver. He checked in daily with local Panthers. He frequently heard gunshots near the office. He and Kathy and other

Weathermen accused the government of a national strategy to wipe out Panthers. He ignored the fact that the Panthers had declared war on the U.S. government. His old friends called him paranoid.

David was arrested for arson after a woman in his collective set off a smoke bomb in a class on police science. He was arrested again for handing out antipolice leaflets to white kids. He fought the arresting police and two policemen were hurt. David was charged with assault with a deadly weapon—a rock. These incidents made him train harder.

On December 9, 1969, Panthers Fred Hampton and Mark Clark were killed by Chicago police. Thousands of black mourners lined up to walk by Fred Hampton's casket in Chicago. Kathy helped to set bombs in empty Chicago police cars in protest of Fred Hampton's death.

Two weeks later, Kathy ran past Jonah Raskin at a huge antiwar march in Manhattan. Angry police were riding horses into the protesters. Kathy saluted Jonah with a closed umbrella like Mary Poppins.

Kathy cheered as Jonah threw stone after stone at a window of the Portuguese airline office. A younger protester whistled "Street-fighting Man" as the huge window crashed to the sidewalk. Someone sprayed OFF THE PIG in red paint on a wall.

Fleeing mounted police, protesters surged west on Forty-ninth Street past Christmas lights in Saks windows. Many carried silk-screened banners: AVENGE FRED.

"I saw what you just did," Kathy said, congratulating Jonah on breaking the window. He marveled that Kathy did not seem the slightest bit afraid, even though if she were arrested and convicted, the penalty would be years in jail. Spurred by Kathy's battle cry, Jonah ran after her and her raised umbrella. He threw another rock that cracked the glass in a Saks window.

Suddenly he was beaten down to the pavement by cops. Jonah watched a policeman chase Kathy hard as she wove through crowds of Christmas shoppers. After thirty seconds, the policeman gave up. Despite his injuries and his predicament, Jonah was exhilarated by his final glimpse of Kathy holding her umbrella high as she disappeared into a sea of people. He silently congratulated her.

Kathy began inviting everyone she met to a "war council" or "wargasm" at a dance hall in a black neighborhood in Flint, Michigan, on December 27. The "open meeting" was being organized by the "macho" women of Weather.

A few weeks earlier, Kathy, Bernardine, Das, and other women had

argued male leaders, including the wild and authoritative J.J., into relin-
quishing leadership positions to women. It was "a military coup." Kathy
had been instrumental in persuading the men that nearly all human interaction was predicated on unfair male authority.

On the afternoon of the Flint wargasm, Kathy entered the dance hall
and was horrified by damp bloodstains on the floor: a black man had been
killed hours earlier by a stray bullet. Plunging ahead, Kathy, Bernardine,
Judith Clark, and Das made a twenty-foot poster of bullets spelling the
names of enemies to be "offed": listed among them were Mayor Richard
Daley of Chicago and Sharon Tate—all representing bourgeois privilege. Sharon Tate, however, had already been murdered by Charles
Manson.

Kathy hung a twenty-foot-long cardboard machine gun from the ceiling. She saw the wargasm as a way to use rock music and free "psychedelic" punch to lighten Weather's image. The women had deliberately
chosen a dance hall as a way to recruit teenage white followers of counterculture leader Abbie Hoffman. (Abbie did not attend.) The problem
was that most teenagers saw the Weather group as "a grim bunch," "a
suicide squad" with "a death wish."

By evening, four hundred kids were pushing against the entrance to be
admitted. Kathy and Das and others blocked the door, frisking them.
Music blared from inside. Admission was $5. But one teenager, typically,
negotiated.

"Look man, I have fifty cents and I got to get back to New York."

"Okay, gimme three dollars."

"Here's one seventy-five."

"Right on."

"Right on" was what Panthers said, raising a clenched fist. In Flint,
Kathy changed the "peace now" gesture of two fingers raised in a V into a
"piece now" sign by extending her forefinger and cocked thumb to imi-
tate the firing of a gun.

Inside, revelers danced as loud rock music thumped. The punch was
spiked with lots of LSD. The main events at the wargasm were speeches.
Outsiders were impressed by the nonchalant way Bernardine and Kathy
talked about having survived prison.

Bernardine flattered, cajoled, and inspired her listeners. Kathy scolded
the crowd. She called white mothers "pig mothers" because they instilled
bigoted views in white American children. She led Weather songs like
"I'm Dreaming of a White Riot."

While Kathy shouted about "doing some heavy shit like political assassinations," some thought privately that she really was saying: Boo! I'm scarier and more important and more committed to world peace than you are.

That night in Flint, Bernardine told the crowd, "We fucked up . . . we didn't fight around Bobby Seale when he was shackled at the conspiracy trial. . . . We didn't burn Chicago down when Fred Hampton was killed."

Referring to Charles Manson's famously bloody and random murders in California, Bernardine said, "Dig it. First they killed those pigs, then they ate dinner in the same room with them, then they even shoved a fork into a victim's stomach. Wild."

Das said that the black revolutionary movement was so advanced that all whites could do to help was fight cops as a diversionary tactic.

Music blasted again. Everyone danced. Kids flying on drugs grew hoarse. Everyone had unlimited energy for listening to the sound of his own voice. The young people stared at Kathy, Das, and Bernardine dancing together—clearly the event's superstars. The women screamed Weather lyrics to the recording of "Nowhere Man," the slow melancholy song by the Beatles.

He's a real Weatherman
Ripping up the motherland
Making all his weatherplans
For everyone
Knows just what he's fighting for
Victory for people's war
Trashes, bombs, kills pigs and more
The Weatherman

Kathy and David began to get together at Flint—at Kathy's instigation. Since "smash monogamy" was still in force, the sexual alliance was not heralded as romantic. Kathy asked David for his "gut check." She meant, Are you man enough to risk your life? Impressed by the blue-collar expression, David admitted he'd never thought of himself as physically courageous.

Another new word of the wargasm meeting was "barbarism," and someone suggested that the group change their name to Vandals, referring to Bob Dylan's line from "Subterranean Homesick Blues": "The pump won't work 'cause the vandals stole the handle."

Suddenly frustrated by arguing with recruits about violence, Kathy and other key leaders marched out in military lockstep. They shouted one another down but stopped short of a decision to go underground. Kathy and Mark Rudd proposed that they become an anonymous and invisible army of fugitives from the law devoted to armed struggle against the government.

Kathy cited historic precedents—going underground meant dodging court hearings, forfeiting bail, and breaking "heavier" laws.

Mark Rudd called for a national campaign of clandestine bombings that would make "anything in the 1960s look like a Sunday school picnic."

Throughout the wargasm, Jonah Raskin scrutinized Kathy; he decided that her talk of violence was mostly metaphor. But he believed her group to be in "an advanced state of disintegration, alternately cogent and mad." They were isolating themselves from the rest of society.

"On the one hand, there was a coherent political analysis [of] . . . imperialism, especially the war in Vietnam, and black oppression in the United States. There was also a firm grasp on the strengths and weaknesses of youth culture and an insistence on the importance of women's liberation. On the other hand, there was a chaotic and frenetic lifestyle, and an intense irrational moral fervor."

Jonah shouted Che Guevara's words: "Revolutionaries are guided by great feelings of love."

Kathy shouted back, "You're sentimental and bourgeois. Don't worry about love, just learn to hate the enemy."

The women were, in general, more uninhibited than the men, although Jonah Raskin twirled a long orange scarf, imitating Mick Jagger. A few guys danced together and tentatively kissed to music by Sly Stone.

Late that night in Flint, Kathy joined women making love on the dance floor. Dancing again, she copied young blacks. She punched and kicked, cutting down invisible enemies as if she were doing karate. She jumped high, winking at admirers, her face red, her curling hair flying and damp with sweat, stamping her bare feet, and shouting at the top of her lungs in unison with the other young people, "EXPLODE, EXPLODE." She returned to New York from the wargasm with a venereal disease.

13

THE "LITTLE HOUSE ON HEAVEN
STREET" GOES TO HELL

*The search of the youth of today is for ways and means to make
the machine—and the vast bureaucracy of the corporation state
and of government that runs that machine—the servant of man.
That is the revolution that is coming . . . [It] need not be a
repetition of 1776. It depends on how wise the Establishment is.
If, with its stockpile of arms, it resolves to suppress the dissenters,
America will face, I fear, an awful ordeal.*

—Justice William O. Douglas,
Points of Rebellion (New York: Random House, 1969)

March 6, 1970, 9:30 a.m., Greenwich Village

Jean Boudin stepped out her door and winced at the sight of a rain
cloud blowing in, and then chided herself for taking the earth's
weather personally. As was her habit, she scanned car bumpers for antiwar stickers. Her favorites were LET SAIGONS BE BYGONES and WAR IS
UNHEALTHY FOR CHILDREN AND OTHER LIVING THINGS. A black truck
driver flashed her a two-fingered V. Jean wished she had the temerity to
flash him the black power fist.

Her first stop was going to be Klein's, a bargain department store on
Union Square, to buy cotton underwear for Kathy.

Although worried sick about her daughter, Jean later realized that she
hadn't a clue about how far Kathy had already gone. Indeed Kathy and
her friends had recently celebrated a serious foray into violence. In honor
of their heroes—members of the New York Black Panther Party—
they'd detonated a homemade dynamite bomb on the Brooklyn lawn of

Nathaniel Burns, a.k.a. Sekou Odinga, under arrest, 1981.

State Supreme Court Judge John M. Murtagh, who was presiding over hearings of twenty-one local Panthers accused of conspiracy to bomb public places.

Far from satisfied with the sympathy bombing, the Panthers, such as the hugely muscled, lethally dangerous, and highly disciplined Sekou Odinga (born Nathaniel Burns), belittled the Weatherman effort, pointing out that "the Murtagh bombing had not done anything to hurt the pigs materially."

Kathy was crestfallen, since she and her group idolized Sekou Odinga as the real thing: a commanding, fearless, black revolutionary who was adept with his gun. For his part, the former gang member from Jamaica, Queens, kept his distance from Kathy's white group.

Currently a fugitive, Sekou was said to have narrowly escaped Manhattan police most recently by climbing out a bathroom window and jumping down five stories.

Sekou rehearsed and planned bombings and murders for months. In a rare failure, he had been thwarted by police while rehearsing a sniper attack on the 46th Precinct across the Harlem River in the Bronx. His plan had been to shoot and kill Bronx policemen one by one as they fled the bomb explosion. To Sekou, it was retaliation: he believed that after many such attacks, individual policemen would be too frightened to patrol black neighborhoods. At that point, the Panthers would establish community control.

A decade later, Sekou Odinga would be the mastermind of a "revolutionary" gang that performed a series of robberies of Brinks trucks—his presence once again a powerful draw for Kathy Boudin and David Gilbert.

The day before her walk to Klein's, Jean had found Kathy leaning into the refrigerator with a motorcycle helmet tucked under one arm. Her eyes were ringed with dark skin. "Are you getting enough sleep?" asked Jean. Kathy strode across the room and put the motorcycle helmet in prime position on the mantel.

"Mine. From the Days of Rage," she said.

If anybody should have been feeling bad about the low turnout for the Days of Rage, it was Kathy. But she declared victory, pointing to the flurry of articles about the "famous Weathermen."

"Where are you living?" Jean asked her daughter.

That day in March, Jean had no idea that Kathy was "crashing" only a few blocks away in an elegant town house on Eleventh Street furnished with Hepplewhite antiques and owned by the absent father of Cathlyn Wilkerson, Kathy's friend dating back to the picket lines in Chester, Pennsylvania.* The nineteenth-century mansion at 18 West Eleventh Street had been the boyhood home of poet James Merrill, who would call it "the little house on heaven street." The town house owner James Platt Wilkerson was a rich Quaker who also owned a chain of radio stations in the Midwest. (The Wilkerson town house could not be altered or torn down by ruling of the city's Landmarks Preservation Commission.) Others staying at the Wilkerson house included Das Oughton, Teddy Gold, Terry Robbins, Russell Neufield, and Cathlyn Wilkerson herself. According to FBI reports, on March 2 Neufield had paid sixty dollars for two fifty-pound cases of dynamite at a factory in New Hampshire and had then brought the cases into 18 West Eleventh Street.

The Fork cadre was arguing about what kind of bombs to make next to

---

*One town house adjoining the Wilkersons' was divided into apartments inhabited by Mel Gussow, drama critic for the New York Times, and actor Dustin Hoffman. The street's other occupants had included the Mark Cross heir, Gerald Murphy, whose style of living had been legendary.

*Attorney Paul O'Dwyer and Leonard Boudin, Harrisburg, 1972. They defended
the Harrisburg seven, who included radical Catholic Father Philip Berrigan.*

carry out plans of jailed Panthers. Suggested sites for explosives were
Macy's, Bloomingdale's, Fort Dix army base in New Jersey during a
dance, and the sundial on Columbia's campus on Easter Sunday. Kathy
was reading a two-volume book called *The Chemistry of Powder and
Explosives* by Jenny L. Davis, which she'd taken out of the public library.

That week in March Leonard was back and forth from Harrisburg,
Pennsylvania, where he was leading secret strategy meetings with clients,
a group of antiwar Catholics led by Father Philip Berrigan. Berrigan was
a saint in Jean's eyes. He and his brother Daniel were household names as
the war-denouncing, church-defying Berrigan brothers who had first
gone to prison in 1968 for burning draft cards.

Leonard had inside information that FBI lawyers were planning to
indict Dan Berrigan for having thrown animal blood on draft files, and
that J. Edgar Hoover believed that Dan Berrigan was plotting to blow up
Washington, D.C., power lines and to kidnap presidential aide Henry
Kissinger.

As Jean headed out toward Klein's, at the nearby Wilkerson town house
Kathy, Terry Robbins, Cathlyn Wilkerson, Das Oughton, Russell Neufield, and Teddy Gold were waking up together. Terry Robbins had

screamed at the others until sunrise about wanting to make bombs with nails in them that killed people. "The government's using them in Vietnam, and people should know what it's like."

As Das Oughton followed Terry Robbins down into the Wilkerson basement that March morning, she looked nothing like a former debutante and Bryn Mawr graduate. At twenty-nine, her skin was opaque and gray-white; she wore broken wire-rimmed eyeglasses, and her hair was cut almost as short as that of a U.S. Marine. She hid her upper torso in a man's black leather jacket. A week earlier, she'd mailed her identification cards and passport home to her parents in Dwight, Illinois.

This morning, Terry was nervous about making his first antipersonnel bomb. He uncoiled and cut pieces of wire. He began to wrap hundreds of roofing nails around dozens of sticks of dynamite. Das hung back while Terry worked.

Upstairs in the parlor, Teddy Gold was making notes for a memoir about Weatherman, while on the third floor, Kathy and Cathlyn were talking about taking a sauna.

Teddy Gold left the house to go buy a book at the Strand bookstore.

About half a mile away, Jean stopped to select a bunch of daisies from a street vendor. At the Strand, she sold back Leonard's mystery books. Suddenly she spotted Teddy Gold entering the bookstore. She called, "Ted, Ted," and when he spun around, she ran to him and kissed him, scratching her chin on his black beard.

Teddy's voice cracked with fatigue and a cold. Jean asked him, "Do you think Kathy will pick herself up and go to NYU Law School in the fall?"

"No," he told her truthfully.

"Is she living in Manhattan?"

"Sort of." They glanced at each other tensely. Then Jean rolled her eyes and they both relaxed into ironic smiles at the inevitability of their generation gap.

All that morning lines concerning the next day's eclipse of the sun had been running through Jean's mind. She'd been doing research about it, primarily to amuse Leonard. The ancient Greeks, it seems, had believed a solar eclipse was auspicious—not surprisingly—and could signal the beginning or end of war. War! Tears suddenly stung Jean's eyes, and she blew her nose.

She hurried along to avoid the rain and couldn't get the phrase "apocalyptic weather" out of her mind. She'd been flipping through an essay by John Ruskin, who believed that bad behavior by people caused calamities such as a plague wind that sucked sunlight up into the sky.

Jean turned back toward St. Luke's Place.

Four blocks away, in the basement of the Wilkerson town house, Terry Robbins had finished constructing most of his first antipersonnel bomb. He crossed two wires. He short-circuited the bomb's timer.

The bomb exploded, hammering him and Das Oughton with nails, gruesomely dismembering them and splattering body parts all over the walls and ceiling. It also killed Ted Gold, who had just returned to the first-floor parlor after his brief trip to the Strand.

Jean was strolling on Fifth Avenue between Eleventh and Twelfth Streets when the terrible explosion caused her to freeze in her tracks, its aftermath rumbling up into her knees from the pavement. Traffic halted and pedestrians looked around wildly in fear and confusion. Car horns suddenly blared. All the solid old mansions on the north side of Eleventh Street between Fifth and Sixth Avenues seemed to shudder. Almost immediately, four fire trucks sped by.

From the end of the block, Jean saw flames erupt from the windows of a town house on West Eleventh Street. Soon smoke surrounded the collapsing town house. "It's got to be the boiler," Jean heard a man behind her say.

In front of the burning house, an FBI agent who had been part of the surveillance team keeping watch on the young radicals quickly snapped pictures of the house's crumpling brick Greek-revival façade. Since the buildings on the block were of significant design interest, he had been posing as an architectural historian.

After inhaling smoke for several minutes, Jean walked away from the crowd. Thoughts rushed fast and furiously through her mind. Thank God she'd recently replaced the boiler in their house. And then she told herself to stop worrying about the explosion, since anyone owning such an expensive piece of New York real estate could damn well afford to lose it.

Meanwhile, on the third floor inside the smoke-filled town house, Kathy was trying not to inhale. She spit out black cinders as she tripped over flaming debris. Since she had been relaxing in the cedar-lined sauna, she had no clothes on. Everywhere large chunks of debris crashed around her. Cathlyn Wilkerson was a few steps behind her. Kathy's eyes and nose were running. Every ounce of will she possessed was aimed at reaching the staircase in the front hall. Finally she staggered, still naked, out of the burning house and into the middle of Eleventh Street. Behind her, an incandescent red glow shined through the shattered windows.

Kathy's hair was tangled, her bare torso and legs scraped and bleeding, her face smeared and sooty. By her side, clutching her, was Cathlyn Wilkerson, clad only in a torn T-shirt.

Nearby the actor Dustin Hoffman chewed gum and stared in shocked silence at the fire. He had fled his apartment in the building next door holding two paintings and a Tiffany lamp. His desk had fallen through a huge hole in the wall. Another neighbor had abandoned his search for paintings stored in his flooded basement after he saw human body parts floating by. It would be a long time before Mel Gussow and his wife, who also lived next door, could speak of the explosion without breaking into tears. The few objects they managed to rescue from their apartment would always smell of smoke.

Another neighbor ran to Kathy and Cathlyn Wilkerson. Susan Hammerstein Wager, who had divorced the actor Henry Fonda years earlier, did not know either girl. Susan took her coat off and wrapped it around Kathy's body.

She and Cathlyn limped after their benefactor into her grand federal house at 50 Eleventh Street and followed her upstairs to a guest bathroom. Susan asked them, "Anybody else inside the house?"

Cathlyn Wilkerson answered slowly. "Yes, maybe two."

Their hostess brought the girls a pile of clothes. She went downstairs to make coffee.

A few minutes later, Jean smiled as she climbed her own front steps. A tangle of wisteria vines clung to the iron banister. She lugged her purchases up her curving interior stairwell. After arranging in a jar of cold water the daisies she had bought, Jean turned on her portable radio to find out more about the explosion.

Meanwhile, inside Susan Wager's house, Kathy washed and dried her face, leaving black streaks on a towel. She pulled a sweater over her head and stepped into brown corduroy pants.

With Cathlyn, she tiptoed downstairs. When the housekeeper asked,

Kathy replied that they were going to Bigelow's drugstore on Sixth Avenue for burn medicine.

Alternately limping and running, Kathy Boudin and Cathlyn Wilkerson used a pay telephone to ask friends about finding a hiding place. Connie Brown refused to give Kathy house keys. Connie was tired of outlaw games.

Kathy had no choice but to ring the doorbell at St. Luke's Place. The two young women bolted past Jean and up the curving stairwell. Jean asked why Kathy was wearing bedroom slippers. Kathy didn't answer. Jean raised her voice. "And where are your house keys? Tell me."

In the dining room, Kathy told her mother in a jumbled rush that her house keys were underneath burning debris in the wreckage of the house on Eleventh Street. Jean dialed the telephone. "Everything is fine," she told Leonard's secretary, speaking slowly and intensely. "Really fine. Please tell Leonard."

The parent of a male friend of Kathy's soon telephoned Jean. The woman had just spoken to Teddy Gold's frantic mother, and was herself very upset. Jean abandoned caution to assure her caller that Teddy had not in fact been one of those inside the house on Eleventh Street.

Later that night, Jean went back over her own sequence of thoughts, trying to remember her initial reaction to the burning brownstone. She recognized the hostility she'd felt toward its rich owners as part of the mysterious bridge between her own innermost angry feelings and her daughter's actions. Jean told herself, "There but for the grace of God go I."

As news of the explosion spread by press reports and word of mouth, Kathy was mentioned most frequently because of her high-profile father. The mental picture of Kathy Boudin crawling naked from a cauldron of death signified the anguishing end of something important to many young people who'd believed they could band together in a "movement" to change the world for the better.

Liz Bogen, Kathy's Bryn Mawr classmate, asked her years later, "I don't get it. You say you're not in favor of violence, but why are you so often on the scene of violence?"

As the news spread, many young people gave up on the idealism of the 1960s. The town house explosion broke their hearts. It was heartbreak that propelled more and more of them to desert the loosely organized civil rights and antiwar movements.

At 8 p.m. two FBI agents arrived at the Boudin home. Jean shooed her daughter and Cathlyn quietly upstairs. She harshly informed the two men that she was busy, then slammed the door.

The next day Jean was too distressed to go outside to look at the midday darkness of the solar eclipse. All Jean knew was that such preoccupations as abnormal weather and friendly chat with neighbors seemed an enormous luxury of the good life that she might never know again. When she finally did leave the house, she saw a sign in a store on Eighth Street: "Teddy Gold died for our sins."

Just before Kathy went to sleep for the last time in her bed at 12½ St. Luke's Place, Jean asked her, "Will I see you again?" Kathy answered, "Not sure."

The *New York Times* condemned Kathy in a long front-page article. Mayor John Lindsay said, "The use of explosives to tear down the system is self-defeating. It's cowardly. No democratic system can live that way. Society cannot permit it."

But in Washington, Kathy's uncle Izzy Stone wrote an eloquent defense of the young bombers. Stone's article, called "Where the Fuse on That Dynamite Leads," was published in his newsletter of March 23. Someone less rigidly devoted to a depersonalized life of ideas might have mentioned that one of the young "bombers" was his own niece.*

Across the country in Denver, David Gilbert was devastated to hear about the death of his best friend Teddy Gold. David had been on his way to the mountains for target practice. At first he believed "the pigs" had killed Teddy. He told Kathy by pay telephone that what he was

---

*Stone wrote:

The Weatherman kids can be seen as distraught children or spoiled brats in a tantrum with a world that will not change overnight. But they are the most sensitive of a generation which feels in its bones what we older people only grasp as an unreal abstraction, that the world is headed for nuclear annihilation and something must be done to stop it. . . . [They] spurn every normal base of revolutionary support and end up squarely in the clouds: the middle class is, of course, no good; the working class corrupted; the college generation determined to sell out; their only hope is the juvenile Robespierres of the high schools. It sounds like the Children's Crusade come back to life, a St. Vitus dance of hysterical politics.

experiencing was far and away the worst feeling of his life. "This is real," he said. "It's life and death; we're not just some college debating society."

Digging in the rubble, New York City firemen found a purse containing ID and credit cards belonging to Kathy Boudin. Rumors spread that Kathy was dead.

Meanwhile Kathy and Bernardine Dohrn started their own rumor that the mangled female torso in the wreckage was that of Pat Swinton, who was not part of the Weather group but was wanted for protest bombings. If the ruse had succeeded, Pat Swinton might have assumed a new identity and eluded police.

Four days after the explosion Kathy called Random House editor John Simon from a coffee shop near Columbia to cancel a lunch meeting.

Workmen digging in the rubble of the town house discovered fifty-seven sticks of unexploded dynamite, four twelve-inch pipes packed with explosives, and thirty blasting caps. When authorities revealed that the detonated bomb had been made with nails—and was thus a device designed to kill people—rumors darkened.

In the days following the explosion, Kathy rode the subway and saw her photograph and headlines on other people's newspapers. She later told an interviewer, "One of the amazing things was knowing how hard the authorities were searching for us and yet they weren't able to find us."

Both Kathy and Leonard relished the cops-and-robbers aspect of their assignations, which took place in coffee shops near Columbia University as well as in the Riverdale mansion of Kathy's former kindergarten teacher, Eleanor Brussel.

Hours before meeting his daughter, Leonard exited not one but two busy restaurants by the back door, in order to elude the FBI agents who were following him.

Leonard ordered his taxi driver to speed to the end of a street that dead-ended on Riverside Drive. There he instructed the driver to make a

---

It is from just such despair that terrorist movements have grown. . . . But these wild and wonderful—yes, wonderful!—kids also serve quite rational political ends.

I ran into an old friend on a Washington street corner the other day who is working hard in a respectable do-good reformist organization, the very kind the youthful radicals despise. I told him I had tried to talk the young people out of the typically American idea that revolution could be "instant" like coffee or iced tea.

"Don't discourage them," was his unexpected plea. "If they stop acting up, we'll never get the Establishment to budge."

fast U-turn in order to confuse any cars following him. This move was repeated several times.

A friend of Kathy's, standing sentry, waited in the doorway to the Brussel house in Riverdale. The sentry watched to make sure no one was following Leonard onto the quiet curving street.

Leonard loved Mrs. Brussel's stone house of twenty rooms, which she referred to as "a little gray cottage." Father and daughter settled tensely on the new back balcony off the kitchen, squinting down the precipitous hill past old trees and rocks to glints of light on the Hudson River.

Leonard begged Kathy to turn herself in immediately for questioning; authorities had promised him that they would not charge her with homicide or transporting explosives across state lines. He was startled by the vehemence of her refusal.

Kathy told him she was preparing to lead an utterly different life— "underground," cutting ties with friends and family in order to fight the state. She still believed she could help to ignite an uprising that would "destroy the system." She had no intention of turning herself in or appearing on March 16 in Chicago criminal court for indictments stemming from the Days of Rage. It was unfortunate but Leonard would forfeit her $10,000 bail. She spoke of the New York town house explosion as a solemn event in history. Leonard rationalized: she was in shock and not showing normal feelings of grief and repentance.

Kathy's decision to hide from the law—and more important, from Leonard himself—forced Leonard to pursue her. She infuriated him by keeping him waiting for hours at designated pay telephones. He was also dismayed because she was endangering his reputation for reverence for the law. Henceforth his public statements were frequently about her and, despite his private fury, he told reporters and acquaintances that as a father he supported her with every fiber of his being.

One morning, Leonard was horrified as he walked past the window of the post office in the lobby of the Harrisburg Federal Courthouse. Taped across a wall were posters announcing in big black letters: WANTED BY THE FBI. There, among the depraved visages of bank robbers with bad teeth, murderers, and escaped rapists was his own precious daughter—her first name misspelled "Kathie."

J. Edgar Hoover had had the "limited edition" poster placed there to threaten Leonard. It displayed three photographs of Kathy taken after her arrest at the Days of Rage. In one of the pictures she looked puzzled, as if focusing on an elusive point somewhere in her own brain.

Kathy Boudin's wanted poster, issued by J. Edgar Hoover, May 1, 1970.

The poster was a death threat; it raised the possibility that Kathy could be shot on sight by a law enforcement official.

The poster also frightened Leonard about the day's work. He was defending Philip Berrigan and his fellow radical Catholics before a jury of ordinary people in Harrisburg. Leonard was not accustomed to dealing with juries; he won his cases by impressing appellate judges with arcane points of law and philosophic entreaties. His daughter's notoriety would surely prejudice jurors against him.

Kathy's wanted poster was also an example of one of Hoover's favorite ploys: inflating the villainous stature of his enemy. It was good for budget requests; it was good for his legend.

Michael Boudin viewed his sister's newspaper headlines for the bombing as disastrous. Whenever he entered a room or an elevator in the United

States or in Great Britain, whispers announced his connection to the famous fugitive. He wondered if Kathy was disturbed and was deliberately trying to ruin his life.

By now, Michael was a small ambling man with long strands of hair combed across his head and a predilection toward rumpled suits. When he started to speak, however, he was lit by his hawklike intelligence. His career was soaring at Covington and Burling, the Washington law firm.

Michael was also fast becoming a fixture at Washington dinner parties. He had a reputation as the perfect extra man. No one knew him well. Indeed, few suspected he was Jewish. His delight at asking questions and his ability to listen meant he excelled at drawing out the women seated on either side of him.

Hugh Cox, Michael's mentor, was slowly becoming his close friend. Since Michael found courtroom histrionics "a cold bath," Hugh Cox encouraged him to spend his time writing and researching briefs. Michael was relieved not to deal with clients. It was Michael's thin skin and feeling of intellectual superiority that made him prefer law books to most people.

Michael was at home in Covington's library of statutes and regulatory law—better than any in the U.S. government. He teamed with Hugh Cox to write successful briefs in support of AT&T's battles against government trust-busting.*

Jean knew Michael's dream was the Supreme Court. "All your genius son needs is a conservative president," said Bert Gross again and again. Jean forced herself to smile.

Kathy was apoplectic: Michael was using his "Harvard-educated brain" to get tax breaks and laws passed to make rich clients richer. The firm partners litigated against government agencies like the FDA to keep potentially dangerous pesticides and drugs on the market.

Kathy alarmed Leonard by disappearing without notice from the New York area three weeks after the Wilkerson town house explosion. Jean's friends whispered that Leonard had probably whisked Kathy abroad—just as they believed he had once helped Judith Coplon travel to Mexico.

But in fact Kathy had driven cross-country with Cathlyn Wilkerson to attend a Weather summit meeting. In Mendocino, California, they joined Bernardine Dohrn, John Jacobs (J.J.), Bill Ayers, Jeff Jones, Mark Rudd,

*Covington represented Du Pont, General Motors, CBS, the railroads, and commercial airlines.

and Howie Machtinger in a luxurious house with walls of glass facing the sea. The house was loaned to them by a supporter.

Kathy was flattered to be invited to the summit meeting, even though Bernardine said that Kathy and Cathlyn were invited only because of their fame resulting from the town house explosion. But more crucially, Bernardine assumed that the two women would support her struggle against J.J., her ex-lover, for leadership.

Bernardine denounced their dead comrade Terry Robbins for his suicidal obsession with bombing. She called him "the mad bomber" of the group, despite the fact that Weatherman members in other cities had been making bombs, too. J.J. fought back. He wanted to escalate armed warfare against the U.S. government. (It was the "heavy" position—intimidating and impressive.) After long self-criticism sessions and fights into the night, Kathy and the other shattered young people came around to Bernardine's position, calling the explosion "a military error."

J.J. was in a tailspin. The young man who had done the most to create Weather intellectually and spiritually was denounced by his former lover. Finally, Bernardine dramatically expelled J.J. from the group. He soon moved to Vancouver, Canada, where he did factory work and sold drugs.

Bernardine had accomplished her goal and, with Kathy and the others, she pledged in a public statement printed in underground newspapers to perform "only symbolic violence" to goad the government. She extolled the three dead Weathermen as "heroic."

That autumn Kathy Boudin and David Gilbert hid out in communal houses—donated by supporters—in the Bay Area and also across the country on farms and in woods in the north Catskills and Adirondacks. Bernardine received money from admiring supporters like actor Jon Voight. Kathy visited Bernardine frequently and the two women were in constant touch by designated pay telephones. Bernardine and Bill Ayers and Jeff Jones lived stylishly for a time on Voigt's houseboat near San Francisco.

It was, they decided, "a hippie period." Kathy joked that Weatherman should change their name to "Eggplant," in acknowledgment of their hippie domesticity—planting vegetables, baking bread and quilting.

Kathy drank wine, smoked hash, and dropped tabs of LSD while lying naked in a grassy meadow, a cherished form of escape. Voices were frequently raised in fights over their mission. They agreed only on the failure of the American dream.

Being underground meant many things to Kathy. It meant shedding a name and identity that had been hers for twenty-seven years. Identity was a recurring crisis. Who were they anyway? The answer depended on who they asked. Heroes. Criminals. Spoiled brats. Phonies. Adventurists. Media stars. The practical problems of "eluding the pigs" kept them busy. Standing next to cops and trading pleasantries with them gave Kathy and David a rush.

Kathy became expert at aliases. She researched old newspapers in local libraries for obituaries of infants who had died at birth. She and the others applied for birth certificates using the babies' names, though Kathy once appropriated the name of a black infant before realizing her error.

They obtained fake passports by using fishing licenses and fake birth certificates, and with the claim that a parent was sick or dying outside the country. It was exciting. They called it an example of "white skin privilege."

On May 21, Kathy and the others produced a "communiqué" from "underground" about a new policy, which they called "strategic sabotage." The communiqué was decorated with the Weather insignia: a hand-drawn red, blue, and green rainbow pierced by a red lightning bolt. It announced that Weatherman had decided to apply the teachings of Che Guevara, the Tupamaros (the urban guerrilla movement in Uruguay), and the Vietcong to tactics in the United States.

The text was confusing: it seemed to be affirming ties to Black Panthers; in fact, Kathy and her friends were backing away from them. In its obfuscation, it mimicked the very establishment politicians Kathy reviled.

The communiqué also delivered a threat: in two weeks a symbol of American injustice would become targeted. Attacking it would protest against the U.S. bombing in Cambodia and the May 14 killings of four students at Kent State by the Ohio National Guard.

When the two-week deadline for an act of symbolic violence came and went with no incident, Jean Boudin was weepy with relief.

Suddenly, two days later, the entire country was shocked when members of Kathy's group walked ten sticks of dynamite into the heavily guarded Manhattan police headquarters and left them on the second floor. The explosion injured seven people and caused damage of several hundred thousand dollars. Policemen throughout the country were devastated and angry.

The Weathermen instantly issued another press release—"a commu-

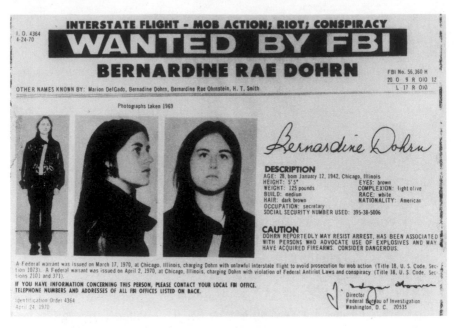

Bernardine Dohrn's wanted poster, issued April 24, 1970, marking her one of Hoover's ten most wanted fugitives. The FBI said that Bernardine called herself a communist revolutionary who advocates widespread terrorist bombings.

niqué" with the trademark rainbow pierced by the thick red lightning bolt. This time it was boastful: "The pigs try to look invulnerable, but we keep finding their weaknesses. . . . They look for us. We get to them first."

It was a high point in Weather public relations. A hundred or more sympathizers rallied to form the Weather support network. William Kunstler, John Simon, Bernardine's sister Jennifer Dohrn, author Marge Piercy, and Drs. Charlotte and Ollie Fein—now living in Brooklyn— were among many who offered food, money, escape routes, and hideouts.

Weather supporters immodestly compared themselves to Underground Railway people, who had provided safe houses for slaves escaping to Canada and freedom. The Weather hero continued to be abolitionist and religious fanatic John Brown.

Kathy rarely slept three nights in the same place. She became accustomed to looking over her shoulder and staying on buses and subways past whatever stop she was headed for to elude "the pigs." It took her three times longer to go anywhere.

Throughout the 1970s, Kathy's group would take credit for more than twenty acts of highly public "revolutionary violence." The only casualties were their own comrades Das Oughton, Teddy Gold, and Terry Robbins. Kathy took part in fewer than half of the actions, but even when she was not directly involved, she was among those choosing the targets for their symbolic value. She also helped to draft press releases.

Kathy drove to Chicago in 1970 to help plant a bomb that again exploded the Haymarket statue in Chicago to commemorate the Days of Rage.

Kathy soon wandered to Los Angeles, where she used several aliases. She was Janet Patricia Scott when purchasing a ten-year-old station wagon. She and David Gilbert headed up to San Francisco where David's alias was Thomas Larsen. Slouched in a torn easy chair in a San Francisco "safe house," David described fights between himself and Kathy in abstract political terms. He predicted that after the race war and the class struggle would come the big conflict between men and women.

Dealing with terrors about Kathy's day-to-day safety and the romance of her new role drew Leonard and Jean together. Bert Gross bluntly told Jean, "Kathy has saved your marriage."

Leonard cajoled and flattered Kathy and insisted on knowing her exact whereabouts. When friends asked, he assured them, "Although I don't know precisely where she is, I know she is okay."

Jean, however, chose to act as if her daughter had utterly disappeared from her life. She was horrified by a friend who theorized that Kathy was underground to keep a safe distance from her powerful and seductive father. As the bereaved mother of a famous fugitive, Jean was accorded great sympathy by friends and new acquaintances. It was as if Kathy's strange and unexpected fame, particularly in underground newspapers, allowed Jean to accept attention and comfort for other unrelated sadnesses.

Jean romanticized her situation, telling a young poet that a man she knew from dinner parties had knocked on her door and asked for Kathy's heavy winter coat. When she pressed him, she claimed he told her, "I'll give the coat to someone, who'll give the coat to someone on a street corner, and that person would finally give it to your daughter."

The FBI circulated an interoffice memo explaining that Weather members trusted no one except their own parents. In this, the Bureau had it

Kathy and her group presented themselves as "anonymous criminals for hire" to break Timothy Leary out of prison. The ex–Harvard professor preached that the drug LSD was a means to get closer to God.

right: despite her rage and competitiveness, Kathy knew Leonard and Jean would do everything they could to keep her from harm.

Kathy's next caper involved a prison break. The former Harvard instructor and youth culture guru Timothy Leary was in San Luis Obispo prison in northern California. He had been convicted of possessing a small amount of marijuana. A patrician-looking man with long white hair, Leary had popularized the motto "turn on, tune in, drop out" after discovering the giddy thrills of LSD and other psychedelic drugs while teaching at Harvard in the 1960s.

In an era marked by rule-averse extroverts intent upon forging new ways of living, few were more deft at exploiting the media than forty-nine-year-old Leary. He'd run for governor of California against "that minor and not terribly bright movie actor Ronald Reagan." Leary's campaign slogan, "Come Together," became the inspiration for his friend John Lennon's song "Come Together."

From inside prison, Timothy Leary now offered $25,000 to any group that broke him out. San Luis Obispo was a minimum-security facility surrounded by a fifteen-foot barbed-wire fence. Leary described it as "the final home for old, beaten, and burned-out lifers." Kathy was alerted most likely to Leary's proposal by Michael Standard, her father's partner and her former boyfriend. Standard was Leary's lawyer.

Soon the Weather group presented themselves to Leary's wife, Rosemary, as "trained criminals." They bragged of their friends in Third World countries like Cuba where Leary could get political asylum.

It is unlikely that in the history of the U.S. penal system, so much educated brainpower had been deployed to mastermind a jailbreak.

Following their orders, Leary waited impatiently for a "dark, cloudy Saturday night."

Finally, on September 12, he put on sneakers he'd painted black, skipped dinner, climbed a tree, and crept along a roof, sweating and gasping for breath. He scrambled down the fifteen-foot wire fence, his sneakers becoming entangled in telephone wire.

A car approached and the door swung open. From inside, two women, one of whom may have been Kathy, handed Leary civilian clothes and false ID papers. The girls slowed in front of a gas station in nearby Morro Bay, where an attendant waved—a signal meaning no police radio alarm had yet been issued.

This was the first of four vehicles involved in Leary's jailbreak. The next was a camper that took him to Oakland; the third was a car that threw police off his track by carrying his prison clothes south, the opposite direction from which he was headed, and dropping them off at a gas station rest room near Los Angeles to throw police off his track. A fourth car monitored police calls on a shortwave radio.

A girl dyed Leary's white hair brown in a car parked on a beach. He looked like a balding businessman. A bumper sticker provided impudent camouflage: AMERICA LOVE IT OR LEAVE IT.

Leary was driven to a safe house outside Seattle, where a candlelit victory celebration included champagne, incense, and homemade bread.

Kathy and her friends soon issued a press release to newspaper editors around the country taking credit for Leary's daring escape. The "communiqué" emphasized youth culture over international revolution, proclaiming that "LSD and grass, like the herbs, cactus and mushrooms of the American Indians and countless civilizations that existed on this planet, will help us make a future world where it will be possible to live in peace."

On the third night of his freedom, Bernardine and Kathy proudly waved newspapers at their new companion, the headlines trumpeting:

"Weathermen Help Leary Prison Escape." It was fun to laugh at J. Edgar Hoover's vow to recapture Leary in ten days.

Their plan was to get Leary to Algeria, but first they counterfeited out-of-state ID cards for him, which he used to procure a Washington State driver's license. (Pictures were not required in that state.) With this document in hand, he flew to Chicago, applied for a passport, and left the country with his wife.

Kathy and David were still crashing off and on in the house they had once taken Leary to on Pine Street in San Francisco. They were not in residence, however, a year later when Leary guided FBI agents to the door.

It became necessary to rationalize the fact that Leary informed on Kathy and her group. Springing anybody from jail was the right thing to do, Kathy told her mother, and, like him or not, Leary had been framed. And if truth be told, the jailbreak had been fun. Furthermore, he had been "his best self" when he risked his life to get out of jail—identifying with revolutionary forces of the world.

Kathy traveled to Manhattan to meet Bill Ayers, Bernardine, Cathy Wilkerson, and Judith Clark in Greenwich Village. They dropped acid and took a subway uptown to catch the Beatles movie *Yellow Submarine*.

As they arrived, flying on acid, the fugitive warriors routinely checked exits. Relaxing, they slid deep in their seats, letting the merry sound track fill their ears.

Suddenly, a man tapped Judith Clark on the shoulder. "Excuse me, could you step into the lobby?" He was an FBI agent who had accidentally recognized her—though not her friends—a few minutes earlier on the subway. One glance told Kathy that he was a "shoe" (their nickname for FBI agents who wore clunky shoes).

Kathy ran toward the closest exit, but once she caught sight of twenty FBI agents in the lobby, she slowed and walked past them unnoticed. (At some point during this period, to disguise herself, she'd had aesthetic surgery that included bobbing her nose.) The next morning Kathy learned that Judith had been captured while trying to swallow pages of her address book. Clark served 180 days in jail in Chicago—for vandalism during the Days of Rage—and afterward she was deemed too risky for Kathy and Bernardine to associate with, since she could be monitored too easily by the FBI.

Angela Davis, Kathy Boudin's high-school classmate, was the vice presidential candidate of the Communist Party in 1980 and 1984. In 1970, she'd purchased guns used by Jonathan Jackson in an aborted attempt to break his brother George Jackson (namesake of Chesa Jackson Boudin) out of Marin County courthouse. She is now a tenured professor at the University of California at Santa Cruz.

Kathy and David decided to stay on the West Coast, no longer believing in the anonymity of Manhattan streets. Besides Judith Clark, Kathy's old high-school classmate Angela Davis, also a fugitive, had been apprehended in New York after taking part in helping two Black Panthers on trial for their lives to escape from a Marin County court. The trial judge and four other people had been killed, including Jonathan Jackson.

In Los Angeles, Kathy and David tried to look like any other young couple. Nonetheless they frequently broke up. Their fights usually erupted about abstractions such as the causes of European colonialism in Africa.

Food was frequently shoplifted, and Kathy liked nothing better than to roll down the windows of her car and floor the gas pedal when on highways and freeways. Some members of the group tried their hand at holding up convenience stores. These risks brought their special high, and as time passed Kathy was becoming addicted to the sensations of danger they aroused.

Once as she was driving an old Plymouth eighty miles an hour on a freeway in Los Angeles, a policeman pulled her over. He fingered her "Kay Kennedy" ID cards. Scenarios involving wildly precarious escapes flashed through her mind. She could barely contain her terror and excitement as he wrote out a speeding ticket. When local police went looking for the address on the driver's license—1423 Cabrillo Street in Los Angeles—it did not exist.

A month later, Kathy was again stopped for exceeding the speed limit. Her adrenaline pumped. This time she gave the California Highway Patrol officer a card that identified her as Patricia Scott. When police traced the car, they discovered it had been sold to a junkyard.

Kathy started and broke off a sexual relationship with a woman in Los Angeles. Together they'd tended a vegetable garden and kept house.

In her fugitive life, whenever she met someone new, Kathy started with a small lie about who she was. Then she built bigger lies, raising self-involvement to an art form. The lies both protected her and gave her the upper hand in the relationship, enabling her to probe another person's psyche without revealing herself. She wrote a poem: "For a Friend Who Didn't Know Who I Was."

Her underground life substituted crisis for a career. While attention to the details of her deceptions did not fill her days, the most banal activities, such as taking her dirty clothes to the Laundromat, became romantically heightened because she had to be vigilant to avoid real danger. Agents had questioned the man who owned the little candy store across the street from her old friend Jennie Simon's house in San Francisco.

Kathy memorized a list of numbers of public telephones and scheduled times to call Bernardine, David, her parents, and other members of her support network. Knowing this, federal agents trailed Weather supporters like Jennifer Dohrn and Lewis Cole, hoping to be able to slap an illegal tap on a pay phone. Yet despite such efforts, the FBI never arrested Kathy.

Sightings of her in the flesh were reported on college campuses. Paul Mattick, her old friend from college days, fantasized that he'd bump into her, take her back to his Cambridge apartment for a good meal, convince her to stop bombing and to live with him.

14

CHANGING THE WORLD

We intend to change the world.

—anonymous Weather member

On January 19, 1971, Leonard exuded prideful prosperity and well-being as he wheeled his luggage in a metal cart toward customs at Logan Airport in Boston. He had just stepped off flight number 751 from London. While the customs official examined his passport, Leonard announced grandly, "I am the lawyer for the revolutionary government of Cuba. My destination is my office at Harvard Law School."

The customs agents exchanged glances, as if to say, "Who is this guy?" Leonard's braggadocio was duly noted by a lurking FBI agent.

In Cambridge for one semester, Leonard and Jean were renting two floors of a charming old house at 26 Gray Street from a Harvard professor on leave. Mornings Leonard bicycled off to his office at the law school, tailed by a slow car containing two FBI agents.

Jean, too, was under twenty-four-hour surveillance. The FBI was hoping that one of Kathy's parents would lead them to her. Crackling static made it clear that the Boudin telephone was wiretapped.

Leonard routinely escaped his FBI tail (parked in the street outside his law office) by wheeling his bicycle down into the labyrinthian basement passageways linking buildings of the law school. He would bicycle underground for a quarter of a mile, then emerge in the street in front of another building, unseen by the FBI agents.

Leonard pedaled his bicycle up one-way streets against traffic. He steered into alleys where he was forced to dodge trash cans, stopping at a popular student restaurant near Brattle Street where he stood impatiently by the pay telephone awaiting his daughter's coded call that sent him on to yet another pay phone and then to her side.

Leonard dispensed imaginative legal stratagems in order to stay in Kathy's good graces, thus empowering Kathy to function as a valued lawyer for her fugitive friends. He helped brainstorm targets for protest bombs, and his rationale for his questionable judgment was his desire to stay close to his daughter. Kathy understood that her father was living vicariously through her high-risk escapades.

After these elating encounters, Leonard doubled back to the pathways under the law school, wheeled his bike into his office, and returned to his law books. Hours later, Leonard took his bicycle back out to the curb under the gaze of bored FBI agents in an unmarked car. They trailed him home to Gray Street.

If his daughter made Leonard's life an adventure, his respectable son, Michael, did not. Leonard was smarting from an incident in the airport in Miami after he and Michael returned from a trip to Cuba. Asked to submit to a body search, Michael agreed. He injured his knee during the search and was unable to ride his horse or take flying lessons for several months.

It was inglorious—at least as far as Leonard was concerned—and he preferred telling friends that Michael had put up a righteous fight, challenging customs officials on probable cause.

Jean was enjoying her Cambridge life. At Harvard ("no less") she was taking courses in prosody and natural science with the biologist George Wald, for whom she anesthetized and dissected a large rat. She invited friends to look through her microscope at a leaf that "sucks up water like a pig."

Overgrown lilacs dominated the lawn parties that Jean orchestrated

ABOVE: *I. F. "Izzy" Stone, brother-in-law of Leonard, teaches Leonard's class at Harvard, 1971.*
BELOW: *Dr. Benjamin Spock speaks to Leonard's class in constitutional law at Harvard, 1971.*

for Leonard behind the Gray Street house; Jean's niece Celia Stone Gilbert was a frequent cohostess. Celia's husband, Wally, sat in an auspicious corner. Leonard told scintillating stories and avoided Celia, "way too bossy," and Wally, "way too condescending."

The rift between Kathy and Jean was widening. It galled Kathy, on the occasions that she permitted Jean to see her, to hear tales of garden parties with "our Celia, the famous younger poet." According to Jean, James Watson and some MIT scientists said that Celia's husband, Wally, was "scary smart," "a damn genius," and "one of a handful of the country's top scientists."

It seemed to Kathy that everyone in the Boudin family had "Harvard-approved" stamped on their foreheads, except, of course, Kathy herself.

Kathy was also vexed when Jean told her that Leonard was advising a new "mystery client." Elaborating, Jean told her daughter that the new client was preparing to risk imprisonment for releasing top-secret Pentagon files that documented Presidents Kennedy and Johnson's lies to the public about the high costs and defeats suffered in waging the Vietnam War.

It was almost more than Kathy could bear, and she shouted her mother down. How could Jean be so stupid as not to understand that it was Kathy and her radical comrades who were going to end the U.S. government's illegal, undeclared war against the Vietnamese independence movement, not some establishment Harvard man who'd been a warmonger?

If Leonard had come within a hairsbreadth of forcing FBI director J. Edgar Hoover out of his job with embarrassing revelations of FBI misconduct in 1950 in the Judith Coplon case, he was currently poised to prevail as the lawyer guiding clients in two highly aggressive actions that would "dynamite the thrones" of both FBI director Hoover and President Richard Nixon.

In addition to being the critical player supporting Daniel Ellsberg, the "mystery man" now determined to stop the Vietnam War with one mighty and illegal public act, Leonard was also secretly advising another group of clients with a similarly desperate agenda.

The other group of clients were twenty antiwar intellectuals who were meticulously plotting to burglarize a small FBI office in Media, Pennsylvania. Their quarry: a thousand secret files detailing superaggressive FBI counterintelligence (COINTELPRO) activities against both blacks and

Leonard and his client Daniel Ellsberg, Pentagon Papers Defense Office, Los Angeles courthouse, April 17, 1973. Note unframed photograph of Paul Robeson on the wall.

antiwar students. Leonard's clients suspected that FBI agents had engaged in hundreds of illegal entries ("bag jobs"), burglarizing and bugging countless offices and homes of people they deemed to be enemies of the government. Moreover, some FBI agents who'd succeeded in infiltrating radical groups encouraged the radicals in self-destructive policies such as the purchase and use of explosives. And if the agents saw ways to foment dissension in the ranks, so much the better.

Since Leonard's clients were desperate to obtain proof of such illicit FBI activities, they formed a secret action group called the Citizens' Commission to Investigate the FBI. The group included Kathy's old friend, Professor Bill Davidon of Haverford College.

On March 9, 1971, they broke into the FBI office in Media, Pennsylvania. There was no alarm system, and conveniently, the incriminating COINTELPRO files were stacked in an open safe.

The theft went off without a hitch.

Meanwhile, Leonard had helped to provide his clients with stratagems as to how best to release the shocking files to newspapers. He made sure that they broke as few laws as possible. For example, they photocopied pilfered documents and took them to friends around the country. The friends, who then mailed documents to newspapers, were unaware of the contents, as per Leonard's advice. By the end of March 1971, shocking proof of illicit COINTELPRO activities would appear in newspapers such as the *Washington Post* and the *New York Times*.

And surprisingly, despite intensive FBI efforts, not one member of the secret group was ever caught. This is due in no small measure to Leonard's charting of their course.

The Media, Pennsylvania, robbery and revelations were a fatal humiliation to the aging and ailing director Hoover. Leonard and his secret clients had crippled the most powerful bureaucrat in U.S. government history. President Nixon declared that his FBI director "had lost it." Nixon began to plan incursions onto Hoover's turf that would involve instigating a highly illegal operation working behind the scenes in the Executive Offices. Thus the Plumbers came into being, and it is possible to cast Leonard Boudin as one of its inadvertent godfathers.

The story of the purloining and release of the Pentagon Papers is much more part of the public record than the Media, Pennsylvania, caper. This is due in no small part to the flamboyance of Daniel Ellsberg.

Over a period of nine months—from September 1967 to March 1968—Ellsberg had sneaked thousands of pages of the pessimistic government study of the Vietnam War out of the RAND Corporation offices in Santa Monica. Ellsberg's colleague at RAND, Anthony Russo, and Ellsberg's two young children helped to photocopy it. Police burst in twice when Ellsberg inadvertently tripped the burglar alarm, but they were easily persuaded that nothing was amiss.

Leonard and Jean had first met forty-year-old Daniel Ellsberg in early spring 1970. Daniel was in superb physical condition. He was a skinny, almost beautiful man—with curly hair and pale hypnotic blue eyes like Leonard. Indeed, he and Leonard were similar: two men who loved righteous battle and insisted on winning. They were restless souls who seemed to be perpetually preening in the gazes of mothers, long deceased. (Coincidentally, both those mothers, Clara Boudin and Adele Ellsberg, were Jews who had become converts to Christian Science. And both had failed to mold their sons into world-class piano prodigies.)

That first evening, the two Boudins and Daniel Ellsberg strolled out to dinner in the Village. Leonard flirted with Ellsberg's likable fiancée,

Patricia Marx, one of the heirs to the Marx toy fortune. Ellsberg needed a good lawyer and Izzy Stone had advised him to speak to Leonard, the expert at using the law to fight government tyranny.

At dinner, Daniel and Leonard sized each other up amid a flurry of wit and classy bonhomie. Uncharacteristically, Daniel and Leonard did not initially fight for the spotlight. Instead, Daniel began by asking Leonard tactful, concerned questions about the older man's pacemaker.

Ellsberg informed Leonard that he had in his possession a stolen and incriminating top-secret "McNamara Study." Knowing what he knew, Ellsberg believed it was his job to "make the study public and stop the Vietnam War." He said he simply had no other choice.

That night Ellsberg's histrionics—he cried as he spoke of witnessing attrocities inflicted on children in Vietnam—unnerved Leonard, as did the younger man's allusions to psychiatrists and recreational drug use.

Explaining to Leonard that he had gone to Vietnam in late 1966, a rabid hawk, while working at RAND, a nonprofit think tank that did studies for the Pentagon, Ellsberg failed to mention that he had enthusiastically played soldier, even attempted to "neutralize" a group of Vietcong with a hand grenade.

But by the evening he met Leonard, Ellsberg was a righteous dove, a conversion based in no small part on the influence of his fiancée, Pat Marx. He dramatically quoted secret documents about U.S. government readiness to deploy atomic bombs.

"It's a First Amendment issue," Leonard said. "The people have a right to know."

After that dinner in Greenwich Village, Ellsberg decided not to choose Leonard as his lawyer. Shrewdly, he worried about Leonard's health and his lack of trial experience. The Spock and Berrigan trials, while famous victories, were thus far the only experiences Leonard had had in facing a jury.

But as soon as Ellsberg told other lawyers about his desire to release purloined, top-secret government documents, they ushered him to the door. Most recently James Vorenberg, a professor at Harvard Law School, had abruptly terminated a meeting, explaining that he did not want to help to plan a crime or be an accomplice in treason.

Six months later Ellsberg appeared at Leonard's house in Cambridge carrying a cardboard box full of documents. Seated in the basement office, Leonard felt the tug of history. "I am not a martyr, I am not as brave as you," he told Ellsberg, "but I will take your case."

He cautioned Ellsberg that released documents must not contain "current military secrets or secret codes and any other information that endangered national security."

It was a serious matter for Leonard to advise a client about how to break the law. Aware of his exposure, Leonard cagily opted to stay in the background—until such time as Ellsberg might be arrested or questioned by the FBI. Daniel Ellsberg declared his willingness to go to prison. Leonard dryly assured him, "I'll protect you from your inner martyr."

Soon after consulting Leonard, Ellsberg deposited heavy boxes of documents with Neil Sheehan at the *New York Times*. Ellsberg had decided against working on a book with David Halberstam, who seemed inclined to cite Ellsberg as a source and not a coauthor. Ellsberg extracted the promise from Sheehan that if the *Times* published the papers, Daniel himself would make final decisions about the time of release and the editing of the contents. Both Ellsberg and Leonard were surprised and upset when, without consulting Daniel, the newspaper printed the first installment of the Pentagon Papers on Sunday, June 13, 1971.

It was, pronounced the nation's elite opinion makers, the most serious leak of government secrets during a war—albeit an undeclared war—in the entire history of the United States. When Ellsberg asked Leonard about whether he would go to jail if his theft became public, Leonard said, "There's a fifty-fifty chance. Somehow stealing government secrets and releasing them to the *New York Times* doesn't have a good ring to it."

Time and *Newsweek* reporters asked Daniel if he had been the *New York Times*'s source. Rumors raged. But on Leonard's advice, Daniel said only, "I'm glad it's out. I'm flattered to be suspected of having leaked it."

Meanwhile the entire country was stunned by what they were reading. The Pentagon Papers were arguably the last straw in public outrage and hysteria against the U.S. government's involvement in the Vietnam War.

Kathy continued to act superior when Leonard and she met, but she understood that she and her revolutionary friends were being left in the dust.

Meanwhile the *Times* was precipitously forced to halt the publication of the second installment of the papers; the Justice Department gained a federal injunction against the newspaper.

It was a real First Amendment crisis, a favorite of Leonard's. And now that the *New York Times* had been silenced, Leonard was confident other newspapers could be persuaded to rise to the occasion.

For the next two days, Daniel Ellsberg, with Leonard at his side, told FBI agents that he was not the person who stole the documents. Then, on June 17, a hot and dismal Thursday morning, two federal agents rang and rang Ellsberg's doorbell in Cambridge. To no avail—the apartment was empty.

Daniel and Patricia had gone "underground" as per Leonard's counsel. Hiding in a nearby un-air-conditioned motel, Daniel was beginning to clash with his lawyer about minor tactical details and timing.

Local antiwar intellectuals, such as MIT linguist Noam Chomsky, hid Daniel and Patricia from the FBI in a series of Cambridge homes. Leonard's experience with Kathy came in handy. He and Ellsberg used pay telephones and code names such as "Mr. Boston," as well as the law school's underground passageways, to stay in touch.

Leonard never satisfactorily dissuaded friends who asked if Daniel Ellsberg had been pedaling the exercise bike in the basement office of the Boudins' rented Cambridge home while the FBI combed the country for him.

Ellsberg invited a writer from the *Washington Post* to pick up heavy boxes of papers to continue publishing the papers. On Leonard's legal advice and in his presence, Ellsberg also ordered the *Post* to deliver a copy to Congress—thus making them public information.

After publishing one section on Friday, June 18, the *Washington Post* was also enjoined by the federal government.

To keep the momentum going, on Monday morning, June 21, again employing the code name "Mr. Boston" and several pay telephones, Daniel Ellsberg passed another section of the papers dealing with the Kennedy administration to the *Boston Globe*. The *Globe* published stories based on the documents on June 22, despite a threatening phone call from Attorney General John Mitchell.

The government quickly moved to stop the *Globe*. But in quick succession, the *Chicago Sun-Times* and the *St. Louis Dispatch* published excerpts of the document.

J. Edgar Hoover ordered a national FBI dragnet for Daniel Ellsberg. But Leonard humiliated his old foe yet again. He set up a television interview with fugitive Ellsberg from "underground." Ellsberg admitted his actions to venerable news broadcaster Walter Cronkite. Daniel soon appeared "from the underground" on the cover of *Time* magazine. This, Leonard decided, was the perfect time for Daniel Ellsberg to surrender to authorities.

Negotiations with the U.S. Attorney's Office about Ellsberg's surrender took place on Leonard's home telephone. After Leonard's telephone line went dead, he said, "I think the line is tapped." The FBI agent was silent. "You think so?" the agent asked at last.

Leonard concocted a ruse that guaranteed Daniel's surrender appear to be what it was—voluntary. Leonard knew how much Hoover needed the fugitive to be photographed as if he had been captured—wrestled to the ground and then handcuffed.

On June 28, the day of Ellsberg's surrender, Leonard drove a "decoy Ellsberg" to the federal courthouse. As soon as Leonard was recognized, press members rushed at him.

Meanwhile Daniel and Patricia arrived quietly with another attorney in the parking lot; they walked calmly through the front door to the U.S. Attorney's Office, where Leonard soon joined them. Daniel was photographed, fingerprinted, and released on $50,000 bail. The record shows "scar to the left of the left eyebrow" from the car accident that killed his mother when Dan was fifteen.

That same day, a Los Angeles federal grand jury indicted Ellsberg for unauthorized possession of documents and writings related to the national defense (a violation of the Espionage Act) as well as theft of the documents. The maximum sentence for each of the two counts was ten years in prison.

President Nixon was sorely vexed. One person to bear the brunt of his wrath was J. Edgar Hoover. First, asked Nixon, why had the FBI failed so miserably at hunting down Ellsberg and his fellow conspirators? And why was the FBI still so clueless about who had stolen those damaging COINTELPRO records from the Media field office. *Time* magazine called for Hoover's retirement. One out of two Americans, according to a poll, felt he was dishonest. President Nixon declared that Hoover was too old and sick to fight Nixon's enemies who, in Nixon's mind, were also enemies of the country.

Nixon told aides that indicting Ellsberg as a traitor was not revenge enough. Nothing less than destroying "that thief" and his coconspirators would do. "I have a feeling we have a hell of an opportunity here," Nixon told Bob Haldeman, "to leak out all these nasty stories [in the press] that'll kill these bastards."

With this goal fixed before him, Nixon went too far. He signed off on the creation of a "dirty tricks" unit that would report directly to the White House. He decided to hire his own ruthless operatives—far more

E. Howard Hunt, convicted Watergate burglar, September 1973. Leonard Boudin's courtroom revelation of Hunt's break-in to the office of his client Daniel Ellsberg's psychiatrist weakened the Nixon presidency.

willing to break laws than the FBI. The operatives were code-named "the Plumbers' unit," since their job was to fix security leaks.

Initially Nixon wanted the Plumbers' hatchet man to report directly to the Oval Office. That way, the president could call him in the middle of the night if necessary. "I want," said Nixon, someone "willing to play cops and robbers games . . . that's as tough as I am, for a change. I can't have a high-minded lawyer like John Ehrlichman [who is] above some crap."

E. Howard Hunt was, according to one friend, "a regular right-wing nut." The retired CIA agent was Nixon's first choice to head the dirty tricks unit. Hunt firmly believed Daniel Ellsberg and Leonard Boudin were key figures in a global militaristic conspiracy to spread Soviet communism. Hunt saw the Plumbers' unit as his own last chance for greatness.

He had been a principal organizer of the disastrous Bay of Pigs invasion of Cuba financed and run by the CIA back in 1961. Anticipating great success, he'd envisioned himself running a new Cuban government, based on a constitution he wrote while on a beach in southern Cuba.

But Hunt had lost control of the invaders and was fired from the operation before it was launched.

Leonard opened the historic pretrial hearings of Daniel Ellsberg in Los Angeles with a show of outrage to Judge W. Matthew Byrne about the "militaristic security stuff out in the hallway," recalled Ellsberg's codefendant, Anthony Russo. "I was terribly proud. This was the Leonard Boudin I'd heard about."

The next day, the metal detectors were gone, and Leonard had positioned himself as the rumpled star of the proceedings.

Ellsberg sat by Leonard's side, drafting questions to Leonard about his long-windedness. Why was Leonard slowing down proceedings with pompous motions? Was it because he lacked the necessary trial experience?

"I need to discuss strategy with Leonard," Ellsberg told people. "This is only the third trial of his life."

In fact, Leonard was stretching out the pretrial for many reasons. First, he was paving the way for an appeal, slowly laying the groundwork for his arguments into the record. He requested, for example, that all evidence against Ellsberg be entered into court record. He petitioned the court to move the trial to the East Coast. The Los Angeles jurors were too susceptible to government propaganda, owing to the fact that one half of the national defense industry was based in California.

Leonard tried to explain to Daniel Ellsberg his second reason for causing delays: it was in their interest to wear down the government until it lost interest and enthusiasm.

But a jittery, dissatisfied Ellsberg accused Leonard of having devoted too much time to the previous case in Harrisburg. "You are not up to speed," Ellsberg fretted. Leonard told Jean that Daniel was "a crybaby, a narcissist." His solution was to act as if Ellsberg was invisible.

Leonard insisted on formal courtroom decorum, discouraging local Black Panthers who were planning to picket. He restrained Anthony Russo, who spoke out in court without being recognized by Judge Byrne. Leonard manipulated Russo (far more radical than Ellsberg) by pretending great fondness for him and nodding vaguely when Russo insisted in late-night meetings that the trial would create a revolution.

Ellsberg began to demand to perform parts of Leonard's job in court, insisting that only he had sufficient expertise to interrogate such important witnesses appearing on his behalf as John Kenneth Galbraith and Arthur Schlesinger. Permission was denied by Judge Byrne.

In his efforts to stay a step ahead of the FBI, Leonard made sure Dr. Lewis Fielding, Daniel Ellsberg's Los Angeles psychiatrist, understood his office was not secure. He was right. Attorney General John Mitchell ordered a wiretap on Fielding's telephones the moment the psychiatrist had rebuffed FBI requests for interviews. The telephone taps were meant to pick up dirt to smear Ellsberg in newspapers. However, "priority" wiretaps sent directly to the agitated President Nixon consisted only of dull conversations.

So Howard Hunt started to prepare to make a "covert entry" into Fielding's office to steal Ellsberg's files; Hunt and Nixon were looking for proof that Ellsberg was sexually perverse.

With "the power of the president" behind him, Hunt recruited his former CIA aide, Bernard "Macho" Barker, his cohort on the Bay of Pigs invasion. Hunt promised a big cash payment and hinted that the mission involved a traitor with access to important American security secrets. Hunt implied that the secret mission might unseat Cuban president Fidel Castro. Barker recruited two of his real estate salesmen—Eugenio Martinez and Felipe de Diego.

Gordon Liddy, Howard Hunt, and the three Cuban Americans checked into the Beverly Hilton Hotel under pseudonyms. (Hunt carried a miniature camera and a red wig along with "pocket litter" in the name of Edward Hamilton.) Only Liddy and Hunt knew the plan.

The next day, two of the burglars were given black deliveryman uniforms, wigs, and thick glasses and told to deposit a large suitcase of burglary tools addressed to Dr. Fielding at the psychiatrist's office. That night, all three Cubans (forgetting to wear gloves) broke a window on the ground floor and forced a door to Fielding's office.

Though they diligently photographed an academic paper by Ellsberg and stole artifacts to confuse police about the reason for the break-in, they failed to find case notes.

The Ellsberg trial opened without a hitch.

Then in the early morning of May 2, 1972, FBI Director J. Edgar Hoover was found dead in his home on his oriental rug. His body soon lay in state in the Capitol Rotunda in Washington. A guessing game began: who was President Nixon likely to choose to replace the most powerful policeman in the world? In the meantime, an interim director was appointed.

Brazenly, behind the scenes, President Nixon was making plans to use the job opening as a lure to influence the judge presiding over the Ellsberg trial.

As the trial gained momentum, Leonard argued that the trial itself was unnecessary because Ellsberg had not, in fact, released any secret government information about the Vietnam War. Rather, all the information published in the Pentagon Papers was already part of the public record in one form or another. This hurt Ellsberg's feelings. It downgraded his heroism.

But the courtroom was Leonard's theater. Martin Arnold of the *New York Times* wrote of Leonard:

> Sixty-one years old, in a rumpled dark blue suit, his black-rimmed glasses dangling from his hand or perched on top of his head as he stands hunched over the lectern thirty feet from the witness stand . . . He appears to have been created by a playwright, and in an earlier era he would be in his shirtsleeves in the courtroom, his hands hooked in his suspenders. Now a bunch of pencils and pens overflow his jacket pockets. . . . Mr. Boudin has sandy white hair, thinning, that is seldom combed. He tosses his head, he smiles, he laughs, he says "quite," he uses them all as a writer uses punctuation.

Ellsberg disliked the fact that Leonard had special permission to stand up and walk around the courtroom "whenever and wherever he wanted because of his pacemaker and bad heart." Ellsberg was longing to fire Leonard and even interviewed other lawyers. But it was not to be; Ellsberg's fate was permanently entwined with Leonard.

Meanwhile Howard Hunt concocted a damaging press release about Leonard's career "as a fellow traveler." Hunt sent it to newspapers across the country. Though later this screed would be labeled "scurrilous and libelous" by Watergate prosecutors, the information in it—assembled by Hunt, the sometime pulp novelist—was picked up by the *New York Times*. Hunt entitled the press release: "Devil's Advocate—The Strange Affinities of Attorney Leonard Boudin."

In it, Hunt described Leonard as possessing "markedly extensive left-wing and Communist associations" as well as having waged "a career-long defense of the Communist Party, Castro's Cuba, assorted spies, perjurers, fellow travelers, conspirators, agitators, and violent revolutionaries." Leonard was, alleged Hunt, someone who could be found romantically cutting sugarcane as a way to help Castro meet Cuba's export commitments to the Soviet Union.

Moreover Hunt wrote: "The art of espionage, of course, is seldom conducted in the open. Nevertheless it has been said with some certainty that over the years Leonard Boudin has been a contact of both the Czech and Soviet spy organizations."

Daniel Ellsberg's birthday party was a fund-raiser attended by Barbra Streisand and all four Beatles. The courtroom itself was filled every day with spectators from the Hollywood movie colony including Streisand and author Joan Didion. Touched by meeting Jean, Didion soon began writing the novel *A Book of Common Prayer* about a girl named Marin who goes underground as an antiwar protester (Marin Riley was the Boudins' downstairs neighbor).

Leonard's struggle with Ellsberg climaxed a few weeks later, while Leonard coached his client for the witness stand. Leonard bluntly told Ellsberg to edit his rambling monologue. A defiant Ellsberg fled to rehearse on his own. He talked and talked until he was lying flat on his back on the floor.

The next day in court, Daniel Ellsberg nervously ignored Leonard's questions. Instead he recited a rambling biography about his motivations for releasing the papers. Leonard stopped Daniel the only way he could. He asked Judge Byrne for a recess. Leonard apologetically cited his pacemaker problems and chest pains. A friend was somewhat surprised to see Leonard swimming laps in the pool with fugitive Bernardine Dohrn outside the Bunker Hill tower apartments. Leonard's heart was apparently just fine.

Daniel and his wife, Pat, berated themselves for not having fired Leonard. But they were too frightened to commit to a replacement mid-trial. After a two-day recess, a subdued Ellsberg sat in the witness stand and followed Leonard's lead in the interrogation. This time he made a credible and compelling witness on his own behalf.

Early on the morning of March 30, 1973, there was a bombshell. A half hour before court was declared in session, a defense lawyer received word of a secret and inappropriate meeting between Judge W. Matthew Byrne and President Richard Nixon. Nixon had, amazingly enough, offered Judge W. Matthew Byrne the job of the late J. Edgar Hoover. It smelled like a bribe! Leonard was furious to learn that his cocounselor had notified Judge Byrne. Leonard preferred to catch the judge off his guard and enact the drama in open court, where it would have had far more impact on the trial. "He was no gentleman in such instances," said Victor Rabinowitz proudly.

Judge Byrne arrived more than an hour late for court that morning, his face flushed. He read (out of the jury's hearing) a hastily prepared speech declaring that he had declined President Nixon's offer to head the FBI. "It's still government misconduct," declared Leonard. But despite his true statement, the trial lurched on.

On May 11, 1973, Judge Byrne called Leonard, the prosecutor, and the defendants into private conference once more. Judge Byrne was apoplectic as he waved an envelope. "Are you going to bring this up or should I?" The envelope contained a Justice Department report that some thugs called the Plumbers' unit, secretly mobilized by President Nixon, had burglarized the office of Daniel Ellsberg's psychiatrist—looking for dirt. President Nixon was blatantly usurping powers that belonged to the FBI and doing crooked things with it.

"Government misconduct," said Leonard, who was shocked by the revelation, even though he'd warned the psychiatrist that his office was probably not secure. "Government misconduct" was Leonard's refrain throughout the trial. Each time, he followed it with the demand that his client be acquitted.

This time, Judge Byrne responded by offering to dismiss all charges. Since this did not constitute an acquittal, Anthony Russo piped up, unrecognized. "Can we think about it?"

Leonard reached past Ellsberg and squeezed Russo's arm, saying hastily, "We'll take it."

The legal victory heralded the collapse of Richard Nixon's presidency.

Leonard soon had another reason to celebrate: his son, Michael, was writing a Supreme Court brief in a pro bono case brought by a group of concerned doctors fighting Dow Chemical's unregulated sale of deadly napalm gas to the U.S. government. Dow was a famous culprit; its name was splashed across photographs of burned Vietnamese children at anti-war marches.*

Kathy at this point was living "underground" in a grim tenement apartment in a black neighborhood only a few blocks from her brother's tastefully underfurnished town house on Dumbarton Street in Georgetown. She asked Leonard why he and Michael pretended that a little legal mumbo jumbo could stop the U.S. government from killing poor people. She was, however, intimidated by both Michael's case and Leonard's coup.

Kathy began plotting a revolutionary bombing to best Leonard once and for all. She and Bernardine settled on the righteous symbolism of detonating a homemade dynamite bomb inside the heart of the domed U.S. Capitol Building, a gesture of support for a national peace protest march in Washington scheduled for March.

Despite strenuous objections from Rennie Davis, the leader of the March 1 antiwar protest, Kathy and Bernardine insisted that such a bombing would draw converts because it was an act of strength that harmed no human beings.

Kathy later said that the Capitol Building was selected as a target because it was "a monument to U.S. domination all over the planet."

Although the FBI accused the Weather group of some forty bombings from 1970 to 1978, many were in fact performed by imitators. The twenty bombings for which Kathy's group took credit in public relations releases included the explosion of May 1970 in Washington, D.C., in National Guard headquarters, protesting the Kent State killings; on May 19, 1972, at the Pentagon after the mining of North Vietnam Harbor and bombing of Hanoi; on May 18, 1973, at the 103rd Police Precinct in Manhattan; after the death of Clifford Glover, a young black boy accidentally killed by police; on September 28 at the Manhattan ITT offices; at the Presidio army base to proclaim the anniversary of the Cuban revolution; in the

---

*Michael Boudin actually brushed up against his father in a wiretap case. In August 1977, Morton Halperin and other key figures assisting Leonard in the Ellsberg trial sued the government (Richard Nixon, Henry Kissinger, Bob Haldeman, and John Mitchell) accusing them of illegal wiretaps, after it was discovered that Daniel Ellsberg was overheard "talking about drugs and sex" on a White House tap of Halperin's telephone.

Michael Boudin was now chief counsel for AT&T at Covington and Burling. He argued that AT&T did not technically assist the government in wiretaps of Morton Halperin's telephone. The U.S. District Court of Columbia found that although the government had violated Fourth Amendment rights of Halperin and his family with a twenty-one-month illegal telephone wiretap, AT&T was not guilty.

Hall of Justice in Marin County after the killings of Jonathan Jackson, William Christmas, and James McClain; and in the Long Island Federal Courthouse in sympathy with prison riots.

Bombs were detonated at the San Francisco and Sacramento Department of Corrections and Prisons after Black Panther George Jackson was killed; at the New York State Department of Corrections on September 17, 1971, after the prison riot at Attica; in the Pentagon on May 19, 1972, to protest the bombing of Hanoi; a stink bomb March 14, 1974, at a dinner honoring Nelson Rockefeller to protest antidrug legislation; a bomb in May 1974, in the Los Angeles office of California Attorney General Evelle Younger, in retaliation for "murder of members of the SLA"; on June 17, 1974, in the Pittsburgh office of Gulf Oil to support the liberation of Angola; on September 4, 1975, in Salt Lake City, Utah, at Kennecott Corporation to mark the second anniversary of the coup in Chile.

It was said that everyone in the Weather group was in love with Bernardine. Dubbed "la Pasionaria of the lunatic left" by *Newsweek,* she made sure of her conquests. There was more to her powers than low-cut T-shirts that showed her tan chest. Certainly Kathy craved her friend's nurturing attentions and stamp of approval. For it was Bernardine who frequently made the decision about which of Kathy's outrageous bomb plans to carry out.

Now the two women disguised themselves day after day as middle-class tourists to "infiltrate" the historic Capitol Building. They searched closets, bathrooms, trash cans, radiators, and basement tunnels to find a hiding place for dynamite. They marked bomb sites and exit routes on a tourist map.

When Kathy and her friend discovered a space behind a five-foot wall of marble in a first-floor ladies' room, she and Bernardine rejoiced. The layers of dust behind the wall made it clear that Capitol janitors did not know about it. The bathroom faced the Washington Monument, fortuitously symbolic. It was also located next to the Senate Foreign Relations Office. Kathy later claimed that the selection of the ladies' room was also a tribute to "the inspiring women of Vietnam who [kept their] beautiful gentle humanity in the face of genocide." It was a ridiculous stretch, but Kathy was trying to dodge women who accused her and Bernardine of imitating the most bullying of masculine power trips.

In the last weeks of February, Kathy found it hard to sleep. Her mind

Saturday, May 20, 1972, one day after Kathy's Weatherman group placed a
bomb in a Pentagon bathroom. The explosion knocked down a thirty-foot hallway
and caused ceilings to cave in. Bill Ayers wrote thirty years later: "It turns out
that we blew up a bathroom and, quite by accident, water plunged below and
knocked out their computers for a time, disrupting the air war and sending me into
deepening shades of delight."

The caption under the front-page photograph in the New York Times *reads:*
*"Searching for clues in Pentagon: Investigators sifting through debris in corridor
after the explosion."*

kept racing down marble hallways, past the barbershop, past the plaque
marking the spot where Supreme Court Justice John Marshall had sworn
in Thomas Jefferson as president.

Foremost in her mind was the anticipation of Leonard's stunned reaction. For Kathy, his minor likes and dislikes were still absolutes. Although
she'd recently considered becoming a gym teacher, she rejected the idea.
"Leonard Boudin's daughter can't be a gym teacher," she said bitterly.
The relationship consumed her, whether she was cursing Leonard or
wistfully admiring him. That it was a losing battle never seemed to occur
to Kathy.

The Wilkerson town house was photographed by many sad young people after the bombing explosion, 1970.

The struggle was in many ways mutual. Leonard's friends described Kathy as the "heat in Leonard's life." He spoke of her as "beautiful and special," adding, "My daughter is tough, tougher than anybody." Yet he still did not understand that Kathy's will was stronger than his own. In order to confound and dazzle her father, Kathy was living a rootless, cramped existence at the swampy periphery of society.*

Kathy trained hard for the Capitol bombing: running, climbing stairs, doing push-ups, and playing basketball. It was scheduled for February 27, the fourteenth anniversary of a Puerto Rican independence attack on the Senate, in which five congressmen were shot. Kathy and Bernardine split up the twenty-four-hour surveillance of Capitol exits with cohorts. Faces and schedules of custodians were memorized. The bomb was set to explode at night.

During a dress rehearsal, one of the Weather women called the night switchboard operator, alerting her of danger, and then timed the watchman's exit.

As the appointed bombing date approached, Kathy felt increasingly

---

*It did not occur to Kathy to follow in the footsteps of her illustrious great-aunt, Sarah Boudin Edlin, who helped hundreds and hundreds of young pregnant women reclaim their lives; Kathy never read Sarah's memoir about her life of good works.

alive. Each of the bombings was a roller coaster of pure terror followed by ecstatic relief when a bomb went off on schedule and without human injury. It was addictive. "It was real. Nothing is as real," said Jeff Jones decades later.

On February 27, Kathy and Bernardine ate yogurt, then dressed in black exercise pants and sneakers. The bombers strapped dynamite to their bodies, joking breathlessly about doing second-unit work in action movies. Kathy and Bernardine walked the timer and dynamite into the Senate and assembled the bomb in the women's room behind the barbershop. Although someone had dropped the bomb while they were connecting wires, it looked fine. They set its clock to explode an hour and a half after midnight on February 28.

They hid outside in shifts and kept watch on the entrances to the building. By midnight, they calculated that the only person left in the building was the night watchman. A call was placed to the switchboard operator: "You will get many calls like this, but this is real . . . this building will blow up in an hour and a half . . . Evacuate the building . . . This is in protest of the Nixon involvement in Laos."

At the switchboard, the woman on duty believed the caller to be male. The watchman exited. The Weather group waited, but as the minutes ticked by, there was no vibrating explosion, no plume of smoke.

It was hard to face the fact that technical problems still plagued them. Kathy and Bernardine realized they had damaged the timer while installing the bomb. This meant it might detonate at any time—people could be hurt or killed. Something had to be done. Kathy and Bernardine had no choice but to risk their lives, steal back inside, detach the broken timer, and carry the whole mechanism out.

Jogging out of the historic Capitol Building, Kathy was in a kind of delirium. She and Bernardine ran and ran. Now they faced a problem; they'd already announced the Capitol bombing. Communiqués, decorated with the Weatherman red, blue, and green rainbow pierced by a red bolt of lightning, had been sent to the FBI and to the press.

Rather than submit to a public failure, they affixed a new timer and sneaked back into the Capitol Building the next day. In the same ladies' room, they reset the bomb with the new timer to go off that night, which was February 28.

At midnight, they called the switchboard again: "You will get many calls like this, but this one is real. This building will blow in thirty minutes."

Taken March 2, 1971, for the Washington Post, *one day after Kathy Boudin and Bernardine Dohrn placed a bomb in a ladies' bathroom in the Senate. It appeared on the front page. The caption reads: "Senate leaders Hugh Scott and Mike Mansfield survey damages to walls of men's room on ground floor of Senate following bomb explosion."*

They watched the night watchman exit. They were jubilant when the bomb finally went off at 1:32 a.m. Not a single person was injured, but walls caved in inside the central section of the Capitol. Windows in seven offices exploded. A bust of Revolutionary War hero Marquis de Lafayette crashed to the floor in the Senate dining room. Calls were made to local newsmen and Capitol police by Weather supporters as far away as Spokane. Moments after the blast, television reporters in radio-equipped cars skidded to a stop at the scene.

Jean Boudin was angry. She celebrated her birthday on February 28. "Other mothers are surprised by flowers," she said to acquaintances.

This time the savvy, post-Hoover FBI dealt the young terrorists a terminal blow. They gave them no credit. Although government spokespersons acknowledged a letter from "Weather," they dismissed it. Attorney

General John Mitchell told reporters that a variety of "crank groups are claiming this action." The FBI claimed to be searching for unidentified males who had planted a bomb in a men's room.

In on the ploy, President Nixon said, "We get these warnings all the time. . . . These are the risks you take in an open society. The important thing is that these great buildings not be closed to the public."

Nonetheless, behind the scenes the U.S. government was focusing on tracking down Kathy and Bernardine and their bomb teams.*

One effect of the bomb was to explode the elegant surface of Michael Boudin's Washington life. It didn't matter that his sister's name was not mentioned in the *New York Times* or the *Washington Post*—it appeared in underground newspapers. FBI agents questioned Michael about harboring Kathy. For a Covington attorney to be a brother of someone who bombed the U.S. Capitol was to make a mockery of everything the firm stood for.

Nonetheless Michael responded calmly when Kathy's name came up at dinner parties. He opened no parentheses and added no new facts. It was as if what she was doing was not that unusual and of no particular importance.

During this period, Michael and Hugh Cox were working on a pro bono brief for the Supreme Court for a black man who'd been evicted from his rented home in Washington, D.C. In *Pernell v. Southall Realty*, Michael cited ancient English common law.

But some combination of shyness and hauteur kept Michael out of the limelight. Another lawyer argued *Pernell* before the Supreme Court. Although Leonard bragged, "Mike is a chip off the old block," Jean's friends did not agree. "One or two cases do not make a career. Michael is spitting in Leonard's eye and Leonard doesn't get it," said Nancy Carlen to her mother, Alice Serber Carlen.

---

*Senator George S. McGovern addressed peers from a spot near the collapsed brick walls and broken windows. "The barbaric act," he said, stemmed from "Vietnam madness. It is not possible to teach an entire generation to bomb and destroy others in an undeclared, unjustified, unending war abroad without paying the price in the derangement of our own society."

Workers painstakingly indexed the 174-year-old fragments of stone and wood on door frames and wainscoting.

Artists began restoring the painted glass window in the dining room.

Joan Baez and her manager, Nancy Carlen, 1984. Joan Baez was briefly a client of the Boudin office. Nancy's father, Robert, who was an art dealer, and his wife, Alice, were childhood friends of Jean. They introduced her to Horace Pippin.

.   .   .

When Leonard and Victor argued a fraud case in Alexandria, Virginia, that year, Michael joined them for dinner.

Walking to a restaurant, Victor gruffly asked Michael what it was like to be the lawyer for AT&T. Michael politely said a lawyer need not take on the coloration of a client. Leonard nodded. Michael said, "In fact, Leonard and I both fight government infringement—the only difference is I am fighting on behalf of corporations. Everybody has the right to a lawyer."

Michael cited family precedent. He reminded Victor that in 1940, Louis Boudin had fought U.S. government trust-busters trying to break the AF of L and CIO unions. Victor said to himself, "Michael thinks Leonard's some kind of crackpot because he works on leftie cases—but he never says so directly."

Kathy spent the next several years ricocheting between feeling very important and utterly worthless. Although she was still drifting from Boston to Berkeley and back and subsisting on the margins of society, she read about important "sightings" of Kathy Boudin in newspapers. The problem was that helping to plant one bomb a year was not exactly a full-time job. She had no home; eluding the FBI was her occupation and achievement. It was hard to remember that one slip might cost her freedom, her physical safety, or even her life. Her patience was frequently strained by old friends who slipped up and forgot to use one of her pseudonyms in a subway, bed, lobby, or public rest room. "Please remember to call me Janet Patricia Scott," she reprimanded sharply. (Other names included Kay Lavon Kennedy, Lydia Adams, Elizabeth Ann Hartwell, and Linda Miller.)

Attorney William Kunstler congratulated Kathy and Bernardine for doing what he dared not. There were still a few people for whom Kathy was a courageous and influential figure. But there was an ingrown quality to her life; for example, her friends were almost entirely other fugitives from the law (some with serious criminal records) and Weather supporters. In Cambridge, San Francisco, and Chicago, she lived in a series of walk-up apartments. Her support network had stopped proffering cash and keys to comfortable summerhouses.

She lived on tofu and yogurt, exercised, exulted in the wiry, skinny body she maintained—and kept on looking over her shoulder. Her close friends in Boston included Mary Moylan, an ex-nun and former member of Father Dan Berrigan's group who'd protested the war by pouring animal blood on draft files. Mary and another woman and Kathy named themselves the Proud Eagle tribe. Members of the "tribe" planted a bomb in a metal box near McGeorge Bundy's office at Harvard. It exploded at one o'clock one morning, twenty-five minutes after someone had telephoned the Harvard police and said, "There is a bomb at Six Divinity Avenue. It is due to go off in six minutes. This is not a joke. Get the janitor out of there."

In autumn 1972, Kathy learned that another bomber on the lam named Jane Alpert—she was not as famous or "heavy" as Kathy and Bernardine and the Weather family—was on her way up to Cambridge to "unburden herself" to Mary Moylan.

Jane Alpert was a lonely fugitive wandering the country entirely on her own. A former classmate of Weather's Cathlyn Wilkerson at Swarthmore, Jane longed to be accepted by the exclusive Weather group.

Jane's first year of planting bombs to protest the war had been harsh but thrilling: she had expected to die for the revolution in a matter of months. After her lover and partner, Sam Melville, was arrested, Jane meekly "retired" and, still underground, earned a little money doing clerical work for a midwestern rabbi. (Melville was killed in Attica during a prisoners' attempt to take over the prison.)

Jane was one of a hundred or so young people, not connected to Kathy's group, who in the 1970s set off bombs for peace or for the hellish joy of protest. In 1972, *The Rat,* an underground Manhattan newspaper, had published diagrams and instructions for making a bomb that "yields one pig car in flames."

A month before meeting Kathy in Cambridge, Jane had a thrilling encounter with the alluring Bernardine in the crowded People's Park in San Francisco. Bernardine took off her blouse to tan herself in a crocheted bikini top. Her hair was dyed flaming red. Jane envied the bond between Kathy and Bernardine, seeing them as "famous women living fulfilled lives: nothing was more important to Kathy and her small group than staying together."

But Kathy and Jane's lives were sadly similar. Both were tiring of their own rhetoric. Evading the FBI had become a boring routine. Kathy worried about getting sick—what if she was recognized in a hospital emergency room? She obsessively examined strangers' faces on subways and buses—looking for FBI agents. Before she went to bed at night, she checked escape routes, opening windows and doors to fire escapes.

Kathy had become afraid to talk to most people. Her ideology also mandated that she despise them. Despicable were reformers who perpetuated the old order by simply improving it a bit. They included antiwar draft counselors, activist lawyers like Leonard, and middle-class blacks. Kathy and her friends cheered each time a plane was hijacked to Cuba at gunpoint.

Despite all the negative theatrics, they were witty in their underground codes. Referring to themselves as "the Beatles" because of their fame, they dubbed their underground identity "the joke." ("Did you tell your new boyfriend the joke?") Nicknames such as "Emma" (for Emma Goldman) and "Harriet" (for Harriet Tubman) were used in long-distance pay telephone conversations.

When Jane Alpert arrived in Cambridge, Mary Moylan took her home to her tenement apartment. A woman was sitting in a rocking chair with her back to the door. When she turned, Jane did not recognize the cheekbones and gleeful smile.

"Hello, Jane, don't you remember me? I'm Kathy Boudin."

Jane was truly amazed. She'd met Kathy at a dinner party at St. Luke's Place and remembered a plump, moon-faced girl. It did not occur to

Manhattan Police Headquarters, 240 Centre Street, as pictured on the front page of the New York Times. *The Weathermen bomb exploded at 6:57 on the evening of June 9, 1970, in a men's bathroom, badly damaged the building, and injured seven of the 150 people inside. The caption under the picture in the* Times: *"Police official walks past hole next to elevator shaft at site of blast at headquarters."*

Jane—as it had to some of Kathy's old friends—that she had had aesthetic surgery on her face. Kathy was now an elfin beauty who looked ten years younger than her age. Like Bernardine, her hair was a now too-bright red color that practically shouted, "Look at me": it was not easy to be a star and an anonymous worker for the revolution.

Kathy told Jane that she wished to discuss ideology. Jane was scared. Jane said she was too hungry and tired and wanted to eat something more substantial than yogurt.

The next day Jane faced Kathy. Instead of saying what she was really feeling—"I am lonely and sorry for the life I led with my late, violent boyfriend"—Jane burst out with, "The goal of feminist revolution is a matriarchy, where the paradigm of society's relationships is that of a mother with her child." She added that intimate relationships between two women tended to be more equal.

Kathy disagreed with everything Jane said. She had, she announced to Jane, experimented with a sexual relationship with a woman, and she had been disappointed to discover the same sort of intense power trips—a seesaw between dominance and submission—as with men.

Jane was shocked by Kathy's bluntness about her personal life. The Weather mode was to be intellectually abstract and obscuring.

Kathy stared unblinking into Jane's eyes. Jane wondered if Kathy was trying to intimidate her or sleep with her—or both. Scathingly Kathy pronounced Jane's feminism "unserious and middle class." For Jane, the most exhausting thing was pretending to like Kathy.

Father Dan Berrigan, himself underground, published a letter in *The Rat* to the famous Weather group pleading with them to give up sabotage and violence.

He wrote:

> By and large the public is petrified of you. There is great mythology surrounding you—much more than around me. You come through in public as another embodiment of the public nightmare which is menacing and sinister and senseless and violent; a spin-off of the public dread of Panthers and Vietcong and Africans and the poor of our country, all of those expendable and cluttering and clamourous lives who have refused to lie down and die on command . . . or to exist in the world as suppliants and slaves.
>
> But in a sense, of course, your case is even more complicated because your choice to rebel is not the passionate consequence of the stigma of slavery. Yours . . . is one of the few momentous choices of American history. . . . Your lives could have been posh and secure but you said no. . . .
>
> As they said about Che, as they say about Jesus, he gave us hope . . . so my hope for you is that you see your lives in somewhat this way, which is to say, I hope your lives are about something more than sabotage. . . . I hope the sabotage question is tactical and peripheral . . . the risk always remains that sabotage will change people for the worse and harden them

against change. . . . No principle is worth the sacrifice of a single human being. . . . A revolution is interesting insofar as it avoids like the plague the plague it promised to heal.

Kathy escaped cramped apartment living to take hikes with David Gilbert in the Adirondacks and in the mountains of northern California. There she and he adroitly turned conversations with other young campers to the latest bombings by the anonymous Weather Underground. "There was popularity, since many people felt the war was just terrible," recalled David, who was "proud to help people feel less powerless in the face of the government."

Leonard had said nobody could elude the FBI indefinitely, but Kathy, it seemed, was doing it. Incredulous friends asked if the feds had stopped searching for her, and were just hoping that she would blow herself up. Others assumed that the government was probably tracking her but holding back on arresting her, for its own reasons. Perhaps they hoped she'd lead them to other underground fugitives. The Communist Party newspaper, the *Daily Worker*, accused Kathy of being run by the CIA, because otherwise her group would have been captured.

David Gilbert was appalled: "That's how much people accept the omnipotence of the state."

15

THE DEVIL'S PARTY

By the close of the year 1973, Kathy and Michael each suffered a loss, although Kathy's was typically more public. As a result, the course of each life changed.

Michael's professional life had been flourishing. Because of the influence of Hugh Cox, Michael still spoke precisely, but no longer with off-putting "College Board words." (Such words as *recrudescence*, for example, which had appeared in his Harvard honors thesis on religious freedom, were of the past. His frame of reference was perhaps his childhood pet turtle Geyser since recrudescence has to do with regrowth of a turtle shell.) Michael had been made a partner at Covington and Burling. The firm still had ties to powerful men in government—its new quarters at 888 Sixteenth Street were a stone's throw from the White House.

Michael's sartorial style was more and more like that of his father. Coke-bottle eyeglasses did not diminish Michael's charm, which was startlingly reminiscent of Jean's. He was a superb listener. Indeed, he and

Jean shared a singular life experience that could be summed up as "listening to Leonard."

Wanting to seem a bit less formal, Michael asked new acquaintances at dinner parties to call him Mike.

He was enveloped in legal writing. Michael preferred corporations as clients. AT&T did not suffer from alarming heart conditions, even if Covington lawyers claimed for corporations the constitutional rights of people. In direct contrast to his father, Michael never spoke of himself. Friends knew only from dinner-party talk with his partners that he won nearly every case he litigated and that his much-admired briefs hinged on impossibly esoteric points of corporate law. They assumed, correctly, that Michael protected the moneymaking practices of corporations like AT&T from government regulation.

Michael was silent on political hot potatoes such as abortion. Friends saw him as a judge-in-waiting. And, appropriately, he did not like to talk about his political views, although at dinner with Stuart Taylor, the legal writer for the *New York Times,* Michael once mumbled under his breath that he sort of liked Ronald Reagan. It was assumed that Michael believed in the untrammeled rights of big business but was humane on social issues such as racial equality.

He appeared to have no romantic interests. He cut an unusual figure: his male friends powerful conservatives, neo-cons; his sister a sixties terrorist; and there was his famous liberal father. He gave four-course dinner parties in his antique Georgetown house. After dessert he handed out scenes from *Coriolanus* or *Macbeth,* assigning roles to his guests. He had an incredible husky voice and was more popular than ever as an extra man in Washington society. He had many women friends who accompanied him to restaurants and to parties. Most assumed he was sexually ambiguous.

Hugh Cox, now sixty-eight, and Michael, thirty-four, were by this time a solid legal writing team. For Michael, it was a transcendent mental connection. Both men read all sorts of books voraciously and were a match in their desire for formality in relationships. Hugh Cox took no credit for legal briefs he helped Michael write. His former protégés (now his partners) used the word *love* in speaking of Hugh Cox. They were warmed by the sight of him in his gloves and hat, walking down Sixteenth Street in Washington, smoking his pipe and turning the pages of a book by Anthony Trollope.

On vacation trips to London, Cox and Michael, and sometimes

Leonard as well, explored old bookshops on Charing Cross Road. Like Michael, Hugh Cox was not given to political pronouncements. He closed arguments about the Vietnam War, saying firmly, "Those people have the right to shape their own destiny, and interference in the end is useless."

But in the spring of 1973, Hugh Cox learned he was dying of cancer. His wife, Ethelyn, continued to drive him every morning to the office. (He was color-blind and had never learned to drive.) And until the end, he walked his old English sheep dog morning and evening along the Alexandria waterfront. In October he died at home.

His memorial service consisted of speeches wreathed in superlatives from good friends who were Supreme Court justices, a former ambassador to Japan, and the novelist Robert Penn Warren. In his memory, Cox's partners presented an American colonial desk to the Supreme Court.

Michael was devastated at the loss. "His life paled, and the ordinary practice of law excited him less and less," said his partner Roberts Owen. Michael inherited Hugh Cox's railroad rate deregulation cases.* He continued to write winning briefs. But his heart was not in them. In his way, he was as widowed as Ethelyn Cox. When he greeted associates in the halls, asking "Read any good books lately?" it was not mere pleasantry. His mind was restless.

Kathy's loss that year was more flamboyant. In the first months of 1973, after a heavy spate of bombing, the United States suddenly pulled out of the Vietnam War. The government had finally responded to the increasing dismay of millions of Americans who'd sat down to dinner every night to watch television news broadcasts of body counts and U.S. airplanes dropping napalm bombs on Vietnamese hamlets.

As a star of the antiwar movement, Kathy suddenly found herself without a mission. Worse still, she was stripped of a romantic persona that had sustained her. "Weather simply fell apart after the Vietnam War ended," said David Gilbert.

But by now Kathy was too militant to stop fighting, although Leonard assumed she was retiring from radicalism. He was relieved that his daughter had not blown up herself or anyone else. Her menacing, preachy communiqués and even the bombings might be, in retrospect,

---

*Now that railroads were floundering and competitive trucking companies were winning away customers, Michael and his firm were arguing that the government should pull back on regulating railroad rates.

Patty Hearst leaves the Federal Courthouse Building in San Francisco. She met clandestinely with Kathy while they were both fugitives from the law.

perhaps, a lively joke, and reflect well on him. Said her mother to Kathy, "Time to go straight, time to grow up."

To make Kathy's life even less thrilling, in January 1974 the federal government dropped two indictments against her and her group of friends. Nevertheless she, David, Bernardine, Bill Ayers, and Cathlyn Wilkerson decided to ignore that fact. They chose to remain underground, as fugitives, even though the FBI had little interest in them.

Kathy and the other core members of the Weather group clung to their identity as terrorists, even as the role became increasingly dysfunctional. Kathy claimed defensively, "Being underground gives us an important pulpit from which to scold and lead the American people." The truth was she did not dare to be ordinary. She quoted the movie *The Wild One*. "Question: 'What are you rebelling against?' Answer: 'What have you got?' " It was no joke.

Her days were, however, depressing. In the dowdy blond wig she sometimes wore, she blended in too well as a house cleaner or as a night-shift waitress in suburban malls. These days she bore little resemblance to the strong-browed young person on the FBI wanted poster.

She scolded strangers about poison in cigarettes and the ozone layer.

A photograph of Kathy Boudin
that her father, Leonard, kept
on his office wall from 1977 until
his death in 1989.

But shrill political arguments that lasted through the night were repetitive. The criticism–self-criticism sessions seemed always to be about sexist "me-first" behaviors of David and Bill Ayers and Jeff Jones.

Kathy was still something of a media star. Rumors surfaced in the *Chicago Tribune* that she was instrumental in the Weather Underground connection to Patty Hearst and the Symbionese Liberation Army, the terrorist group that Hearst had joined after they'd kidnapped her. In fact the two famous upper-class rebels had met in June in an unheated Pennsylvania farmhouse and shared stories of eluding "the shoes and the pigs."

Early in 1974, Jean was rinsing lettuce and listening to public radio station WBAI. Suddenly she heard the words "Kathy Boudin." A radio announcer was explaining that Kathy was one of three women leaders of the Weather Underground who had mailed a tape of poems to the radio station. They were from a self-published book called *Sing a Battle Song*.

Then Jean heard Kathy herself reciting "Sisterhood Is Not Magic," a poem inspired by arguments with Bernardine about what to do after the end of the Vietnam War. It was dated summer 1973.

Whatever did witches do
*About how to save the "devil's party," * . . .
and best serve the peasants' needs . . .

Jean jotted down a phrase from Kathy's poem—"lovers among witches"—as she dialed her niece Celia in Cambridge to discuss Kathy's poem. She had not seen her daughter in almost a year.

Jean later wrote an essay for *Ms.* magazine in which she explained how she'd taught herself to count small blessings, like the sound of her daughter's voice on the radio.

Leonard saw Kathy frequently and more than Jean. Jean made do with his secondhand reports of risky reunions. But she encouraged Kathy's high-profile "underground" friends to come by St. Luke's Place to get a night's sleep, or to cash checks, or to meet her for a nourishing snack at Anglers and Writers, her favorite restaurant down the block. Ex–Weather member Kit Bakke, now in nursing school, brought her small daughter to dinner. Unlike most parents of Weather members, Jean and Leonard were respected—to a point. Jean sat the young people down by the fireplace and forced them to answer her questions, which ranged from the humorous: "How does a revolutionary terrorist dress to plant a bomb in middle America?" to the unanswerable: "How can you plant bombs that might kill people?"

Kathy silenced her mother. "Revolutionaries are often destroyed by soft feelings for loved ones."

Kathy was speaking more and more intensely about the struggles of blacks in the United States. It seemed to be the "what's next" for Weather. Kathy quoted W. E. B. Du Bois's book *The Souls of Black Folk*, written in 1903 about heartbreaking disappointments of blacks during the years of Reconstruction after the Civil War.

For Leonard, the question remained: Why did Kathy experience society's ills so personally and the tragedy of black oppression so intensely?

But her parents failed to see how much Kathy feared exchanging her "revolutionary identity" for a diminished position in the family hierarchy. Kathy continued to be infuriated by Leonard's ever-increasing pride in Michael. Jean was openly sentimental about Celia's marriage to her childhood sweetheart, the charming, gat-toothed, and shy Walter "Wally" Gilbert. It was rock solid. Wally was also researching patent law and management issues in order to create a biotechnology firm named

Genentech, which promised to be worth millions of dollars. Jean and Leonard planned to acquire stock.

On April 24, 1974, Michael learned that he'd won the Supreme Court case *Pernell v. Southall Realty* for the black man in Washington, D.C., who had been evicted from his rented home. Justice Thurgood Marshall wrote the majority opinion.

On Christmas Day, Leonard rushed to his deserted office. Ever the competitor, he had decided to contact Justice Marshall as well. His goal: to stop FBI surveillance of his client, the Socialist Workers Party. He saw an opportunity to use "the Boudin knifing technique": a surprise attack. (Government lawyers hardly expected a counterattack on Christmas.) Leonard dictated a petition on behalf of the Socialist Party to Justice Marshall, requesting the stay of an injunction against FBI surveillance at the next week's Young Socialist convention. A single Supreme Court justice has the authority to grant a temporary stay. (Leonard had obtained an injunction from the District Court. On appeal, however, the U.S. Court of Appeals from the Second Circuit had sided with the government. That decision left the FBI free to monitor the convention.)

The next morning Leonard found a clerk in the deserted Supreme Court Building in Washington and asked him to take the petition to Justice Marshall. Leonard was accompanied by his young associate, Herb Jordan, who loved playing "David vs. Goliath and using the federal judiciary system as the weapon."

It was highly unusual when, an hour later, Justice Marshall summoned Leonard for oral argument in a big room lined with books. Justice Marshall addressed Leonard by his first name; they'd judged a moot court at Harvard Law School. Despite the fact that Leonard called the older man "Justice," he was not humble.

Marshall was undoubtedly curious to see Leonard Boudin again—he had of course recently lauded Michael Boudin's succinct and persuasive brief in the Pernell case. Leonard opened the twenty-minute session by saying that there were FBI informers in the Socialist Workers Party. Leonard said, "It's worse than life under the czars of Russia."

Justice Marshall raised his palm like a traffic cop. He joked. "Stop. I've never been to Russia, Leonard, and I never intend to go there."

Three hours later, a clerk brought Leonard the written decision. He had lost, but Leonard seized upon a small triumph. The Court outlawed the FBI's historic practice of reporting to the Federal Civil Service the names of people attending the Socialist convention.

Supreme Court Justice Thurgood Marshall wrote the majority opinion on a pro bono case won in April 1974 by Michael Boudin that ensured the rights of a Washington, D.C., tenant. Soon afterward Leonard appealed to Justice Marshall for a stay of injunction against FBI surveillance of a Socialist Party meeting.

Soon afterward three women including Kathy (according to Jean) detonated dynamite in the headquarters of the Department of Health, Education, and Welfare in Washington, D.C. The ensuing Weather communiqué criticized HEW for treating women as poorly as the Bureau of Indian Affairs treated Native Americans. Bureaucrats doled out meager welfare payments, while making no plan to alleviate long-term misery.

The bomb went off, but the action was a dud, in no small part because the FBI once again did not credit the Weather group to the press.

In 1975, Kathy stalled when David Gilbert formally asked her to go back to Manhattan with him. He was eager to join forces with Judith Clark, she being more committed to violence after serving her short jail term. Judith was humbly assisting a group of black men who were ex-addicts and aides at a detox center located at Lincoln Hospital in the South Bronx. They saw themselves as a new generation of the lethal Black Liberation Army; their code name was "the Family."

David was galvanized by news that the ex-Panther fugitive Sekou Odinga was seriously thinking of joining the Family. Sekou was talking about robbing banks to finance a separate black state within the United

Bank security photograph of Black Liberation Army member Joanne Chesimard, a.k.a. Assata Shakur, during a robbery, August 1971.

States. Judith quoted Sekou to Kathy: "Bank robbery is a form of capitalism by illicit means."

David still saw Sekou as the most courageous native revolutionary with a gun. For his part, Sekou was determined to stay out of jail, where he believed he would be tortured or killed by police in retaliation for declaring war on them. He was working at a dry cleaner and selling African artifacts in the South Bronx. The Family was also planning to break high-profile black prisoners out of jail. The first on their list of prisoners was Assata Shakur, whose birth or "slave" name was Joanne Chesimard.

Kathy wrote loving poetry to Assata Shakur, a fierce and astonishing young woman who'd been accused of multiple murders of police. Fast-thinking and beautiful, she was small and moved with the purposeful speed and grace of a ballet dancer. Assata—Joanne Chesimard—was known to thousands of blacks as the "soul of the original Black Liberation Army," the short-lived, small underground group dedicated to killing policemen, whom they portrayed as "occupying armies in the ghetto."

Joanne Chesimard was born in Flushing in 1947 and named Joanne Deborah Byron by her mother, a schoolteacher. She was raised in

Georgia by her grandparents, who owned a stretch of beach. She once avoided rape by a black gang at the home of a gang member's parents by suddenly smashing lamps and vases as fast as she could. Joanne ran away as a young teenager to Greenwich Village, where she worked as a bar girl who inveigled white men to order expensive drinks. By the next year she was reading Hart Crane and T. S. Eliot. She was "duped" into taking part in a school play extolling Thomas Jefferson, a slaveholder whose Declaration of Independence did not include her as a woman and a black.

While at Queens College, Joanne became a Black Muslim and joined an offshoot of the dying Black Panther Party called the National Committee to Combat Fascism. She took the African name Assata Shakur; Assata means "she who struggles" and Shakur means "the grateful."

On the day that Assata Shakur married Louis Chesimard, April 2, 1969, he and other leaders of the New York Black Panther Party chapter—the Panther 21—were coincidentally arrested. Within a year, the marriage was annulled, and the jailed Panther leaders had been replaced by a small group of angrier blacks, including Assata, who were adept with guns and who called themselves the Black Liberation Army.

They were determined not to repeat the Panthers' mistakes, which included public meeting places easily penetrated by police and FBI informers. The corrosive ideology of the clandestine Black Liberationists outlived them—and become pervasive among angry black youth.

Assata Shakur went underground with the Black Liberation Army to help perform "revolutionary executions." The Black Liberation Army issued a communiqué dated May 19, 1971, claiming credit for killing two Harlem policemen, one white man and one black man, at a Harlem housing project. When the white policeman had gone down on his knees to beg for his life, he was hit with twelve machine-gun bullets. As a result, law enforcement agencies around the country mobilized. As Sgt. William Moriarity said, "They are killing men because of their color, which is neither black nor white—but blue."

Black Liberation Army members delivered a package to the *New York Times* containing the communiqué and a live 45-caliber cartridge. The communiqué read in part:

> The armed goons of this racist government will again meet
> the guns of oppressed Third World Peoples as long as they
> occupy our community and murder our brothers and sisters in

the name of American law and order—the guns of the Black Liberation Army will mete out real justice. We are revolutionary justice. All power to the people.

Then, almost a year later, on January 28, 1972, another "Army" communiqué claimed credit for "executing" a black policeman and a white policeman outside the Shrimp Boat restaurant on the Lower East Side. Afterward angry and frightened police put out a national alarm for the arrest of four Black Liberation Army members and declared that five more, including Assata Shakur, a.k.a. Joanne Chesimard, were wanted for questioning.

Authorities believed that Assata Shakur had been at the scene of gunfights that had resulted in bleeding, dying policemen. Some of her supporters insist, however, that her main occupation had been to make fake IDs for Black Liberation Army members and other black fugitives.

The policemen were vulnerable targets. Although civilians tend to define policemen by their guns, few police fire or even draw guns on duty. They are not shy, on the other hand, about using less violent means to get even with criminals, such as "subduing" a dangerous suspect, particularly a "cop killer," by beating them harshly with fists and clubs.

At that time, gun training for rookies was limited to a week. For six intense days, the recruits reviewed safety measures and such issues as how to clean a gun, when and under what rare and specific circumstances they could use it (a gun was to be kept holstered until absolutely necessary). Finally, on the seventh day, they practiced shooting a hundred rounds at targets on a shooting range. The police recruits were taught the terrifying facts of how difficult it is to shoot a gun while someone is actually shooting at them. A policeman rarely had time to aim his gun. He squeezed the trigger as many times as he could while pointing it in the direction of his adversary.

There was more to Assata Shakur's participation in horrific bloodshed than faking identification cards. She was present during at least one shootout on the New Jersey Turnpike on May 2, 1973.

The bloodbath had erupted near dusk after a state trooper began to tail the white Pontiac driven by three Black Liberation Army soldiers, including Assata Shakur and Zayd Malik Shakur (known also as James Coston). Zayd was the man for whom Bernardine Dohrn and Bill Ayers would name one of their sons. He is also the birth father of Tupac Shakur, the gangsta rapper and recording star. (When someone asked the precocious little boy what he wanted to be when he grew up, he said, "A revolutionary.")

Assata claimed that State Trooper James Harper stopped her car on the Jersey Turnpike only because the occupants were black and the car had a broken taillight. In reality, however, a national alarm had been issued for the "underground soldiers" because of the police murders.

Two more state troopers speeded to the white Pontiac. Witnesses diverge about what happened after State Trooper Harper ordered Assata and the others to pull over. State Trooper Werner Foerster began struggling with Sundiata Acoli and was shot to death with his own gun. Also killed was Zayd Malik Shakur, leaving Tupac fatherless. Bill Ayers would pay tribute to Sundiata Acoli as a fellow freedom fighter at the end of his memoir.

The government prosecutors accused Assata Shakur of starting the shootout "on command" and then fighting policemen. Assata denied both charges and claimed that she'd been standing with her arms raised in the gesture of surrender when she was shot in the forearm and shoulder. Two doctors, witnesses for the defense, testified that bullet scars on her shoulder and severely damaged arm supported her side of her story. Paraffin tests on her hands showed that she had not fired a gun.

In her autobiography, Assata avoids details of the fatal fight. She prefers to write of police retaliation. Nonetheless, her own descriptions of her trigger-quick reflexes in other pressurized situations make it impossible to believe that Assata was not slugging it out in the thick of battle.

Assata fought for her life with a collapsed lung, an arm partly severed from her body, and one leg shackled to a hospital bed.

Her taut poems describe her struggles against police and "amerikan kourtroom justice." She wrote of Zayd Malik Shakur's death:

STORY
You died.
I cried.
And kept on getting up.
A little slower.
And a lot more deadly.

With Kathy still undecided about whether to join David, he hitchhiked to Lincoln Hospital in the South Bronx in 1975 to check out "Doc"

Mutulu Shakur (whose birth name was Jeral Wayne Williams), the highly articulate, boyish leader of the Family. (Doc was now the stepfather of four-year-old Tupac Shakur.) He was also a skillful acupuncture counselor at Lincoln Hospital Detox Center, established after community sit-ins in 1970. The center was run with millions of dollars of city and state funds. Doc was pioneering a cure for drug addiction using acupuncture and the writings of Malcolm X. He hoped to raise an addict's self-esteem by demonstrating that his pain and his addiction were in no small part based on white oppression. (He hung photographs of Assata Shakur and Che Guevara in his office.)

Doc's rise and fall was based on idealism that had soured into base criminal acts. He was recruiting his patients for armed robberies of local cocaine dealers and Brinks trucks for "revolutionary purposes." Doc did not tell David Gilbert that he had recently bungled a grandiose robbery in Pittsburgh. He'd tried to steal sacks containing $1.44 million being carried out of Kaufman's department store to an armored car. (One of Doc's men—a recovering drug addict—panicked and his back went into spasm, causing him to shoot his gun by mistake. Doc's acupuncture treatments had not cured the man's back problems.)

Judith Clark's small group of angry white women radicals assisting Doc Shakur had named themselves the "May 19 Communist Group"—to honor the birth date of Malcolm X and Vietcong leader Ho Chi Minh. The name also referred to the fact that the short-lived Black Liberation Army had killed ghetto policemen on May 19. (That May 19 was Kathy Boudin's birth date was seen as significant by Kathy and some of her friends.) The May 19 Communist Group included Susan Rosenberg—the go-between with the blacks—and Silvia Baraldini, a daughter of an Italian diplomat.

The leader was Marilyn Buck, whose father had been fired as an Episcopal priest in a black diocese in Austin, Texas, for criticizing the church for moving too slowly on civil rights. Marilyn Buck had recently escaped from Alderson prison where she'd been serving a ten-year sentence for gunrunning.

The women believed they must play subservient roles, since the black struggle was not their own. Thus they followed orders, renting and driving getaway cars for Family robberies. They also purchased guns and ammunition and set up safe houses. The women were not disturbed by Family members' use of heavy drugs. (Sekou Odinga was the rare nonuser.) It was part of black culture, the women told one another.

Mutulu "Doc" Shakur, whose birth name is Jeral Williams, was the mastermind of the deadly and ill-planned Brinks truck robbery in Rockland County, 1981. He had attempted the robbery many times before executing it.

.   .   .

Meanwhile in Los Angeles, Bernardine and Kathy received a series of flattering letters from Emile De Antonio, a respected documentary film-maker. "De" was eager to make a laudatory film ("a film weapon") about Weather. He wrote that he admired Weather's "sense of adventure" and the "tender loving care" they put into bombings.*

The filmmaker was excited by a new Weather manifesto distributed in the summer of 1974, called *Prairie Fire: The Politics of Revolutionary Anti-Imperialism*. The essay hinted that Weather was softening its stance and looking for a wider group of supporters. (They'd self-published forty thousand copies.)

---

*A positive film would be a change of pace for De. Like Kathy, he worked in the "scold and criticize" mode. His documentary *Point of Order*, for example, was constructed from televised videotapes; it was a brilliant attack on Joe McCarthy, ending in a scene of dementia: Joe McCarthy sitting in the Senate raving about communists while people walk out.

De was a Harvard man who called himself "a half-baked radical who lived by his wits."

Like many serious people, De was disturbed by the disappearance of the movement with the end of the Vietnam War. He decided that if the militant Weather group was trying to reach a larger audience, a TV documentary was the next logical step.

De promised Bernardine and Kathy that his film would reach millions of people on television. It would revive idealism among Americans who seemed numbly content with President Gerald Ford.

De wrote: "The film would sell on the Underground's undeniable dramatic appeal. You have created a masterstroke of political theater which not only reveals the police state, but that it's possible to beat it." He scribbled at the bottom of a letter, "It belongs on film. Bang. Bang. Bang."

David Gilbert and Judith Clark jeered at Bernardine's desire to make a film that "would soften our image." But Bernardine, Bill Ayers, Jeff Jones, Eleanor Raskin, and even Kathy were developing a holy zeal about the idea of raising children: a good way, they were beginning to believe, to make a better future.

David called Kathy a "clean revolutionary who wasn't willing to put her safety on the line." She accused David of being out of touch with reality. He answered, "Well, white America is only about four percent of human reality."

But the filmmaker—as well as Kathy and David—gravely mistook the national mood. By 1975, people wanted to forget all about the Weather Underground. The public needed comforting and soothing after the Vietnam War, rather than goading and prodding. Weary peace marchers were stunned to realize how little they knew of the workings of their government. President Nixon had been unmasked as a thug, and two more presidents had lied to the American people about the waging of a hopeless, undeclared war.

In January 1976, David hitchhiked to Chicago for a "Hard Times conference" of a handful of bickering people still committed to the movement. Blacks criticized whites for not focusing on black self-determination. Women attacked men for sexism. Attendees agreed only that the movement had fizzled. A few "optimists" like David predicted its revival due to economic crises.

Bernardine summoned De Antonio to Los Angeles. Although the meeting was near his hotel, it took him two hours to follow her "heavy security" precautions. The obstacle course increased his ardor.

Bernardine and Bill Ayers greeted De Antonio in a vegetarian restaurant. Bernardine ran the meeting according to rehearsed power plays. She won total control of the filming.

Kathy was caught between Bernardine and David. To appease Bernardine, Kathy reluctantly promised to appear as one of five stars of the "image-softening documentary." But Kathy appeased David, too. She consented to move to Manhattan with him in a few months to do "armed struggle" with Judith Clark and the black Family. Kathy insisted, however, on living separately from David. She wanted to develop apart from "his arrogant will and sexist attitudes."

Kathy joined subsequent meetings with De over the next six months in restaurants and busy sidewalks. She and Bernardine approved content, location, cinematographer, and editor.

Film editor Mary Lampson apologized when she met Kathy, Bernardine, Jeff Jones, and Bill Ayers—for not being radical enough. She said, "I am at a different stage." Kathy magnanimously brushed aside her apology.

Meeting on a bench in Central Park, Kathy, Bernardine, Jeff Jones, and Bill Ayers told De Antonio that they'd turned down thousands of dollars to do a television network documentary.

When asked how he planned to shield their identities, cinematographer Haskell Wexler said he would not use ski masks. He did not want them to look like they'd just robbed a supermarket. Kathy played lawyer. Relaying Leonard's counsel, she warned Wexler to expect to be called by a grand jury when the FBI learned of the film. She made him and Mary promise not to cooperate, at the risk of prison sentences.

De asked if he should get a gun for the filming. He cited the police killing of Black Panther Fred Hampton. "If you're going to be armed, I'd like to be too."

"Don't be ridiculous," Kathy said. "We're not going to be armed. If we're surrounded, we'll just come out."

De suggested that his presence would be protection. "The cops still don't kill filmmakers in this country." Haskell Wexler and De each put up $5,000 of their own money to finance the film.

During the next weeks, the Weather group argued about what not to say in front of cameras. They agreed to be "up," very positive about the future.

On the film's start date, De Antonio and Haskell Wexler and film editor Mary Lampson waited anxiously for instructions from their subjects. They were supposed to go to a safe house somewhere in Los Angeles.

Hours passed. Two days passed. (The tactic, frequently used by Panthers, demonstrated who was in charge.)

Finally, a messenger arrived with orders to proceed with filmmaking equipment to a pay telephone. At a second pay telephone, the three filmmakers were put in a car and ordered to don opaque black eyeglasses. After they arrived at the safe house, Kathy and Bernardine kept the filmmakers waiting yet another full day.

The next morning, Kathy, Bernardine, Jeff Jones, Cathlyn Wilkerson, and Bill Ayers strode in. Smiles vanished when they saw a large sheet of gauze filmmakers had hung across the living room. They sat, uneasily facing a large mirror. The camera was to shoot their reflections in the mirror through the gauze. One by one Kathy and her friends peered into the camera to make sure the gauze hid their faces.

De dared not ask his "heavy" subjects basic questions such as how many they were or how they stayed in touch. He marveled aloud that the whole state was mobilized against the young people. (In fact it currently was not.) De told himself he was "sitting with Robin Hood."

Bill Ayers opened with a dissonant statement. "We are not a terrorist group and it is irresponsible for people to make that conclusion."

Haskell Wexler was snowed. He believed the radicals were "very sensitive to one another and to us as people." Wexler missed the point. His subjects were politicians trying to "act appealing." Kathy sometimes used tough street language: dropping *g*s at the end of verbs like *eating* and saying "ain't" and "fucking"; but for the filmmakers she was her most genteel self.

During filming Kathy began by introducing herself, somewhat pompously. She described "a turning point" in her life. She'd been driving with a black woman down a street in Cleveland. A riot was raging and there were soldiers with rifles. Kathy was taking the woman to fight for welfare money to feed her children. Kathy panicked, but the woman turned on the radio and sang along with it. She told Kathy, "We're gonna get our welfare today and my people gonna get what we need." Kathy waxed romantic: she'd gone to Cleveland to help poor people, but welfare mothers had taught her courage. She gave no hint that she viewed her Cleveland experience as a failure.

Kathy and her friends ate lunch with chopsticks from a common bowl. De watched reverently, correctly assuming the influence of the Vietcong. Sounds of backfiring cars made him jump. He longed to rehearse an escape plan.

That night, Kathy's group retired to a bedroom for a self-criticism session about unrealistic "Hollywood" expectations. They went to sleep in a heap on the floor.

Kathy woke at sunrise and found De staring miserably at the camera. He said plaintively that Kathy and her friends had been trying too hard to obliterate what was human and personal about themselves.

But the second day was worse. Kathy made disorienting attempts at self-effacement: she announced an "anonymous" poem—obviously written by her—about her empathy with Black Liberation Army member Assata Shakur, and then she said of herself: "I am a black revolutionary, and by definition that makes me part of the Black Liberation Army." She recited:

FOR ASSATA SHAKUR—

> *. . . You moved among your people*
> *Carefully choosing the moment of attack.*
> *And when they hunted you hard*
> *I was an invisible supporter working on another front*
> *And when you were captured, sister, I wept for all of us.*

Kathy's identity problems cast a shadow over the film. The paean to Assata Shakur was meant to appease Judith Clark and David Gilbert. It blatantly contradicted Bernardine's "softened" message. (Kathy did not mention the fact that she and David had agreed to steal a car for a big robbery whose funds would help Doc Shakur and Sekou Odinga break Assata Shakur out of prison in New Jersey and finance her escape to Cuba.) Jean saw Kathy's poem as "untrue romance." It was another attempt—in the name of virtue—to do away with her white identity. Kathy was "talking big."

Kathy recited a second "anonymous poem" about having been inside the exploding Wilkerson town house. Then Kathy asked rhetorically, "What is the best way for us to make a film that moves other people, that moves many people to feel that they can make a revolution in this country?"

De prompted: "Tell us how you . . . a woman of a certain age, in the United States . . . reacted this way, you had these fears, you had these strengths, you had these ideas, and so you've come to this place in American society."

Kathy spoke of weeping at the parade of Soviet guns and tanks in

Havana in 1961. Bill Ayers chimed in that part of being politically mature was to admit fear. (The guys had been painfully and painstakingly educated to express feelings by Bernardine and Kathy.)

Jeff Jones added, "Fear, yes. Every time—I think—for all of us. I know for me, every time I see a policeman, I have this rush of adrenaline. And I take a defensive stance, in a martial art type of sense. I mean, not a fighting posture but an alert posture. I remind myself who I am, what my name is, what my various numbers are, where I'm going, where I've been."

Bernardine made a stab at justifying her politics. "I was a much more fearful person growing up in this society than I am now because now the fear is a real fear, it's not paranoia, it's not fear of the unknown. It's a very tangible thing. And that doesn't make it go away at all."

Haskell Wexler commented that life underground sounded worse than hiding in a basement and being fed through a hole in the door. Kathy cheerily disagreed. "We circulate freely. Some of us have regular jobs and do aboveground organizing."

Bernardine brushed off criticism of their abrasive ways. "We were a revolutionary movement that started with the student base—and most everybody was not mature enough to make that transition without making mistakes." But she hastened to add, "There's no question that we're special, we're professional revolutionaries."

The revolutionaries spoke about their mission for three long days. Afterward, De declined to smoke a celebratory joint. He laughed at himself; smoking marijuana was a minor crime compared to Weather bombings.

To say good-bye, Kathy and her friends held hands in a circle with the filmmakers. They presented De with a quilt they'd made, embroidered with the words THE FUTURE WILL BE WHAT WE THE PEOPLE STRUGGLE TO MAKE IT.

The next day, Kathy made a mistake that put the FBI on the filmmakers' trail. At her request, Haskell Wexler agreed to film her and Cathlyn Wilkerson talking to striking doctors at nearby Martin Luther King Hospital. Kathy wanted to prove how effective she was at organizing while underground.

Although Kathy routinely hid her face from surveillance cameras in banks and drugstores, she totally missed the video camera on the hospital roof aimed at the strikers. Security guards closed in with questions about Wexler's camera. Kathy and the filmmakers ran.

Three weeks later, the surveillance video reached the FBI in Washington, revealing Kathy to be very much the subject of a movie. Although the FBI had stopped tracking her, they suddenly feared a movie would embarrass them. The truth was that after all this time only two members of the notorious Weather Underground had been caught despite millions of dollars of government expenditures.

Soon afterward, four FBI agents pretended to fix a flat tire at the curb by Haskell Wexler's house. One man photographed Wexler's car. A man peered through binoculars. De called the New York bureau and shouted, "Get your fucking gumshoes off our back."

The filmmakers sat up nights asking themselves, Where was the leak? Kathy authoritatively repeated Leonard's adage: they must not assume that the FBI knew everything and was omnipotent and at the same time they must not think that the FBI knew nothing.

Haskell Wexler held a press conference explaining why he was refusing to surrender his footage to the FBI. It was about artistic rights. The unfinished documentary became a national preoccupation. Newspaper editorials argued against the government. They maintained that the case resembled instances in which the government tried to force news reporters to reveal sources.

Leonard agreed to be legal counsel to film editor Mary Lampson after she, along with De Antonio and Wexler, was subpoened by a Los Angeles grand jury.

Kathy knew she was impressing Leonard. He enthusiastically coached the filmmakers for grand jury hearings. They continued to edit the film in secrecy. Leonard was confident he would win, and sure enough FBI subpoenas were withdrawn.

Jean disliked the film, even though she loved the sound of Kathy's voice. There were no visuals, the speeches ponderous and impersonal and long-winded, the subjects invisible. One viewer called it "a film in chains." Jean was jolted by the sweetness of the disembodied voices on the sound track, a reminder that Kathy and her friends were young. Jean told herself, "Who but young people and madmen can be so certain of answers in life?"

Jean spent the month of May 1976 writing poems in a solitary, "neat-as-a-pin" log cabin at the MacDowell Colony for artists in the New Hampshire woods. After not hearing from Leonard for a week, Jean called his secretary. Upon learning that he was in Washington, she did not ask for his telephone number or request that he call her.

Jean attended the film's official opening in early June, without Leonard. She pretended to friends that she had not yet seen it.

When the movie ended, acquaintances sitting behind Jean gripped her shoulders and whispered, "How did you like it?"

"Like it?" repeated Jean, feeling an inexplicable anger. Her emotions seemed to be all over the place. "I want to see it as often as I can." Judith Clark and Susan Rosenberg, representing the May 19 Communist Group, picketed the screening. They accused Kathy and the other documentary stars of selling out.

Suddenly Bernardine quit Weather. She denounced her past seven years as having been based on serious errors. It did not faze her that she was reversing herself on beliefs of which she had been certain enough to wage war on the U.S. government.

Instead of saying she wanted to tend to her private life, which now included two small boys, Bernardine claimed she had been "too male-identified," ignoring the fact that she and Kathy had been running the show for some time.

Kathy and Eleanor Raskin supported Bernardine. David angrily walked out on Kathy. Jeff Jones walked out on Eleanor. Kathy ignored the true cause of the collapse of the Weathermen. The country was tired of them.

16

THE SECRET SITS IN THE
MIDDLE AND KNOWS

While we dance round in a ring and suppose,
The secret sits in the middle and knows.

—Robert Frost

In 1977, Kathy and David moved to Manhattan to assist in the preparations for the jailbreak of Joanne Chesimard, a.k.a. Assata Shakur. The young couple made arrangements to live separately. Mutual friends from Cleveland soon introduced Kathy to a mother of two small children who needed a roommate to share expenses. Rita Jensen lived in a spacious, sunny cooperative apartment on Morningside Drive. The ivy-covered, eight-story brick building was near Columbia University, five miles north of St. Luke's Place. It had sweeping views of Harlem to the northeast.

Rita Jensen and Kathy bonded as soon as they met: they had a lot in common, including a poorly concealed layer of emotional tension. Rita described herself to Kathy as "the only welfare mother to graduate from Columbia Journalism School." She was an award-winning reporter, having written an exposé about New Jersey police who'd purchased tenements under secret names, then burned them to collect insurance money.

Rita was fragile: her nerve endings had been rubbed raw by an abusive first husband. A small-boned young woman with probing eyes, she wore big sneakers and little hats. She reminded friends of Jean Boudin.

Kathy moved in with Rita on Morningside Drive, and neighbors observed that "they were openly affectionate" and assumed they "were an item." Although Kathy was also sleeping over at David's apartment on Saturday nights, she drew close to Rita and her small children, helping with laundry, planning meals, and cooking. She accompanied Rita to PTA meetings, although Rita resented Kathy's attire at the meetings. "She was Kathy Boudin. She didn't have to dress up for anyone or anything. I am not such an aristocrat."

Kathy introduced David (calling him James Hartwell) to Rita as "the man I've chosen to be the father of my child." She did not say that David, now thirty-four, was the rare available man with whom she could be Kathy Boudin.

Rita disliked David: he was a rival for Kathy's affections and he was impossible to oppose in argument; a voracious reader, he reeled off historical facts about the exploitation of Africa by European businessmen. He had an intimidating moral certainty.

Rita made fun of his obsession with radical economic history as a filter for his life, including his refusal to eat sugar. (David and Kathy believed that sugar was an inexpensive, addictive, and nonnutritious food that rich people historically encouraged poor people to eat.)

Kathy finally told Rita that taunts about David hurt her feelings. So Rita stopped joking about how tired she was of sitting in her rocking chair in her living room on Morningside Drive and arguing with David's upside-down butt—literally, since David combined hours of political lecturing with his yoga shoulder stands. (As author Marge Piercy noted, David was truly at home only in the world of ideas.)

David was living in nearby West Harlem with an elderly black roommate named Erwin Hendricks. David had too many confusing aliases. When friends telephoned and asked Erwin Hendricks brusquely, "Is your roommate there?" Hendricks thought they were ill-mannered, but in fact, callers did not know what name David was using.

Working for a local moving company under the name Lou Wasser, David explained his erudition by saying he was a struggling writer. A coworker found him "decent, sensitive, and political"; he was poor and once borrowed eight dollars to pay his rent. He brought his vegetarian lunch in a brown bag.

David argued with Rita Jensen that white-dominated society had nothing left to offer blacks. He, Kathy, and Judith Clark visited Doc Shakur to hear reports of Assata Shakur's impatience to get out of jail. Sekou Odinga had joined the Family and was going to be in charge of the break-out. He and Assata were old friends. Kathy read a poem by Assata that Sekou Odinga had smuggled out of the minimum-security prison in Clinton, New Jersey.

> *. . . I have been kicked by the lawless,*
> *Handcuffed by the haters.*
> *Gagged by the greedy.*
> *And if I know anything at all,*
> *it's that a wall is just a wall*
> *and nothing more at all.*
> *It can be broken down.*
> *I believe in living.*
> *I believe in birth.*
> *I believe in the seat of love*
> *and in the fire of truth.*
> *and I believe that a lost ship,*
> *steered by tired, seasick sailors,*
> *can still be guided home*
> *to port.*

One morning in early October 1977, Kathy put on a blond wig and boarded a crosstown bus. She was on a critical Underground mission, per instructions from Sekou Odinga. At a car rental agency on East Eighty-fifth Street, she listed her home address as the Empire Hotel, near Lincoln Center. Her name: Elizabeth Hartwell. The branch manager of LaGuardia Econo-Car hired her as a clerk despite her baggy cotton pants and crooked brown eyeglass frames.

Kathy was poised to help steal a rental car that would be used in a robbery to finance the prison escape of Assata Shakur. Although the manager initially pegged "Elizabeth Hartwell" as "slovenly, unambitious and a drifter," he was pleasantly surprised by how meticulously she wrote up rental agreements.

Eight months later, on the humid morning of June 25, 1979, Kathy traveled to the Econo-Car's midtown office on Forty-third Street. Still posing as Elizabeth Hartwell, she wore the blond wig as well as brown eyeglasses that her roommate Rita said made her look like a raccoon.

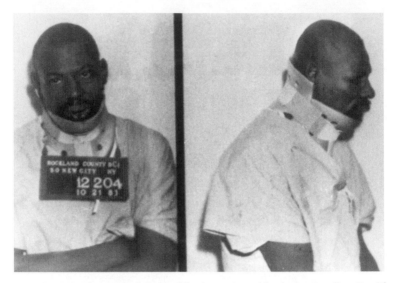

Sam Brown was arrested in Rockland County with Kathy Boudin, David Gilbert, and Judith Clark.

Kathy watched a customer fill out a car rental lease. She had zeroed in on Edward Anderson the instant he explained that he would be flying home from La Guardia Airport late that night. Giving him car keys, she instructed him to leave the Ford station wagon at the Econo-Car Rental Agency's lot at La Guardia Airport. She knew that the car would not be logged in, since clerks would have left.

A few hours later, Kathy handed a duplicate set of the Ford station wagon's keys to Sam Brown. Garrulous and insecure, Sam Brown was, like Kathy, a new recruit to the Family. He was twenty-two and had been enlisted by Doc while a patient for cocaine addiction at Lincoln Detox. Sam Brown talked a good game, even though a listener might soon see that colorful stories about his past contradicted one another. (His and Kathy's fates would be intertwined; they would be tried together after the Brinks robbery, and Sam's false evidence against Kathy would put her in even greater jeopardy.)

That night, as Kathy expected, the Ford station wagon was returned to the airport lot. Within an hour Sam drove it away using the keys Kathy had given him. It was not reported missing or stolen. Per instructions, Kathy quit her job at the car rental office by failing to show up for work the next day.

. . .

During this time, Leonard was showering his daughter with courtly invitations to stroll in flower gardens at the Cathedral of St. John the Divine. Although Kathy forced him to take precautions before meeting her, in fact many Columbia graduate students and professors recognized their new neighbor, and Kathy's name was mentioned during more than one faculty meeting.

All Leonard seemed to want out of life was Kathy's return to his name. He assumed that Kathy's underground activities had petered out. He knew that Bernardine Dohrn and Bill Ayers were making plans to surface and to surrender to authorities, as was Cathlyn Wilkerson.* But Kathy sternly lectured her father. "Being underground isn't about being happy. It's about doing what you feel is right."

Leonard particularly hated Kathy's recital of David's analysis of the economy of Africa, whose people had lived miserable lives on the continent of deepest human history. Leonard said that Kathy was not black, nor was she a slave trader living on that distant continent.

Leonard was pushing his daughter too hard. He failed to see that he himself was a central figure in the drama: paradoxically, in order to convince Kathy to return to ordinary life, he would have had to accomplish the impossible—to vanquish himself.

Kathy gloried in the fact that, as an absent personage living underground for idealistic reasons, she lent serious status to the Boudin brunches. Kathy was more terrified than ever that if stripped of her glamorous and dramatic revolutionary attachments and subterfuges, she would be the dullest person in Leonard's circle of admirers. (Celia's husband, Wally, had, as expected, won the Nobel Prize in chemistry and was poised to amass a fortune in Genentech.) Without her attachment to a blinding ideal far bigger than herself, Kathy saw herself as a failure. She would be a woman, no longer young, whose work was waiting tables and cleaning houses.

. . .

*Authorities believe that Bernardine Dohrn helped with robberies. She stole credit card information that was used to apply for ID cards for the May 19 women.

Kathy is believed to have used ID cards in the name of Mary C. Baker to rent a car for the robbery of the armored car in a mall in the town of Greenburgh, New York.

Walter Gilbert, Cambridge, Massachusetts, 1980: Walter Gilbert (left) and coworker celebrate news that Gilbert shared the Nobel Prize in chemistry for his work in gene splicing.

Leonard and Jean were delighted to take under their wing a beautiful twenty-six-year-old poet named Binnie Klein. She was subleasing an outdoor studio in the woods on a private road by Compo Beach in Westport, Connecticut. Jean and Leonard met Binnie while visiting her landlady, Ruth Krauss, a bohemian poet with flowing gray hair.

Binnie teased Jean about the way she'd eat cottage cheese and herring while standing over the sink. "It's about being Jewish," said Jean. "Somehow after all these years it tastes better like this." Binnie got tears in her eyes when Leonard said how terribly proud he was of Kathy. Jean prudently did not tell Binnie she'd recently strolled with Kathy in the town of Westport.

Leonard seemed "blown away" by Binnie and her typing speed—a hundred words a minute. He asked her to help him write his memoir. Lying back on Binnie's bed, he spun stories of famous people and legal battles won while Binnie typed. One night, after Jean went to bed, Leonard and Binnie sat in the living room.

"How old are you, my dear?" Leonard asked Binnie.

"Twenty-six."

"That's a passionate age," said Leonard. "Why I recollect Kathy was twenty-six when she went underground and Jean was twenty-six when I met her." (Jean had been twenty-two.) Leonard had observed how stories of Kathy's heroics had captured Binnie's imagination and how Binnie adored Jean.

Then Leonard kissed Binnie passionately. Binnie was scared. Yes, there'd been a flirtatious vibe between them, but Leonard was ignoring the fact that Jean was sleeping only six feet away. Moreover, it disturbed Binnie that Leonard cited the two women in his life before kissing her. It felt like incest. Binnie saw herself as a free spirit, but Leonard was forty years older. She sometimes thought Leonard was masking a lot of sadness and was "more a persona than a person"—almost a husk. She ran her hand down his chest and felt his pacemaker lodged there, the size and shape of a pack of cigarettes. It frightened her.

Leonard pointed to Binnie's studio. "Let's go."

She answered, "I'm not comfortable with that."

Quickly, Leonard said, "Nor am I." And that was the end of it.

A week or so later, Jean traveled again to MacDowell Colony in Peterborough, New Hampshire, her fourth visit. On the airplane on the tarmac at La Guardia Airport, she wrote a letter in a small spiral notebook to Madi Leof. Jean described MacDowell as a haven "where I will brood over words which are just as meaningful or less as / all other ongoings." Madi worried about Jean's marriage. There had been many recent "Leonard sightings." Someone had bumped into him hurrying alone on the Boul Mich in Paris on New Year's Eve. Someone else said he had been sitting close to Barbra Streisand at the Polo Lounge in the Beverly Hills Hotel. Bert Gross saw him eating borscht with a lovely blond woman at the Kiev deli in the East Village.

That summer, the exhilarating brunches on St. Luke's Place included legal seminars on strategy about Kathy's surrender. Leonard explained that Cathlyn Wilkerson's problem was worse. On her way back to ordinary citizenship, Cathlyn had to face a charge of negligent homicide because her family had owned the Eleventh Street town house.

Manhattan District Attorney Robert Morgenthau and his wife, Lucinda Franks, were invited to brunch. Morgenthau was the person who could dismiss the old legal charges against Kathy in New York stemming from the town house explosion. Lucinda, with Tom Powers, had written the Pulitzer Prize–winning articles on Diana Oughton. No one remembers that the Morgenthaus ever came to brunch.

Kathy was now Leonard's most prized client, due in some part to the decrease in exciting cases since the demise of the movement. Leonard was, however, making good money litigating against the government about the tax-exempt status of the Scientology group. He argued that it was a religion.

Leonard soon opened a delicate conversation with Bob Morgenthau about reducing charges against Kathy. Leonard also commenced informal negotiations with Chicago authorities to dismiss charges against Kathy for jumping bail.

While walking with Kathy in the park at the Cathedral of St. John the Divine, Leonard reported insider conversations he'd had with a judge about Cathlyn Wilkerson's surrender. She was going to receive a mild sentence.

But Leonard was soon warned by District Attorney Bob Morgenthau to stay out of the Wilkerson case because he had a conflict of interest.

Leonard asked Jean to invite the author Thomas Powers and his wife, Candace, to dinner. The Powerses had never met the Boudins and found the invitation perplexing. They were invited by Leonard for two reasons. First, Leonard wanted them to report back positive things about Kathy to Tom's friend Lucinda Franks Morgenthau, wife of the Manhattan district attorney. Second was the possibility that Pulitzer Prize–winning authors Tom and Lucinda might be influenced to write about Leonard.

Throughout the dinner party, Tom marveled at Jean's pride in her aristocratic position on the left. She was the match of any Palm Beach hostess. He stared at a motorcycle helmet sitting incongruously on the Boudin mantel. It was not until saying goodnight that Leonard proudly volunteered the information that the helmet was Kathy's from the Days of Rage.

Bernardine Dohrn and Kathy remained close. They went to the movies and to a Pete Seeger concert at a church on the Upper West Side, where they sat in the first row, clapping and singing. Many assumed Bernardine and Leonard had had an affair. In any case, Bernardine was under the spell of the Boudin family. She and Kathy spoke wistfully about practicing law.

The "Family" waited two and a half months, until September 1979, before using the Ford station wagon, stolen with Kathy's assistance. It was used in a successful robbery that took place at gunpoint at a Bamberger's department store, located at the Garden State Plaza, a mall in Paramus, New Jersey.

Afterward, the robbers drove the Ford station wagon to the parking lot of a nearby restaurant, the Fireside Inn, in Rochelle Park. It was 11:12, and they hastily ditched it and piled into a van, the second escape vehicle, rented and being driven by the attractive Marilyn Buck, acting as "the white cover."

Marilyn Buck, the leader of the May 19 Communist Group, steered the van, with robbers crouched in the back, twelve miles to the George Washington Bridge, where police pulled up alongside her. (The van was "a legit ride," meaning it had been rented, not stolen.)

Coldly in control and acting as a decoy, Marilyn flirted with policemen. Seeing a young white woman with a cute, round face, police dropped back.

After the Bamberger's robbery, the Family, under the leadership of Sekou Odinga, took nine months to pull themselves together to break Assata Shakur—code-named "Cleo" for the operation—out of jail. A successful escape would establish the Family's legend among blacks both inside and outside of criminal life. It would humiliate a legal system Family members saw as unfair to blacks.

Assata Shakur was living in a single-story brick structure named South Hall at Clinton Correctional Facility for Women in New Jersey, biding her time. Security was lax. (Previously she had been kept at high-security prisons for men.)

A woman with a heart condition guarded the visitors' area. A guard with a two-way radio drove visitors to the prison entrance. Neither was armed.

Sekou Odinga was the only Family member to visit "Cleo." After one visit, he was pulled over for speeding on the New Jersey Turnpike. (As for Kathy and David, speeding provided him risky thrills.) Sekou Odinga presented false ID cards and was released. But the infraction endangered the whole plan, since police checked recent motor vehicle violations after a crime as huge as the one he was planning.

He did not cancel the prison break. Assata believed she was in physical danger in jail.

On October 24, 1979, ten days before the scheduled jailbreak, David and an unidentified white woman, who was probably Kathy, rented a blue van from the Family Rental Center on Grand Avenue in Baldwin, Long Island. The blue van was an "escort vehicle" for the jailbreak, scheduled for November 2, 1979.

At 2:45 that afternoon, Sekou Odinga signed in at Clinton prison under a fake name and stepped into the trailer that was used as the reception area. He was not asked for ID nor was he searched for guns. He soon hugged a sweaty "Cleo" and passed her a .357 Magnum revolver.

Minutes later, two other members of the Family forced a guard at gunpoint to take them to the visitors' room, where they joined Sekou Odinga and Assata Shakur. She pointed her gun at the female guard. Sekou ordered one man to handcuff the guards.

Assata and her rescuers herded the handcuffed guards into the prison van. Waiting outside the prison and playing backup was Doc Shakur (in the blue van rented by David and probably Kathy).

Sekou hid Assata for two nights in a safe house in East Orange, New Jersey. Marilyn Buck drove Assata and Sekou in the trunk of another car to Pittsburgh, Pennsylvania. Assata had her teeth fixed and her hair straightened while waiting for two months to escape to Cuba. She was given $50,000 in robbery proceeds.

Furious and frightened, police launched the biggest manhunt in New Jersey history. It was front-page news. A white prisoner at Clinton warned a guard not to talk to authorities about the jailbreak. "You're not dealing with a bunch of two-bit niggers. These people are organized."

To celebrate the euphoric success of the prison break, Kathy and David became pregnant a few days after the robbery.

Doc Shakur used robbery proceeds to obtain a mortgage on a mansion on Strivers Row in Harlem, where he'd continue his acupuncture work with addicts. He'd been locked out of Lincoln Hospital by police on orders of New York mayor Ed Koch, who accused the staff of running a revolutionary cell with taxpayers' money. (Indeed, staff attendance was lax; the cost of treating each addict had tripled.) Doc was bitter about losing the three-quarter-million-dollar-a-year budget, which he'd also used in part as patronage.

After Assata's dramatic escape, the Family started calling themselves "the Army" in honor of the original Black Liberation Army.

There were three levels of command: Five blacks including Sekou Odinga and Doc Shakur made up the "primary team," who performed robberies. Beneath them, the second tier consisted of the four white women of the May 19 Communist Group. They followed orders. (The white women's support of primary team members was not based on sexual connections; they were lesbians.)

Each May 19 woman had at least five support people to help her; they were not given money from robberies. David and Kathy supported Judith Clark. Judith did not tell Kathy and David that the blacks were using more and more robbery proceeds for cocaine.

Kathy's revolutionary work took precedence over her safety. In fact, as the events of the next two years played out, Kathy would also desert her child, although not as definitively as Kathy's grandmother Celia Roisman had deserted Kathy's mother Jean by dying in childbirth. Kathy's desertion of her son was similar to that of Ethel and Julius Rosenberg, whom Kathy saw as heroes for sacrificing themselves and the welfare of their two boys in pursuit of higher principles.

Kathy was taking natural childbirth classes at the Maternity Center Association, across Central Park on Ninety-second Street. She and David asked earnest questions. For as long as she could remember, Kathy had scrutinized middle-class attitudes through a lens loosely based on socialism. But motherhood seemed different: normalcy seemed suddenly precious.

Kathy decided she needed a stable income. Her jobs were low-paying and sporadic: she had recently served chicken and ice cream to spectators at the U.S. Tennis Open tournaments in Forest Hills. She received $355 a month in welfare benefits, under the alias Lynn Adams.

By April, Kathy was five months pregnant. After much ambivalence, she applied to the Paralegal Institute on Nassau Street in Manhattan. For all her feminist moralizing, she was prepared to be a legal secretary, not a lawyer. On her application, Kathy claimed to be "Ann Harriet Appelbaum," thirty-one years old—five years younger than her actual age.

Kathy had found the real Ann Harriet Appelbaum in a 1970 Barnard College yearbook. Kathy filled out a baptismal certificate purchased from a store specializing in religious items. She used "Ann's" baptismal certificate to obtain a Social Security card as well as a New York Public Library card.

On "Ann's" paralegal application, Kathy cannily invented experiences close to her own life. She listed employment by a Hackensack, New Jersey, research company where "Ann" had coordinated campaign surveys during the 1976 senatorial campaign of Howard Metzenbaum, a liberal Democrat from Cleveland, Ohio. (Kathy was combining her work for welfare mothers in Cleveland with Metzenbaum's campaign.) She wrote, "I have always worked very hard. I am dependable and conscientious and have done well in my field."

Kathy was the best student in many years to graduate the thirteen-week paralegal course. Her exam scores were perfect.

Unbeknownst to Kathy and David, Sekou Odinga quit the Family in fury that summer after condemning Doc Shakur's latest robbery plan.*

Doc had spotted cash being loaded onto a silver Brinks truck outside a small Chemical Bank in Nanuet, Rockland County, three miles west of the village of Nyack.

Doc and Sekou were by now competing for leadership. Sekou vetoed the Rockland job because there were too many unknowns involved in robbing an armored car in broad daylight in a town of whites. He believed that escaping blacks would be too visible. (Neither the primary team nor the intellectual May 19 women did adequate research; they would have discovered that, surprisingly, Nyack's population was nearly 30 percent black, and the town had been a stop on the Underground Railroad just before the Civil War.) More important, Sekou felt the bank was

---

*In the preceding months other ambitious robberies had failed. For example, on February 20, 1979, Doc and Sekou fled empty-handed after trying to rob an armored car picking up cash outside a Korvettes store in Greenburgh, New York. One guard simply refused to open the truck.

Meanwhile, Doc and Sam Brown were also performing "nickel and dime" operations—robberies of cocaine dealers on first floors of Upper West Side apartment buildings. A paid street informant would tip Doc that a dealer was or was not wearing a gun or was flush with cocaine and cash. Although easily frightened, Sam Brown was highly motivated because he was using a lot of cocaine. Sam had a seriously violent streak; he seemed to enjoy hitting people.

The Family was also robbing United Parcel Service trucks in order to buy cocaine from a Cuban family who dealt out of six rooms at the Colonial Hotel on 112th Street near Columbia University.

too far from the Tappan Zee Bridge, the only escape route to Manhattan. Police would have ample time to set up a roadblock.

Nonetheless, Doc began rehearsing the robbery without Sekou. He scheduled it for autumn 1980. This time Doc promised that all cash proceeds would go to the robbers, instead of one third going to black revolutionary activities.

The bottom line: Doc was broke without his sinecure at Lincoln Hospital. Worse yet, he was unable to control his own and his group's growing cocaine use. Much to the consternation of Sekou Odinga, who viewed drugs as counterrevolutionary, robbery money was being spent mostly on cocaine. Large sums disappeared from the safe.

One man traded an automatic machine gun for cocaine. Doc cried when his car was confiscated and the mortgage holder moved for foreclosure on his house. He feared Sekou would use his moral advantage to gain control of the group.

Days before her baby was born, Kathy traveled to Harlem to undergo unorthodox acupuncture treatments at Doc Shakur's brownstone clinic. This is despite Kathy's later claims that she never met any robbers or knew who they were. The acupuncture treatments would, it was hoped, make the fetus turn around before it was born. As it was, the baby was in position to be born feet first instead of head first.

Kathy went into labor on August 20, 1980, while out to dinner with David. They counted breaths during the difficult delivery at Columbia-Presbyterian Hospital. David played a cassette he had made of music by Smokey Robinson and Nina Simone.

Despite Doc's acupuncture needles, the baby boy came into the world feet first on the way to the delivery room on August 21, at 6:10 a.m. The healthy seven-and-a-half-pound baby had a small abnormality—one toe had two parts to it, probably a result of Kathy's use of drugs.

David laughed as he described to a friend from Kenya the birth of his beautiful son. Since he had been born feet first, the infant's head had not been squeezed by forceps. He had dark brown hair and an impish expression that reminded David of his father, Sam. David said the baby came dancing feet first into the world. So John Mwangi, the Kenyan, suggested the baby be called Chesa, which means "dancer" in the Swahili language. The name also had an underground meaning: it evoked Joanne Chesimard, a.k.a. Assata Shakur, in whose honor the baby was conceived.

David wrote to his son from prison a dissonantly upbeat history of the fourteen months of their life together. "Chesa, your arrival into the world was the most exciting change in our lives ever. We loved to look at you and hold you. You wanted to be held all the time—which was very nice, but sometimes difficult because we did have other things that we had to do."

One afternoon in late September 1980, Doc and the primary team soldiers (minus Sekou Odinga) attempted to rob the Brinks truck in Nanuet. They squatted for two miserable hours in the cargo area of a rented U-Haul van parked by a McDonald's restaurant across Route 59 from the small drive-in Chemical Bank. But the silver truck never appeared. (They did not yet realize that the truck made the Federal Reserve Bank run only on Fridays.)

Meanwhile, Judith Clark and Silvia Baraldini (the white decoys) waited a mile away inside a rented van by a vacant Korvettes department store, the designated switching point. Disguised as respectable suburbanites in wigs and suits and makeup, Judith and Silvia carried .38-caliber revolvers.

Sekou reluctantly joined Doc for the second attempt at the Nanuet robbery. But Sekou countermanded Doc's orders about the proceeds: money was to be divvied up to support revolutionary activities such as rallies and bombings of police stations—as well as among robbers.

Again, the silver Brinks truck failed to appear.

Kathy was unable to commit to a name for her baby for six weeks. She called him many nicknames, such as "my eensy beensy" and "froggy" (he slept with his legs pulled up under him). The Capitol bomb had also been referred to as an "eensy beensy." Kathy finally agreed to the name Chesa.

The elated parents belted Chesa into a Snugli and went on a hike in upstate New York, the child resting on David's chest. It was here that Kathy and David officially named their baby Chesa Jackson, his middle name for George Jackson, the Black Panther who had been killed while trying to shoot his way out of a California prison, since Chesa was born on the anniversary of Jackson's death. Kathy noted that Chesa liked the peacefulness of the country breezes.

On his birth certificate, the baby was identified as C. Jackson Adams. No father's name was filled in. As befit his family background, he started out in life with a kind of alias.

Sitting on buses and in the park by the Cathedral of St. John the Divine, Kathy asked other mothers over and over again about all aspects of Chesa's physical and emotional well-being: Did his feet turn out too much? Was he too alert? Why did he cry? Was he too sleepless? He wanted her to hold him all the time. Was that okay? Should she wait to see if he walked okay before she had his toe operated on?

Although Kathy had made a rational decision to become a mother, she was surprised by how attached she became to him, even though he was still crying too much.

Kathy and David quarreled because David wanted to help bottle-feed the baby, but Kathy refused. Nonetheless, Kathy and her close friend Nancy Gear took turns breast-feeding each other's infants. David accused her of sexism. The two parents were living separately.

Chesa was enthralled by a new mobile and was content to play without crying for eleven minutes. (Kathy timed him.) Kathy said, "We tried the Jolly Jumper—a swing thing—every possible little thing that people had around their houses, but he wanted Mama's arms."

In May, Doc and Sekou again tried to rob the Chemical Bank in Nanuet for a third and fourth time. Both times the Brinks truck did not appear. (The Army also failed at two attempts on a Chase Manhattan Bank in the Bronx.)

When Chesa was a year old, David assigned a meaning to the baby's use of the word *ca* while pointing at a new object or person. "We all went wild with speculation on what 'ca' meant to you . . . you said it while pointing at a cat, so we thought it meant 'cat.' Then we thought 'car.' "

David concluded that Chesa was using the word to define the separation between himself and the world. *Ca* meant "that thing out there." David wrote, "Quite the little philosopher."

Kathy's growing feelings of love for her child kept on catching her by surprise. She began moving away from the May 19 Communist Group. Kathy was reading Chesa books she had liked at his age, particularly *Pat the Bunny*. ("Put your finger through hole and pat soft bunny.")

That summer Kathy and David took Chesa camping for three weeks in California. They'd bought a used 1975 kelly green Toyota Corolla from a man in Woodside, Queens. Kathy registered it in Connecticut under the name Linda Miller. She obtained a Connecticut driver's license under that name and rented a mail pickup box, very close to the *Advocate* newspaper, where her roommate Rita Jensen was working as a reporter.

David moved to an apartment of his own in Washington Heights, making it easier for Kathy and their son to sleep over. David and Kathy were reading a book called *Right from the Start: A Guide to Non-Sexist Childrearing.*

Meanwhile, despite Sekou's disapproval, Doc was still dreaming about the million-dollar sacks he had glimpsed a year earlier in the back of the silver Brinks truck at the small Chemical Bank in Nanuet, Rockland County.

Doc sneaked behind Sekou's back to schedule a fifth attempt to rob the Chemical Bank in Nanuet for October 1981. Doc was more desperate than ever to pay his mortgage. He also needed cocaine. He again broke Family rules by declaring all proceeds of the Rockland robbery would be distributed to Army members, with nothing for revolutionary activities.

Doc now knew that the Brinks truck made the pickup only on Fridays, but instead of simplifying his Nanuet robbery plan as a result of four previous failures, he complicated it.

Judith Clark and Susan Rosenberg had cruised around Rockland and reported back to Doc that a lot more money was loaded onto the Brinks truck on its next stop, a mile away. The larger haul was at Nanuet National Bank in crowded Nanuet Mall. Doc decided to wait until the last possible minute to decide where to rob the Brinks truck. If the haul was piddling at the smaller bank, he would follow the Brinks truck a mile and rob the truck at Nanuet Mall.

Meanwhile, Doc had lost key people. Thus he promoted Sam Brown to the primary team, despite his debilitating drug use. Whenever the "Big Dance" (the code name for the robbery) was mentioned, Sam said, "Yeah, we're going dancing," and ran in circles, pretending to be weighed down by sacks of money.

Rehearsals for the fifth try at the Nanuet robbery were held at a park by tennis courts near 155th Street and Riverside Drive, under the Henry Hudson Parkway. Doc did not tell his men he was sneaking behind Sekou's back: everyone knew Sekou was out of town. Whites were not invited to rehearsals. One man told Doc, "Make sure those crackers get their shit together."

In rehearsals, Doc coached Sam Brown, urging him to strengthen his arms; he was to carry bags of money. When another recruit brought two of his call girls to a session, Sam Brown complained about the security breach.

At one practice session, Doc drove a yellow van right behind the "armored car." A robber pretended to be a guard and went for his gun. Others jumped out of the attack vehicle, but Sam Brown hung back, afraid. Sam was reassured by primary team member Mtayari Shabaka Sundiata, who explained that he was going to save time by instantly killing the Brinks guards. It would be better than waiting for guards to go for their guns.

Robbery attempt number five took place on Tuesday, October 6. Once again five keyed-up, armed men squatted for two hours in the cargo section of the "attack vehicle." When only a few bags of cash were loaded from Chemical Bank into the armored Brinks truck, Doc was too upset to follow his plan to trail the Brinks truck to the larger bank at Nanuet Mall.

Once again, on October 13, the Army arrived at Chemical Bank too late. Hyped on cocaine and frustration, they drove slowly around ranch houses and woodlands. Attempt number six had failed.

When he returned to New York and learned that the Nanuet robbery was still being planned behind his back, Sekou was enraged.

He immediately went to Nanuet and drove along the Brinks truck's pickup route. He then told Doc that all stops it made were too dangerous. Sekou again warned that the bank at the Nanuet Mall was a riskier target than the small Chemical Bank; the mall was too far from the Tappan Zee Bridge. It meant that police would have still more time to erect a roadblock at the Tappan Zee Bridge. Sekou called it "sure death."

But after two other aborted robberies in the Bronx, Doc decided to make a seventh attempt at the Nanuet job, once again without Sekou's knowledge. Kathy Boudin would be enlisted for the seventh attempt.

Chesa looked uncannily like his maternal grandfather's baby pictures. Aware that neither of his children resembled him physically, the delighted Leonard sat with Kathy and his only grandson more and more frequently in the gardens at the Cathedral of St. John the Divine.

David Gilbert was pointedly not included. Leonard knew David was his rival as far as Kathy's surfacing was concerned. Members of the Boudin family whispered of David Gilbert's "harsh influence." For the two arrogant and brilliant men in Kathy's life, this was shaping up to be the fight of their lives. They transmitted accusations through Kathy.

The truth was that David Gilbert did not want to surface. And if Kathy surfaced, it would be difficult for David to see her or his son without being detected by police. David did not want to step back from his commitment to the Army. It gave him what he later called "an exciting secret identity and a chance to make a contribution without expending a lot of time or taking huge risks." He had developed "a service relationship mentality" toward the blacks, which gave him "the best of both worlds."

David feared he would not have a significant place in Kathy's aboveground life, since he was not famous like her father, her uncle Izzy, or Kathy herself. Kathy reinforced David's worries by telling him of Wally Gilbert's Nobel Prize and describing a party Jean had attended for one of Wally's mentors, James Watson, author of *The Double Helix*.

Leonard also organized Boudin family reunions at the stately stone Riverdale mansion of Eleanor Brussel, Kathy's kindergarten teacher and Leonard's friend and confidante of nearly forty years. It was clear that Eleanor, seventy-eight and eyes snapping with enthusiasm, still considered the Boudin family trysts to be naughty larks.

Eleanor broke speed limits driving Leonard in her blue Peugeot to meet Kathy and Chesa and David in an apartment in East Orange, New Jersey. What Leonard did not know was that the apartment was the Army safe house used by Assata Shakur.

Kathy left Chesa with her roommate, Rita, and slept over on Saturday nights at David's apartment. One night at around eleven, after a quarrel about taking Chesa to see Leonard without David, Kathy dashed into the street alone. By now, autumn 1981, Kathy and David could not stop quarreling over Leonard's desire to have her surface. Pressure on Kathy increased when Leonard told her of the possible early release of Cathlyn Wilkerson from prison. She had served less than a year of her three-year sentence at Bedford Hills Correctional Facility.

On October 20, the night before the Rockland robbery was attempted yet again, Kathy tensed for her role. David ignored the fact that Kathy was terribly unhappy.

Kathy's fright was heightened by the fact that her specific tasks depended on Doc's last-minute decision. If Doc decided to follow the

Brinks truck from the small Chemical Bank to the larger bank at crowded Nanuet Mall and rob it there, Kathy and David's U-Haul van would be the "primary switch vehicle." Kathy would then be serving as the decoy in the front seat of the getaway van, filled with guns, over $1 million in stolen money, and robbers high on cocaine and adrenaline. If the robbery went off at the first bank, Kathy and David were to drive back toward Manhattan inconspicuously behind the fleeing robbers, ready to abandon the U-Haul to the robbers at any sign of police. Kathy and David were then to run away, hitch rides, or get themselves back to Manhattan by bus.

If the robbery was aborted (as it had been in previous attempts), Kathy and David would return the rented van and pick up the baby from the sitter.

At 9:30 in the morning of October 20, David waited on West 108th Street in the small green Toyota while Kathy took Chesa, now fourteen months old and still nursing, up to the apartment of his baby-sitter, Ana Vasquez. Kathy was dressed in "respectable guise"—an imitation brown leather jacket, brown boots, and green corduroy pants. Kathy was thirty-seven and very thin. She was not wearing the blond wig; her dark curling hair was combed. She carried identification in the name of Barbara Edson.

David was inconspicuous near Columbia University, with his shoulder-length dark hair and bushy beard.

The two parents hoped to pass casual inspection by suburban police. As the "white edge," or decoys, Kathy and David were to blend into the crowd of suburban commuters driving home through the hamlet of Nyack during rush hour.

After taking Chesa up to the baby-sitter, Kathy ducked back inside the green Toyota. Nancy Gear pulled her car up to bring her own baby to the same baby-sitter. She volunteered to take Chesa to play in the park later on. Kathy thanked Nancy, adding that she and David expected to be back by five o'clock, but if not, she asked if Nancy would take Chesa back to the baby-sitter.

At times such as this Kathy told herself that to risk her life or the lives of other people for a greater good was permissible, even mandatory. Kathy also told herself that she would be back before five o'clock, even though the bank robbery was scheduled for four o'clock. The plan was for Kathy to travel forty-five miles to Manhattan during rush hour and jump on a subway while David returned the U-Haul rental truck—all in time to pick up her baby at 5 p.m.

Kathy was also assuming that if the robbery took place, it would be a success and that no blood would be shed. This, despite the fact that all participants—including the guards—carried guns. The Army had recently murdered a guard at a similar robbery, for which Judith Clark had been lookout. The crime had taken place four months earlier on the morning of June 2 in the Bronx at a small Daitch-Shopwell shopping plaza on the Boston Post Road near Mount Vernon. The Army had netted $292,000. Brinks was offering a $100,000 reward for information leading to the robbers' arrest. Kathy may not have been a direct participant in that robbery, but she knew of it and the murder of a fifty-nine-year-old Brinks guard named William Moroney by Army member Tyron Rison.

After leaving Chesa, David drove the green Toyota to the Bronx. Carrying a heavy knapsack, probably filled with guns and ammunition, he and Kathy walked two blocks to Kingsbridge Moving and Storage Company at 230 West 230th Street. David signed papers to rent an orange-and-silver-striped U-Haul truck. His alias, James Lester Hackford, belonged to a retired New York City policeman. Authorities also believe that David had also rented another escape vehicle—a white Oldsmobile. Two white women of the May 19 Communist Group (believed by authorities to be Marilyn Buck and Susan Rosenberg) were to park and wait in it at a Texaco station in Nyack.

Kathy and David hung a burlap cloth between the passenger seats and the back of the U-Haul. They pasted metallic contact paper inside the back windows to hide crouching robbers. The contact paper actually put the robbers at a disadvantage: they were unable to see potential crises outside the van.

David and Kathy then drove to the quiet suburb of Nanuet, past a few shoppers at McDonald's, Jack La Lanne, and a Pathmark, and finally around to the rear of the abandoned Korvettes store. Back here, all but hidden from view, was the "switchpoint," a small loading area.

It was early afternoon. There was nothing to do but wait, with dry mouths and pulses racing, to find out if, where, and how successfully the robbery had been performed.

By one o'clock, Doc was steering a red Chevy van (contact paper also covering its back windows) through suburban villages surrounded by woods. The van was filled with cramped, armed members of the primary team, again high on cocaine. Judith Clark was steering a rented tan Honda behind Doc and his men. She and Silvia Baraldini were disguised for war in tweedy jackets, slacks, and gray wigs.

Moments later, Doc parked at the small Chemical Bank. He cursed his bad luck as he watched armed Brinks guards hoist only one white canvas money bag into the back door of the silver armored truck.

James Kelly, age forty-eight, drove the silver Brinks truck on Fridays, on "the Federal Reserve run," past quaint towns, tract houses, malls, and banks. He was a relaxed, talkative man to whom the drill of drawing guns while loading money sacks had the feel of a child's game. In the tight space in the back of the Brinks truck, separated from James Kelly by bulletproof glass, guards Joe Trombino and Peter Paige were feeling nostalgic. This Friday was, after fifteen years, their last scheduled run together. Peter Paige was being transferred to a new route.

It took Doc a split second to decide not to rob the silver armored truck at Chemical Bank. He was still furious that only one bag of money had been loaded onto the Brinks truck. He swore as he trailed the truck to the larger bank at Nanuet Mall.

At 3:45, he and his soldiers pulled into Nanuet Mall. A nervous primary team man with a mustache and sideburns—born Donald Weems but now calling himself Kuwasi Balagoon—jumped out of Doc's red Chevy van and strolled to a bus stop just outside the mall.

He stared at the silver Brinks truck parked ten feet away from the mall's rear entrance.

Balagoon watched Brinks guards Joe Trombino and Peter Paige wheel a cart into the mall.

Inside the Brinks truck, James Kelly moved from the driver's seat into the passenger seat to fill out the last entry on a clipboard of the day's stops. The two other guards, Peter Paige and Joe Trombino, soon reappeared, wheeling three heavy sacks of money to the rear of the truck. In the passenger seat, Kelly hit the release button for the back door. While Peter Paige pointed his gun to the ground, Joe Trombino lifted one bag of money into the rear compartment.

Kuwasi Balagoon jumped up and ran toward the white canvas sacks of money, shooting his gun. Simultaneously three men in ski masks and ski suits sprang out of the red Chevy, also shooting at the two guards.

One of the robbers waved his gun at shoppers walking out of the mall, keeping them at bay. Trombino fired one shot and then was hit in his shoulder and upper arm by a bullet that almost tore his arm from his shoulder. "I got no arm," he shouted. (He survived, only to be killed in the World Trade Center terrorist attack on September 11, 2001.)

Inside the front of the Brinks car, James Kelly heard loud claps and assumed it was "firecrackers because the week before when I was there some young kids were throwing these little firecrackers down. At first I thought it was that, until I seen the expression on Mr. Paige's face completely change and I realized what happened."

To gain precious seconds, the robbers gave Peter Paige no chance to aim or drop his weapon. He was executed by two different robbers as he stood by the back of the Brinks truck, his gun pointed downward.

One masked robber ran around to the front of the Brinks truck and shot out the glass. He narrowly missed killing James Kelly, who ducked. Flying glass knocked Kelly out.

Sam Brown hung back in the red van until the shooting paused. Wearing several layers of clothing, including a yellow ski suit purchased for him by Doc, he ran to the back of the armored truck, reached over the bleeding Joe Trombino, and lifted canvas money sacks smeared with blood. Sam Brown picked up two more sacks from the ground—six sacks in all, three containing $759,000 from earlier pickups, three with $839,000 from the Nanuet Mall bank. In his haste, he left sacks containing $1.3 million. He broke three fingernails dragging the sacks to the red van.

The robbery was over in forty seconds. No Army member had been hurt. They slammed the doors of the red Chevy van shut. Doc hit the gas pedal.

The robbers were jumping up and down as they crouched in the back of the red van. Meanwhile, Brinks driver James Kelly staggered out of the front seat of the silver truck. He was unaware that he had a concussion and facial cuts.

"I climbed in the back of the truck. Blood was like chocolate pudding all over the floor. I sat Mr. Trombino down next to Mr. Paige. At that time I didn't know Mr. Paige was completely out of it. Some woman came running over; she said she's a nurse. I soon lost composure of myself. I locked myself in the truck [crying and saying over and over 'They shot my friends'] until a police officer from Clarkstown talked me into getting control of myself and coming out."

17

MURDER IN NYACK

David turned off the motor of the orange-and-silver U-Haul. He and Kathy were a mile away from the robbery site and still parked behind the vacant Korvettes store.

David peered at Kathy, who was terribly frightened. To distract her, David asked her to get out and check the sliding back door of the U-Haul. Standing behind the truck, Kathy blocked David's view of the spot where the red van would enter.

Since David saw life through a filter of political absolutes that he sometimes failed to live up to, he later wrote, "Part of why I turned to talk to her came from a realistic sense that she was feeling shaky. Part of it came from a sexist arrogance that I am better at tactical military work than my partner—which isn't true."

Unseen by Kathy and David, Doc's red van swerved into the Korvettes parking lot. Oddly, Doc did not see David and Kathy's U-Haul, either.

Thirty seconds later, David spotted the red Chevy van. He made a critical mistake. Panicked and relieved, he drove the U-Haul toward the red van. His instructions had been clear: he was to wait hidden behind the vacant Korvettes for Doc to drive over to him.

In the heat of the moment, neither he nor Kathy nor Judith Clark and Silvia Baraldini, in the tan Honda escort vehicle, nor any of the blacks, high on fear, victory, and cocaine as well as adrenaline, realized that in this new meeting spot where they now converged all three vehicles could be seen from the living room of the lone house whose windows faced the parking lot.

This was precisely the sort of deadly error that, in the past, had been seized upon and corrected by the absent Sekou Odinga.

Kathy's jaw muscle clenched as she heard the robbers exult about the successful robbery. There was bright blood on the canvas bags. The primary team men were still dressed for combat in ski suits, white bullet-proof vests, surgical gloves, and ski masks. They dragged four sacks containing $798,000 into David and Kathy's U-Haul. Two other sacks, which contained $800,000, were carried to the trunk of the tan Honda.

In the house facing the parking lot, a young woman was writing a college economics paper. Through her living-room window, she had paid little attention to the tan Honda and the red Chevy van entering the parking lot. The cars had disappeared from her view. But the vehicles reappeared, and she watched a black man waving a rifle jump out of a side door of the red van and climb up into the back of a third vehicle—a silver-and-orange U-Haul truck.

The young woman ran outdoors to try to see license numbers, but all the running men had vanished, along with the Honda and the U-Haul truck. In a frenzy to leave, they'd abandoned the telltale red Chevy robbery van—doors open and motor running. The young woman ran inside her house and called the local police.

"A red van?" the policeman asked. He was already in the process of transmitting reports of the robbers escaping from the mall. Police from all over Rockland County were converging on Nanuet.

The telephone description of the frenzied black men with guns climbing from a red Chevy van into the orange U-Haul truck helped police plan roadblocks. David and Kathy had inadvertently dealt a fatal blow to the Army's escape.

Three minutes later, David was steering the orange U-Haul truck east through Friday rush-hour traffic toward the hamlet of Nyack. He turned at the Kentucky Fried Chicken sign, driving past signs on the right side of the road: WEST NYACK CARES, CENTRAL NYACK CARES.

David made a left turn toward the crowded entrance ramp leading to the New York State Thruway. He was calming himself by breathing long, deep breaths, as he did in his yoga workout. Another three minutes and he would be across the Tappan Zee Bridge and home free. Judith Clark was driving right behind David in the tan Honda, with $800,000. The rest of the money was in the back of the U-Haul, along with the six men who had just killed at least one person. At this point in the operation, the Army primary team was utterly dependent upon the "crackers" in the passenger seats of the U-Haul. The robbers could not see out the windows, which were covered by contact paper. As they listened through the stapled burlap partition to David's upbeat reports of traffic conditions, it was clear to them that Kathy (the other "cracker") was falling apart.

Moods plummeted all around when David reported that a uniformed white policeman had driven up onto the road in front of them and parked his police car across the Thruway entrance ramp, partially blocking access.

Whenever a robbery occurred in any part of Rockland County, Nyack police sped to this intersection and set up a roadblock. The spot was key in the easterly escape to the Tappan Zee Bridge.

Only five short minutes had passed since the vehicle switch. A police siren blared. In the back of the U-Haul, the Army men were exploding with fear and frustration. They scratched frantically at the corners of the contact paper, but it was tightly glued on. It was impossible to see what was happening. Meanwhile, Judith also spotted the police car. She signaled David and cut ahead of him, steering toward the police car.

Parked squarely in the middle of the highway, the young Nyack policeman, Brian Lennon, pointed a shotgun at the passenger side of the U-Haul windshield. The muzzle faced Kathy.

Three minutes earlier, and less than half a mile away, Brian Lennon had been on coffee break at the Village Donut Shop on picturesque Main Street in Nyack. His portable radio had broadcast an urgent "101" for him to call the office. He ducked into his car and followed two other Nyack policemen—Sergeant Edward O'Grady, the officer in charge on that fateful day, and Detective Arthur Keenan—each driving an unmarked Nyack police car to the intersection.

Radio transmissions had alerted each of them that an armed robbery had taken place a few miles away at Nanuet Mall, and that after killing at least one Brinks guard and stealing almost $2 million in currency, the six

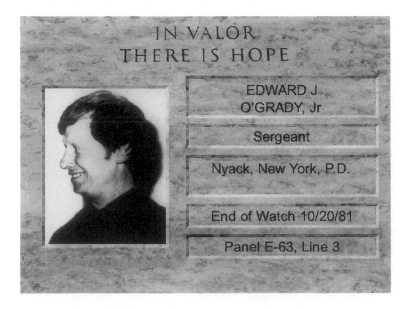

IN VALOR
THERE IS HOPE

WAVERLY L
BROWN

Police Officer

Nyack, New York, P.D.

End of Watch 10/20/81

Panel E-32, Line 1

ABOVE: *Waverly "Chipper" Brown was a popular policeman killed during the Brinks robbery at the roadblock in Nyack. The only black policeman on the force, he'd served in the United States Air Force after the Korean War. He gave away turkeys to poor families on Thanksgiving. The third man killed was Brinks guard Peter Paige.*

BELOW: *Sergeant Edward O'Grady Jr., age thirty-two, was one of three men killed in the Brinks robbery in Nyack on October 20, 1981. He had served two tours of duty in Vietnam and had been a policeman for eleven years. He planned to practice law when he retired.*

IN VALOR
THERE IS HOPE

EDWARD J
O'GRADY, Jr

Sergeant

Nyack, New York, P.D.

End of Watch 10/20/81

Panel E-63, Line 3

robbers—all black men—had escaped in a red Chevrolet van and then switched to an orange-and-silver U-Haul truck.

Red-haired Sergeant Edward O'Grady had been a cop for eleven years; he was skinny and tall and strong for his size. He had served two tours of duty in Vietnam and was a volunteer fireman. He was a stubborn man—conscientious to a fault. As ranking officer, he was in charge of the roadblock.

Behind Sergeant O'Grady's was a third police car, driven by another popular Nyack policeman, Officer Waverly "Chipper" Brown, the only black man on the force. When he heard the call, Brown had been parked at the Exxon station some thirty feet off the entrance ramp.

Following O'Grady's radioed instructions, Lennon parked his car across the lane leading to the entrance ramp and pointed his gun at the orange-and-silver U-Haul van. But unlike the robbers, neither the U-Haul driver nor the woman passenger was black. Although this was a huge relief to Officer Lennon, he kept his gun trained on the van.

There were two passenger cars in front of the orange-and-silver U-Haul. The first was the tan Honda driven by Judith Clark. The second was a new tan BMW being driven by a local woman named Norma Hill. Norma was in a hurry. She and her elderly mother were doubling back to a dry cleaner near Norma's shoe and handbag store across from the Nanuet Mall. Norma had forgotten to pick up her daughter's private-school uniform. Also in the BMW was a manila envelope containing nearly $15,000 in cash from the store.

Norma was scheduled to host a dinner party with her husband at the Rainbow Room for advertising executives from all over the world. She stepped on the gas pedal. It looked to her as if policemen were giving someone a ticket. She slowed to ask Brian Lennon if she could pass. "Move on," nodded Lennon curtly. She and her mother sailed by, only to get stuck in commuter traffic.

In the tan Honda Judith Clark also passed Brian Lennon, safely if temporarily out of the roadblock and the clutches of the police. Suddenly police sirens blared. The two policemen in the unmarked Nyack police car pulled up close behind the U-Haul as it was barreling toward Brian Lennon and the Thruway entrance.

Twelve feet in front of the U-Haul, Officer Brian Lennon was still pointing the muzzle of his shotgun at Kathy's side of the windshield. David braked and stopped.

Ahead of the roadblock by some fifty feet, Judith Clark braked. She got out of the Honda and stood on tiptoe to see what was happening behind her. Norma Hill noticed her standing under the road sign. Judith's clumpy gray wig looked odd, but she seemed like one more rubbernecking commuter. Nearby in another car, two more white May 19 Communist Group women screeched to a stop.

Although Nyack police had used emergency tactics to corner the U-Haul, they still doubted that it was the right vehicle because of its two white occupants. Their radios were reporting another orange U-Haul truck, identical to this one but driven by blacks, that was traveling south toward New Jersey.

Kathy raised her arms and inched out of the passenger side of the U-Haul. Staring at the shotgun pointed at her, she hunched over, as if her stomach spasmed. Jumping down to the highway, her eyes open wide, she raised her palms higher.

David Gilbert also raised his hands high and slid out of the driver's side of the U-Haul. He was far less frightened, telling himself he had arrived at this spot after years of thought and physical training for "armed struggle."

Officer Lennon waved Kathy and David over to the grassy side of the road. As part of the "white edge," Kathy's main job was to keep her cool and distract police by presenting an innocuous flirty presence.

Instead, Kathy edged a few steps toward the Thruway, distancing herself from the U-Haul. Officer Chipper Brown got out of his car. The black policeman trained his shotgun on Kathy. Kathy turned to Sergeant O'Grady, who'd gotten out of the second police car behind the U-Haul. "Tell them to put the gun back," she shouted to him in an earnest, fearful tone. He stepped cautiously around the U-Haul and toward Kathy. Apparently convinced by the authority in Kathy's voice and by the fact of her and David's white skin, he put his handgun back in his holster and turned to tell Chipper Brown to put his gun away, too. "I don't think it's them."

Later O'Grady's wife, Diane, said with sadness and bitterness, "Look, a girl my age asks him in a scared voice to put away the gun. Of course he did what she asked."

Kathy was looking from side to side trying to figure out what each policeman was doing. And although she was murmuring sounds of appeasement, Kathy was stepping away from the roadblock.

Detective Keenan stepped out of the police car behind the orange U-Haul. He circled it. Opening the door Kathy had just exited, he stuck his head in. The robbers behind the burlap drop cloth froze. Their euphoria had crashed to murderous fear. Kathy again yelled to O'Grady, "Tell them to put the gun back."

Sergeant O'Grady shouted to Lennon, "Put the shotgun back. I don't think it's them." Shrugging his assent, Lennon bent into his own car and locked his shotgun under the dashboard.

Meanwhile, Detective Keenan nervously popped open the glove compartment inside the passenger area of the U-Haul. Nothing looked out of the ordinary. Inches away and hidden by the burlap, the robbers crouched and listened, motionless.

Keenan backed out of the U-Haul truck and circled to its rear. He jiggled and then yanked the back door handle. It was sealed from inside. He walked to Kathy and, grabbing her arm, he pointed his thumb at the rear cargo section of the U-Haul truck. "I want to know what's in there."

Just then, one of the robbers pulled the metal door open a crack. He saw flashing red police car lights. Turning quickly to the others, he said, "It's on." One robber dropped an ammunition clip before loading his M-16 rifle.

Detective Keenan heard a ping as the ammunition clip fell inside the truck. Another robber shouted, "Go," and another lifted the metal door.

The rear door of the U-Haul truck clanged upward. Two men holding handguns and a third holding an M-16 automatic rifle sprang from the truck almost simultaneously and crouched on the highway in identical military stances. Behind them three more men leaped out.

There in sleepy little Nyack, in the middle of a crowded Thruway entrance ramp on a road filled with rush-hour commuters, the robbers began firing rounds of bullets at anyone wearing a police uniform. Within seconds, the road was transformed into a battlefield.

Officer Keenan rolled and dived to the side of the road, returning fire from behind a pine tree, unaware he had been hit twice. The fact that he was out of uniform saved his life.

The black policeman, Chipper Brown, fell instantly. He was raked with bullets, his chest torn open. He had no chance to fire his gun. As Ed O'Grady tried to reload his .347 Magnum revolver next to a police car, one of the robbers shot him repeatedly with an M-16 rifle.

Sam Brown, the most frightened of the robbers, was the last to jump out of the U-Haul. He forced an ammunition clip into his 9mm handgun and shot rapidly at three uniformed policemen. Recognizing Judith Clark's tan Honda parked in front of the U-Haul, he ran toward it.

The Army's roadblock strategy was a shambles, for which they later blamed their white supporters. As soon as police appeared, Judith Clark was supposed to have parked her car in front of the police cars, blocking them. Now, although she had in fact parked, her car was not blocking police. As per the plan, the two other white May 19 women had abandoned their car on the highway so that the blacks could at least jump in it and flee.

Meanwhile, across the Thruway traffic slowed. Michael Koch, a burly and extroverted young parole officer and Vietnam veteran, braked his camper. Although not in uniform, he had his gun. He spotted policemen talking to a thin, straggly-haired woman in a brown leather jacket who was standing on a grassy knoll.

Hearing the familiar sounds of guns and battle and seeing a small army of black men appear out of nowhere, Michael Koch told himself, "This is 'Nam in Nyack." He could not imagine what was going on, but when a small movement caught his eye, he jumped out of his camper.

The wiry, straggly-haired white woman whom he'd seen talking to police had broken away from them and now was weaving through traffic and dodging cars. Kathy'd crossed the road, knees pumping, and was fleeing on her own.

Koch unholstered his gun and ran after her.

Back at the roadblock, Doc had been trying to steer the U-Haul around Brian Lennon's police car; he rammed into it, then pulled alongside it. The battered U-Haul began spurting antifreeze. David and Doc peered at Brian Lennon, trying to figure out what he was going to do next. David's was the coolest head; unlike the other Army men, he was not high on cocaine, believing it destructive to brain cells.

As police shot at David Gilbert from behind, he ran to Judith Clark's tan Honda, still parked a few car lengths ahead.

Sam Brown also reached the tan Honda and lay across its hood, firing three or four shots back at police before his gun jammed. He fell off the Honda, cursing as its occupants took off. He was stranded.

Sam Brown tried to commandeer a station wagon filled with local people, but the driver stepped on the gas pedal. Then Brown looked ahead and saw that the tan Honda had stopped for him—someone swung the back door open. He streaked toward it.

From inside the back of the Honda, David pulled in the injured Brown. The back of Brown's head had been shaved by a bullet; he was bleeding and missing a patch of hair. Judith Clark was in the front passenger seat. The driver, May 19 member Silvia Baraldini, was bleeding from a bullet wound. She'd shot herself in the leg trying to draw a gun. Sam Brown screamed at Baraldini, "Get me out of here," and passed out.

Surrounded by blasts of bullets, a local pediatrician named Ronald Dreyer threw himself down on the road behind his silver Oldsmobile, leaving the motor idling. He held his breath as he listened to rounds of automatic gunfire, then single shots. He peeked out and into the muzzle of a shotgun pointed at him by a bank robber.

Kathy was across the highway and running for her life. Galloping after her, Michael Koch was reliving his combat days. He shouted "Halt!" and waved his badge and gun, not realizing that in a denim shirt and with long hair and a beard, he looked nothing like a policeman. Finally he caught up with her. "Halt!" he shouted, grabbing her.

Kathy thrust her hands above her head.

"Police, don't move," Michael Koch shouted over the noise of passing cars.

"Are you crazy?" Kathy asked with the same earnest authority that had disarmed Officer O'Grady.

Then, her hands still raised, Kathy wrestled away from Koch's grasp and started running again. Koch pursued her. He grabbed a clump of her hair and held on, putting the muzzle of his gun against her neck. Panicking, she said, "He shot him. I didn't shoot anyone." Frisking her, Koch found no weapons. He pulled her coat down over her arms to pin them against her body, then pushed her back toward the scene of the shooting.

"Are you crazy?" she shouted again, resisting.

"How many are there with you?" Koch asked.

Kathy finally took her own *Bust Book* advice and did not answer. Koch dragged and pushed her back to the roadblock.

When they reached it, Koch handcuffed Kathy with cuffs belonging to Detective Arthur Keenan. The air smelled of gasoline and burning gunpowder. Police cars sat in the middle of the road, windshields shot out. Other cars were at a standstill bumper to bumper. Police began shouting questions at Kathy, who lowered her head. From a departing car, one of the robbers screamed, "Forget about Kathy. Leave her. I don't care."

The Army men cursed and screamed at one another. They had shot in all directions and bullets were later found hundreds of yards away in gas pumps at a station across Route 59. The robber who had trained his shotgun on Dr. Dreyer used it to nudge the pediatrician away from his Oldsmobile. Screaming to his companions to join him, the robber got into the Oldsmobile and tore off into Nyack on Mountainview Avenue.

To Michael Koch, the scene looked like the aftermath of a brutal wartime battle: two policemen lay bleeding to death. Police shouted into their radios for medical aid, giving conflicting descriptions of the fleeing suspects.

Kuwasi Balagoon ran over to Norma Hill; she and her mother were still stalled in traffic. He poked a machine gun in her face and ordered her out of her BMW. When she did not immediately obey, he yanked the car door open and grabbed her shoulder, ripping her suit. He threw her down on the road. She screamed at him, "Let my mother alone." Ignoring her, he dove into Norma's car next to her shaking mother, skidding past the police. Michael Koch raised his gun to shoot him, but Norma Hill scrambled off the ground and tackled him. "Don't shoot," she said. "Please don't shoot."

Michael Koch leveled his gun at Norma Hill. He assumed she was working with Kathy, but Norma rapidly convinced him that her BMW had just been stolen with her mother in it. Kathy was still standing next to Michael Koch, hands cuffed behind her back, head still bowed.

Suddenly Norma shrieked and pointed frantically to her BMW where a body was rolling out onto the road. She raced to her mother as several people screamed that the elderly woman was dead. Norma turned her over, fully expecting to see her riddled with bullet holes. To Norma's relief, her mother was dazed but unharmed. Two bystanders crawled over to help. Norma dragged her mother out of the line of fire.

Norma watched her BMW, with Kuwasi Balagoon at the wheel, speed after Dr. Dreyer's silver Olds up Mountainview Avenue and into Nyack. Michael Koch ordered Kathy to lie facedown and spread-eagle. Kathy lowered herself to the cement highway, where she lay next to the dead black policeman, Chipper Brown. A puddle of his blood merged with antifreeze from the battered U-Haul and oozed at her. By her side, Dr. Dreyer, the pediatrician, was kneeling, trying to start Officer Brown's heart. "Who are you?" he asked Kathy. Twisting her head up, Kathy said, "Don't shoot me. Don't let them hurt me. Just please don't let them hurt me."

Two policemen stopped an ambulance transporting a heart attack victim and lifted Officer Brown into it. The vehicle raced to Nyack Hospital, where he was pronounced dead on arrival from three bullet wounds—in his chest, thigh, and shoulder.

It was now 4:05 p.m., only fifteen minutes since the silver Brinks truck had stopped at Nanuet Mall.

Officer Chipper Brown had been very popular. Hundreds of people had felt good greeting him on a daily basis. Brown was forty-five and had served thirteen years in Nyack. He had been in the air force after the Korean War and had two daughters serving in the air force overseas. Divorced, he spent a lot of time with his teenage son, Gregory. He set an example for black schoolchildren and spent hours of off-duty time urging them to eschew drugs and to do well in school. Every year he bought more than a dozen Thanksgiving turkeys for indigent neighbors. Among the many people who felt they had lost a personal friend at Chipper's death were his fellow members of the local NAACP and the Elks organization.

Meanwhile, his young partner, Sergeant Edward O'Grady, battled for his life at the same hospital. Many people in Rockland County had gone through school with Ed O'Grady. He was a Vietnam War veteran and, with his wife, Diane, he was raising a family of three children: Edward Jr., age six, Patricia, two, and Kimberly, six months. He was taking courses in criminal justice at St. Thomas Aquinas College.

On the operating table, Sergeant O'Grady was treated for massive bleeding caused by three bullets that had shattered his liver, his diaphragm, and his kidney. He died an hour and a half after doctors started working on him.

The two dead policemen were valued members of the small Nyack community, whose citizens would not forget or forgive their murders in coming decades. Nor would townspeople overlook the fact that big-city blacks and whites claiming to be fighting for the greater good of blacks had gunned down and murdered the town's only black policeman.

Robbers in three escaping cars—their own tan Honda, the stolen silver Olds, and the BMW—sped up narrow, twisting Mountainview Avenue, passing signs reading SLOW, CHILDREN AT PLAY, 15 MPH. They skidded through the quaint, riverside hamlet of Nyack. With the tan Honda leading the way, all three cars swerved up on the front lawn of one ranch house on Mountainview Avenue. Police sirens blared in the distance.

Shouting at the others to hurry, David stumbled over the rocks in the driveway. The robbers loaded guns and divided ammunition. Judith

Clark had four rounds of .380 ammunition in her purse and a .380 semi-automatic pistol. They embraced, cursing, crying, laughing, at the miraculous fact that they had shot their way out.

David whispered words of encouragement to the bleeding Silvia Baraldini and to Sam Brown, semiconscious on the backseat of the tan Honda. It was David who made the decision to go on in two cars and to abandon the easily spotted BMW, doors open and windshield wipers running. One robber ran toward the surrounding woods, where he buried his gun.

With the silver Oldsmobile in the lead, the two cars sped feverishly on for several miles. Judith Clark drove the Honda, with David in the passenger seat and Sam Brown lying in the back.

Driving by, South Nyack police chief Alan Colsey, age twenty-nine, spotted the tan Honda. Instantly he wheeled his car around and chased the robbers at eighty miles an hour through the residential streets of Nyack. Judith Clark lost control of the Honda and crashed it into a pole. The Honda then careened into a cement wall at Sixth Avenue and Broadway, directly in front of a stately house owned by Helen Hayes, whose long lawns sloped down to the Hudson River.

Two hundred yards ahead, the silver Olds escaped, speeding south past the Nyack Police Station.

David crawled out of the wrecked Honda. He began talking in a working-class Boston accent to distract Chief Colsey, so that Sam Brown and Judith could grab guns. Neighbors thronged, asking if anyone needed help. Chief Colsey shouted, "Keep back. Get away. They may be armed." David shouted, too: "We need help. My friend is hurt."

Colsey drew his gun and pointed it at the three robbers, saying, "Don't move. Get out of the car with your hands up." Colsey kept his gun trained on David and Judith until other policemen arrived. Glancing over the roof of the tan Honda, Colsey was horrified to see a school bus stop. Children leaned out of the windows to see the commotion.

Then Colsey and policeman Jim Stewart pulled the wounded Sam Brown out through the back window. Brown fought them as they peeled layers of clothes off him and found his ammunition clip hidden in his sock.

In automobiles and on foot, Doc, Marilyn Buck, Silvia Baraldini, Kuwasi Balagoon, Sundiata, Chui Ferguson, Edward Joseph, and at least one

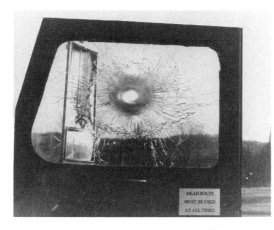

The robbers shot to kill guards inside the Brinks truck, Nanuet Mall, 1981.

RIGHT: *Kathy Boudin, Nyack Police headquarters, October 21, 1981.*

BELOW: *David Gilbert, Kathy's ex-husband and the father of Chesa. A brilliant economist, he is serving a life sentence in a maximum-security prison for his participation in robberies with the Black Army. Note David Gilbert's bulletproof vest and blackened eyes.*

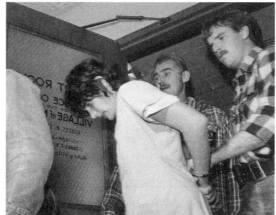

more May 19 woman, who authorities believe was Susan Rosenberg, escaped from Rockland.

Back at the roadblock, Officer Brian Lennon told Kathy to stand up. He pushed her into his police car, her hands still cuffed behind her back, her face smudged. Kathy said that her name was Barbara Edson. Officer Lennon was in a terrible rage against the small and silent woman. He was also baffled; he knew bank robbers did not attack and gun down policemen.

Steering past familiar quaint boutiques on Main Street on the way to the police station, Officer Lennon's mind raced with confusing theories about how his silent passenger might have arrived at this low spot. She was older than she had first appeared; there were fine lines at the corners of her eyes and a crease between her brows. He told her, "Because you wanted the shotgun put away, now there's two cops shot." She said nothing.

Eight hours later Kathy wore shackles on her wrists and ankles, big white slippers, loose brown prison pants, a large green shirt, and blue sweat jacket with the letters R.C. JAIL.

She sat with David and Judith in a small meeting room in the Nyack village hall. Kathy was trying to look inconspicuous.

Outside, grieving and terrified townspeople gathered. Rumors flew. Although it was after midnight, no one wanted to go home. They kept telling one another what they'd been doing when they learned about the robbery and shootout.

The whole episode was a stunning first for the riverfront community of sixty-five hundred inhabitants, many of whom commuted to Manhattan. Everyone knew someone who'd been at the mall. There had never before been a policeman killed in the line of duty. "Give them the electric chair," shouted a teenage boy. Others took up the cry.

Inside the meeting room, three unlikely bank robbery and murder suspects faced the arraigning judge. David was doing his best to look nonchalant. By his side, the slight Judith Clark slid down in her chair, grinning. (It was a nervous habit that did not endear her under present circumstances.)

Judith whispered something to David, then said, "I want a lawyer. I've been asking for a lawyer all afternoon." Not underground, she gave her real name. Sam Brown, who was being arraigned in a hospital bed,

John Castellucci, thirty-four, Nyack, 1981. The Rockland County reporter who investigated the Brinks robbers. When he learned Kathy's identity, John had felt a flash of complicity with her. He had taken part in the 1968 Columbia University student uprising. But he instantly understood that the Brinks robbery was an entirely different kind of violence. He recalled his dislike of the guilt-tripping tactics of fellow students who'd claimed that daring to be violent made them more serious and committed to such ideals as racial equity.

gave the alias "Sam Boines." Kathy and David also gave aliases, although only cockeyed optimism kept them from assuming that FBI fingerprint records would soon reveal their identities. The judge read the list of murder and bank robbery charges. The Brinks guard Peter Paige was dead. The police officer Waverly Brown had died, as had Sergeant Edward O'Grady.

Kathy was trying to look tough and inconspicuous at the same time. John Castellucci, a young reporter who later wrote a comprehensive book about the robbery, was confounded by the three suspects. He noted that "Barbara Edson" appeared the least confident. When Kathy asked for a lawyer, she sounded apologetic, as if she were sorry for taking up a busy man's time.

David, Kathy, and Judith had fantasized about situations like this one many times. All three knew stories of radicals who'd been arrested throughout U.S. history. They remembered how Alexander Berkman, captured after failing to assassinate Henry Frick, president of U.S. Steel,

July 1917 anarchists Emma Goldman and Alexander Berkman were romanticized
by Kathy Boudin and David Gilbert. Goldman and Berkman spent time in jail
for fighting the draft.

shored himself up by telling himself, "I am a brave revolutionary." John
Brown declared at his hanging that he was proud and happy.

The judge charged Judith, Kathy, and David one at a time, as they sat
in front of him, with multiple counts of robbery and felony murder.
They were by state law liable for any killings that took place during the
failed holdup and subsequent shootout.

At around 2 a.m., authorities in Nyack finally allowed Kathy a telephone call. Instead of calling her father, Kathy called Weather supporter
and radical lawyer William Kunstler, who lived in a brownstone on Gay
Street, near St. Luke's Place.

Margaret Ratner Kunstler answered Kathy's telephone call. As soon as
the operator asked her to accept a collect call from a correctional facility,
she groggily handed the phone across the bed pillows to her husband.
Kathy identified herself as "Barbara Edson" and said she needed legal
help. She asked if Kunstler had heard of something happening in Nyack.
He had not. Failing to recognize her voice, Kunstler hung up after telling
her to call back the next morning.

Sometime during that night, David and Judith were beaten by police, suffering bruised arms, broken noses, and swollen, blackened eyes. Kathy was not beaten. The police had learned her identity and were aware her father was a powerful lawyer.

The next morning, Kathy called the Kunstlers collect once more and this time said to Margaret, "You know my father, Leonard." At that Margaret realized who the caller was.

Having the news of her participation in the disastrous robbery broken by William Kunstler, a rival lawyer, gave Kathy leverage. She was forcing Leonard to compete with Bill Kunstler to be her lawyer. Unlike Leonard, Kunstler was an experienced criminal lawyer. His clients had included Jack Ruby and the New York Panthers.

Kunstler immediately telephoned Leonard at his office. Kunstler persuaded Leonard's secretary, Sherry Wertheimer, to put a reporter from ABC-TV news on hold.

Leonard's reaction to the calamitous news about his daughter was swift: How soon could Bill Kunstler pick him up and drive up to Nyack? Leonard needed someone with Kunstler's experience in criminal proceedings.

Leonard ran the eight steps down the short hallway to Victor Rabinowitz's office. Wisps of his longish white hair were standing on end. Struggling to push his arm into his suit jacket, Leonard said, "Let's go. Bill Kunstler's driving to Nyack. Kathy's been arrested on a murder charge."

Outside, Victor spotted Bill Kunstler, his wife, Margaret, and Jean folded into Kunstler's little blue Saab.

On the drive to Nyack, Jean held Leonard's arm. Bill Kunstler tersely recited Kathy's version of events. Leonard and Victor asked key questions, trying to pinpoint where Kathy was during the robbery and during the shootout. Jean posed her face in a tense smile. Her eyes smarted. She was determined not to cry for Leonard's sake. She regretted that she happened to be dressed in black; she did not want to look as if she were mourning for Kathy's life.

Leonard's friends worried about his heart condition. This was a terrible blow, particularly in view of his recent efforts to have Kathy surrender peacefully. He'd just been released from the hospital after a month of treatment for a serious bout of endocarditis. The viral illness had flared after a trip to Ecuador to visit a young lover who had previously stayed with him and Jean at St. Luke's Place. Victor and the Kunstlers knew nothing of Jean's bad heart and her recent operations.

Leonard and Jean Boudin, October 21, 1981, outside Nyack courthouse, surrounded by the press after talking with their daughter, Kathy, about her arrest for murder and robbery.

As William Kunstler steered the way to Nyack, Victor recalled his own daughter Joni's arrest in Albany, Georgia, although Kathy was being accused of crimes that seemed on the surface to bear scant relation to political principles. He thought sadly that if there were any truth to charges, she'd gone crazy.

Other friends were horrified, too. In Chicago, Andrew Patner, a biographer of Izzy Stone, was angry that Kathy had done such a bad thing to Leonard. "He devoted his life to fighting inequities in 'the system' but always through legal and orderly means." The elderly southern civil rights activist Virginia Durr wrote to a friend from her home in Wetumpka, Alabama: "What puzzles me more than anything else about the whole thing is how such a smart girl could do such a dumb thing. She stayed with us once for several days, and while very polite and pleasant, she was absolutely impenetrable, neither Cliff nor I could understand her position in the least, nor can I understand it now."

Few saw Kathy's Army codefendants as anything but hardened criminals, con artists, and drug addicts. Even those who claimed to "get the

Robin Hood aspect of robbing the rich" were appalled. "In broad daylight, at a crowded shopping mall?" asked Alice Carlen. "Why would such a smart girl risk her life on such a stupid plan?"

Particularly irked were those old leftists who used the term *revolution* seriously or with irony. One problem was, for them, that a revolution was analogous to a religious miracle. It was never expected to happen at close hand; even the Revolutionary War was safely in the distant past.

Victor admitted his quandary when pressed. "Of course, I never really took part in a revolution, except perhaps in my mind."

Kathy's friend Connie Brown, now a psychologist, had her own interpretation. Connie knew of Leonard's powerful grip on Kathy's feelings and mused that Kathy had finally figured out how to get the man's absolute attention, while also protecting herself from him by putting prison bars between them.

18

MY DAUGHTER LOVES THIS
COUNTRY VERY MUCH

The five graying intellectuals from Greenwich Village looked lost in the crowd outside the Rockland County village hall. Jean kept staring at Leonard as if she'd just asked him an important question.

An hour later, Jean, Victor, Leonard, and the Kunstlers were led into a squad room filled with uniformed policemen arriving from all over New Jersey, New York, and Connecticut. They were paying respects to two of their own who'd been murdered by terrorists who bragged of gunning down policemen.

To her jailers, Kathy seemed self-possessed, even after a sleepless night in a small, solitary holding cell. They dubbed her "the ice princess."

To Victor, however, Kathy looked shaken up and as helpless as he felt. She sat on a metal folding chair, staring straight ahead and wearing prison pajamas, manacles on her wrists and ankles, and terry-cloth slippers.

"Are you okay?" Leonard asked her. The concern in his voice touched

Jean more than his words. Like Judith Coplon years earlier, Kathy was moved by the compassion in his voice.

"Yes," Kathy said.

"Are you hurt?"

"No."

"They are feeding you?"

"Yes."

"And nobody tried to incapacitate you?"

"No."

"Good."

"What did you eat today?"

Kathy shrugged.

"Drink water," interjected Jean. "Remember to drink water."

"What have you told them?" asked Leonard.

Scores of agitated policemen pushed into the room to glare at Kathy and her visitors. Two men in Connecticut uniforms forgot they were holding lit cigarettes and burned their fingers.

Leonard said, "Don't say anything else, and you'll be fine."

Leonard hugged Kathy and whispered that he loved her. Jean reassured her, "Leonard will take care of everything." Bill Kunstler felt proud to be part of the intimate moment between Leonard and his daughter. Watching Leonard in court, he frequently pictured him wearing a laurel wreath and lecturing to applauding Roman senators.

Leonard made it absolutely clear whom he respected and whom he did not respect. Bill Kunstler knew that Leonard was contemptuous of him for chasing headlines and not doing scholarly research.

The squad-room visit felt ceremonial, as if each of Kathy's visitors had a formal part to play. It was also like a nightmare in which they all suddenly found themselves at the funeral of someone they loved: worse yet, they were also forced to talk to and comfort the dead person. Bill Kunstler told Kathy he would see to her arraignment and bail.

Kathy asked in a low voice if someone would pick up the baby. She assumed he was at the home of his baby-sitter.

That night the evening's national news featured Leonard and Jean, looking frail, outside Rockland County jail. Leonard spoke with authority, saying he'd had a "long personal discussion" with his daughter.

Standing nearby, Bill Kunstler could not resist a microphone. He told a television reporter, "What are you all getting so excited about? This is a garden variety robbery. Because these are radicals and there are whites and blacks together, you're making a big deal of it. This is nothing more than a regular robbery."

Leonard scowled and silently fired him. Leonard had not yet developed a strategy—and such public statements could be damaging. On the ride home Kunstler stopped for gasoline. Victor asked Leonard as cars whizzed by, "How could two parents of a small helpless child do something so risky? I know parents who take separate airplanes just to protect their kids."

Leonard did not answer.

Back in Manhattan Kunstler parked in the Columbia University neighborhood. Leonard and he ordered hamburgers at the West End Bar, a student hangout. Margaret Kunstler and Jean went around the corner to fetch Chesa. Leonard wasn't able to eat anything. To keep himself together, he mused aloud about defense strategies. He needed to find an explanation for Kathy's presence at the roadblock that would also separate her from the murders of two policemen and the Brinks guard. He knew she'd told Michael Koch, "I didn't shoot anybody, he did." It sounded like an admission of complicity.

Leonard theorized that when the two policemen were shot, quite possibly Kathy was already in custody and unarmed. In that case, she was not an accessory to the murders of the two policemen. (Leonard was grasping at straws. Kathy had not been in custody, but running away. And if she had known about the robbery, she was criminally liable.)

Jean and Margaret Kunstler soon returned, carrying Chesa and extra diapers and formula. Twenty minutes later, Bill Kunstler delivered grandparents and the crying baby to St. Luke's Place.

The next morning, Leonard spoke a single sentence to microphones thrust at him outside his home. He rubbed his furrowed brow. "I can only say that my daughter loves this country very much." It was what he had told reporters about Judith Coplon. Leonard was disturbed by memories of the Rosenbergs' execution by the government for conspiring to commit treason. The cards were stacking up for a fight for his daughter's life.

When a reporter asked Leonard, "Will you be defending your daughter?" his answer was, "No comment."

Leonard agonized: it had been his fault for bringing "crazies" around the house while Kathy was growing up. Jean comforted him. She did not say that Leonard's preoccupation with his clients had been part of what had caused his daughter to emulate them.

To Leonard Jean said, "They were family. You and I loved them."

Kathy's action immersed Leonard in feelings of failure, a state that he loathed. When he was not thinking up ways to get charges against her dismissed, Leonard was trying to make sense of his own life, constructing arguments that distanced himself from Kathy and the robbery.

Leonard would prevail in one critical way: he finally grasped that Kathy was willing to die to prove that she could lead a life more heroic than his own. He began to concede victory privately to Kathy: otherwise, he knew that Kathy would continue to court destruction and death if only to outdo him. He understood that he must act as if he believed that Kathy was more moral, more courageous, and more successful at helping mankind than he was.

At sunrise on the Friday following the robbery, the town of Nyack was occupied by three hundred frightened policemen. They surrounded the village hall and courthouse, and stood on street corners, lawns, and rooftops. They fingered rifles, Uzis, and a Thompson submachine gun. Not so long ago, these robbers had broken Assata Shakur out of jail, and most of them were still at large.

In a few hours, a judge would decide if there was enough evidence to keep Kathy, David, Judith, and Sam Brown in jail. There was little doubt as to the outcome.

The police feared that among the hundreds of courtroom spectators there might be terrorists poised to kill policemen. Guns, bomb-making manuals, wigs, and money wrappers had been found during FBI and police sweeps of the robbers' apartments. In East Orange, New Jersey, the rented Army safe house had been found to contain police duty rosters and what seemed to be an assassination "hit list" of individual police and maps of six Manhattan North police precinct houses where bombs could be placed.

Another "hit list" contained the name of Theodore Appleby, the New Jersey judge who had sentenced Assata Shakur, as well as Ku Klux Klan members. Targets also included the headquarters of the International Association of Police Chiefs, the FBI–New York City Police Department Joint Terrorist Task Force, the Ninth Precinct in Manhattan, New Jersey state troopers, and, in Boston, "certain pigs."

The FBI had opened every drawer and dusted papers and surfaces for fingerprints in Kathy's Morningside Drive apartment and basement storage bin. They found little in Kathy's bedroom (renamed Area L) except tan envelopes containing papers. The envelopes contained the detritus of a life that had stalled for some time at an intersection, and then suddenly jumped off the map.

There were food stamps and welfare forms, a New York birth certificate and a vaccination record for C. Jackson Adams, as well as an application to New York University Law School. ID papers for "Lydia Adams" included a New Jersey driver's license, Social Security card, a New Brunswick, New Jersey, library card, and a Colorado birth certificate.

Other finds linked Kathy to the rental of other cars used in robberies. They were ID cards in the names of Elizabeth Hartwell, Elizabeth Mahoney, Judith Paige, Linda Miller, Harriet Applebaum, Marjorie Rossiter, and Charlotte Sanders, as well as receipts from a wig store and blank baptismal certificates. Finally, there were two handwritten notes: the first about "a red van and dudes with payroll," and the second about "how to get rid of a tail."

Leonard protested the FBI search, which had been performed without a signed warrant. He had similarly protested the seizure of contents of Judith Coplon's pocketbook. But this time around, the FBI won, claiming they had confiscated only things in plain view. They also noted that escaped robbers could have been hiding in the apartment.

Leonard, Jean, Victor, and attorney Martin Garbus took almost an hour to make their way through the jittery crowd to the Nyack courthouse, which was draped in purple and black mourning cloths. Television cameras recorded Leonard's arrival. Many townspeople were angered by Leonard who, they felt, had a self-important demeanor. He knew he had never made such an ignoble entrance to court.

A police car pulled up to the courthouse, and Kathy, Judith, David, and Sam Brown, chained to one another, were hustled in. Police flinched when women supporters greeted the prisoners with upraised arms and clenched fists. They also chanted "Free the Land" and "October 20, Freedom Fighters." Women of the May 19 Communist Group wore checkered scarves around their necks, in imitation of Palestinian terrorists.

Inside the courtroom, Leonard greeted Kathy with a big, almost congratulatory hug. It was critical to demonstrate respect in public. Kathy's response was minimal and almost imperious.

The judge opened proceedings. Within minutes, Sam Brown fell for-

ward, his head in his lap, moaning in pain. Like his three white codefendants, Sam's hands were shackled and locked to steel chains around his
waist. But unlike them, his feet were bare, except for a piece of one black
sneaker, and he wore a metal neck brace. To one spectator he looked like a
slave at a slave auction. Staring at Sam Brown, Jean was reminded of the
painting by Horace Pippin of John Brown shackled at his trial.

Police had broken Sam Brown's neck while torturing him and trying to
get him to confess to murder. In the courtroom, one policeman told Sam
Brown to "act like a man." Another pulled his head up off his chest.
When lawyer Susan Tipograph shouted, "You're torturing him," a
policeman in the back of the courtroom who was holding the leash of a
large New York State Police dog said, "Oh, really, what a pity."

District Attorney Ken Gribetz held up the death certificates of police
officers Waverly Brown and Edward O'Grady, as well as that of Brinks
guard Peter Paige, saying, "This I submit is evidence of murder." Sitting
by Kathy, Leonard put his arm around her. Kathy looked politely drained.

Murray Kempton, the respected New York columnist, observed that
Leonard had two modes of treating Kathy: first, he hugged her, kissed
her, and gazed at her with adoration as if he were her lover. In the other
mode, he pressed his thumb and forefinger to the corners of his own lips,
urging her to smile, as if she were a small child.

Kathy seemed to be pretending she was invisible.

Sam Brown was moaning loudly. Guards carried him to the bathroom.
When he returned, his green prison pants fell to his ankles, exposing his
bare buttocks. Kathy and lawyer Susan Tipograph, sitting on either side
of him, bent to pull up his pants.

As expected, the four defendants were charged with robbery and three
counts of second-degree murder. They were held without bail and taken
back to cells.

News organizations around the world produced page-one stories con-
demning the Brinks robbery and murders. They wrote that Assata
Shakur and Kathy had masterminded the massacre. The robbers were
named "Boudin and Co." Journalist Robin Reisig, who was interviewing
Kathy for *The Nation,* asked, "Hasn't the robbery cast a slur on the left?"
Kathy answered in a pleasantly surprised tone, "I never thought of that."
An October 23 editorial in the *New York Times* dismissed the robbery as
"lunacy."

The *Times* ran a sympathetic article about the former head of the FBI
New York office who'd lost his job in a dispute with the Justice Depart-

ment over surveillance methods used on Judith Clark. The subtitle was "An Element of Vindication." (Her suit against the FBI was pending.)

Kathy steadfastly refused to participate in a lineup for eyewitnesses, saying that lineups were used traditionally to frame blacks, but finally, at 7:10 p.m., on May 26, 1982, after months of negotiating, she forced police to carry and drag her to a lineup for eyewitnesses. She was shackled and chained.

Leonard and his lawyers, who now included Martin Garbus, Victor, and Leonard Weinglass, negotiated desperately for Kathy's right to keep her earrings on. (She said, "I have not taken them off in three years.") Leonard insisted her shackles be hidden by a blanket. In return Kathy reluctantly agreed to remove her eyeglasses and not to lower her head, which would taint the identification process.

Much of Leonard's jockeying over technicalities was his way of causing problems for the state, but he was also working to convince Kathy to cooperate with a legal system that she professed to hate, and that was his life. To horrified and fascinated friends, Kathy and her father seemed to have been preparing for this family tragedy for decades.

Leonard filed motion after motion against Kathy's jailers. He submitted requests to have the New York felony murder statute declared unconstitutional. He claimed that applying it to someone like Kathy, who was an accessory to a murder (not a direct participant in the murder), bases the attempt to convict for homicide on a chain of legal fictions and piles inference upon inference.

He attempted to block the court's subpoena of Kathy's Bryn Mawr senior honors paper as a sample of her handwriting. The judge warned Leonard that so many battles were beginning to look like admissions of guilt.

Kathy's roommate Rita Jensen accused Kathy and David of trying to follow in the footsteps of the martyred Julius and Ethel Rosenberg. Rita angrily refused Kathy's request that Rita refuse to cooperate with a grand jury, which would have meant jail for her and separation from her two daughters.

The *New York Times* continued to depict the armed robbery as a grand finale to sixties idealism. The *Times* condemned Kathy's avowal of nonparticipation while fleeing. Assuming she was the gang's leader, her words sounded like a cowardly lie.

Members of Leonard's firm were pressed into service. Ellen Winner was assigned a suit against Rockland County for forbidding contact visits between Kathy and Chesa. Friends like Paul Potter, Kathy's suitor from the days of Cleveland SDS, dropped out of their own lives to help. Paul deposited pamphlets in bookstores and coffee shops. He and Victor mailed out hundreds of appeals for financial help in which Leonard wrote with pride of Kathy's courage. There was little response.

Leonard made arrangements to adopt Chesa, but it was difficult to care for the baby. He and Jean were seventy years old. "We'd never heard of Pampers," said Jean. "I was reading the instructions by the hall light while Leonard was trying to put on the Pamper. We didn't know how to undo the stickum. The baby was crying."

Bernardine Dohrn and Bill Ayers quickly took Chesa into their Manhattan apartment. They said they already loved him and were prepared to raise him as a brother to their two small sons, Malik and Zayd.

Leonard berated Bernardine daily by telephone about the lower-middle-class black and Hispanic children who were in the majority at preschool P.S. 9. "My grandson must attend a traditional school. The little children are roughnecks and have no manners." Bernardine found him infuriating.

Kathy's birthday was seven months away. Reports circulated that she was suicidal. Her "support group"—including Bernardine, Paul Potter, and Drs. Charlotte Phillips Fein and Ollie Fein (also from Cleveland SDS days)—sent photocopied letters inviting fifty people to sew Kathy a "Friendship Quilt." Jean sewed a ribbon that spelled out MOTHER on her square.

In Washington, Michael was profoundly shaken by his sister's arrest for bank robbery and murder. Friends of Michael's, like Matt Nimetz, who'd worked in the White House under Lyndon Johnson, agonized: if Kathy's bombing of the Capitol had not damaged Michael's career, her arrest for murder would certainly do so. Leonard telephoned his son frequently, but Michael was the rare lawyer in Leonard's circle who was not pressed into working on Kathy's behalf.

To shake up his life, Michael decided to add a weekly commute from Washington to Cambridge, Massachusetts, to teach, in the fall of 1982, a seminar in evidence at Harvard Law School. During the second semester, he taught antitrust. It was a gargantuan workload.

Judge Michael Boudin in his office at Harvard Law School, 1998. As a sitting judge on the prestigious Second Circuit Court, Michael has written opinions against such issues as affirmative action.

In the self-published history of Covington, Michael's new job was described: "Somehow with all this teaching, he continued a heavy burden of work at the firm at the same time. He was constantly on the move, back and forth."

During this time, David Gilbert presented an ongoing problem for Leonard as he maneuvered for control over Kathy and the handling of her defense. Leonard telephoned Sandy Katz, a criminal lawyer who'd defended members of the Panther 21. Leonard said, "I need a favor."

When Leonard entered the crowded lobby of the Harvard Club to meet Sandy for lunch, a hush fell. He was a newly familiar face on television news programs. Leonard winced as one NYU law professor turned away.

Leonard and Sandy Katz unfurled starched napkins under the high ceiling and stuffed deer heads. Leonard wasted no time in asking Katz to represent Kathy's codefendant, David Gilbert, "the father of my grandson," adding that he himself was broke and that David had no money. Sandy refused. He did not believe Leonard's cry of poverty. It took, Sandy thought, a lot of nerve. It seemed as if Leonard believed Sandy an inferior who'd feel honored to work for Leonard without pay.

Sandy remembered all too well how Leonard had devastated him when he was a law student and working at Leonard's firm. After his first week, Sandy wrote up his legal research. Leonard scanned it, then he ripped the pages into small pieces and tossed them at Sandy.

Leonard soon forfeited a down payment on a summerhouse in Westport, Connecticut; he needed the money for Kathy's defense. He called emergency night meetings of friends, delivering passionate speeches about Kathy's high ideals to Alger Hiss and screenwriter Walter Bernstein. But Leonard was silent when asked about the robbers. He was throwing his entire being into separating Kathy from her codefendants.

David and Judith fired their lawyers. Following Sekou Odinga (now also in custody), they refused to cooperate "with a corrupt legal system skewed against their black codefendants." David loftily asked for a trial at the World Court of The Hague. He pressured Kathy to join him.

Leonard worried that at any point Kathy was a hairsbreadth away from also refusing to defend herself. He argued that David and Judith were sacrificing their whole lives because they were embarrassed that they could afford good lawyers.

Kathy was using her political skills to hang on to precarious alliances with her parents and her codefendants. She was relieved and shamed by the hundreds of thousands of dollars spent on her behalf.

She dazedly surrendered bits and pieces of her will and her privacy. Guards sneered at requests for vitamins, writing paper, toilet paper, or a brighter lightbulb to read by.

In late November, Leonard appeared at a hearing in Brooklyn before five judges of the appellate division of the state supreme court. He asked the judges to move Kathy's trial out of Rockland County. He said that each person in that community had experienced the robbery as an invasion into his or her home.

Meanwhile jailers were afraid that Kathy might escape from the fifty-two-year-old decrepit Rockland County jail. Doc Shakur was eluding a massive manhunt, as were several other Army members. A map detailing plans to escape had been confiscated from David Gilbert.

Thus at four o'clock on a gray afternoon in late October, an eight-car convoy filled with thirty heavily armed local and state police and FBI agents swooped down on the jail. Kathy and Judith Clark were pulled out of solitary cells and into a drizzling rain. As per procedure, Kathy had no time to grab personal belongings. Nor were she and Judith told where they were being taken. They were locked into a gray van with black windows. Guards trained rifles at Kathy's head. Helicopters buzzed overhead.

The convoy crossed the Tappan Zee Bridge against rush-hour traffic. At 5:20 p.m., they pulled up at the maximum-security Metropolitan Correction Center in Manhattan—twenty blocks south of St. Luke's Place. Ken Gribetz told reporters that the move also would save Rockland County $1 million in security costs.

Leonard fought for every possible advantage. He visited Kathy as her lawyer and thus was permitted a private room. His letters to her were marked "attorney-client privilege" and were in theory not opened by prison authorities.

Jean urged her unhappy daughter to work on an affidavit describing the inhuman conditions of her solitary confinement. "Stop telling Leonard how bad things are. Be a writer. Write it."

"It's not that Kathy has had a breakdown," Leonard said to reporters, "but she cannot sustain herself."

Jean advised Kathy, "The best way to get out of prison or a mental institution is to respect the hierarchy. Do not make the guards the enemy." Kathy's transition over the next years to model prisoner would be based on these words of Jean's. Jean instructed her to "make believe you are the perfect prisoner." Jean told Kathy that now that she was a "con," she must "con" authorities. "Act obedient. No power games," said Jean. She repeated, "Do not make the guards the enemy."

Leonard did his best to charm individual guards. No detail was too small, no problem insurmountable. He established chatty relationships with wardens and their deputies. He campaigned to get Kathy out of isolation. He and Jean urged Kathy to talk to people, even other prisoners. They wanted her to speak to people outside her group who might make her question her need to sacrifice herself to an ideal of equality for blacks.

Kathy wrote the affidavit about the inhumane conditions of her solitary confinement.

> I live in solitary confinement. At 5:30 a.m., I wake up in a room 12' by 8'. I see my mother two times a week, attorneys, and

have brief exchanges with guards. I have not been allowed to talk with my codefendant [Judith Clark]. I am not allowed to talk with other prisoners. I cannot have friends visit me from outside prison.

At 6:30 a.m. I hear a bang on my door, and my breakfast tray is placed on my open toilet seat. My room is 12′ by 8′ with only a bed, a toilet, and a sink in it.

For the first four weeks the entire lighting in my cell consisted of one 60-watt bulb over the toilet at one end of the room. In order to read I had to sit on the open toilet or move my bed next to it to catch the light. After a month my eyesight had severely deteriorated. . . .

The only window has bars on it and looks only into walls. There is a sense of day or night, but nothing in between—no sun, no ability to see the sky, no sense of the weather, just gray light or darkness. I have not had any fresh air since my arrival here. I am not allowed to exercise on the roof with other women.

I live in a box cut off from the rest of the world. If I do not want to spend 22½ hours sitting or sleeping and eating on my bed, I can walk six steps in my room, turn around and walk six steps back to the back wall. I get somewhat dizzy. These conditions are designed to break me not only mentally but also physically.

Over a two-week period in late November the temperature in my room ranged from 85° to 95°. I had to take off my clothes in the presence of male guards and to live in front of them in bra and underpants, using a wet towel to keep water on my body. I had to sleep nude on the floor to try to get below the heat.

I am in a cage cut off from all human relationships.

No matter how well I behave I must remain in this box. The notion of endless solitary confinement can only be designed to present to me a very bleak and inhuman future, to try to destroy me as a political person, as a woman with a heart and soul, to break me physically, and to make me a defendant at trial unprepared and unable to defend myself.

Kathy ended with her greatest sorrow: she was not allowed to touch Chesa when Jean and Leonard brought him to visit. Security was the reason given. Weapons could be hidden in diapers. Officials refused to reconsider, even though Kathy volunteered that he be searched.

> At the start of the visit the Unit Manager . . . said, "If you touch your child even once, the visit will be immediately discontinued." . . . Every time my child would nearly place his hand on my knee, I would jump away for fear the visit would be discontinued. . . . I could not express my love for my child, and he, of course felt that . . . he could not feel my body. He could not smell me. I cannot express in words the pain that such cruelty inflicts on both me and my child.

Leonard insisted Kathy call him daily on the prison telephone. Standing near her, Judith Clark did not conceal her contempt as Kathy acknowledged Leonard's reports of bonding with yet another prison official who might persuade the commissary to update its ways and order granola. Her powerful father was calling in every favor, pulling every string, and working every angle.

Paul Mattick, Kathy's old friend from Haverford College, tried and failed to visit Kathy on three consecutive weekends. Frightened for her life, he drove down from Bennington College in Vermont, where he was now teaching philosophy.

Paul was permitted to see Kathy on his fourth visit. Kathy sat up straighter at the sight of Paul through a thick glass window. Kathy slumped as she realized that nobody had informed her of Paul's attempts to visit.

Paul later was assigned the task of bringing Chesa to visit Kathy. When Chesa vomited in the car, Paul comforted him by saying that he too would throw up if he were on his way to visit his mother in jail.

Leonard's increased dependence on his wife was remarked upon by all who knew them. They were working as a team more than ever before. Kathy had indeed unified them. Jean set to work recruiting distinguished visitors for Kathy. It was important to demonstrate to her that she did not need guns and violence to make a difference. The well-known and illustrious visitors who trooped to five different prisons included Dr. Ben Spock, Dave Dellinger, Noam Chomsky, and Philip Berrigan. Kathy received them politely, saying little. They encouraged Kathy to defend herself to the best of her ability.

Dr. Charlotte Phillips Fein began to publish a mimeographed "Kathy Boudin newsletter" with updates on pretrial motions and political pronouncements, such as Kathy's views on black liberation and on the "government's attempt to criminalize political prisoners." There was an address for financial contributions. Utterly decent, Charlotte said stoically, "I love Kathy, but that doesn't mean I love everything she does."

Leonard and seven other lawyers filed a writ of habeas corpus arguing that Kathy was being punished by high-security isolation in advance of her conviction. The habeas appeal alone cost Leonard nearly $180,000 in lawyers' fees and required over eighteen hundred hours of work.

On January 7, 1982, a few hours before his appeal was going to be adjudicated, Leonard was outmaneuvered. Guards woke Kathy. She and Judith Clark were hustled out of their cells and driven to Woodbourne, a high-security state prison for men, outside the jurisdiction of the judge who would later that day decide in favor of Leonard's habeas corpus petition.

At Woodbourne, Kathy was again in solitary confinement, but this time in a row of cells with Judith, Sam, and David. Sam Brown was in terrible shape, in physical agony, and in terror of more torture. David tried to shore him up, speaking compassionately through cell bars, even though he believed Sam lacked "political consolidation."

When a guard overheard Kathy tell David, "I've got to get out of here," FBI agents attempted to pressure Kathy into turning on her co-defendants.

Kathy and David's priorities were clear: they might lie to the U.S. government about what they and their codefendants had done. They would not, however, denounce, deny, or act against their loyalties to what they perceived to be the higher cause. Jean was infuriated by Kathy's sanctimony.

At Woodbourne, Kathy and Judith were finally permitted to touch their children. Jean said, "The first time we all went to Woodbourne, the baby clung to me. He wasn't the slightest bit interested in Kathy. But the second or third time, he sat on Kathy's lap. Then he reached his little arm into her blouse, and she gave him a bottle. Suddenly his whole body remembered her."

A letter from David to Kathy alluding to Assata Shakur's newly published autobiography was smuggled in inside Chesa's diaper.

When accosted by reporters, Dan Pochoda, an attorney who was working pro bono on Kathy's behalf, repeated one of his favorite maxims: "The test of a civilization is how it treats the people it dislikes."

During this period, Leonard engaged Sam Brown in games of "telephonic" chess. He was desperate to keep Kathy's new enemy close. Brown was spinning stories for the FBI and claiming that he'd seen Kathy at robbery planning meetings.

Leonard allowed Brown to win chess games. Leonard also pretended to be considering the possibility of representing Brown in a civil case against the police who'd broken his neck. Brown clumsily fed what he viewed as Leonard's sense of importance, addressing letters to Leonard with "His Greatness."

Leonard also brought Chesa to visit David and asked David "as the father of Kathy's small child" to lie on Kathy's behalf. He asked David to testify that Kathy had not known that a robbery was planned that day in Nanuet.

Despite Leonard's accusations to the contrary, the delays in Kathy's trial were almost entirely due to Leonard's pretrial stalling tactics. He was wearing down the courage and resources of Rockland DA Ken Gribetz, who was terrified of the big-city lawyers running Kathy's defense.

19

A SAFE HARBOR

In October 1984, Michael Boudin astonished his friends and acquaintances in the legal and political establishments up and down the Atlantic coast by mailing out printed announcements of his marriage on September 14 to Martha Amanda Field.

The ceremony had taken place in Martha Field's austere book-lined house on Irving Street in Cambridge. Women friends, who included Michele Slung, the writer of an influential column for the book section of the *Washington Post*, were surprised. Who was Martha Amanda Field? How had she snared the "bachelor prince"? They soon learned that Michael's bride was a professor of constitutional law at Harvard Law School. Michael had apparently found a safe harbor with an unconventional woman who possessed an incredible legal intellect and a strange past.

Several women sent flowers to the new bride, welcoming her to Michael's home on Dumbarton Street. But they soon learned that

Martha Field,
Freshman Register,
Radcliffe College,
1966. She married
Michael Boudin on
September 14, 1984.
She is a professor of
constitutional law at
Harvard and has
written essays for law
journals arguing for
legal rights of
mentally retarded
children.

"Marty" Field had not the slightest interest in moving to Washington. To make matters odder, just after the ceremony, Michael began commuting up to Philadelphia to teach antitrust law for a semester at the University of Pennsylvania.

It was rumored that Marty was eccentric: although she'd married only once previously, her three small children had three different fathers, each more brilliant than the next.

Jean instantly got the point of Marty Field, although the two women took no pleasure in each other's company. Jean said, "Martha plays tennis. She teaches constitutional law at Harvard. She has a house on the Cape. She is very WASPY. She is a second-generation Radcliffe girl, a Harvard aristocrat, who clerked for Supreme Court Justice Abe Fortas. She loves the law, and very importantly—she has three children." Jean had picked up on Michael's yearnings for a family. Jean noted that Marty was a compassionate person, and indeed her law review essays argued for constitutional rights for mentally retarded people.

Despite her unconventional way of forming a family, Marty Field was a formal person. Unlike Michael's mother, Marty had little vanity.

Marty Field was no stranger to scandal: her mentor Abe Fortas had resigned from the Supreme Court over what was at the time said to be a financial impropriety. One of President Johnson's last acts of office had been to nominate Justice Fortas as chief justice. (In fact, Fortas resigned because of J. Edgar Hoover's threat of blackmail: an FBI agent had visited Fortas in 1968 to inform him of Hoover's "concern" that Fortas had been seen at a homosexual bar. It was left to President Nixon to appoint Fortas's successor as well as the chief justice. Thus did Hoover deliver a history-changing coup de grâce to the liberal Supreme Court.)

Marty Field's background was unusual, although not as unusual as that of her new husband. Her mother, Adelaide Anderson Field, had been a southern belle who fled Memphis to attend Radcliffe. Upon graduating, she'd become a reporter and editor for *Life* magazine, a prestigious job rarely held by women. After divorcing her first husband, she moved to Brookline, Massachusetts, where she edited *Child Life* magazine and raised her daughter.

At Washington dinner parties, Michael began mentioning his stepdaughter—Adelaide Maria Field—by name. He was speaking a bit more personally and clearly loved taking responsibility for his new family. Said his friend Henry Sailer with great affection, "Mike and Marty are the most eccentric couple of my acquaintance."

Despair and ill humor knocked Kathy down like an ill wind. She started a poem about the small act of cruelty that had disproportionately shattered her: a guard threw garbage into a bag containing a picture of Chesa. She was in a fugue state; she seemed unable to cry. She would be kept in jail for twenty-seven months without bail being set.

Jean urged Kathy to see prison rules as similar to those imposed by Weather collectives. "At least you have your thoughts to yourself," said Jean, referring to the cruel criticism–self-criticism sessions.

Jean blamed herself. "Maybe there weren't enough rules when you were growing up." She continued, "You are surrounded by prisoners in worse pain. Help them. They need you."

"What about helping myself?"

"Helping them will get you out sooner," said Jean. "Think of it as a public relations campaign to get into a good college."

The firm of Rabinowitz, Boudin, Standard, et al., was in turmoil. Attitudes were changing. Young women exploded with regularity at

Leonard's "sexist attitudes." Money was in short supply. Leonard was sacrificing everything to Kathy's cause. He was, said his partners, bankrupting the firm.

Victor grew increasingly alarmed when Leonard announced that because of his overwhelming expenses for Kathy's defense, he was going in partnership with a New Jersey lawyer to represent drug dealers in Manhattan. Leonard said that Michael Kennedy had a lot of money and represented drug dealers. Leonard's partnership with the New Jersey lawyer ultimately brought in no cases.

Leonard had hired a City College professor and jury demographics expert named Jay Schulman to survey people's opinions of Kathy in Rockland.

Jay Schulman discovered that over 99 percent of people interviewed by phone thought "Kathy and her ilk" were guilty. Strangers shouted, "Kill the suckers," "Hang them," "Put them in the electric chair." Jay Schulman agreed to defer his payment. He was never paid.

Leonard wanted the trial set in the Bronx where blacks could be recruited as jurors. He succeeded in changing the trial venue twice, but each time it was set in another middle-class suburb whose residents were disturbed by the apparition of big-city crime. Changing the venue of the trial was Leonard's potent tactic. District Attorney Ken Gribetz was becoming more and more frightened; he knew he was no match for Leonard's warrior spirit.

Kathy was transferred to New City jail during jury selection. She dejectedly told a reporter that mothers had forbidden children to play outside because they were afraid Kathy would escape and harm them.

The courthouse was ringed with concrete barricades. Policemen on horseback guarded the entrance. Despite Leonard's objections, police frisked spectators with metal detectors.

Wire mesh had been hastily nailed over all windows. Defendants were shackled and a special metal chute had been constructed as their entry.

Kathy was still being watched twenty-four hours a day. Guards scrutinized her in front of television screens and typed summaries of her movements every fifteen minutes.

Between bouts of panic, Kathy crocheted garments for friends and for Chesa. Her cell toilet had a red-and-blue crocheted cover. She made many toilet covers while waiting for her trial.

The pretrial hearings at the Surrogate Court building in Goshen, Orange County, were raucous and scary. Kathy, alone of the defendants, maintained courtroom decorum—a triumph for Leonard.

When the judge forbade Judith Clark, David, and their lawyers (for the fourth time) to wear New African Freedom Fighters' armbands, lawyer Susan Tipograph said, "I think your long robe is silly, but I'm not stopping you from wearing it."

"Human rights," said Judith Clark, also speaking without the judge's permission.

On the morning of June 2, 1983, many spectators and all defendants except Kathy refused to stand when the judge entered the courtroom. Police suddenly dragged one black spectator out, beat him, and arrested him for creating a disturbance. Judith Clark screamed, "Fascist dogs. Fascist dogs." Court was recessed.

At the start of the next session, Kathy's able attorney, Lenny Weinglass, rose to ask the judge to affirm that spectators had been beaten. The judge refused. Lenny Weinglass calmly described the disruption and beatings for the record. He protested the warlike setting for the trial, which, he said, unfairly prejudged his client's guilt.

One afternoon Jean walked out of court next to journalist Robin Reisig. "I am so angry," Jean said. "Why is Kathy doing this to us?" Norma Hill, the chief eyewitness against Kathy, bumped into Michael Koch in the municipal parking lot. Authorities feared for her safety; she still had a round-the-clock police guard. The man who had captured Kathy shook Norma's hand. "I almost shot you at the roadblock. I thought you were with Kathy." Norma Hill fainted.

At the start of David and Judith's trial, they announced that they planned to boycott the proceedings. (Kathy's case was still in pretrial.) Judith shouted that she and David were freedom fighters, not defendants.

David and Judith played basketball in a room under the courtroom during much of their trial. Judith became pregnant and had an abortion.

Sekou Odinga was the only witness they called in their defense. David and Judith also made a rare appearance in court to salute Sekou Odinga when his own trial commenced. David spoke up without permission. He said, "I just want to greet you, Comrade Odinga, and express my respect for you for twenty years of commitment and self-sacrifice for the New African people, and all oppressed people. Stay strong and I am really thrilled to have someone speak the truth in this courtroom for a change. Free the land."

On September 14, 1983, hours after David was convicted of multiple counts of murder and armed robbery, he and Kathy were married by a prison chaplain at Orange County jail. They wore matching state-issue green pants and shirts. David's sentence was seventy-five years to life in prison. Without his unruly beard and bushy hair, he looked like a young man who might be found in a suburban ranch house. His nose, however, was swollen, crushed by police. Her fate still undecided, Kathy looked older than her forty years.

Leonard had brokered the marriage. His reasons were complex. Publicly it was stated to be in the interests of his grandson. It allowed Kathy and David to communicate by telephone about Chesa. It would cut red tape for Chesa's visits to David, whose name did not appear on the birth certificate.

Private reasons were more complex. Leonard had listed David as a defense witness in Kathy's upcoming trial. David had agreed to lie under oath. His testimony was the foundation of Leonard's claim that Kathy had not known anything about the Rockland County robbery.

Jury selection for the joined trials of Kathy and Sam Brown was spellbinding. Martin Garbus introduced each potential juror to Kathy. The deference he showed her was a self-conscious cue. He asked prospective jurors: "How do you feel about a father defending his daughter?" The jurors seemed unable to take their eyes off Kathy and Leonard. Kathy looked impassive, not quite present. Seated close to her, Leonard displayed anguish at each mention of her name. The formal tragedy appeared to be happening to him.

20

THE BARREL OF A GUN

Political power comes out of the barrel of a gun.
—Chairman Mao

David Gilbert was growing more and more uncompromising. He was awed by the steadfastness of his codefendant Sekou Odinga, who would not discuss the Rockland robbery with police despite the fact that Sekou had refused to take part in it.

During the fifth week of Kathy's pretrial hearings, David told Leonard he had changed his mind. In a dramatic turn, David dealt Leonard's defense of Kathy a fatal blow, sealing her fate.

He explained patiently that he did not want to besmirch his fellow defendants by lying on the witness stand that Kathy had been duped by them into taking part in the robbery.

Leonard talked himself hoarse: Why was David again sacrificing the well-being of "your helpless child and his mother" to loyalty to a group of murderers? Under extraordinary pressure, David remained curiously calm. He said he would testify only that Kathy had not been in on planning sessions. David was undoubtedly thinking of Julius Rosenberg,

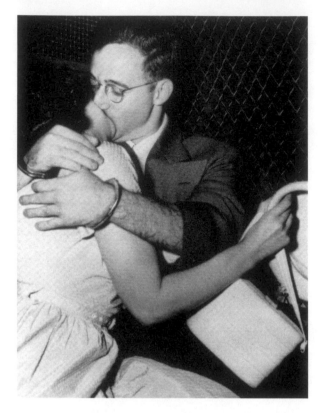

Julius Rosenberg and his wife, Ethel, leave the courthouse in 1950 after their arraignment. Rosenberg's refusal to exonerate his wife was a historic lesson for David Gilbert.

whose commitment to political ideals had precluded his testifying to his wife's innocence.

Leonard formally removed David from the witness list. He changed Kathy's plea to guilty. He told Jean he had never felt lower in his life.

Lenny Weinglass made the public announcement. He said that the case had been only "marginally tryable from the start." Weinglass said the guilty plea was justified because by now the public had a far different picture of Kathy. She had been decorous in court and well-behaved during her thirty months in prison, unlike her codefendants. Kathy was no longer perceived as the "leader of the Boudin gang." She had also voluntarily taken a lie detector test that seemed to indicate that she did not, at this point in time, see herself as a violent person.

Leonard was wracked with alternating pain and fury: Why had Kathy thrown away her life? Was it to ruin his reputation and life? "The case was a rare public defeat for Leonard, and I believe that was part of Kathy's intent," said Leonard's friend, Andrew Patner.

Leonard began scrappy negotiations to shorten Kathy's prison sentence. He asked for eight and a half years to twenty-five years for robbery only. He again argued that Kathy was not legally responsible for the murders of the two policemen because she was in custody when they were killed. When Brinks guard Peter Paige was murdered, she had been a mile away.

When asked, Leonard promised that Kathy would not raise her fist in the black power salute in the courtroom. Judge David Ritter and District Attorney Ken Gribetz were terrified of a public outcry against a show of leniency toward someone who appeared to be a remorseless murderer.

After a week of pleading and arguing, Leonard could not do any better, however, than a term of twenty years to life for one count of felony murder of Brinks truck guard Peter Paige and a second count of first-degree robbery.

In exchange for a guilty plea of only one count of murder and one of robbery, the prosecution agreed to drop eleven counts of robbery, assault with weapons, and—most important—two counts of murder.

Kathy looked dazed in the crowded courtroom in April 1984, as she admitted that she went to Nyack as part of a robbery plan. She addressed the widow Diane O'Grady. "I feel terrible about the lives that were lost, the tragedies. I knew, given the nature of the incident, the other individuals would be armed."

Kathy's "dramatic reversal seemed to come out of the blue," noted the *New York Times*. A drawing of Kathy depicted her cheekbones as ugly slanted slashes, her eyebrows a third dark slash. It was the portrait of a villain.

Despite the *Times* description, Kathy's statement was not a serious reversal. Many spectators noted no evident remorse. She did not mention her role as a decoy or the fact that she had tricked the policemen into putting away their guns. Most important, Kathy said, "I was there [in Nyack] out of my commitment to the black liberation struggle and its underground movement." She added that she mourned the death of Mtayari Shabaka Sundiata (born Samuel Lee Smith), the primary team member who had been killed by police in a shootout in Ozone Park, Queens, days after the Rockland robbery. (It had been his idea to kill drivers of Brinks trucks to save time.) Kathy's tribute to the dead shooter stirred barely audible signs of exasperation.

The truth was that Leonard's pretrial gambits had, as he'd hoped, frightened and exhausted DA Ken Gribetz. Delays had drained their finances. Taxpayer costs for Kathy's trial had been estimated by reporters as between $2 million and $6 million.

Condolence letters to Leonard and Jean poured in from scores of people. They were similar to those sent when a family member dies. Sally Goodman, the beautiful wife of Leonard's now deceased college friend Paul Goodman, wrote of the anguish she felt for Leonard, his wife, and for Kathy.

Kathy's formal sentencing took place a week later, on May 3, in White Plains. Kathy wore a tweed suit and leg irons as she and her lawyers and her family faced Judge David Ritter in chambers.

Father and daughter each spoke as if directing their words to historians. Lenny Weinglass introduced Leonard. There were hints of something sad in Leonard's citations of sympathetic letters from highly placed judicial officials.

Her father's speech flattered Kathy. It also distanced him from her. Kathy, he said, had caused him and Jean great difficulty and pain. He nonetheless saluted his daughter for her idealism as if she'd won a major victory.

Kathy soon urged Leonard to "pull every string" to ensure her assignment to Bedford Hills Correctional Facility for Women, situated in a rich, WASPy, woodsy suburb, only a forty-five-minute train ride from Manhattan. The train would allow Chesa to visit weekly.

Leonard asked everyone he knew, including Victor Navasky, the publisher of *The Nation* magazine, "Do you know anyone who knows the governor?" Leonard was laying groundwork for a pardon.

Assignment to Bedford seemed the logical next step, but as Kathy said to Jean: "Little normal has happened to Judy and me yet." Kathy joked that on the positive side, she had heard rumors that security at Bedford Hills was being fortified in anticipation of her and Judy's arrival. Hammering and drilling was under way for sentry stations and razor wire spirals on walls.

Bedford already had one famous inmate: Jean Harris. She'd been convicted of murdering her lover, a philandering doctor named Sy Tarnower, author of a popular book, *The Scarsdale Diet*. Jean was a former headmaster of the Madeira School in Washington, D.C., alma mater of Kathy's late comrade, Das Oughton.

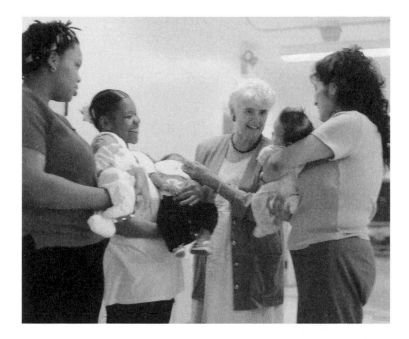

ABOVE: *Sister Elaine Roulet, the Roman Catholic nun who has worked miracles for thirty years at Bedford Hills Correctional Facility. She helped to provide a well-stocked playroom for mothers and children and arranged it so that today new mothers can live in a nursery with their infants up to the age of sixteen months. Sister Elaine also works with dying women and the criminally insane.*

BELOW: *Bedford Hills Correctional Facility for Women, 2001. Extra wire fences were added for the arrival of Kathy Boudin and Judith Clark.*

With the support of a young assistant activities director named Elaine Lord and a nun named Sister Elaine Roulet, Jean Harris had been part of a miracle at Bedford. The three women had managed to cut through a maze of negativity and red tape to establish a nursery at Bedford Hills, where an incarcerated mother could live with her baby until the child was sixteen months old.

The promotion of Elaine Lord ("Lordie," as guards affectionately called her) to warden as well as the utterly benign presence of Sister Elaine Roulet would turn out to be fortunate for Kathy, her decades in prison becoming a period of partial if belated maturing.

Kathy arrived at the Bedford Hills guard station inside a navy-and-white Department of Corrections van in early 1984, with guards again pointing guns at her head.

Her personal possessions, in state-owned garbage bags, included prescription eyeglasses, photographs of Chesa, and provisions from her parents and friends—raisins, raw wheat germ, powdered miso soup, Haines dried soups (miso, tomato, and mushroom), whole wheat fig bars, multivitamins, tranquilizers, painkillers for headaches and toothaches, valerian, and herbal tea bags.

Kathy was undoubtedly stunned by the sight of Bedford Hills: unkempt brick buildings bereft of landscaping. It had been the campus of a prep school. There were, Kathy knew, six houses where prisoners lived, a Laundromat, a visitors' center below Superintendent Elaine Lord's office, a school, a medical facility, and a fenced flat yard with weeds and fog lights.

Kathy was fingerprinted and photographed against a cinder-block wall. As directed, Kathy took off her clothes and a guard put them in a plastic garbage bag. Warnings bombarded her. "No body-punching." "No wrestling." "One girl to a bathroom or you get charged." She was handed disinfectant soap and escorted to an unpainted communal shower. The guard ordered her to use the disinfectant soap to wash her hair, with its new wiry gray strands. "We don't want nobody bringing in body lice."

After showering, Kathy was allotted a large black garbage bag containing a tangle of used clothing in varying sizes, each labeled KATHY BOUDIN and her number: 84-G-171.

The number reflected yet another identity. It meant Kathy entered Bedford in 1984; "G" meant Bedford was her first official prison residence, and she was the 171st prisoner to arrive that year. She was forbidden to step out of her cell without pinning on a badge with her picture and prison number. A replacement cost her $1.50.

The garments in the garbage bag included:

> 1 big, heavy, dark green coat
> 1 dark green jumper
> 1 yellow jumper
> 2 dark green slacks
> 4 green blouses
> 2 pair pajamas (yellow)
> 1 brown flannel robe
> variously sized pieces of underwear
> 2 pair shoes
> 1 pair boots

In a new slouchy jumper and shirt, Kathy was declared "stated down" (a term of approbation used by guards and prisoners meaning "complying with regulations").

Kathy marched back across campus, surrounded by tense guards. The air smelled of frying fat. Hundreds of women stared through cell windows. They were in lockdown, due to the arrival of a "big-shot Black Army terrorist." As her parade advanced, guards shouted "Kathy Boudin, 84-G-171" back and forth, her name resonating. She would always be "a tracker" because of the seriousness of her crime: guards called her name as she moved from building to building.

Inside her temporary quarters, Kathy and guards strode down a narrow corridor lined by metal doors. Each door had a tiny rectangular glass window. Behind each window was a woman prisoner. Smells of their lives wafted down the corridor—cloying perfumes, hairspray, nail polish remover, sweat, shower soap, indigestion, and deodorants. Guards bragged about the "spic and span quality of the cells." "At Sing Sing, some guys don't clean themselves."

Kathy's cell initially smelled of disinfectant and was the size of a bathroom in one of the homes in nearby Bedford. A thin cot was bolted to the floor. The state also provided a hot plate, a stationary clothing rack, a small locker, a sink, a toilet without a lid, and a little table.

Kathy was not in control of when she woke up, what she wore, where she went, and to whom she spoke. Even her mental activities were curtailed: the Bedford prison library consisted of twenty-five books. Sounds of footsteps, cursing, slamming doors, and loudspeaker announcements filled her solitary cell.

During those first weeks, Kathy frequently heard a woman sobbing. It was a young black neighbor also locked in solitary confinement. Kathy's mother urged her to speak to the crying woman. The woman confided to Kathy through cell doors that because she'd had a fight in the nursery, her baby had been sent away to her grandmother. Kathy suggested she write a letter to the baby. When the woman admitted her inability to write, Kathy said the woman could dictate a letter to Kathy.

Jean urged Kathy to begin writing a letter to her own baby about their months together. The supercheerful, even bouncy letter was authored with David.

Kathy also crocheted a pom-pom with a long cord and attached it to her ceiling light, which she could now turn on without getting out of bed. Like other prisoners, Kathy was counted in her locked cell at 11:15 a.m., 4 p.m., 8:15 p.m., and 10:15 p.m. There was also an unofficial count by guards at 11:30 p.m., 2 a.m., and 4 a.m.

In the morning, just before six, Kathy was awakened by slamming of doors (her door was partly opened and then banged closed) by the guard walking up and down the corridor. "Wake up, now. Okay, up. I'm up. You're up."

The day's "count" was taken to make sure each woman was alive and present. After rising, Kathy stood in her cell and placed the palm of her hand in the small window of the closed door—just large enough for one hand. Guards joked about the girls in scanty Victoria's Secret night-gowns. Kathy was no longer sleeping in the nude; a T-shirt was welcome protection.

More dehumanizing were strip searches of prisoners by male guards after visitors left. The women stood in a line, dropped their pants, bent over, and showed their lower-body orifices to guards. Kathy would learn in time to schedule visitors one after another to reduce the number of strip searches.

Meanwhile Bernardine was becoming more and more "pissed off" at Kathy. She accused Kathy of acting selfishly by forcing Chesa to undergo emotional experiences that destroyed his peace of mind. Separation from Kathy after their weekly visits was excruciating for him. Bernardine worried about his sanity. Reports from his teachers and psychiatrists were dis-

Chesa Boudin, age twelve, 1992, photographed by his grandmother Jean Boudin during a voyage to Europe.

mal: he cried and kicked and punched other children. He suffered mild epileptic seizures.

Nonetheless Kathy's letters to her father about Chesa's visits remained cheerful. One took the form of a single page of dialogue in play format about her disapproval of G.I. Joe toys, made by the company that employed Chesa's other grandfather, Sam Gilbert. It was titled "A Birthday Gift for Dad: Conversations with Chesa."

Bernardine fought Kathy's influence by frequently "forgetting" Chesa's scheduled visits to Bedford. Her husband, Bill Ayers, said that they were "a pain in the ass."

Chesa asked Kathy over and over about the Brinks robbery. "What went wrong with the plan again?" He made Kathy promise to accompany him to a supermarket when she got out of prison. He asked her how old he would be when she was released.

"Twenty."

"Why not ten or fifteen?"

The small boy cursed Kathy, climbed up a tree, and refused to leave at the end of visiting hours. "And I hate you, I hate you," he screamed, "for leaving me behind and for getting in jail." He demanded to see the spaces where Kathy slept and wrote letters to him; he could not understand why this was forbidden him.

The separations and indeed his entire life seemed unbearable. Two psychologists said Chesa blamed himself for having been left behind by Kathy and David. Chesa believed it was because he was unlovable. Chesa hid in closets; he beat his head against the wall. He was a violent, troubled boy. Psychologists also said he was showing early signs of autism.

Other prisoners also cursed Kathy: guards were using Kathy and Judith Clark as a reason not to show up to escort prisoners to meet visitors. The guards claimed that they had their hands full doing heavy surveillance of Kathy and Judith. Finally, Latina and black prisoners sneaked a petition around the yard addressed to Superintendent Elaine Lord citing "prisoners' human rights" and asking that Kathy and Judith be admitted to the general population.

To everyone's amazement, Kathy and Judith were released by Superintendent Lord into the general population. Kathy relished lining up with other prisoners to go to the cafeteria. A good dinner was a gray hamburger with a spoonful of brown gravy.

Kathy's admission to the general population—by popular demand—was highly unusual, but Superintendent Elaine Lord was an unusual woman. (Of course, Lord took no chances: if a prisoner was observed talking or eating next to Kathy, the other woman became suspect and her surveillance was sharply upgraded.)

Kathy and Superintendent Elaine Lord soon began and ended an intimate relationship. They became uneasy rivals.

As Kathy's old friend Jonah Raskin said: "The relationship [with Lord] was an example of Kathy's complex response to authority and people representing authority such as her father." He noted that Kathy paradoxically flourished in situations where lines of authority and power were rigid. Paul Mattick, Kathy's friend from college, said, "Well, Saint Teresa got to be intimate with God, so it makes sense that Kathy was close with the warden."

Elaine Lord was tough, smoldering, progressive, and empathic. She wore a ribbon necktie and blazer, with a collage of the twenty-plus keys to her kingdom hanging from her trouser belt. She held a master's degree

Superintendent Elaine Lord, Bedford Hills Correctional Facility, 2001.

from the State University of New York at Albany. Her job would overwhelm most sensitive people: it drove "Lordie" to seek God's help and she soon became an ordained minister. She took to wearing a black robe and white collar as she swept through crowds of prisoners in the cafeteria, cells, and the yard, taking notes in longhand while dispensing histrionic "God Bless You's" left and right, like an old-fashioned evangelist. Nobody escaped her ministrations, and her hoarse, overwrought greeting could bring women to tears. (She reactivated the grievance committee to which prisoners brought problems. Several members of the committee were prisoners, and Elaine Lord made certain the committee responded positively to most prisoner grievances.) But Superintendent Lord was no pushover. She liked to say that prisons "might" provide opportunities for prisoners," adding, "but they must make changes themselves."

Superintendent Lord soon started what she called "the first self-governing prison unit in the state." The best-behaved prisoners lived at Fisk Cottage with unlocked doors and gardens. She urged long-term prisoners to apply. Guards jeered: lifers were getting open space. But Lordie patiently explained: at Fisk, such prisoners would be less angry and less likely to make trouble.

Once settled at Bedford, Kathy cut ties to another women's institution. She instructed Bryn Mawr College not to print her address on class lists or to send her mailings. Recalling Kathy's contempt for the bureaucracy of Rockefeller Hall, Jean worried all over again that Kathy would lose her temper and be destroyed by instigating a losing battle against the "cruel and senseless rules" of prison.

At 8:15 one morning in autumn 1984, her ID tag pinned on her purple T-shirt, Kathy dutifully followed twelve other prisoners—ranging in age from seventeen to seventy-four—across the yard. Accompanied by guards, they straggled into a depressing cinder-block room. It was Kathy's first day as a teacher's aide in a literacy class. The prisoners were mostly black and Hispanic. Although a few were literate in their native languages, they were all unable to read or write English.

The literacy classroom was heavy with resentment. On the walls were letters of the alphabet and dusty posters of well-known black people. The women sat at two long tables. Nearly all of them were suffering from crises such as homelessness, AIDS, and separation from their children. Many had used drugs and had difficulty concentrating.

By 9:30, most had disappeared for "call-outs"—to medical appointments, counseling, the visiting room, an Hispanic committee meeting, a dentist, a drug program, job training, and transfers.

Class work consisted of each woman filling out a sheet of multiple-choice questions based on single paragraphs unrelated to prisoners' lives. Hours passed as Kathy marked the workbooks, lining each woman's answers up to a chart. The depressing activity gave her headaches. (Kathy's postcollege employment years outside prison had been equally depressing, but she had been consoled by clandestine missions.)

During this time, Kathy began to teach a woman in her cell block to read. The work gave her satisfaction and even fleeting feelings of heroism. She was changing a life. The woman's gratitude touched her. Kathy chose texts that she knew would be emotionally gripping: an oral history of a family from Puerto Rico, the life story of a battered woman, a narrative about the poor treatment of black women in jail.

Kathy felt disappointed and sorry for herself when the woman was transferred away from Bedford. "I was having stimulating discussions but I didn't have enough time to teach her how to read," said Kathy to Jean.

"Teach another woman. You will feel good."

Kathy began to dream of early release based on good works.

Another student presented herself. And then another. By early 1987, Kathy was trying to quit her job as a literacy teacher's aide. It was boring. It was pretty much fruitless. But then a temporary teacher asked students to write about themselves. The teacher also urged a reluctant Kathy to compile a journal of student writings in both Spanish and English. Kathy slowly edited women's stories of battering, drugs, unemployment, and separation from children into a volume. She began to feel touched and enlivened by the work.

When another teacher quit, Superintendent Lord asked Kathy to take over the class until the end of the term. Prisoners did not teach classes at Bedford Hills; it was an honor.

The unorthodox gesture was based on Superintendent Lord's respect for Kathy's tutoring of women in and out of programs.

On her first day as a literacy teacher, Kathy impulsively pushed the two long tables together. She then screened a movie about the new secret and deadly epidemic of AIDS, which afflicted women at Bedford Hills. The classroom was suddenly alive with emotion.

The next day Kathy brought in vocabulary sheets.

The women were frightened: many had used intravenous drugs or had worked as prostitutes. Kathy asked the class: Should you take the AIDS test? Questions flew: What if I am pregnant and test positive? Should I tell my mother? Kathy wrote *antibodies* on the blackboard. Women spoke of fear of the tests. Authorities punished people who tested positive. They were denied medical help, trailer visits with family, future custody of their children, and chances of parole. They faced charges of assault with a deadly weapon for actions that would be dismissed as misdemeanors or minor disciplinary infractions if they were not considered dangerously infected.

Kathy soon proposed that the class write a play about AIDS called "Our Play." The women improvised dialogues: One pretended to tell her mother she had AIDS. Another played her mother. Kathy recorded dialogues on squares of newsprint. Stories emerged. Weeping and fighting about whom to turn to about the dangers and shame of AIDS, Kathy and the women slowly invented and memorized a play.

The women performed the play for other prisoners, amid tears and applause. Officials traipsed to Bedford Hills from South Orange, New Jersey, England, and South America to witness "inmate-to-inmate" teaching.

Miraculously, besides finding punishment, defeat, failure, endless rewriting of her life, and genuine sadness, Kathy found a life's calling inside prison walls. The limiting physical nature of imprisonment forced her to abandon some of her grandiosity. The work with fellow prisoners about the tragedy of AIDS changed Kathy. Although still bitterly unhappy, she slowly became a vividly helpful and authoritative presence in the prison.

Chesa was more preoccupied than ever with jail and jailbreaks. He kept asking people why his parents, unlike the parents of all his school friends, were in jail. He blew out candles on a cake at prison to celebrate his birthdays. His tantrums were getting worse.

One day Chesa asked his father to watch him run. He ran down an aisle between the long metal tables as fast as his legs could carry him. The boy asked, "You can run that fast, right? So Daddy, can't you break the window and run real fast and get away?"

Bernardine was exasperated. She told Leonard she and Bill loved Chesa and wanted to make him a real member of the family. She had decided to move to Chicago primarily to put distance between Chesa and his overbearing grandfather as well as his parents.

Kathy experienced the request for guardianship as a second loss of her son. It meant Chesa would be hundreds of miles away and would visit infrequently. Leonard declared Bernardine's ultimatum ludicrous. After all, Kathy's incarceration was temporary, was it not? As weeks passed, Victor gently pressured Leonard, who pressured Kathy during a Sunday visit. She was wounded. Voices were raised.

Kathy wrote "to Leonard especially, but to both of my parents" and cited the "level of anger and misunderstanding between us" on two long yellow sheets of legal paper. Her message was that in 1981, she had become a child again and "you became a full parent at age seventy."

The letter was dated: "Sunday after our meeting," and it started in poem form since Kathy found it easier to reveal herself in stylized format. She accused Leonard of depriving her of motherhood and of seeing her as a weak person who was pushed around by her friends. Most important, both her parents treated her as if she had wasted her life. She said she could not continue to accept their help when she also felt that they neither respected nor liked her.

> *There is no reason to tear our own flesh and blood with the barbed wire of our words and feelings. You have committed these months to protect me and free me, these last years of your lives.*

She wrote that although she felt Leonard's love, she knew that he and Jean hated her for destroying the last years of their lives.

> *When I try to exert my opinions or my views if they conflict with you, you want me weak so that I don't have the ability to change my friends views or do what I think is right*

She observed that her choices and mistakes reminded her parents of their own failures—or what they believed to be their failures.

> *You remind me of my own failures by telling me of them over and over as if I don't know them well enough.*

Kathy politicized her fight to control Chesa's future. She'd been doing a lot of reading about mothers in prison and noted that Leonard's anger and contempt toward her were parallel to negative attitudes of society and prison personnel.

> *The prevailing notion is that mothers in prison are irresponsible etc. and therefore should be mainly grateful if they get to see their children. . . .*
> *It is not right that Chesa be raised by Bill & Bernardine with all decisions being made by them. . . .*
> *We obviously need help between you and me for mediation, communication etc.*
>
> > *love,*
> > *me*

Bernardine won. She moved Chesa away to Chicago, probably saving his life, although the troubled little boy refused to learn to read for years.

On the day that Chesa left Manhattan, Kathy forgot to meet with a young woman who feared she had AIDS. The woman later consoled Kathy; she had felt awful when her child's foster parents moved away.

Judith Clark was accused of plotting to escape and was put in solitary. As a result, Kathy was put in lockdown, her diaries confiscated. Leonard wrote many letters to Superintendent Lord about Kathy's treatment: Kathy had also failed to receive letters he had sent her (stamped attorney-client privileged communication); his birthday gift of an electric type-writer had disappeared; a visitor waited in vain for Kathy all day in the visiting room.

21

EVERYTHING I KNOW
ABOUT THE LAW

Michael was forty-eight, and one of the few human beings on earth to whom Leonard spoke as an equal. Michael's friends were amazed; they decided it made for a highly unusual father-son relationship. Michael was still in the process of shaking up his life. He decided to retire early from Covington, in order to accept a government position that had been held by Hugh Cox as a young man and one that usually went to people with less experience than Michael. In 1987, Michael joined the Justice Department as acting chief of antitrust. He continued to commute to Cambridge to be a father and husband.

Michael loved his new job. Instead of making the best argument for a client, he was deciding for the public good. Senior members of the Justice Department were impressed. Total recall was the least of Michael's intellectual skills.

The *Wall Street Journal* announced a ruling by Michael in a big chunk of print. (Leonard carried the clipping in his wallet next to a letter of gratitude to Kathy from a fellow prisoner.) Michael had sued to stop bankrupt Eastern Airlines from selling eight gates at the Philadelphia International Airport. Michael argued successfully that the deal "threatened to lessen competition in the provision of airline passenger service" and to increase ticket prices.

Meanwhile Kathy was finishing a master's thesis for Norwich College in Vermont on teaching adult literacy and AIDS awareness in prison. Her thesis mentor was Ruth Meyer, the psychologist who'd had the affair with Leonard when Jean was institutionalized. Despite "family feuding," Kathy's thesis was also vetted by Bernardine's husband, Bill Ayers, now working in Chicago as an expert in educating deprived children.

Indeed, members of the old Weather cadre were still tight: Eleanor Stein was Kathy's ardent day-to-day supporter, and Eleanor's son was close to Chesa and his stepbrothers, despite the thousand miles between their homes. The group's overblown ambitions had been tempered by adulthood. Bernardine had made the most visible transformation: despite the fact that she had been denied admission to the bar in New York and Illinois, she was behaving like a pillar of the community, studying legal problems inherent in the children's court in Chicago from a perch at Northwestern University.

Eleanor Stein Jones was working as a lawyer for the state of New York. Her husband, Jeff Jones, wrote articles about such people as State Comptroller Carl McCall for a state employees' newsletter.

Bill Ayers said that raising three fine boys was his proudest achievement. Bill's second proudest achievement, he said, his voice shaking, was living underground ten years without getting arrested. He wore an earring and seventeen tattoos, including the colorful Weather rainbow with a lightning bolt through it. His business card described an "educator, activist, peacemaker, cyclist, and flash of lightning."

The group was dealing with the past with a kind of amnesia about violent actions. Bill Ayers recollected his adventurous violence with practiced jokes. "Guilty as hell, free as a bird, it's a great country," he said. He also said his three sons were incredulous to hear that Bill had burned his draft card to protest the Vietnam War. "Burned your credit card?" asked one little boy. "Man, I'm not that stupid," Bill said.

Eleanor and Jeff Jones were looking forward to the next phase of their lives. They purchased a piece of rural land in the Adirondacks for a

Bill Ayers, August 2001, former Weatherman, stomps on U.S. flag. As a result of their friendship with Kathy Boudin and David Gilbert, Bill and Bernardine Dohrn raised Chesa Boudin.

Weather group retirement, although they did not all plan to live in the same bedroom or even the same house after all these years.

John Jacobs (a.k.a. J.J.), the founding spirit of the Weather group, had been living in Vancouver since Bernardine threw him out. His pseudonym was now Wayne Curry. He did blue-collar work and sold marijuana. Canadian friends assumed he was an embittered former hippie. Wrote Kevin Gilles in *Vancouver Magazine* in November 1998, "They had no idea of how much he had to be embittered about."

Since the average woman was locked in Bedford for less than three years, Kathy and Judith Clark were long-term and influential residents. Two excellent poems by Judith were published in *The New Yorker*.

Few had earned Kathy's powers and creative freedom in the New York State correctional system. "Kathy's practically running the prison," said Susan Kapit. "But that's Kathy."

But to keep her powers, Kathy had to, in one sense, operate underground again. Superintendent Elaine Lord was jealous of her turf. Despite Kathy's elevated status as helper, beloved teacher, and leader, she was nonetheless a disenfranchised prisoner who had to endure strip searches and locked doors. Elaine Lord was the authority. A whim of the warden could be the death of Kathy's privileges and powers. Superintendent Lord preferred Kathy as an anonymous prisoner.

For a reunion in 1986, high-school classmates asked Kathy to telephone them collect. They met in a big living room filled with inherited Biedermeier furniture on the Upper West Side of Manhattan, overlooking Central Park.

They took turns talking to Kathy on the phone. The classmates asked about Kathy's struggle to do good works in prison. After the telephone call, they held hands and blurted memories.

Afterward, they sent Kathy a group letter:

> *You are innovative and successful in your situation (of course, you're Kathy Boudin), and you are inspirational to others. Keep it up!*
>
> > *Love,*
> > *Flo Mason*

> *There has been such connectedness here tonight, and you have been so centrally a part of this, and there is such poignancy in your absence and presence among us.*
>
> > *Love,*
> > *Kate*

> *. . . and there were you and me and Amy sitting on the corner of Broadway and 50th Street (is that right?) writing a one-act play and basking in being totally outrageous. That image never fails to give me some humor and perspective about myself . . .*
>
> > *Love to you,*
> > *Karen*

I remember proudly telling colleagues at the Post—*where I was working at the time—that I had kissed you on a date way back when and that you had a terrific sense of humor. Be well.*

John Gruber

I most remember your spirit and energy and doing a joint project in the tenth grade before the class. We talked about you tonight and the support for you here is tremendous. I hope your spirit today is as I remember and that you look forward to the future with high hopes. Hopefully we'll have another reunion in 25 or sooner and that you will be able to be among us.

Love,
Bob F.

By 1988, five years after being transported to Bedford Hills, Kathy was supervising prisoner-to-prisoner AIDS counseling. It started when several Hispanic women asked Superintendent Lord if Kathy could teach them to tend to terminally ill AIDS patients in the infirmary.

Kathy, Judith Clark, and others were soon playing cards and knitting with patients. Inmates requested classes by medical experts about AIDS. Within a year, Kathy and other inmates were teaching the classes.

One prisoner, Ada Rivera, was astonished at how much life improved after Kathy counseled her about her AIDS affliction. Things had been bad before: "When I carried my food tray into the mess hall, women just got up and left me sitting by myself. They threw away forks and spoons I used rather than washing them. They cursed and refused to step into a shower after I used it."

But after two years of the inmate-run AIDS education programs, Ada Rivera said, "We eat together, drink together. We could be sucking a lollipop and it will be passed to a friend. Life has actually become more meaningful because of inmate AIDS counseling program; as odd as it may sound, the virus actually changed my life for the better."

Kathy began to teach classes in parenting. It was only while addressing tearful, less fortunate mothers behind bars that Kathy started to face some of her own guilty feelings about abandoning Chesa. "Why did I commit a crime knowing that if I was caught I couldn't take care of my baby?"

Kathy became adept at writing grant proposals for such programs as College Bound, which allowed prisoners to earn college degrees from Marymount Manhattan College. She invited other colleges to donate services of professors. She finished another classroom project: a guide-book for fearful new prisoners. One woman wrote that she had expected guards to beat her because she was gay. Another wrote that she'd expected to be raped by gay prisoners.

In the spring of 1989, Kathy was awarded her master's degree in education, a first in Bedford history. Kathy's kindergarten teacher, Eleanor Brussel, Chesa, Jean, and Leonard watched other prisoners accept high-school equivalency and cosmetology certificates. When Kathy was called to the podium, she received a foot-stomping standing ovation.

On hearing about the ceremony, Victor said, "There's no doubt that Kathy has been rehabilitated in prison. In fact, she should be graduated with honors." Kathy and her mother seemed to close part of their rift.

Leonard felt increased pangs about his own mortality when Izzy Stone died in mid-June 1987. He grumbled about the *New York Times* obituary extolling Izzy's "scholarship, wit and lucidity" as well as his "integrity, inspiration and annoyance for decades." It was official. Izzy was a great man.

Leonard said, "You remember how the great humanitarian said he was hungry? He clapped three times and Esther came running with his dinner on a plate."

Izzy's memorial service in the Ethical Culture Society auditorium was described in a third *New York Times* article titled "600 Share Laughter and Memories at a Service Honoring I. F. Stone." Leonard's speech was great. He said, "Izzy's style was unusual. He once described Franklin Roosevelt as a master of the art of changing the subject."

In early September 1989, Leonard was forced to write to Kathy weeks in advance to ask if she could see him. Kathy had been too busy counsel-ing—or so she said—when Leonard had recently showed up on impulse and without an appointment.

Leonard was campaigning to represent China's international trade and banking interests. Jean and he flew to China in October, despite Jean's month-old heart surgery. She and Leonard were both cardiology patients of Nobelist Bernard Lown at Harvard.

The week before Thanksgiving 1989, delegates to the Angolan mis-sion at the UN trooped dejectedly into Leonard's office, as if to a funeral. Leonard pointed to a photograph of himself as a young man at a labor conference. "I was really handsome in those days," he said cheerfully. By the time they left, the Angolans were giggling.

On Thanksgiving, Leonard ducked out of St. Luke's Place to lead a "grandchildren parade" made up of Chesa, Bernardine's other two sons, and Michael and Martha's children to the deserted firm office now in a loft building on Astor Place. He bought them slices of anchovy pizza. They played while he scribbled notes to associates about his Palestinian clients, who'd been denied the right to an embassy in Manhattan. He was also cataloging hundreds of cases from all over the world for two huge books, one on conspiracy law and the other on contempt of court.

Home again, Leonard hosted Bernardine and Bill, Michael and Martha, and their families. Bernardine teased Leonard about his chess victory over Zayd's entire fifth grade class at the University of Chicago community school. Leonard said sheepishly, "I didn't hold back."

After eating Thanksgiving turkey, Leonard suddenly became nauseated. He and Jean ducked into a cab. He was admitted to nearby St. Vincent's Hospital while suffering a massive heart attack.

Leonard regained consciousness fitfully. He was in a fair amount of pain, with plastic tubes sticking into his body. Jean swore she made Leonard smile by admonishing him for "staging" the heart attack to compete with Izzy.

The next morning Bernardine drove Chesa to Bedford Hills to tell "Chesa's other mother" that Leonard was dying. Kathy and Chesa made a booklet about Leonard. Chesa wrote on page one, "Everything I know about the law I learned from Leonard."

Jean and Kathy reassured each other and wept by telephone. "We are lucky we knew a great man." But Kathy was reeling. Among her many feelings was the fear that she'd rot in the bowels of the prison system. There had seemed no predicament too overwhelming for the "Boudin knifing gambit" and Leonard's other wily manipulations of powerful people. Who could take his place?

One junior lawyer at the firm was crying as he telephoned another two days after Thanksgiving, 1989. "Ding, dong, the witch is dead," he said. He and she probed the complexities of loving and hating Leonard.

Corliss Lamont was badly shaken. He had footed expenses for many of Leonard's successful Supreme Court cases, including a suit against the postmaster general for opening "subversive mail" and then querying the addressee to see if he wanted it. "Great Spirit," he said aloud, "you will not be forgotten."

Leonard's obituary in the *Times* was shadowed by two detailed paragraphs describing Kathy's public actions: the town house explosion, Weather Underground bombings, the Brinks robbery, and her twenty-years-to-life prison term.

Listed were famous clients: Ben Spock, Julian Bond, Paul Robeson, and Daniel Ellsberg. Judith Coplon was not mentioned. Michael made a rare public statement. He said Leonard "was very saddened" by Kathy's imprisonment, and "there is no more to say than that." Michael did not add that Kathy's problems had worn his father out.

On January 26, the night before Leonard's memorial service, Jean shared her bed at St. Luke's Place with Helena Kennedy, now an influential British barrister and chat-show host. Helena had flown in with journalist Jon Snow. Jean and she lay talking into the night of "pain, love, and Leonard's bad heart."

Michael presided over the emotional memorial service on January 27 at the Community Church on Madison Avenue. Jean declined to address mourners, but selected a maxim by Reinhold Niebuhr on the church sign: LAUGHTER IS THE BEGINNING OF PRAYER. "Poor Jean" (as Leonard's friends called her) was an erect figure in a mannish fedora that contrasted with her delicate beauty. Something inside Jean had relaxed. Leonard would never run from her again.

Bea Gilbert, Doriane Kurtz, Bill Ayers and his three long-haired sons—Chesa, Malik, and Zayd—Dr. Ben Spock, Eleanor Brussel, and Georgette Schneer were among hundreds of unhappy people in the modern auditorium, draped with Buddhist and Muslim flags.

In his husky voice Michael described his relationship with Leonard as "perfect." "Relations with Leonard from my viewpoint were always sunny. He was for me a perfect parent, wise and devoted, considerate and charming, and I told him so."

"Who's he kidding?" said Bert Gross aloud. Victor's sister, Lucille Perlman, was also incredulous. She asked herself, "How has Michael emerged as the big player in the family?"

Edith Tiger wondered: "Suddenly here's Michael, a hired hand for the ruling class, brushing his hand over his hair like Leonard, pausing in mid-sentence like Leonard. Nobody knows him, and he is saying how his relationship to Leonard was perfect."

Helena Kennedy, wavy hair cascading down her back, brought a breath of scandal. In a Scottish brogue, the young woman praised Leonard for giving her so much of his time when she had been far less distinguished and so much younger than other London lawyers of his acquaintance.

Kathy had asked Helena to read one of Kathy's poems in which she recalled that her father picked her out of the ocean when she was five years old.

> *He was my net . . .*
> *But the years bring tears that cannot be caught.*

Kathy concluded the poem with a question: Who can believe me when I say it was really almost perfect between us?

Oddly Kathy and Michael both described their relationship with Leonard as "perfect." At least, said Bert Gross, Kathy's claim was poetically equivocal.

Corliss Lamont thundered his speech like Billy Graham. He spoke of "thirty-seven years of [my] work with Leonard when he broke"—but corrected himself—"I was going to say 'broke the back of the government.' "

Victor explained that following Leonard's expressed wishes, he was "not going to tell the whole truth." He praised Leonard's courage during the cold war.

Bernardine could still heat a crowd, despite added girth and a skirt that covered her knees. She hinted at incestuous ties to Kathy and to Leonard by remarking that Leonard never knew how to introduce her, calling her "daughter-in-law and friend."

Bernardine brought the house down (not literally at this juncture) when she waved to Chesa and quoted him: "Everything I know about the law I learned from Leonard." "Leonard had," said Bernardine, "remained infuriatingly the same." The word *infuriatingly* hung in the air as Bernardine walked confidently off the stage.

An empty seat on one side of Jean was a reminder of Kathy's absence. References to Kathy made people sadder. Friends whispered that Kathy had decided that her presence, in cuffs and accompanied by hovering helicopters, would turn the memorial service into a circus. Jean sensed a deeper problem: Kathy was terrified of what she might feel during a fleeting visit to the world outside prison.

Leonard's death rocked the law firm, although not a single client left. Victor tore up pages of the ledger book containing drafts of Leonard's love letters to Doriane.

One junior partner sat on the floor of Leonard's office, holding her breath as she read more than a hundred love letters from women, stored in a bulging file drawer. Several letters were from a woman who had worked at the office: "I was just thinking of you darling when the phone rang and there you were"; "Your letter arrived today and I hugged it as I wanted to hug you."

Between file folders, a secretary found an uncashed check for $5,000.

Jean told friends, "My life is our Kathy, doctors, pills, and the movies." She dragged Dinky Romilly to an afternoon screening of *Hiroshima, Mon Amour*. To Jean, Dinky's affair with Leonard was part of the blurring past.

Kathy took charge of her team of lawyers. Now it was up to her to pull her own strings. She tried to imagine how Leonard might solicit and deal with powerful people. She was hard on Lenny Weinglass, denying remarks she'd made in previous meetings.

Kathy asked David for a divorce. He refused: they would not be able to speak by telephone about their son. But Kathy was in love with a young Hispanic inmate who was jealous. (Jean tacked the girl's drawings on the dining-room door and asked friends in a cheerful voice what they knew of lesbian love affairs.)

When Kathy's friend was released, it brought home to her why she should not get attached to fellow prisoners. But it was too late to cancel divorce proceedings. David had committed to it.

In 1990, Michael was nominated by admirers (many of whom were coworkers in the Justice Department) to the U.S. District Court in Washington, D.C. President George H. W. Bush's senior advisers were not deterred by the fact that Michael's sister was serving a prison term for murder and armed robbery. But this was the wrong judgeship. Petty crimes were brought before him. Michael did not enjoy listening to lawyers spin defenses of drug dealers. He yearned to ponder issues of law and public policy.

He and his wife, Marty, were tiring of the commuting marriage. At last, in 1992, Michael issued an uncharacteristic public statement. "I need to devote time to my family," he said, and quit his post to move permanently to Cambridge.

A vacancy soon occurred in the prestigious Second Circuit Court of Appeals located in Boston. Conservative members of the Bush administration prevailed and Michael was appointed. The *New York Times* heralded the "unusual appointment of an unusual man—a twist that might perplex Mendel and fascinate Freud." The newspaper called Michael "the oddest offshoot of his family's extraordinary tree . . . a nonconformist, but only within his illustrious and iconoclastic family."

This was a simplification of Michael's course. Corporate law was almost as central to the zeitgeist of the late 1970s and 1980s as his father's work in labor law had been in the 1930s. And like Leonard, Louis, and Izzy, Michael was fascinated by the judiciary and saw the Supreme Court as a locus of power.

On March 31, 1993, Michael wrote an opinion in favor of mentally retarded residents of Pineland Center in Maine. He cited legalistic points, but added that it was not in the people's interest to lower standards of care.

Jean was failing. She slowly climbed stairs at St. Luke's Place, reporting cheerfully that blood pressure pills were canceling out heart medicine. She couldn't pull on underwear; her knees were painfully arthritic. She'd enjoyed a Robert Altman movie at Lincoln Center that featured a shameless womanizer, welcomed upon his return home by his wife. "He was terribly appealing," said Jean, laughing. "They always are."

She presented herself as if watching her was still a treat, and it was. To a wardrobe of two custom-made suits plus hand-me-downs from women friends she added a blue floral blouse, purchased for $3.50 at the Junior League Thrift Shop near Bedford prison.

When she learned she was dying, Jean felt vindicated. After years of trying not to think about death, even trying to die, and then trying not to die, she found herself relieved it was at last approaching. "From what I'm told, I'll finally get a good night's sleep," she told friends.

Jean entertained royally from her hospital bed. She showed visitors snapshots of herself and Chesa greeting the captain on the *Queen Mary*. Friends brought grandchildren to witness her cheerful end. The past faded. Jean had retouched it into great stories. She discussed her dying as matter-of-factly as if she were moving to a small, elegant apartment in Paris.

Michael stood at a distance in the hall outside Jean's hospital room. He extended his hand to visitors, assuming a formal receiving line posture.

Tupac Shakur, the most famous gangsta rapper, was murdered in a drive-by shooting at the age of twenty-five in Las Vegas in 1994. His stepfather, Mutulu "Doc" Shakur, was the mastermind of the Brinks robbery in Nanuet Mall. His mother, Afeni Shakur, was a member of the New York Panther 21 and a friend of Joanne Chesimard a.k.a. Assata Shakur.

Victor noted that Jean's public show of vulnerability appeared to disturb him.

There was no obituary to mark Jean's passing. Jean's friends had assumed Michael was taking care of it. He was not a man who made mistakes in such matters.

Tupac Shakur, Doc's stepson, had become the most famous and controversial gangsta rapper recording artist of his generation, as well as a talented budding movie star. Tupac was as detested by white adults as he was loved by hundreds of thousands of young fans, both black and white. A target in several shooting incidents, he was finally gunned down by vengeful members of a gang in a street in Las Vegas in 1996 at the age of twenty-five. His violent life and violent death made him a myth.

Michael Boudin was still a powerful circuit court judge, who would in four years vote to end affirmative action to aid members of racial minority groups in high schools and colleges in Maine, Rhode Island, New Hampshire, and Puerto Rico. The petitioner in this case was a white girl who had narrowly missed admission to Boston Latin School.

Small accidents of fate and politics had prevented Michael from

The prisoners who are AIDS counselors of Bedford Hills Correctional Facility. Kathy Boudin, second from right. Precious Bedell, her protégée, second from left, back row. Under Kathy's leadership, prisoners were taught to help one another with the scourge of AIDS.

achieving his heart's desire. (Despite speculation, his disappointment had nothing to do with his sister.) He was becoming a bit too old to be appointed to the Supreme Court. Presidents were cannily appointing younger justices with an eye toward their having more years on the bench, and therefore a greater impact on history.

A campaign for Kathy's clemency was conducted in secrecy at the end of 1994. Kathy did not want to alert Diane O'Grady, the energetic widow of the slain policeman Ed O'Grady. Kathy and her lawyers feared Mrs. O'Grady would protest to Governor Mario Cuomo and organize a picket line of policemen and their families at the prison.

By telephone, Victor Rabinowitz told Eleanor Brussel, whom I was interviewing, to ask me to leave her living room while she read Victor her polite letter on Kathy's behalf to Governor Cuomo.

The campaign had ignited after a casual remark by a political reporter to Governor Cuomo in the last days of his term. (Kathy's friend and protégée at Bedford, the vivacious Precious Bedell, launched a similar campaign at the same time.)

Four lawyers set to work—without fees—on Kathy's appeal for clemency. A letter from Jean pleading for Kathy's pardon had been put aside after a previous appeal by Leonard. It described Kathy's courageous run for help when Jean tried to commit suicide. Jean's friend, the author Judith Viorst, wrote swearing to Kathy's nonviolent nature. Michael wrote, too.

Norma Hill, the chief eyewitness against Kathy, was an unexpected clemency supporter. She was now a rich lonely widow and visited Kathy frequently. The two women had become close friends as they compared notes about the ruinous effects of the shootout on their lives. Norma wanted to write an article for the *New York Times Magazine* describing her relationship to Kathy and about Kathy's good works. She wanted to meet Chesa. Kathy said no. It was not the right time for a press campaign.

Someone in the Rockland County DA's Office leaked news of the clandestine clemency campaign; a neutral article appeared in December in the *New York Times*. The *New York Post* ran a hostile editorial. Only Channel 9 in Manhattan covered the demonstration at Bedford Hills prison organized by Diane O'Grady at which three hundred policemen in uniform carried placards: DON'T FREE KATHY BOUDIN. Diane O'Grady and her sister-in-law drove hundreds of miles to put petitions for signatures in supermarkets and gas stations throughout New York State.

Victor told Kathy not to get her hopes up. But then someone from the governor's office telephoned to ask for more documents and Victor changed his mind. He said he was expecting the appeal to be granted. "Hoping it will be granted?" I asked. "Not hoping," he replied, "expecting."

Days passed. Cuomo did not grant clemency to Kathy or to Precious Bedell. Victor became morose and took to his bed with pneumonia, unusual for a man who eschewed umbrellas and never caught a cold. Word went out that Kathy was fine; she had not allowed herself to believe she would be freed at this point.

In spring 1997, Danny Glover, the black movie star, read a poem written by Kathy to a crowd of several hundred people as part of an event sponsored by PEN American Center, a group of writers devoted to writers beleaguered by governments around the world.

Danny Glover mistakenly identified Kathy as a resident of death row.

No one corrected him. The appellation seemed to fit Kathy's desire to identify herself as less fortunate.

Two weeks later, on the evening of May 18, 1997, PEN gave its annual awards to writers in United States prisons. The lachrymose ceremony was held at the New School in Greenwich Village. It was known in advance that Kathy was sharing first prize, in absentia of course, for poetry.

After someone recited a poem by a male prisoner containing the line, "I died the day I was born," lights went out. A huge video screen was filled with Kathy, her bangs waved, her eyes shadowed in dark skin. She was wearing a pale blue shirt. The garment marked her honored status: blue was worn only by guards. She was poised behind a lectern and in front of a dinged blackboard.

Kathy silently scanned a page of writing and cleared her throat. The poem was called "Our Skirt" and employed a skirt that Jean gave to Kathy when she was fourteen and Jean was forty-five to illustrate how much Kathy now missed Jean.

> *"It's from Paris, " you said*
> *as if that would impress me*
> *who at best had mixed feelings*
> *about skirts.*

I was struck by the music of her contralto voice. Her tongue formed silibant *s*s and staccato *t*s, like a tap dancer elegantly tapping his toe and then his heel.

Kathy's poem went on to describe how much she loved the cotton skirt decorated with splashes of black and white paint. She remembered how it had moved like ocean waves as she danced at a high-school party.

> *And over the years your skirt became my skirt*
> *until I left it and other parts of home with you.*

> *Now you are eightyyy and Iiiiaammm—*

Kathy's words *I am* dissolved into a wail. Her eyes widened in startled apology. She closed her lips to silence the sounds of weeping. "Excuse me." The sweetness of her apology spiked emotions in the auditorium.

Kathy started to recite the line again—"Now you are eighty, And I." She began to cry harder.

This time, she rolled her eyes in humorous exasperation at her loss of control. She started the line again. Stopped again. By now there was no emotional distance between her and the several hundred people in the audience at the awards ceremony. Many people clapped, rooting for Kathy to distance herself from her sadness.

"Excuse me," Kathy finally said. She started reading again, this time breaking down into a single graceful sob. There was no contorting of nose and mouth. Her physical attempts to overcome vulnerability were far more poignant than words.

Kathy stepped away from the lectern, unembarrassed about crying in public. She seemed at ease with being a public person. A slim young black woman in a red sweater appeared and then enveloped Kathy in a hug that looked unconditional. They disappeared into each other.

The person operating the video camera said in a pedagogic tone, "It's fine. Read another poem, Kathy."

Kathy stepped back up to the lectern. The audience was waiting to hear her recite another poem. But instead Kathy continued with "Our Skirt," shakily stepping over its emotional minefields, describing herself at fifty and Jean at eighty, sitting across from each other in the prison visiting room.

> *Your soft gray-thin hair twirls into style.*
> *I follow the lines on your face, paths lit by your eyes*
> *until my gaze comes to rest*
> *on the black and white,*
> *on the years our skirt has endured.*

It was hard that day to resist Kathy Boudin; her worn lovely face illuminated the dreary evening. Hard glamour. Serious glamour. Tragic wretched-of-the-earth glamour.

The crowd applauded. Kathy is like us, they seemed to say, although braver, more foolhardy, more famous. The audience of book writers and activists was not afraid to crawl inside Kathy's pain. The clapping went on and on.

Kathy wrote a letter discussing John Brown's violence in service of a cause greater than himself to novelist Russell Banks, whose novel about

John Brown, *Cloudsplitter,* is narrated in the first person by Brown's pathologically self-loathing son.

Kathy's letter led Noel Ignatiev, former Progressive Labor activist and prizewinning author, to assume that Kathy condemned Brown's tactics but not his cause.

J.J. died on October 20, 1997, in Vancouver. The ex-Weatherman leader was fifty years old. His girlfriend said his death was one of his finest moments. She had summoned paramedics to their basement apartment, where they found him in the midst of an anguished fit. He was dying of cancer, which made his skin ultrasensitive, so much so that when a female police officer gently patted him and whispered that he was doing fine, he slugged her in the face. "He fought all the way," said his girlfriend. "The police said he was one of the strongest sons of bitches they'd ever seen."

In a turn of events more reminiscent of Groucho than Karl Marx in the winter of 1999, one of Kathy's codefendants was welcomed back to her native Italy as a national hero. Silvia Baraldini had served seventeen years in Danbury Federal Prison for key roles in sixteen Black Army bank robberies. Fifty-one, white-haired, short and stocky, and a breast cancer survivor, Baraldini disembarked in Rome from a jet owned by the Italian government, while a thousand people threw rose petals and screamed, "Freedom." (Silvia was an Italian citizen, and her pardon had occurred as part of a political trade with the Italian government.)

Silvia's triumph took place three thousand miles away—a safely romantic distance—from the Nanuet Mall and the highway near Nyack. The Italian press portrayed her as a courageous fighter against the unjust U.S. government. Many urged her to run for president of Italy.

After the terrorist attacks in the United States of September 11, 2001, however, Baraldini's luck would change. Frightened Italians whispered that she was a terrorist, likely to be in league with those who had bombed the World Trade Center and the Pentagon. People stopped visiting her. They feared FBI tails.

Bill and Bernardine were justifiably proud that Chesa had become a good student and was attending Yale, a decision that would have jarred Leonard's fantasies of a Harvard degree for his grandson. Perhaps that was the plan. Chesa rigged the telephone in his dorm room so it didn't block collect calls from his incarcerated parents. Chesa felt an outsider at Yale and made arrangements to spend his junior year in Chile.

As Thanksgiving 1999 approached, Kathy was more depressed than usual by the anniversary of Leonard's death. Her spirits lifted when her favorite protégée, Precious Bedell, was miraculously freed—after twenty years. Although the separation hurt, the sudden reversal in her friend's case gave Kathy hope for her own freedom. A small picture and front-page headline in the *New York Post* on November 22 read: "Baby Killer to Go Free." The picture showed a black woman wearing a V-neck sweater over a white T-shirt. A bracelet on her wrist suggested important jewelry, so dignified was her posture and physiognomy. In fact, the bracelet was a cuff attached to a chain that circled her waist.

Precious Bedell was a free woman, due to smart legal work and the influence of movie actress Glenn Close. A judge agreed that laws had been broken during her trial: Precious Bedell should have been present when evidence against her was shown to a jury. Instead, Precious was made to wait in the vestibule of the Valle Restaurant, while jury members toured the bathroom where Precious, high on crack cocaine, banged her two-year-old daughter's head over and over, allegedly because of her table manners.

An accompanying *New York Post* column was titled, "Glenn Close Should Hang Her Head in Shame."

Like so many of Kathy's women friends, Precious began attending classes to prepare for law aptitude tests.

Precious Bedell's fluky release went against the climate of the time. Parole boards and judges were getting tougher in New York State. A death row was being constructed in Bedford Hills, next to the nursery. Due to Leonard's masterly legal work, Kathy had only one conviction of felony murder and one for robbery, but parole board members were aware of the context of the shooting of the two Nyack policemen. Authorities said privately that Kathy had gotten a break, primarily because Leonard had exhausted the state's resources and resoluteness by delaying the trial.

Six hundred uniformed policemen gathered every year to mourn for-mally the murders of the two Nyack police officers in Nanuet on the anniversary of their death, October 20, at four in the afternoon. Two low metal-encased eternal lights beamed weakly on a granite memorial embedded in the grassy lawn by the southbound entrance to the New York State Thruway, across from a McDonald's restaurant.

Just as the day began to chill to night, policemen from all over New York State stood at attention in rows. The hundreds and hundreds of fitted navy uniforms with medals, holstered guns, and orange rope epaulettes looked powerful. In contrast, their faces looked sad. Also present were retired police chiefs in baggy, black civilian suits. A bagpipe band in kilts and feathered hats opened the ceremony every year. They march in, playing "Amazing Grace." Around the edges of the police lines, plainclothes detectives talked into walkie-talkies. They mingled with several hundred other local people.

One local person in that crowd is always Gregory Brown, the startlingly handsome U.S. postal policeman and son of slain black policeman Waverly Brown. Gregory Brown customarily stands by the late sergeant Ed O'Grady's sister.

Without warning and toward the end of the ceremony, two earsplitting ceremonial gunshots always ring out. Absent on most years are two survivors of the shootout. Retired policemen Brian Lennon and Arthur Keenan are too emotionally overwrought to participate in the annual ceremony.

In 1998, the seventeenth memorial service had been attended for the first time by U.S. congressman Charles Schumer, a liberal and a gun-control advocate who was campaigning for the Senate. He promised in a deceptively mild tone that, if elected, he would come back here to mark the anniversary of the murders every year of his life. He said, "I can assure you that I will do everything I can to make sure that the people responsible for the deaths that occurred here remain where they are."

In the year 2000, newly elected senator Schumer returned to address a larger crowd at the same spot. A huge crane dangled hundreds of feet above him. A CBS television crew was recording the event for a news piece on *60 Minutes* about a bid for clemency by imprisoned May 19 Communist Group member Susan Rosenberg. No one seemed to be aware of Silvia Baraldini's pardon.

The memorial ceremony was dignified. No one mentioned Kathy's name. Police chaplains and other local officials spoke briefly about the two policemen who gave their lives to protect the community from "murderers and terrorists." Another speaker read a letter from Diane O'Grady. It was a message of thanks and included her promise to remember mourners in her prayers.

Diane was too distraught to attend this year's service. The reason: her son Ed Jr. was a helicopter pilot on an escort ship to the USS *Cole*, the navy vessel attacked three days earlier by "terrorists abroad" in Yemen.

Kathy soon invited me to Bedford Hills to ask me about the memorial ceremony on the highway in Nyack. She told me of her desire to make formal apologies to families of the men killed during the Brinks robbery. She'd created a project that would entail teaching classes of other prisoners about how to make amends to crime victims. "You can help me," she said.

I mentioned Gregory Brown, explaining that he attends the memorial ceremony in Nyack every year for his father.

"Who?" she asked.

"Waverly Brown's son."

"Really," Kathy marveled. "I never knew the guy had a son."

Kathy wrote poignant poems about her incarceration. She lectured other prisoners about making amends to crime victims, but in the twenty years since the Brinks robbery she had not learned that Waverly Brown, the young black policeman slain by the BLA in Nyack moments after she'd convinced him to put away a gun, had had a teenage son. I wondered if the facts of the robbery were too terrible for Kathy to absorb. She seemed oddly disconnected from that reality.

President Bill Clinton left office nine months later. One of his last acts was to pardon Susan Rosenberg. The *60 Minutes* newscast had been skewed to Susan's point of view. Acknowledging the fact that she was arrested with some seven hundred pounds of dynamite, Morley Safer took Susan at her word that she had not been present at the Brinks robbery. Immediately following her release, she took the subway to Coney Island to see the ocean. She soon began working on a newsletter for AIDS patients at a synagogue in Manhattan.

At 6:30 one Friday night in July 2001, hundreds of Rockland County families in T-shirts walked from Main Street, Nyack, to the sparkling gray-blue river in silence. It was a protest rally and the climax of a campaign against Kathy's first bid for parole. The protesters had amassed thirty-five thousand letters to Governor Pataki.

Earlier that day in Manhattan, on Thirty-third Street, the O'Grady family, the Paiges, and the Browns assembled to speak of their losses to parole board members. Ed O'Grady Jr. cried when a parole board member asked Waverly Brown's daughter what memories she had of her father. The young woman replied, "None."

The evening protest ceremony was about Kathy. A minister so subtly asked God to keep Kathy in jail that listeners relied on faith to understand the prayer. Families of the slain policemen and Brinks guard Peter Paige sat in the front row of the podium.

There were no powerful politicians or celebrities on the podium, just assistant district attorneys and assemblymen. There was a lone stringer from a wire service and one woman from a local TV station. Between speeches the moderator thanked by first name scores of volunteers who'd sold T-shirts and had stuffed envelopes. In the audience, neighbors alerted one another to a long cover story on Kathy in *The New Yorker* magazine, describing events from Kathy's point of view.

The interview had been brokered by Victor Kovner, a high-powered lawyer who was connected in publishing circles. Kovner was asked to help at a meeting of members of Kathy's loyal support group including Lenny Weinglass, Eleanor Stein, Victor Rabinowitz, Jeff Jones, and Linda Bakiel (a lawyer whose clients include Puerto Rican nationalists accused of violent acts).

Spectators at the Nyack ceremony listened to Greg Brown say that he was not comfortable in crowds. "I ordinarily have very few words, but I am here to give my father a voice." The moderator invited Greg to bring his children to next year's twenty-year memorial service on the highway. "We want to see what their grandfather can't see."

At the end of the ceremony, the crowd surged uphill out of the park, past a brick building with graffiti and across Main Street to surround the post office porch. Each person held a blue plastic light.

Led by Greg Brown and Diane O'Grady, townspeople stepped up to two red-and-blue mailboxes on the post office porch, picked a letter to Governor Pataki out of the overflowing mail sacks, and mailed it. These letters urged Governor Pataki not to grant Kathy Boudin parole. When the mailboxes were full, most of the crowd disappeared into the night.

Family members of the slain policemen and Brinks guard stood in a cluster in front of the post office. Someone thanked a volunteer who was to drive some of the thirty-five thousand letters up to Albany. They could not afford stamps for the letters.

A half hour later, Ed O'Grady Jr. sat on the curb outside his aunt's suburban house, three blocks from the post office. He talked about why and when he proposed to his girlfriend, about how he didn't tell his mother how close he came to going on the mission against international terrorists that killed his buddies on the USS *Cole* in the Persian Gulf, about the hubris of his application for a U.S. Navy fellowship to Stanford for a Ph.D. in aeronautical physics. "Then I'll find out if I'm as smart as I think I am."

He mentioned a rumor that Kathy's son, Chesa, wanted to go door-to-door canvassing in Rockland for support for his mother. Ed said his own mother had made up an excuse to be with him the first year he was away from home at Annapolis on the anniversary of his father's death.

Ed was fascinated by a TV documentary that tracked a Texas family's obsession with the killer of their father. "They think of the murderer every morning when they wake up."

Ed Jr. did not think that was a good idea. "If my mom thinks about that woman first thing every morning, that means Kathy Boudin is winning."

In preparation for Kathy's hearing in front of two parole board commissioners, two weeks later, in August 2001, robbery eyewitness Norma Hill wrote letters of support to a Rockland County newspaper and to the parole board. Kathy also asked acquaintances to petition the board and to contact Senator Charles Schumer. He was asked not to speak out against Kathy's parole. The publicity campaign climaxed in Kathy's radio broadcast answering telephone queries for several hours on the day before the hearing.

Kathy was understandably frightened at the start of the closed parole hearing. When a commissioner pointed to sacks of letters they had received about her case, she looked stunned. One commissioner told Kathy that they were familiar with her good works in prison. They added that they did not want to debate facts of her case.

The two parole commissioners facing Kathy were not people who used poetry, irony, or idealistic politics to blur distinctions between legal and illegal acts. Furthermore they had been appointed by Governor George Pataki—and were not sympathetic to Kathy.

"Did you attempt to escape from the roadblock [after the Brinks robbery]?" asked one commissioner. "I did not attempt to escape," Kathy claimed. "I was standing there in surrender with the police. I was scared. I had never had guns at me before."

Throughout the hearing the commissioners tried to pin Kathy down: Why had she been present when so many acts of violence were taking place? Why had she continued on the path that led her to wake up in the morning and drive to Nyack to participate in a violent crime?

Kathy denied knowledge of what "they" were doing in the town house. And Kathy said that she had not taken part in Weather bombings. Such evasive testimony undermined her vows of remorse.

Her denials were, however, a basis for Lenny Weinglass's subsequent suit asking the State Supreme Court to throw out the parole board's decision.

That day in August, parole commissioners probed, ostensibly to determine if Kathy would again act violently against perceived social injustices if released from prison. Said one commissioner, "And one of the things that I think we need a little focus from you on is that you were not an eighteen-year-old child who was easily swayed [at the time of the Brinks robbery]. Try to explain to us or try to make us understand what would motivate you to participate in this kind of crime."

Kathy answered, "From the day I understood that people were killed, I was completely horrified basically with myself for being there."

A commissioner chided, "That wasn't the first day you participated or were part of an organization that believed in violence to accomplish what you call civil goals."

Kathy answered, "I was—I want to say that I was never involved in violence directly."

Kathy explained that she had grown up surrounded by family and friends who were committed to helping society and people. She cited the burden of having such a successful brother and father. "I wanted to be the best—a hero." She added that other people's poverty made her feel guilty.

The commissioner responded that when a person decides to be a hero, "There are warning signs and there are bells that ring. And if you were normal, as you are, and I hope I am, we are able to read those signals. But sometimes it takes two or three for the message to get across. But we read these signals—you got out of the [town house] building safely, fortunately. That's a signal [to ask yourself] who am I with, what am I doing, what are these people doing?"

One commissioner deftly added that they were not accusing her of any crimes in the Wilkerson town house explosion. (Such an accusation, since charges had been dropped, would undermine a negative parole board decision.)

Kathy supplied no good answer when asked why she hadn't stopped revolutionary activities after the three deaths in the town house bombing.

She said that after her three friends were killed, she believed that she had to demonstrate her commitment to them by going underground. "[It] was my way of saying that I will continue at least to do what their lives were dedicated to. I was not personally involved in violence, but lending my support to those who were, and that was wrong."

She wisely refrained from reciting her poetic line that had been quoted in *The New Yorker:* "I am responsible for not being responsible."

Kathy interrupted the two parole board commissioners eight times. Prisoners defer to parole boards for obvious reasons.

One commissioner pressed: "To associate yourself as intently as you did, with counterculture philosophical organizations that were espousing destruction of government and using violence to accomplish their means puts this whole thing and you in a different category than a person who was out there with the banners fighting the Vietnam War."

Kathy cited her social work in the prison and vowed to do good works on a small scale if paroled.

The commissioners had reason to distrust Kathy. They wondered aloud why she had not devoted herself to social work when she was underground. "You could have worked in a soup kitchen or become a volunteer in some organization. You had many different identities. You had jobs. You were not alone in a room with the blinds drawn. You had the ability to do something constructive and yet you didn't do it."

> QUESTION: So how'd you get involved in this robbery?—
> KATHY (interrupting): I'm going to get to that.
> QUESTION: All right, that's—
> KATHY: —I think I had jobs, I worked in odd jobs and took care of kids and finally decided, and I lived in a sense—maybe the best word, way of thinking of it, I developed an idea in my mind that I was underground and that simply, the very identity of being underground, gave me a certain moral identity. I saw myself as Joan of Arc in a—

QUESTION: So during that time, you didn't associate with people, the Weathermen or—

KATHY: —Well, the Weathermen fell apart in 1975, and from the 1970s to 1975 I was associated with them. My work was not doing violent work, but organizing conferences and educating people.

Kathy went on to interject that she knew nothing about the men who committed the robbery in Rockland. She had, she said, never met them and assumed they were probably former Panthers whose goals in the black community she identified with. She further maintained that "someone named Bob contacted David, David and I went out to a restaurant, he asked if we would ride in a truck that was going to be sitting in a parking lot. I think because I had no idea who the people were—"

"That sounds incredulous," a parole commissioner broke in, meaning *incredible*.

"—It does but it's true—"

The commissioner said, "I have to interrupt you. That sounds incredulous." Kathy repeated that she did not know the robbers, and the commissioner said, "Your history, your association—"

"—But it's true."

The commissioner continued, "It's incredulous to believe that you didn't know you were going out to do this, you were going to sit in the van—"

"—I knew I would be sitting in a van and helping people to escape from a robbery. The question is why. How—" she said. "If I thought of violence happening, I would not have been there." She explained, "I denied risk."

One parole commissioner alluded to Kathy's self-centeredness, and told her that psychological reports made at the time of her sentencing were going to be weighed.

The commissioners worried aloud about Kathy's statement that she'd blocked out the likelihood that in an armed robbery people could be hurt. What was to stop her from doing something similar again?

A commissioner asked, "While you've been incarcerated, you've focused on helping individuals, and it's a rather narrow life in prison. When you get out of prison—I believe you'll start by helping individuals, but at some point you might look around again and see the inequities in society."

Kathy asked to read a written statement. The commissioners politely suggested she leave it for them to read. But Kathy read it aloud anyway. It was an expression of what she would feel upon "walking out of the prison gate."

> I will gently touch the air that surrounds me like a shawl. It is autumn and the leaves are floating in circles of reds, browns, and oranges.

The recital was an abrupt change of tone. Kathy continued.

> I have another journey to make. I must cross that river of sorrow into the past where the flames burn the spirits. I will approach and look for your faces, to find your eyes and look directly at you, to go back again to that day, to kneel at the place where I lay on the ground, to retrace my steps and to tell you that your ghosts haunt me, to wail with the flames, oh, if I could only replay that day, I would not have been there, I would not have gone. I would not have my hands in any way touching the tragedy of that day. I lower myself onto my knees and pray, as I have learned in prison, to the larger force that we cling to, if I could only push back the clock and remake the past. . . . My journey cannot be taken without facing your eyes and those of your loved ones who went on without you. If there were only a place where the living and the dead could meet, and tell their tales and weep. I would reach for you, not so that you could forgive me, but so that you could know that I have no pride for what I have done, only the wisdom and regret that came too late.

Instead of waiting two days, the commissioners announced a few hours later that parole was denied. Kathy gamely told supporters that she'd never expected to be released. Lenny Weinglass filed a suit in the state court asking the court to void the parole board's decision. He argued that the board had not considered Kathy's good works in prison and her sentencing judge had said she might be paroled in twenty years.

After the extensive publicity campaign for parole, Elaine Lord punished Kathy. Declaring that Kathy had been illicitly discovered in the computer room, Superintendent Lord stripped her of all powers. She was fired from all the children's programs and college degree programs. Her new job was washing dishes in the mess hall.

When Kathy appealed, her job was upgraded. She was assigned to tend to the terminally ill.

Kathy's publicity was irrelevant to the parole campaign. Kathy knew publicity would not sway the parole board. She also knew that virtually no one convicted of murder is released on the first parole bid. Yet Kathy used the parole hearing as an excuse to jump feet first into the media.

Besides everything else, Kathy also knew that such a gigantic publicity gambit would threaten the warden. One might surmise that Kathy wanted to be famous more than she wanted to succeed in prison or to get out of prison.

An ill-timed interview with Bill Ayers appeared in the *New York Times* in September 2001. The interview, conducted right before the terrorist attacks on the World Trade Center and the Pentagon, proclaimed Ayers's fantastical belief that it might be necessary again to bomb government buildings.

Ayers was appearing in the *Times* to publicize a memoir of his Weather bombing days—replete with high-energy jokes, clever metaphors, and secret messages, as well as an unscrupulous politician's rewritings of historic fact. He allotted one sentence to the "mischief" his group had performed with the Black Liberation Army. He referred to the bomb placed in the U.S. Capitol building as an "eensy beensy," a pet name Kathy had also used for Chesa. He also chose to brag of "the balmy day" on which his Weather group had bombed the Pentagon and mused about the importance of doing it again.

When an august group called the Chicago Humanities Committee withdrew an invitation to speak, Ayers waged a war in the pages of the *Chicago Tribune*, claiming that it was he, not the committee, who'd canceled his speech. Bernardine, who'd been photographed looking fiercely haughty with Ayers for his *Times* interview, soon found herself battling her employer, Northwestern University, whose board was trying to fire her.

Ayers and Bernardine saw Chesa Boudin's academic successes as a private and public triumph. They passed around a paper Chesa wrote at Yale, in which he described himself as having been an aggressive and disturbed little boy. He said that he had hit his head against walls and refused to learn to read until he was nearly ten years old.

The paper mused about the dark theme of Chesa's life: Who was he to fault for his wrenching separation from his birth parents? Chesa righteously elected to blame "the system." It discriminated against blacks and had punished his birth parents for taking up the black cause.

Chesa recounted a poignant argument with a black childhood friend whose mother was also incarcerated at Bedford Hills prison. The friend insisted—each time he and Chesa met—that it was not a racist society that had put their mothers in jail. The women had been responsible for their own criminal actions.

Then Chesa's friend was jailed, as a teenager, for armed robbery. Chesa visited him in jail. The old argument flared up. The friend said that he alone was to blame—as a human being and a man—for acts that led to his incarceration.

Chesa disagreed: privileges of the system had saved Chesa himself from a similar fate. Hundreds of thousands of dollars were spent on psychiatry. A network of people rescued him. Otherwise, he too might be in prison.

Leonard Boudin's hero was Louis Boudin, a moralist who performed intellectual services for underprivileged people using the law, which he considered holy—and at which he knew himself to be a master—to curtail government power.

Leonard also believed he knew better than judges, legislators, and police. But despite the fact that he advised his beloved clients about breaking the law in the name of conscience, Leonard guided his career for the most part in accordance with the laws of the land, employing the law to win fight after fight against the government. Confounded by Kathy's actions of "conscience"and unwilling to admit he'd ever made any mistakes, he was profoundly distressed to find it difficult to sum up the course

The Trial of John Brown, *painted in 1942, by artist Horace Pippin, a childhood friend of Jean Boudin. The violent abolitionist John Brown loomed large in the imaginations of the Boudin family circle.*

of his life's work. Unlike his brother-in-law Izzy Stone, Leonard was not confident enough to admit he'd ever been wrong about anything.

Leonard was a flawed person, an egoist, as great political players frequently are. He saw himself as a hero because he helped his clients by invoking the U.S. government's protections for dissenters. Leonard defended many idealistic and grandiose intellectuals who opposed the government and then tested the largesse of its laws. He was a hero to his radical friends and relatives. He had to be politically adroit to maintain his establishment position as well. He was in fact admired by the legal establishment—which included his son, Michael.

While Leonard won cases that shaped the legal canon, Kathy asserted her authenticity by physically attacking the system and its laws in the name of justice. It and Leonard himself were, in her view, very powerful and very fraudulent.

· · ·

Leonard believed that Kathy had injured his reputation. As Kathy's defense costs skyrocketed, he'd consulted tax lawyers. He said that he suffered financial wounds as a result of her actions. He argued that the $1.5 million he'd spent on Kathy's defense was a tax deduction, a critical business expense. If his own daughter was convicted of murder and armed robbery, who would hire Leonard to defend them?

Kathy has come to loom larger in the media than Leonard ever did, but she has endured ceaseless hardships for her prized fame. Long ago, she sacrificed "respectability" and creature comforts, and later her mother-hood and freedom. She views herself primarily as a public figure and even now divides people into two groups: "my supporters and my detractors."

Fourteen months after Kathy's parole bid, in December 2002, a front-page *New York Times* article heralded Chesa as a success story. Photographs of him and the proud Bernardine Dohrn Ayers also appeared in *People* magazine.

Chesa had won two prestigious graduate fellowships—the Rhodes and the Marshall. David and Kathy learned of his accomplishment by reading the *Times*. He went on to graduate summa cum laude from Yale.

Reporters were awed by obstacles—imposed upon him by his birth parents—that Chesa had thus far overcome. Chesa spoke to the press mostly in his "aboveground" persona. He said he was named for the Swahili word for "dancer," omitting the Joanne Chesimard reference. He declined to talk about his parents' activities. "Different times require different tactics."

The *New York Times* reporter noted that Kathy and David had missed Chesa's Little League games, his high-school graduation, and his Phi Beta Kappa award ceremony, but Chesa said he wasn't angry anymore; he was, he said, lucky that he'd had four parents instead of two. His aboveground persona slipped when he added, "My parents were all dedicated to fighting U.S. imperialism around the world. I'm dedicated to the same thing."

Kim O'Grady, the daughter of the slain policeman Ed O'Grady, was disturbed to read of Chesa's two-day struggle to reach his incarcerated parents to tell them his good news. Kim said to herself, "I haven't talked to my father in twenty years."

A columnist wrote an article entitled "Being the Son of Left-wing Terrorists Means Never Having to Say You're Sorry," and asked readers to contribute money to a Nyack policemen's scholarship fund. Over five hundred letters containing checks totaling $14,500 were delivered to Nyack in the next week.

In spring 2003, the state supreme court concurred with Lenny Weinglass's suit and ruled that Kathy's parole hearing be voided. The decision was noted in the *New York Law Journal:* "[Kathy] had nothing to do with the murders of three people, two of them police officers." The article remarked on two of Kathy's illustrious relatives, Judge Michael Boudin and her late father, the prominent civil rights attorney. It also mentioned Weinglass's argument: the sentencing judge had said in chambers—refusing to repeat himself in open court—that Kathy might be paroled in twenty years based on her conduct in prison, should the parole board see fit.

Unless the state attorney general appealed the decision, Kathy might face two parole hearings in a six-week period: first, the court-ordered rehearing; then, in August, her second parole hearing.

Victor Rabinowitz claimed that Kathy had won a moral victory. It seemed common sense, however, that after being attacked by Kathy's lawyers in the courts, the parole board would dig in its heels.

So it came to pass, in May 2003, two members of Governor George Pataki's parole board faced Kathy Boudin. They opened by literally telling her to back off: she had inched her chair too close to them.

One commissioner asked Kathy if she recognized names of five of her Brinks codefendents. "I'm not sure," she said. This time, the board went on record by describing the Rockland robbery in detail.

Kathy responded weakly, "It's a terrible crime. I feel like it is horrendous to listen to it." She repeated her claim that she had not told police to put their guns away, but admitted for the first time publicly that, frightened by the shooting, she ran. (Previously she claimed she had not tried to escape.) She said she didn't know until she was "in the police car or in the police station" that anybody had been killed.

A commissioner remarked that clearly the men she was involved with were not going to Nyack to play a game of Mahjong. "They were there with weapons and took an incredible amount of money and wanted to get away, and things would certainly happen. You were aware of that."

Kathy reiterated that she'd been a last-minute recruit. "And I had a belief system that said it's all right to risk human life, if it has to be for a greater good."

She insisted, once again, that she'd never been involved in violence directly.

For example, she'd had, she said, no idea whatsoever that anyone was building bombs in the Wilkerson town house. She just happened to be there the day that three young people were killed, after living with her parents for two months while recuperating from mononucleosis.

She again insisted that she'd supported the Weatherman organization as an educational group only. She said that she'd never had anything to do with bombs or guns.

Once more—although Kathy was saying with anguish that she was sorry for past actions—she was not admitting what a great number of those actions had been.

She did say that taking part in the Nyack robbery had been wrong—and criminal. She said, however, that she'd helped to facilitate the robbery, but had had nothing to do with its planning.

The commissioners asked in several ways if by agreeing to take part in the robbery she'd in fact been helping to plan it.

When asked, she said she'd assumed that the robbery money was going to be used to create health clinics and recreation centers in the black community.

"Blows me away," said one commissioner, stating that at age thirty-seven Kathy'd surely known that there were such things as banks and loans and that a million and a half dollars doesn't just "plop out of the sky."

Kathy again said that she was sorry and seemed anguished.

A commissioner asked her if she helped in the robbery because she felt she had done nothing else big enough. She agreed: her life had been mundane after the Weather group broke up.

A commissioner asked politely why Kathy hadn't warned the Nyack policemen at the roadblock, saying "look out or watch out" instead of putting them at greater risk.

As the session drew to a close, the commissioners seemed more warmly disposed to Kathy. Kathy said, "I think fortunately, I've changed. I have matured."

"Certainly we hope so."

"I'm going to be sixty next week."

"You look really good for sixty."

"I appreciate that, I know I have gray hair."

For the record, a commissioner read a list of Kathy's good works in prison: she'd been a bench carpenter, porter, building maintenance worker, librarian, group counselor, group leader, mother's legal rights counselor, general clerk, and teacher.

"Late bloomer, as it were," said the commissioner.

"Oh God, that's so true," said Kathy.

She added, "And so many people got hurt [because of the robbery]. She did not mention Chesa; but one commissioner said, "Including your own son."

Kathy admitted in a rush that it had taken her some six years to begin to connect to her feelings of guilt for having left Chesa. She'd made the emotional connection, she recalled, only after Chesa climbed up into the tree at the end of visiting hours and screamed at her how stupid she had been to have committed the robbery and left him behind. Kathy's admission was surprising—six years was a long time to disconnect from that painful truth.

Kathy offered to show the commissioners a photograph of Chesa. After politely deferring Kathy's request, one commissioner remarked that despite what Chesa said, in fact Kathy was a very bright woman.

Kathy responded, "Bright has nothing to do with being emotionally screwed up, which I was." She soon revealed new plans to become a therapist after studying at Columbia Teachers College upon her release. She hoped to live in Brooklyn Heights with her good friends the doctors Charlotte and Ollie Fein.

After the warmth of the exchange at the end of Kathy's hearing, the commissioners denied her parole in harsh language: her many achievements in prison were clearly outweighed by the serious and brutal nature of the crimes for which she pled guilty.

Many people who liked Kathy were sad. Said John Castellucci, "No matter how irresponsible a parent she was or how much she's lying about past violence, Kathy has been in prison for twenty-two years. I think she's paid her debt to society. I don't believe she would be a danger to society if released."

Nonetheless it seemed likely to Chesa Boudin that in August 2003 the parole board would again refuse to free Kathy. Public opinion was very negative about famous terrorists since the 9/11 attacks on the Pentagon and the World Trade Center.

A lively, romantic documentary film called *The Weather Underground* opened in late spring. It featured Bill Ayers, Bernardine Dohrn, Naomi Jaffe, and David Gilbert. Ayers carried a baseball bat as he recalled events of the Days of Rage and walked the route of the protest.

Kathy Boudin was conspicuously absent from the film. Her name was not even mentioned in the long segment on the Wilkerson town house bombing. Once—and only for a split second—the camera swept across her plumpish young face among scores of others on the FBI wanted poster. David Gilbert spoke steadfastly of taking responsibility for his actions. He did not say that he now spent nearly twenty hours a day alone in his cell or that he was allergic to much of the food at Attica prison. The group's role in the Army robberies was referred to only in a few sentences of print about David that appeared at the end of the credits. It looked as if Kathy's old comrades were supporting her version of events to help her get out of jail.

The Weather group was again attempting to rewrite history. And the public relations geniuses almost succeeded. Victor Rabinowitz's sister Lucille Perlman was one of many people who wondered if Kathy's group was trying to write Kathy out of history, at least until she was released from prison.

Letters supporting Kathy's bid for parole in August 2003 came from hundreds of people, including Bishop Desmond Tutu and aristocratic conservative William F. Buckley Jr. Nonetheless Kathy's attorney Leonard Weinglass warned Kathy that in light of the politics of the situation she must not expect to be paroled for at least a year and a half. Her supporters were saying that the decision to keep her in jail was coming directly from George W. Bush's White House.

Kathy's parole hearing took place midafternoon on Wednesday, August 20, 2003. Soon afterward, in a stunning reversal, she was granted parole. Kathy telphoned Weinglass, screaming and crying at the news. She was going to be a free person sometime during the next four weeks.

The arguments that Jean took part in more than seventy years ago at the Leof table in Philadelphia loom over Kathy's turbulent life. She has spent twenty-two years in prison for acting out her own ill-conceived romance of liberation theology.

Unlike Kathy, Dr. Leof never presumed to solve the great questions; he simply wished to discuss them. He asked: "If a man is good to society but not to his family, is he a good man?"

Dr. Leof asked his wife Jennie, "If I talked like John Brown, would you call me meshuga? How can any man break the law and then presume the exoneration of history?"

He added, "When is a man justified in making war on his own government? Is the answer 'never'?"

Dr. Leof liked to recite Walt Whitman: "I am not asleep to the fact that among radicals as among the others there are hoggishnesses, narrownesses, inhumanities, which at times almost scare me for the future."

Notes

Preface

xiii The bereaved mother in the Didion novel is married to a jocular progressive lawyer named Leonard, an amoral man who sells guns to unnamed Latin American countries. The couple has a daughter who goes underground as a violent antiwar protester.

xvi went to see Jean Boudin in 1992: I am indebted to Jean Boudin for interviews as well as personal photographs and access to papers.

xvi Also visiting Jean: Bert Gross was a professor of economics at NYU and an expert on full employment. I am indebted to him for hours of recollection.

xvii malign forces: Michael Standard, interview, 1996.

xxiii Four years later: Kathy Boudin conversations, Bedford Hills prison.

1: Leonard Boudin—Deep Background

4 Louis's parents: Bert Gross, interview, 1994.

4 spoken English: Jean Boudin, interview, and letter from Anna Pavitt to Louis in Louis Boudin papers, Columbia University Library.

4 "Boudin walks out": After losing a fight with pro-Soviet John Reed about a phrase written by Karl Marx, Louis renounced party politics. Louis did not believe that the Russian Revolution would ignite worldwide revolutions. Russia was not, as per Karl Marx, an advanced industrial society. Following Louis's example, Leonard never joined a political party.

4 her favorite person in the world: Leonard assumed in later years that the family had suffered extreme discrimination against Jews: punitive military service, taxation, and pogroms—massacres of Jews by rowdy Russians, sometimes to celebrate Christmas. By 1900, more than 2 million Jewish people had left Russia. Leonard Boudin, Columbia University Oral History Project, 1994.

5 featherbedding: Sarah Boudin Edlin, *The Unmarried Mother in Our Society* (New York: Farrar, Straus, and Young, 1954).

5 told as a joke: Jean Boudin, interview.

5 After graduation from law school: Victor Rabinowitz, interviews 1992–93, and Leonard Boudin, Columbia University Oral History Project.

5 "a parasite": David Kairys, ed., *The Politics of Law, A Progressive Critique* (New York: Pantheon, 1982); Victor Rabinowitz, "The Radical Tradition in the Law."

5 Henry Street Settlement: Leonard would proudly cite in later years the fact that Herbert Lehman, the future governor of New York and a rich German Jew from the banking

family, taught Joe Boudin English at the Henry Street Settlement. Leonard Boudin, Columbia University Oral History Project, interviewed 1984.

6 neckties in a sweatshop: Edlin, *The Unmarried Mother in Our Society.*

6 William Edlin: The Yiddish newspaper featured fiction by Isaac Bashevis Singer, naïve poetry, news stories about U.S. criminal courts, the romantic meanderings of Jewish housewives, socialist opposition to World War I, and news of events such as the Sacco and Vanzetti trial.

8 Jack London and League for Industrial Democracy: Louis Boudin papers at Columbia University Library.

8 "the smartest little boy in America": Bert Gross, interview.

8 "mediocre and dull": Leonard Boudin, Columbia University Oral History Project.

9 a harsh lesson: Leonard swore by a lesson in the smug chess autobiography of J. R. Capablanca, who as a twelve-year-old played against the reigning Cuban champion. Leonard was convinced that the man was superior to him because of his extensive experience. After losing two games, Capablanca saw something subtle in the third game that revealed his opponent's sense of his own weakness and gave Capablanca the necessary courage and confidence to win every game that followed. Bert Gross, interview.

9 Leonard's boyhood relationship to Morton Gould: Bert Gross, interview. Morton Gould later won the Pulitzer Prize and was honored by the Kennedy Center, crossing the line between popular and highbrow musical composition.

9 Joe cursed his sweeping losses: Bert Gross, interview.

10 foreclosed mortgages: Leonard Boudin, Columbia University Oral History Project.

10 Paul Goodman: Paul Goodman, *The Break-Up of Our Camp, Stories, 1932–1935,* ed. Taylor Stoehr (Santa Barbara, Calif.: Black Sparrow Press, 1978).

10 his lover: Bert Gross interview.

12 autobiographical short story: *The Lavender,* 1931, and Georgette Schneer, interview, 1995.

12 Leonard corresponded with Paul Goodman: Paul Goodman correspondence, Harvard Library.

12 Delaware Cliff Camp: Professor Herbert Robbins, Princeton University, interviews, 1992–1994.

14 could mean its opposite: Bert Gross and Edith Tiger, interviews, 1994. I am indebted to Edith Tiger for sharing many memories and papers.

14 softened jawline: Ruth Gilbert, interview, 1994.

14 Harvard Law School: Leon Friedman, interview, 1992.

14 fire hydrants: Georgette Schneer, interview, 1994.

14 Lomax: Georgette Schneer Phil Foner, interview, 1995.

15 City College newspaper: Many of the Jewish students at City College rejected traditional faith. One article in the April Fool's parody issue reviewed a "speech" by a rabbi from the American Jewish Congress. The article accused Hitler of trying to arouse "feeling against our race by maliciously charging us of being atheists."

15 overdue rents and mortgage payments: Paul Goodman correspondence, Harvard Library.

15 "early connection with the working class": Leonard Boudin, Columbia University Oral History Project.

16 Louis's poor eyesight: Bert Gross, interview.

17 Mortgage Commission: Leonard had been recommended for the job by one of his law professors, Maurice Finkelstein, a friend of Louis Boudin, who also wrote about the U.S. Constitution. Leonard disapproved of his professor's cruelty to slow students. "I

suppose I learned how not to teach from him," he said years later. Yet many students and protégés would one day criticize Leonard for his cruelty to those he considered of inferior intelligence. Leonard Boudin, Columbia University Oral History Project.

17 "my real love, labor law": Leonard Boudin, Columbia University Oral History Project.

18 Louis . . . opposed the Communist Party: Victor Rabinowitz, interview.

18 canoe: Bert Gross, interview.

2: *Before Me There Was Nothing*

19 born . . . on leap-year day: Jean Roisman Boudin, interview.

19 Celia Roisman: Lila Roisman, interview, 1996.

20 Jennie Roisman: Richard Roisman, interview, 1996.

20 "bi-everything": Lila Roisman, interview.

21 Charles Roisman, black jazz clubs, and "prince of charm": Ruth Gilbert, interview.

21 Roisman pickle company: Lila Roisman, interview.

21 "a thinking place": Jean Boudin, interview.

22 Madi's home: Alice Carlen, interviews, 1993–1995.

22 Students . . . jockeyed for an invitation: Blanche Orr, interview, 1994.

22 brilliant and restless: Bert Gross, interview.

22 Horace Pippin: The painting *Country Doctor* had been sold to the Leofs by their friend Robert Carlen (who would marry Alice Serber), and it would be the high point of a 1995 Pippin retrospective at the Metropolitan Museum. Morris Leof lent *Country Doctor* to playwright Clifford Odets, who did not return it.

Jean would pace Madi's third-floor bedroom helping her to write articles. One essay called "Horace Pippin: The Odds Are Against Him," syndicated in Sunday newspaper supplements. It read: "Horace Pippin is a tall open-faced man, [who] smiles often and has a loud unrestrained hearty laugh." It concluded, ". . . although Dr. Albert C. Barnes, owner of the most comprehensive collection of modern art in the world, calls Pippin the most important Negro painter ever to appear in America, Mrs. Pippin, until two years ago took in laundry to pay household bills." Courtesy Robert Carlen archives.

22 reread Freud: Eric A. Gordon, *Mark the Music: The Life and Work of Marc Blitzstein* (New York: St. Martin's Press, 1989).

23 scarlet paint: The Blitzstein family had serious glamour: when the Moscow Art Theater's production of Maxim Gorky's *The Lower Depths* had come to Philadelphia in 1923, the great Gorky honored Marc's father, Sam Blitzstein, by staying at his Girard Avenue home. Gordon, *Mark the Music*.

23 Brown was hanged: In John Brown's last speech, he said: "Now, if it is deemed necessary that I should forfeit my life for the furtherance of the ends of justice, and mingle my blood with the blood of millions in this slave country whose rights are disregarded by wicked, cruel, and unjust enactments, I say let it be done."

25 Harry Kurnitz: He went on to write movies such as *The Thin Man* and *Once More with Feeling*, which was based on one of his novels. Jean's smart-alecky jokes about Harry's foibles fed his myth. No one minded the fact that he pilfered small amounts of money. Harry was supporting himself by turning out romances for *Redbook* magazine using female pseudonyms. Jean made up an opening line for one of his stories: "When I felt this small new life within me . . ."

25 Marc Blitzstein: After years of study and performances in Europe, Marc Blitzstein

would compose Marxist morality operas for Broadway theaters and concert halls. He wrote the best English translation of Brecht's *Threepenny Opera*. He was Leonard Bernstein's early mentor. Jean Boudin, interviews, and Gordon, *Mark the Music*.

27 Ben Snellenberg: Alice Carlen, interview. Despite opposition from gentile property owners, the Snellenberg brothers, former peddlers, had transplanted their menswear stalls from the Jewish ghetto market in the late nineteenth century. Their large store flourished several blocks north on the cosmopolitan Market Street. See Dennis Clark, "Irish-Jewish Relations in Philadelphia," and Edwin Wolf II, "The German-Jewish Influence in Philadelphia's Jewish Charities," in Murray Friedman, ed., *Jewish Life in Philadelphia, 1830–1940* (Philadelphia: Ishi Publications, Institute for the Study of Human Issues, 1983).

27 "male admiration": Bert Gross, interview.

27 Jewish culture: For an informative look at Jewish life at this time, see Friedman, ed., *Jewish Life in Philadelphia*.

27 student Communist Party: Jean Roisman Boudin, FBI transcript.

28 navy ROTC: Bert Gross, interview.

28 Jean quoted Madi on the constitutional Nineteenth Amendment, passed ten years earlier giving women the right to vote. If Jean was going to vote, she must be educated. In later years, Jean downplayed feminism, preferring to attribute her youthful spunk to the altruistic beliefs of Thoreau and Marx.

28 "after one glimpse of his dimples": Andrew Patner, *I. F. Stone, A Portrait* (New York: Pantheon, 1988).

29 *I. F. Stone's Weekly:* Izzy's independent newsletters would gather international acclaim during the Vietnam War era. His would be the first article in the *New York Review of Books* to condemn the United States' involvement in the war in Vietnam. He considered himself "American to the core and radical to the end." Robert C. Cottrell, *Izzy, A Biography of I. F. Stone* (New Brunswick, N.J.: Rutgers University Press, 1992).

29 Nicola Sacco and Bartolomeo Vanzetti: Sacco and Vanzetti were sentenced to death by a judge who many believed was prejudiced against anarchists. Despite appeals, the state Supreme Court and the U.S. Supreme Court refused to intervene. An advisory committee headed by President Abbott Lowell of Harvard found no reason to commute the sentence.

29 "leftist infighting": I. F. Stone, *In a Time of Torment—A Nonconformist History of Our Times, 1961–67* (Boston: Little, Brown, 1989), author's preface.

30 Jean graduated from Penn: Jean Roisman Boudin, FBI file.

30 Leonard . . . removed himself from arguments: Bert Gross, interview.

31 reading at "322" and Jacob modeled on Poppa Leof: Alice Carlen, interview; Ruth Gilbert, interview.

31 *Awake and Sing*: Margaret Brenman-Gibson, *Clifford Odets: American Playwright* (New York: Atheneum, 1982).

32 "immense beckoning sweetness": Anatole Broyard, *Kafka Was the Rage: A Greenwich Village Memoir* (New York: Random House, 1997).

3: The Most Gorgeous Couple of the Left

33 Leonard and Jean were married in Manhattan: Boudin marriage license.

33 real daisies into the wedding cake: Jean Boudin, interview; Bert Gross, interview.

34 gloomy wife, Eva: Eric Gordon, *Mark the Music: The Life and Work of Marc Blitzstein* (New York: St. Martin's Press, 1989).

35 "sharp as a tack": Georgette Schneer, interview.
35 an acquaintance from Philadelphia: Jean Boudin, interviews. Also, Leon Berkowitz file, Smithsonian Institution, archive of American Art 4166–4175.
36 The love in his classroom: Donna Fecteau, interview, 1998.
37 so frequently and fondly: Ruth Gilbert, interview.
37 bare loft: Gordon, *Mark the Music;* Jean Boudin, interviews.
37 dark miracle: Gordon, *Mark the Music.*
37 Leonard shivered: Bert Gross, interview.
38 "forced marches": Jean Boudin, interview.

If *The Cradle Will Rock* seems simplistic, there were in fact similar union fights taking place throughout the country. By March 1937, the *New York Times* was printing a regular column called "Day's Strike Developments." U.S. Steel ("Big Steel") caved in and agreed to accept unions. But the smaller companies ("Little Steel"), including Bethlehem, Youngstown, and Republic, were holding out against unions: News clippings; Gordon, *Mark the Music.*

38 opening-night benefit: Jean Boudin, interview. As opening night approached, Jean heard disturbing rumors that congressmen were unhappy about the operetta's radical views on steel strikes. Congress did not want to fund anticapitalist artists.

Marc Blitzstein invited everyone he knew to the final rehearsal on June 5. He worried that antiunion congressmen might find a way to keep the opera from opening. Some members of the WPA thought the production too expensive. But cast members, plus a controversial chorus of blacks and whites—as well as Marc himself—were being paid the minimum $23.86 a week by the WPA: Jean Boudin, interview; Gordon, *Mark the Music.*

39 Leonard huddled inside: Bert Gross, interview; Jean Boudin, interview.

4: A Revolutionary Childhood

40 died in childbirth: Jean Boudin, interview.
40 Margaret Mead: In 1928, Mead's brilliant and best-selling anthropology monograph, *Coming of Age in Samoa,* had helped create the new social science of anthropology. Despite Mead's fierce independence, she and Jean had much in common. Mead had also been raised in the Philadelphia area and had attended the University of Pennsylvania. Like Jean, Mead was always scribbling deeply felt "nonfiction" poems about peaks and valleys in her emotional life. The two women flourished as seekers of big new ideas, although Mead was far more original. They differed in other ways. For example, Mead believed in God as the force of love and order in the universe, and Jean believed in the potential of her fellow man.

Mead had requested that her pediatrician, the tall young Dr. Benjamin Spock, break several taboos. Jean was amazed to see friends of Mead (and Dr. Spock) trooping toward the delivery room with a movie camera, tripod, floodlights, and wires. Dr. Spock remembered six people, all crowding around "Mead's obstetric area painted bright pink with mercurochrome."

There was no precedent for filming a baby's delivery. But Mead believed it a service to her infant daughter—because she also believed a person was most him- or herself at the time of birth. She filled at least one notebook with early observations of her daughter, Mary Catherine Bateson, carrying on a family tradition. Mead insisted on remaining awake in order to observe the baby's delivery—unheard-of at that time in the United States. Mead was also a friend of Jean's hero, Eleanor Roosevelt, another rare progressive and brainy woman in public life. Committed to "saving" dying primitive cultures by recording them for history, Mead was turning her attention to "saving" her own culture by revising outmoded child-rearing conventions.

I am indebted to Mead's daughter, Mary Catherine Bateson, and to her book *With a Daughter's Eye* (New York: William Morrow, 1984), as well as to Pulitzer Prize–winning historian Carleton Mabee, author of "Margaret Mead and a Pilot Experiment in Progressive and Interracial Education: The Downtown Community School" (New York State Historical Association), for sharing recollections and observations.

40 maternity pavilion: *Academy Bookman*, vol. 15, no. 1, 1962; President's Report, French Hospital, 1939.

40 in a panic: Jean Boudin, interviews.

40 In French Hospital: Mead and Jean shared services of pediatrician and gynecologist Dr. Claude Heaton, whose progressive book on child-raising annotated the high rate of infant mortality in Harlem. Heaton's name appears on birth certificates of Michael and Kathy Boudin. Mary Catherine Bateson, interview.

41 log of observations: Jean Boudin, interviews.

41 feeding on self-demand: Margaret Mead, *Blackberry Winter: My Earlier Years* (New York: William Morrow, 1972). Jean did not follow every step in Margaret Mead's trailblazing path. Mead refused to downplay her own ideas in order to protect a man's ego. Her first husband became a minister because as a girl Mead had dreamed of herself as a minister's wife. She was, however, traditional enough to hide the fact from her second husband that she was doing housework, but her reason was that it made him feel guilty.

41 Dr. Ben Spock without crediting Mead: Mary Catherine Bateson, interview.

41 parent-run elementary school: Carleton Mabee, historian, interview.

41 The Downtown Community School was a supplement to the existing Little Red Schoolhouse, and both primary schools sent students on to Elisabeth Irwin High School.

The Little Red Schoolhouse had been founded back in 1921 as a progressive school in the public school system. Elisabeth Irwin High School had been founded in 1941. At the outbreak of World War II, the city school board closed the school down. The teachers bought the building and took it private. The tuition was high: $1,400 per student. Music, art, and drama were required courses, and intellectual competition was intense.

In the 1950s, teachers would be hired who had been forced out of other jobs by Senator Joe McCarthy and other congressional investigators. Many parents were drawn to radical ideas, and left-wing politics was an integral part of classroom discussions. Angela Davis, *Angela Davis: An Autobiography* (New York: Random House, 1974).

42 "Stalinoids": Dwight MacDonald, notes for a speech to the Downtown Community Board. Courtesy Michael MacDonald.

42 Leonard's blood boiled: Jean Boudin and Carleton Mabee, interviews.

42 Paul Klee: Paul Mattick, interview, 1993.

42 "the Great God Geyser": Mary Catherine Bateson, interview.

43 scorned tough language: Martha Ullman West, interview, 1994.

43 swanky cars: Susan Kapit, interview, 1993.

43 "real classy place": Fred Gardner, interview, 1994.

43 Leonard's professional life: Victor Rabinowitz was hired along with Nanette Dembitz, a niece of Supreme Court Justice Louis Dembitz Brandeis. Victor Rabinowitz, *An Unrepentant Leftist* (Ann Arbor: University of Michigan Press, 1996).

Victor would have been annoyed to be told that there was a sense in which he exemplified F. Scott Fitzgerald's dictum: "The very rich are different from you and me, soft where we are hard." Victor scoffed at "softness" or "tender-mindedness" in favor of rule-governed objective reasoning.

43 appropriated Victor's credo: Michael Standard, interview.

45 intellectual snob: Sherry Wertheimer, legal secretary to Leonard Boudin, interviews, 1998.

46 on behalf of their client: Leonard sprang to the rescue of a client with explosive energy. He was horrified to learn, for example, how Metropolitan Life made the salesman with the lowest weekly sales stand in a corner with a dunce cap on his head. Leonard Boudin, Columbia University Oral History Project.

Leonard and Victor appealed to the State Labor Relations Board about Metropolitan Life Insurance Company. The two lawyers charged the company with maintaining an illegal company union. When employees formed an independent union—Local 30 of the United Office and Professional Workers—Met Life refused to bargain with the new union. Then Met Life fired all forty members of the independent union. Leonard Boudin, Columbia University Oral History Project; Victor Rabinowitz, interview.

47 debated what the spectacle: Rabinowitz, *An Unrepentant Leftist*.

47 as time passed: Bert Gross, interview.

47 a partner's salary: Bert Gross, interview.

48 *Amalgamated Utility Workers v. Consolidated Edison Co. of New York:* Supreme Court transcript.

48 "went down the shore": Bert Gross, interview; Jean Boudin, interview.

48 lobbied for raises: Leonard Boudin, Columbia University Oral History Project.

5: Sword and Fire

50 further inside himself: Jean Boudin, interview.

51 "She was a stunning presence": Robert Riley, interview, 1997.

52 12½ St. Luke's Place: The house had been purchased for $5,000 by Robert and Marin Riley, fellow parents at the Downtown Community School; since the Rileys could not afford to repair the rain-damaged floors and walls of the entire four stories, they sold the top two floors for "next to nothing" (under $5,000) to Jean and Leonard, who promised to be wonderful neighbors and who came with the high recommendation of school director Eleanor Brussel. Robert Riley decorated the store windows at Lord & Taylor and later joined the costumes and textiles department at the Brooklyn Museum.

52 ran hand in hand: Richard Kostelanetz, interview, 1998.

54 Victor was to argue before the U.S. Supreme Court: Victor Rabinowitz, interview; Supreme Court transcripts.

Provision 9(h) of the Taft-Hartley Act gave the government the right to ask all elected union leaders to sign a "loyalty oath" swearing they were not communists. Furthermore, Congress declared that unions organized by liberals who had associated with communists were illegal.

Congress was trying to get rid of union leaders who, it was feared, might act under the partial influence of the Soviet Union and against the interests of American workers and companies. Congressmen feared such union leaders might foment strikes in order to weaken the U.S. economy. Supreme Court of the United States, October term, 1948, American Communications Association, *CIO et al. Appellants v. Charles T. Douds individually* and the American Labor Relations Board, Second Region.

Victor cited important abstractions: the loyalty oath deprived union representatives of the freedoms of thought, expression, and association. Victor argued that in the Taft-Hartley Act, Congress was depriving union members of their choice of representatives by putting unconstitutional requirements on union leaders. Furthermore, union leaders who refuse to sign loyalty oaths were not necessarily communists and ought not to be deprived of their right to represent union members, and, if necessary, to strike.

Victor's brief was not as melodramatic as that of the government, whose lawyers quoted alarming data, gathered by the House Un-American Activities Committee (HUAC), that the Soviet Union encouraged strikes in the United States before the two countries became war allies (H. Rep, no. 1, 77th Cong., 1st sess.). The government lawyers also cited terrifying allegations by congressional committees that the Communist Party was trying to take over unions in order to foment strikes in the U.S. defense industries.

The government argued that belief was not the issue—but was an indication of potential conduct. Although Justice Hugo Black, in dissenting from the Court, called the loyalty oath "thought control," the majority of justices agreed with Congress.

54 great basketball player: John Castellucci, *The Big Dance: The Untold Story of Weatherman Kathy Boudin and the Terrorist Family That Committed the Brinks Robbery Murders* (New York: Dodd Mead, 1986). I am indebted to John Castellucci for his generous help, his reporter's notes, and his meticulous research into the Brinks robberies and the jailbreak of Assata Shakur.

54 Michael was the best student: Francine Fontaine, interviews, 1995.

55 darkly mischievous: Margaret Ullman West, interview, 1994.

55 drawings of Hiroshima: Mary Catherine Bateson, interview; Francine Fontaine, interview.

55 Bob Serber: Alice Serber Carlen, interviews.

Bob Serber had been second in command of a concentration of physicists led by J. Robert Oppenheimer, working at the top-secret laboratory.

Charlotte's exact location was secret. Her cryptic letters home to "322" from Los Alamos (with random postmarks) were always mailed on to Jean in New York.

A few days after the second bomb exploded over Japan, Bob Serber telephoned his sister, Alice, in Philadelphia to reveal his close connections to the event. He spoke of his awe at the sight of the first successful bomb test in Nevada. He also had witnessed the bombing of Nagasaki from one of the airplanes carrying bombs. Jean refused to contain her pride in her old friend. After the war ended, she repeated his stories about living in the top-secret laboratory.

55 "dropping the atom bomb": Al Socolow, interview, 1998.

56 disabled man: Mary Catherine Bateson, interview.

56 Roisman family's seder: Jean Boudin, interview.

56 terminally ill: At Clara's death a few months later, Joe Boudin endowed a lecture series at NYU Law School in her name. The gesture enraged Leonard, who saw it as his father's puerile attempt to make up for his cruelties.

57 "His life was charmed": Andrew Patner, *I. F. Stone: A Portrait* (New York: Pantheon, 1988).

57 Izzy on Palestine and Israel: Jean Boudin, interview.
57 Izzy was the first journalist: Robert C. Cottrell, *Izzy: A Biography of I. F. Stone* (New Brunswick, N.J.: Rutgers University Press, 1992).
57 "anti-ideologue": Eleanor Brussel, interview, 1994.

6: There Is No Proof

58 "great love of my life": Eleanor Brussel, interview.
58 convicted in Washington: *United States of America v. Judith Coplon*. On petition of writ of certiorari to the U.S. Court of Appeals for the Second Circuit.
58 stealing government documents: Skulduggery was in the air. Among documents in Coplon's purse were internal FBI documents that had been stolen twice previously. These were personal files of Jay Lovestone, the ex-communist and New Dealer (and a friend of Louis Boudin). First, the files had been stolen from Lovestone by rival party members. Then in 1944, Lovestone's files were stolen a second time, during a clandestine break-in by the FBI into the files of one of Lovestone's rivals. Now Coplon had allegedly stolen at least part of the file a third time! Harvey Klehr, John Earl Haynes, and Fridrikh Igorevich Firsov, *The Secret World of American Communism* (New Haven, Conn.: Yale University Press, 1995).
58 Although Leonard later claimed that it was purely by chance that he was appointed by the court to the Coplon case, in fact Coplon specifically asked the judge to appoint him and two associates from his firm. FBI director J. Edgar Hoover scribbled an internal memo: "These stinkers! Coplon's request for their [Leonard and his associates'] services surely places her . . ."
59 Coplon later wrote: Paul Wilkes, "The Left's Lawyers' Lawyer: A Profile of Leonard Boudin," *New York Times Magazine*, Nov. 17, 1971.
59 fell in love with Coplon: Belle Harper, interview, 1996.
59 Lamphere pounced: Robert Lamphere, interview, 1998; Robert J. Lamphere and Thomas Schachtman, *The FBI-KGB War: A Special Agent's Story* (New York: Random House, 1986).
60 Venona communiqués: The incredible story of the Venona communiqués, which were the FBI's secret trail to Judith Coplon, began on a battlefield in Finland during World War II where a farmer found a partly burned KGB codebook. In November 1944, William "Wild Bill" Donovan, OSS (Office of Special Services) chief, and rival of FBI director J. Edgar Hoover, secretly negotiated to pay the Finns $10,000 for the codebook and other coded materials. At that point, the United States was still allied with Russia, so the purchase horrified the secretary of state, who did not want to be accused of spying on his Soviet friends. He ordered that Donovan return the codebook to Russia. Wild Bill Donovan reluctantly obeyed his superior, but Donovan also clandestinely copied the codebook.

    As soon as the secretary of state returned the KGB codebook to the Soviets, they abruptly changed the KGB codes that had been used for espionage messages sent to and from the United States from early 1944 to May 1945.

    Meanwhile Donovan gave his illicit copy of the KGB codebook to the Army Security Agency, which assigned it to one of its best cryptnalysts, Meredith Gardner, to be deciphered.

    Meredith Gardner was a shy loner, a brilliant linguist and former college professor, who spoke six or seven languages, one of a handful of Western scholars who read Sanskrit. He was said by colleagues to have taught himself enough Japanese in three months to work on breaking Japanese codes during World War II (Lamphere, p. 82).

Working in what had been a girls' dormitory near Washington, D.C., Meredith Gardner set out to penetrate the KGB code. He was aided in this task by an eager special agent named Robert Lamphere, who believed he was more aggressive about sniffing out Soviet spies in the United States than FBI director J. Edgar Hoover.

Who was Special Agent Robert Lamphere? He had been twenty-three, "baby-faced, but hard-lipped" (according to the *Sunday Worker*, August 10, 1947) when he joined the FBI, where he soon found something to replace his father and mother, who had recently died. Born in 1918 in Coeur D'Alene, Idaho, in the mining district, Lamphere left after fighting with his father. He became an itinerant miner in hard-rock mining camps in Idaho, Montana, and British Columbia. On his father's instructions, he did not go home to attend the man's funeral.

Lamphere traces his father's family back to 1669 when they settled in Rhode Island. His paternal grandfather lost an arm in the Civil War and afterward was an administrator in the Treasury Department. The unusual man also wrote a book on the organization of the federal government, and he published a pioneer newspaper in Minnesota.

Lamphere had been the youngest of a class of fifty aspiring agents who believed the FBI to be an elite crime-busting outfit of "straight arrows." The FBI knew more, he believed, than anyone else about nearly everything from guns, to how to testify in court, to how to speak to civilians ("yes sir" and "no sir" regardless of their station). He proudly wore a gold badge, a white shirt, a snap-brim hat, and a Western-style belt that held up his gun holster and his .38 pistol, and carried a locked briefcase.

Nonetheless criticism leaks into Lamphere's memoir. "I always had the feeling that someone was looking over my shoulder, checking up on what I was doing and how I was doing it. In fact some of the FBI discipline verged on thought control. The unfortunate impact of the stringent disciplinary system was a dampening of the spirits of the men in the FBI."

Lamphere disobeyed Hoover by refusing to tattle on colleagues' infractions like coffee breaks, which were forbidden. "Those agents who did tell tales were dubbed submarines and wouldn't last long at the FBI."

In autumn 1947, Lamphere was transferred to Washington, D.C., to supervise the Bureau's antiespionage division. Unlike criminal cases, spy cases rarely brought closure. Trails of suspects started with a first-name initial and then met dead ends. From 1945 to 1949, Meredith Gardner kept trying to decipher the KGB code. It seemed impossible: besides the code, the KGB had substituted names for people and places and things. It had assigned numbers to letters and to words and then added a random number to the whole thing that was contained in a single-use cipher pad.

Lamphere assisted Meredith Gardner by giving him a bunch of duplicate onetime pads "sent mistakenly by someone in Moscow." (These pads were probably stolen by the FBI.) Using the partially deciphered code, Gardner was trying to decipher a backlog of dated KGB messages, also provided by Special Agent Lamphere, and which FBI agents had stolen from the New York offices of Amtorg, the Soviet purchasing office in New York (Harvey Klehr, John Earl Haynes, and Fridrikh Igorevich Firsov, *The Secret World of American Communism* [New Haven, Conn.: Yale University Press, 1995]).

In 1948, after three years' work trying to crack the Venona code, Meredith Gardner began slowly decoding stolen messages dating from early 1944 to May 1945. He decoded messages to the KGB that turned out to be top-secret letters from Winston

Churchill to President Harry Truman. (The trail would also lead to British spy Kim Philby.) The decoded messages led the FBI to assume the guilt of Julius Rosenberg and to an anonymous woman spy working inside the U.S. government. (The FBI soon believed that woman to be Judith Coplon.) Hoover would also use Venona communiqués to try to justify accusations against Alger Hiss. The Venona communiqués between Coplon and a Russian agent decoded by a language genius named Meredith Gardner would not be made public until the 1990s. They would be viewed by many as justification for Hoover and Senator McCarthy's fight against communism. Gardner himself was very sad about the Rosenbergs' executions. "Those people at least believed in what they were doing," he told his wife.

60 not reliable: Venona communiqués; NSA.org; Thomas Powers, interview, 1998; Harvey Klehr interview, 2002; Klehr and Hanes, *Venona: Decoding Soviet Espionage in America* (New Haven, Conn.: Yale University Press, 1999).

The Venona spy-to-spy documents were never used in court for many reasons. The government feared opening up a can of worms. A good defense lawyer might ask questions that endangered government secrets. For example, Director Hoover did not want to alert the Soviets that his cryptographers were slowly breaking the Venona code. Besides which, the messages between spies were not admissible as evidence. They did not name names, and could have been tricks or mere boasts by Russians sending them.

60 unlikely to have happened: Victor Navasky, interview, 1999; Thomas Powers, interview, 1998.

63 "Yes and I love him": Curt Gentry, *J. Edgar Hoover: The Man and the Secrets* (New York: Penguin, 1991).

63 Gentry, *J. Edgar Hoover:* An internal FBI memo was soon leaked (probably by a rival of Director Hoover) to the *Herald Tribune* newspaper. The FBI memo, dated November 9, 1949, ordered the hasty destruction of the phone tap records. It read:

> The above named informant [TIGER] has been furnishing information concerning the activities of the subject. In view of the imminency [sic] of her trial, it is recommended that this informant be discontinued immediately, and that all administrative records in the New York office covering the operation of this informant be discontinued . . . it is believed desirable that the indicated records be destroyed.

Hoover punished Truman by feeding "discoveries" of communists in his administration to Senator Joe McCarthy.

66 tizzy of reorganization: Gentry, *J. Edgar Hoover.*

67 at the heart of Leonard's tumultuous career: Hoover's career took off before World War II when, in 1936, President Franklin Roosevelt asked him to gather information on possible subversive activities of communists and fascists in the United States. To avoid legal and political problems, the work was to be done in secret under the authority of the State Department. The FBI soon employed practices such as blackmail of congressmen and other government members, surreptitious entry, safecracking, mail interception, telephone surveillance, coaching and paying witnesses, microphone plants, trash inspection, disorganization and penetration of groups, falsely labeling group members as confidential informants, and mailing anonymous accusatory letters to target groups' spouses. Bernard A. Weisberger, "The FBI Unbound," *American Heritage Magazine* (Sept. 1995).

As Hoover gained momentum, he flourished as a kind of mini-government under six presidents, despite setbacks such as the "personal and departmental disaster" that he suffered at the hands of Leonard Boudin in the Judith Coplon case. Although Leonard's war against Hoover might look to some to have been unequal, the young lawyer was "psyched" to win: he was armed with his belief in his fierce brain and in the Bill of Rights and the Constitution.

67 Paul Robeson's last Carnegie Hall concert: Jean Boudin, interview.

67 "The Purest Kind of Guy": Eugene Dennis, interview, 1998; Peggy Dennis, *The Auto-biography of an American Communist: A Personal View of a Political Life 1925–1975* (Westport, Conn.: Lawrence Hill & Co., 1977).

67 debates about Judith Coplon: Victor Rabinowitz, interview.

68 opened her mail: Gentry, *J. Edgar Hoover.*

68 disingenuously: Leonard Boudin, Columbia University Oral History Project.

68 aftermath: Gerald Gunther, *Learned Hand: The Man and the Judge* (New York: Alfred A. Knopf, 1994).

68 Coplon did not breathe freely: Despite Judge Learned Hand's assertion of Coplon's guilt, the highly independent jurist wrote a stern warning:

> Few weapons in the arsenal of freedom are more useful than the power to compel a government to disclose the evidence on which it seeks to forfeit the liberty of its citizens.
>
> All governments, democracies as well as autocracies, believe that those they seek to punish are guilty; the impediment of constitutional barriers are galling to all governments when they prevent the consummation of just that purpose. But those barriers were devised and are precious because they prevent that purpose and its pursuit from passing unchallenged by the accused, and unpurged by the alembic of public scrutiny and public criticism. A society which has come to wince at such exposure of the methods by which it seeks to impose its will upon its members has already lost the feel of freedom and is already on the path to absolutism.

Judge Hand angered Leonard and Victor by qualifying his decision:

> For all the foregoing reasons, the conviction must be reversed; but we will not dismiss the indictment for the guilt is plain, and it is possible on another trial. . . . The examination of the "confidential informant" may go far enough to show that he was not a "wiretapper."

Learned Hand also wrote:

> Perhaps also the powers of the bureau to arrest without a warrant should be broadened; and perhaps it would be desirable to set limits—as for example in cases of espionage, sabatoge, kidnapping, extortion, and in general investigations involving national security and defense—to the immunity of wiretapping of those who are shown by independent evidence to be probably engaged in crime. All these are matters with which we have no power to deal and on which we express no opinion; we take the law as we find it; under it the conviction cannot stand.

After he delivered his opinion on the Coplon case, Learned Hand also became a target of hate mail. As he wrote to Justice Felix Frankfurter on December 19, 1950: "You would be amused at my Judy Coplon mail: [It says] the Jews bribed us to let her off and we are now rich because, being 'rats,' 'curs,' 'traitors,' etc., we cashed in 'big.' I will

own that I am a little disturbed at the constant note of anti-Semitism; but the rest enter-
tains me." Gunther, *Learned Hand.*

69 Coplon illegally visited Mexico: Jean Boudin, interview.

7: Are Communists Part of an International Movement?

70 slowly losing her sanity: Jean Boudin, interview.

70 rapped on the bathroom door: Bert Gross, interview.

71 dwindling law practice: Victor Rabinowitz, interview: The firm's demise was not, however, the breakup of a happy family. Leonard had told his partner Sam Neuburger (who
had litigated the famous Scottsboro Boys case, taken up by the Communist Party, alleg-
ing the rape of a white woman by black teenagers) that Sam was "useless" because he
wanted to solicit "lowly" criminal cases. Sam, said Leonard, was incapable of reflecting
on intellectual aspects of the law.

72 North Korea was "a pain in the ass": Twenty-eight publishing houses in the United
States turned down Izzy's book, *The Hidden History of the Korean War.* It was published by the left-wing Monthly Review Press in the spring of 1952.

Izzy worried that the United States would become overwhelmed if it insisted on
fighting on behalf of right-wing governments in the Far East. In fact, many historians
trace the origins of the Vietnam War to President Truman's containment policy in
Korea. Phillip Knightley, *The First Casualty: From the Crimea to Vietnam: The War Correspondent as Hero, Propagandist, and Myth Maker* (New York and London: Harcourt
Brace Jovanovich, 1975).

72 Albert Camus and Jean-Paul Sartre: George C. Herring, *America's Longest War: The
United States and Vietnam, 1955–1975* (New York: Wiley, 1979).

72 Yale medal to Victor's father: Michael Standard, interview.

72 Louis Boudin dies: "Louis Boudin Dies, Labor Lawyer, 78," *New York Times,* May 31,
1952.

Authority on the Constitution had served as chairman
of American ORT Unit.

Louis Boudin, the noted labor lawyer and authority on constitutional law,
died Thursday night after a long illness. His age was 78.

He had served for many years as chairman of the board of directors of
American ORT Federation and as a director of World ORT.

In his legal work, Mr. Boudin represented many AFL and CIO unions in
important court cases. He refused, however, to take part in factional fights
between the two labor groups, although he fought relentlessly against racke-
teering and corruption in the trade union movement,

In 1907, Mr. Boudin's book, *The Theoretical System of Karl Marx,* was published here, and later the volume was translated into many languages. The
book is used in the economics departments of several universities as a standard
text on the philosophy of Marxism. After leaving the Socialist Party in 1919,
Mr. Boudin quit political activities and devoted his time to his law practice,
writing, and numerous charitable and community endeavors. In July 1946, he
flew to France to take part in the first postwar conference of the World ORT
Union of Paris. An outstanding legal victory was won by Mr. Boudin when the
United States Supreme Court sustained his view that utility workers were entitled to the protection of the Wagner Act.

SOME KEY DECISIONS.

He represented the unions involved in disestablishing the company union of the Western Union Telegraph Company and won a four to three decision from the New York State Court of Appeals that white-collar workers were covered by the State Labor Relations Act.

He was a frequent contributor to law reviews. With ORT, he served for many years as editor of *The Economic Review.* In 1932, he published a two-volume work, *Government by Judiciary,* which traced the growth of power of the United States Supreme Court and attacked the high court's judicial power. The work was lauded by Prof. Henry Steele Commager of Columbia University.

73 the sun had gone down: Bert Gross, interview.

73 solace from women: Sandy Katz, interview.

73 Izzy decided to found: Andrew Patner, *I. F. Stone: A Portrait* (New York: Pantheon, 1988).

In one early newsletter, Stone railed against "a Mad Hatter quality" rampant in the United States, heading "toward fascism and folly." The country was beginning to discard "all the precious faith in freedom," and "all that made [it] a proud name in the eyes of the world is being dirtied and destroyed and degraded."

73 bright red undershirt: Edith Tiger, interview, 1992.

74 Joseph McCarthy: Athan Theoharis and John Stuart Cox, *The Boss: J Edgar Hoover and the Great American Inquisition* (Philadelphia: Temple University Press, 1988).

74 McCarthy's was one of three congressional committees. The other two were the Senate Subcommittee on Internal Security and the House Committee, which called the most witnesses. Victor and Leonard also represented people interrogated by employers such as the New York Board of Education and the Coast Guard.

76 Izzy founds the Emergency Civil Liberties Committee: Edith Tiger, interview.

78 Victor Brudney declines offer to be Izzy's staff lawyer: Leonard Boudin, Columbia University Oral History Project.

79 suspend civil liberties: The Subversive Activities Control Board was established by the Internal Security Act of 1950, which passed despite President Truman's veto. Izzy called it "the greatest danger to democracy."

79 Leonard's legal strategy: Leonard and Victor were not the only lawyers fighting the FBI. For example, on the West Coast, there was the firm of Barney Dreyfuss and Norman Leonard. Others included David Rein in Washington.

79 "a smiling fool": Victor Rabinowitz, interview.

79 case looked "good": Victor Rabinowitz, interview.

80 Ann Braden: Griffin Fariello, *Red Scare: Memories of the American Inquisition* (New York: W. W. Norton, 1995).

80 Carl Braden and his alleged coconspirators were jailed and released on $10,000 bond. Carl Braden and his wife, Ann, were among those indicted for sedition in bombing the house.

At his trial, Carl Braden swore he was not currently a member of the Communist Party. Informers (recruited by the House Un-American Activities Committee) testified that he was a communist and as such planned to stir up trouble between the races, take all land away from the whites, and give it to blacks. (This was based on Marcus Garvey's early suggestion that some southern states cede territory to blacks, a suggestion that was discussed by some communists and black groups.)

Prosecutors confiscated books from the Braden house as evidence of his communism—books by Dostoyevsky, Turgenev, Marx, Lenin, and Tolstoy.

Leonard professed not to care about Braden's politics. When Braden referred to prominent people as "executive members of the ruling class," Leonard found himself blanking out. He was thinking, "Hmmm, that's Carl." He objected to Braden's mixing politics with simple legal questions: Do you have the right of free speech or don't you? Do you have to answer questions or don't you? Do you have a right to belong to a political party or don't you? Victor Rabinowitz, interview.

81 Dorothy Parker: Jean Boudin, interview.

81 Lionel Stander hearing: Eric Bentley, ed., *Thirty Years of Treason: Excerpts from Hearings Before the House Committee on Un-American Activities 1938–1968* (New York: Viking, 1971). When asked what he did for a living, Stander said, "I am an actor. I have been a newspaper reporter. I have been a director of various stage entertainments for the Red Cross, the air force, the Kiwanis, junior and senior chambers of commerce, Elks, Moose, and other organizations with animal names." Leonard and Stander had devised a straddling strategy. First Stander refused to answer "the sixty-four-dollar question," explaining he had sworn a noncommunist oath twelve years earlier to the same committee. He then stood, albeit flamboyantly, on First, Fifth, and Ninth Amendment privileges. When a congressman tried to interrupt him, Stander raised his voice: "If any of these charges are true, why haven't I been indicted?" he asked. His voice boomed out over yet another reproach. "I was asked a twenty-five-minute question and I can't even give a two-minute answer. I don't think that's fair." Stander interrupted an interrogator's droning question about why communists advocate violent overthrow of the government, saying, "I don't know about the overthrow of the government. This committee has been investigating fifteen years so far and hasn't even found one act of violence." Stander shouted over orders to be quiet. "I know of a group of fanatics who are desperately trying to undermine the Constitution of the United States by depriving artists and others of life, liberty, and the pursuit of happiness without due process of law . . . and also a group of ex-Bundists, America Firsters, and anti-Semites, people who hate everybody including Negroes, minority groups, and most likely themselves."

81 Leonard himself "cooperated" to some degree: Leonard Boudin, FBI files, FOIA.

As he had hoped, Leonard's answer signaled the liberal establishment that he could be trusted. The *New York Times* reporter Peter Khiss would write an internal *Times* memo dated May 1962: "When called as a witness before the House Un-American Activities on June 12, 1956, Leonard Boudin swore, 'I have never been a member of the Communist Party. I am not a member of the Party at the present time, and I don't expect to be one. . . . I have never taken orders or directions from anybody including the Communist Party and I don't expect to do so. I have never been under the discipline of the Communist Party of the United States. . . . I have never been a member of the Young Communist League . . . and have not paid dues or have any recollection of having made financial contributions to the Young Communist League or the Communist Party.' "

In the memo kept in Leonard's *New York Times* file, he is described as a responsible member of the legal establishment.

83 Hoover decides to indict Leonard for perjury: As Hoover pressed, each witness against Leonard declined to swear in court that Leonard had been a Communist Party member. A labor lawyer named Henry J. Bender admitted it was only his passing opinion that Leonard was a communist. In the late 1940s, Bender had represented the right-wing faction of the United Office and Professional Workers Union and had fought Leonard, who represented the communist faction. The professional former communist Louis

Budenz refused to testify in Leonard's presence. He said that his health would suffer, his memory was failing, and he was not legally competent. FBI file, Leonard Boudin.

83 boiled down to an unreliable informant: Maurice Malkin was on the FBI payroll and was dying to testify, but Hoover knew a good lawyer could prove he was inconsistent.

83 Maurice Malkin admitted to having been a communist. He bragged about beating up opponents of the Party at union elections. Malkin was currently living in Mexico City and filing reports to the FBI about a group of people from the United States and Europe who were selling arms and information to both sides in the cold war. Maurice Malkin, *Return to My Father's House* (New York: Arlington House, 1972); Leonard Boudin, FBI files; Victor Rabinowitz, interview.

83 Leonard and Izzy cannily attached: When General Electric workers went on strike, Kent had picketed, and was fired by the company. (He had painted a mural, *Electricity and Progress,* for the 1939 World's Fair and was currently finishing a company calendar.) He sued to finish the calendar, but refused, he claimed, to paint out a *picket* fence.

Kent's troubles came to a head in 1950 after he went to Paris to speak to the French Chamber of Deputies asking that they ban nuclear weapons. While in France, he accepted an invitation from Russia to speak on the same subject before a special session of the Supreme Soviet. He then traveled on to Sweden for another peace conference of leftists, and helped to write the Stockholm Appeal, calling for a ban of nuclear weapons.

When Kent returned home, the State Department notified him that he was grounded, his passport invalid: he had crossed into Eastern Europe without applying for a visa. Kent instantly requested another passport to go to Ireland to paint. State Department officials assured Kent privately that if he signed a sworn statement that he had never belonged to the Communist Party, his request might be reconsidered. He readied himself for public legal fight, declaring, "We are interred in America." Rockwell Kent, *This Is My Own by Rockwell Kent* (New York: Duell, Sloan, and Pearce, 1940).

84 Dear Kathy: ECLC papers, Columbia University Library.

84 Kathy poised, Michael furtive: John Simon, interview.

85 it was raining: John Simon, interview.

85 FBI agents: Jane Lazarre, "Conversations with Kathy Boudin," *Village Voice,* Feb. 14, 1984; Jean Boudin, interview.

86 Doriane Kurtz: Doriane Kurtz, interview, 1999.

86 whispering desperately into the telephone: Jean Boudin, interview.

87 toast "to my loving friend": Georgette Schneer, interview.

87 Kathy ran . . . to the public library: Robert Riley, interview.

87 Kathy's unnatural composure: Jean Boudin, letter filed by Leonard asking for pardon for Kathy.

87 St. Vincent's Hospital: Victor Rabinowitz, interview.

88 Silver Hill: Jean Boudin, interview; Marcia Rabinowitz, interview. Silver Hill still exists today and is an expensive sanitarium ($1,200 a day) habituated by actors, entertainers, and artists. Nick Nolte, Liza Minnelli, Michael Jackson, Mariah Carey, and Billy Joel are among those who have used it as an alcohol and drug rehab clinic.

88 ears and chest: Marcia Rabinowitz, interview.

89 Leonard spoke of Jean's suicide attempts: Michael Standard, Eleanor Brussel, Ruth Gilbert, Victor Rabinowitz, Alan Lelchuk, interviews.

90 clay pieces of a mother and child: Ruth Gilbert, interview.

90 law students: Judge Shirley Fingerhood, interview, 1996.

90 Kathy was coping: Bert Gross, interview.

91 Kathy thought of the Willcoxes' golden retriever as her own: Kathy Boudin, conversations, 1996.
92 ordinary rules did not obtain: Joanna Grant, interview, 1995; Paul Mattick, interview.
93 vulnerability was contagious: Jean Boudin, interview.
94 Jean's difficulties with Leonard: Ann Waldman, interview, 1994.
94 "the other woman" was still hovering: Jean Boudin, interview.

8: Leonard Wins the Legal Fight of His Life

96 victory brunch: Leonard had won the right-to-travel case at the Supreme Court. Supreme Court Justice William O. Douglas had affirmed Leonard's argument in the majority opinion: ". . . the right to travel is part of the 'liberty' of which the citizen cannot be deprived without due process of law. . . . Where activities or enjoyment, natural and often necessary to the well-being of American citizen, such as travel are involved, we will construe narrowly all designated powers that curtail or dilute them.
97 on what government would do if all witnesses said they were guilty: Jean Boudin, interview; Leonard Boudin, Columbia University Oral History Project.
97 "Public opinion was the problem": Leonard Boudin, Columbia University Oral History Project.
97 Baez fired Leonard: Nancy Carlen, interview, 1995.
97 Kent's pink Cadillac: Edith Tiger, interview, 1993.
97 Prague: Leonard enjoyed the romantic pangs of solitary travel. The trip to Prague was a literal escape from home, a gesture he relished in many forms. He would be picked up in Prague by the Sterns and driven in a big black Mercedes to their luxurious government-owned villa, with superb plumbing and a year-round garden. The Sterns coddled Leonard, who had developed a bad cold. He sipped clear soups and slept. Although the Sterns were appalled by the economic deprivation of neighbors, they and their eleven-year-old son took trips to Russian seaside spas, collected antiques, and were tended by four servants, plus a gardener and chauffeur.
97 I am indebted to Nancy Carlen for interviews and counsel, as well as papers from the Robert Carlen archive.
99 Leonard enjoyed the FBI tail too much: Edith Tiger, interview.
99 Esther chiding Jean for flirting: Edith Tiger interview; Bert Gross, interview.
100 Izzy kissed: Jean Boudin, interview.
100 No one danced like Leonard: Jean Boudin, interview.
101 Elisabeth Irwin: The high school was housed in a small brick building on the outskirts of Greenwich Village. Teachers dressed in T-shirts and sneakers. Students addressed the principal, Rudolph Smith, a New England WASP, by his nickname, Rank. After Kathy became famous in the 1970s, Rank told reporters she was "a person who was rather quiet, thoughtful and intelligent." Interviews: Josh White Jr., Richard Kostelanitz, Susan Kapit, John Castellucci, Andrew Zelman.
101 as the most popular leader: Susan Kapit, interview.
101 young Fidel Castro: In January 1959, Fidel Castro and his small band of armed young Cuban guerrilla fighters had captured Havana and routed the army of right-wing military dictator General Fulgencio Batista. The young hero Fidel would be a model for Kathy and her peers. They would, for example, romanticize his stays in prison and try to emulate his good works there. While a political prisoner on the Isle of Pines, Fidel Castro was said to have started teaching literacy classes, and read books by such thinkers as Kant, de Beauvoir, Freud, Marx, and Dostoyevsky.

Fidel Castro also smuggled a manifesto out of Isle of Pines prison to his sister. The manifesto was said to have been written in invisible lemon juice between lines of ordinary correspondence. In language that reminded some followers of President Franklin Roosevelt, Castro secretly proposed to nationalize electric and telephone companies and formulate profit-sharing for manual laborers and white-collar workers in large industries such as sugar. He swore he would confiscate the wealth of anyone and his heirs who had misappropriated public funds.

> No weapon, no force is capable of defeating a people determined to fight for its right. . . . When we speak of the people, we don't mean the well-to-do, the conservatives of the nation, who reap the advantages from any oppressive regime, from any dictatorship, any despotism, bowing down before every master in turn. . . . We mean the great unredeemed masses . . . , cheated, betrayed . . . , longing for justice . . . , ready to give its last drop of blood for something it believes in. . . . And when we speak of battle, we refer to the six hundred thousand Cubans without work; the five hundred thousand farm workers living in miserable huts, working for months and starving with their children during the rest of the year; the four hundred thousand industrial workers and laborers, robbed of their retirement funds; the one hundred thousand sharecroppers who live and die working land that does not belong to them; the twenty thousand self-sacrificing teachers . . . , shabbily treated and poorly paid; the twenty thousand small merchants, debt-ridden, ruined by the economic crisis; and the ten thousand young professionals—medical doctors, engineers, lawyers, veterinarians, dentists, pharmacists, journalists, painters, sculptors, those who leave the university filled with hope, only to find themselves in a blind alley, every door closed. . . . To all of them we say: Here you are! Fight with all your might for liberty and for happiness.

As soon as the articulate, long-winded socialist intellectual Fidel set up the new revolutionary government, he was hailed throughout the world. Fidel was quoted, extolled, and photographed with his trademark glossy black beard and olive-green fatigues and rifle with telescopic sight. Robert Quirk, *Fidel Castro* (New York: W. W. Norton, 1993).

In the beginning, the *New York Times* extolled Castro as a visionary with high hopes for his poverty-stricken countrymen. It noted that Castro was clear about his anti-Russian beliefs: he was unwilling to trade one despotic government for another. He wanted Cuba to stand up against all world powers—the United States, the Soviet Union, and China. Quirk, *Fidel Castro,* 158.

At first President Dwight D. Eisenhower supported Fidel Castro's sudden overthrow of Cuba's decadent right-wing dictator. To the great relief of the U.S. government, whose businessmen owned billions of dollars in sugarcane fields and refineries alone, Fidel Castro initially promised not to seize private property. Quirk, *Fidel Castro,* 111; *New York Times,* Dec. 19, 21, 28, 29, 1956; Jan. 1, 3, 4; Feb. 24; Mar. 14, 25, 1957.

101 Learned Hand: Michael wrote a lucid and compassionate appreciation of Judge Hand in his law review piece: *Stanford Law Review* (January 1995); book review, Gerald Gunther, *Learned Hand: The Man and the Judge* (New York: Alfred A. Knopf, 1994).

102 Kathy was the best student: Francine Fontaine, interview, 1995.

103 Jean fibbed about her language skills: Bert Gross, interview.

103 Angela Davis was an intensely timid: Angela Davis, *Angela Davis: An Autobiography* (New York: Random House, 1974).

Since the end of World War II, Angela Davis's host, the Reverend William Melish, and his father, Reverend John Melish, had been fighting a losing battle to keep jobs at their church. They were suspect because of their progressive views—and had been upper-echelon members of the Communist Party. They had collected money for Russian War Relief and had been charged by members of the Episcopal Church with associating with "atheists, communists, agitators of world revolution, totalitarianism and almost everything which denies the Christian doctrine of man."

The Reverend William Melish had angered parishioners by inviting new neighbors who were blue-collar workers and Puerto Rican to join the church. Accepting a position with the Quakers in the emerging civil rights movement, Reverend Melish invited southern leaders to visit his home. The Melishes received hate letters about Angela Davis living with them. Money was scarce, although the money accompanying a distinguished French Peace Prize rescued them for two years. *Angela Davis: An Autobiography* (New York: Random House, 1974).

Like Kathy, Angela Davis would be accused of taking a traditional female sidekick role in a horrific crime, even though authorities knew she had killed no one.

104 picketing Woolworth's: Jennie Simon, interview, September 1994.

105 "go all the way": Susan Kapit, interview.

106 College Board test scores: Leonard Boudin, Columbia University Oral History Project and Francine Fontaine, interview.

106 Michael's senior honors thesis: "The Free Exercise of Religion Clause of the Constitution, a Study of Supreme Court Interpretation Since the Civil War." A thesis presented by Michael Boudin, 1961, Harvard University Library.

108 Robert Johnson: Leonard Boudin, FBI file; Robert Johnson, memo to J. Edgar Hoover.

At first Robert Johnson had curtly said, "Yes," "no," or "pending" when Leonard called the State Department about the status of a client's passport application. The two men had relaxed over time into real interchanges. By 1958, Robert Johnson and Leonard were having dinner and a glass of wine every month or so. Victor Rabinowitz, interview, 1992; Leonard Boudin, FBI file.

108 *The Cowards:* A novel by Josef Skvorecky (New York: Ecco Press, 1958). Jean Boudin, interviews.

109 Hoover wanted to enlist Leonard: Leonard Boudin, FBI file.

9: Kathy Was Somebody Serious

110 "great souls": Liz Bogen, interview, 1999.

110 "For god's sake Kathy": Fred Gardner, interview, 1996.

110 named after John D. Rockefeller: The grandfather of New York state governor Nelson Rockefeller had been persuaded by Bryn Mawr's early president, M. Carey Thomas, to donate funds to build Rockefeller Hall, the Gothic stone dormitory with wide gloomy hallways. Rockefeller had spread his influence throughout the world, funding the medical school in Hong Kong and much of the University of Chicago.

111 Mary Thom: In later years Mary Thom worked for women's rights as executive editor at *Ms.* magazine. As an author, she wrote a history of the magazine and the second feminist movement. Kathy is very present in Mary's mind, although she has not seen her since college days. "Kathy gets you into a certain mind-set and it's just an amazing place to be."

112   Placid campus: *Bryn Mawr College News*, Sept. 22, 1961.

    Bryn Mawr has a fascinating history. It was founded in 1885 by a rich all-male group of Quakers from Philadelphia, including Dr. James Carey Thomas. It was situated on thirty-two acres, landscaped by the upper-class firm of Frederick Law Olmsted, the creators of Manhattan's Central Park. Dr. Thomas was concerned about proper Quaker training for young women such as his daughter, who called herself M. [Martha] Carey Thomas. The college was soon taken over by Dr. James Thomas's strong-minded, even bossy daughter, a Cornell graduate, who believed that she knew best about virtually everything.

    Bryn Mawr thrived on fertile conflict. On the one hand, there was the demure image of a "Quaker lady" as envisioned by rich male founders. They wanted a religious college to turn out a gentlewoman of a "higher and more refined class of Philadelphia society" whose "satin bonnet, silk dress, kid gloves, perfect slippers [harmonizes] with her face, which is both intellectual and holy."

    But, on the other hand, there was the reality of the unholy leadership of Martha Carey Thomas. Although the classroom building Taylor Hall was built in "muted grays" of local Fairmount stone, there was nothing muted about M. Carey, whose ambitions soared far beyond the domestic accomplishments of her mother. Leo Dolenski, archivist, Bryn Mawr College, interview, November 1995.

    Thomas's revolutionary vision was clear: like truth, the right to a fine education was not confined to men or women. It did not occur, however, to her to extend the privilege of fine education to men or women who were not rich. Nor was a Bryn Mawr education available to blacks. "M. Carey Thomas was a sacred monster," said historian Catherine Stimpson. "She believed in women's rights for privileged women, but campaigned actively against admitting blacks to the college. One black woman was admitted, but not permitted to live on campus."

    Wanting to attract wealthy young women, M. Carey Thomas designed Rockefeller Hall with private suites, and basement rooms for maids' living quarters as well as for hairdressing, laundry, and a grocery store. (She did not want students to be distracted from study by domestic chores.)

    President Thomas and her rich female lover, railroad heiress Mary Garrett, flouted convention by living in a magnificent mansion in the center of campus named the Deanery. It was enlarged and refurbished in 1907 by a donation of $100,000 from Mary Garrett, who, with the help of a male designer from Tiffany's, filled the lavish drawing rooms with Tiffany glass and Persian rugs. The two women and their staff of six servants entertained fascinating intellectuals from all over the world. They were stunning visual proof of how well two brilliant and wealthy women might live "in sin," flouting patriarchal rules. Helen Lefkowitz Horowitz, *Alma Mater* (Amherst: University of Massachusets Press, 1984).

112   societal responsibility: The students joked about M. Carey Thomas and her radical bluestocking ways. We misquoted the M. Carey Thomas aphorism "our failures only marry" as "only our failures marry." Seniors substituted risqué lyrics (which they did not seriously mean) in one of M. Carey's many pageant songs, singing ". . . and we your daughters living up to thee/we'll name our bastards after M. Car-ey."

    The first wave of students at Bryn Mawr, in the late nineteenth century, had been radicals. The mother of Isamu Noguchi, the sculptor, was from the Midwest. After Bryn Mawr, she became the mistress of a married artist in Japan and gave birth to Noguchi out of wedlock.

113 Kathy was openly envious: Marcia Rabinowitz, Joni Rabinowitz, Jean Boudin, interviews.

113 It was thirty-five more years before there was a newsworthy sign of change in race relations in Macon, Georgia. The *New York Times* reported it as front-page news in December 1998: A highly qualified black man named Sanford D. Bishop Jr. was elected to the House of Representatives by the predominantly white rural district that includes Albany. Bishop had previously represented a black district, until the Supreme Court ordered redistricting, and then he had actually represented the new white district exceedingly well, until the election. It was, said the *Times,* a case of "the old prejudices giving away to a more pragmatic politics of racial cooperation and interdependence." Bishop won four out of ten white votes.

114 Ernesto "Che" Guevara: Che was literally poster person for activist students in the United States. Posters of him were a rallying point in protest marches in Paris, Washington, Tokyo, Bombay, and Baghdad. The revolutionary poet from Argentina was a restless soul who read German philosophers for relaxation. He had been the leader of victorious guerrilla fights against Batista, and was now head of Cuba's Banco Nacional. The nickname "Che," which is Argentine slang for "pal," was given him by Castro. Jean liked Jean-Paul Sartre's description of Che as "the most complete human being of our age."

In 1965, Che left Cuba to spread socialism around the world; he was killed fighting in the jungles of Bolivia. Upon his death, Castro called him the ideal socialist man. There is a four-story mural of Che in Havana's Revolution Square. Cuban schoolchildren begin their day with a secular prayer to grow up to be like Che. *Insight Guides: Cuba* (New York: Houghton Mifflin, 1995).

114 Leonard and Victor represented Fidel Castro's revolutionary Cuban government: After a brief 1957 visit, the English writer Graham Greene described prerevolutionary Havana in his novel *Our Man in Havana* as a degraded place "where every vice was permissible." Havana had been the prostitution capital of the Western Hemisphere. Tourists getting off planes were shown photographs of thirteen-year-old prostitutes of both sexes to buy for the weekend. A joke circulated: When asked what he wanted to be when he grew up, a child in Havana responded, "A tourist."

Gangsters like Meyer Lansky, personal friend of dictator Fulgencio Batista and adviser on gambling reform, ran high-stakes gambling at the Riviera Hotel. They made huge fortunes from liquor, drugs, gambling (despite allegations of rigged games), and prostitution. Lansky is said to have deposited more than $3 million in Batista's Swiss bank account.

115 Fidel Castro had been grossly insulted by the U.S. government: Fidel Castro later estimated that the CIA had launched twenty secret attempts on his life. A director of the CIA expressed surprise; he claimed he knew of only five attempts.

115 Kassana Worszeck: Michael Standard, interview; Victor Rabinowitz, interview.

116 plight of the maids: *Bryn Mawr College News* clippings and Professor Ariel Loewy, interview, 1994.

119 Das was a gifted teacher: Bill Ayers, *Fugitive Days: A Memoir* (Boston: Beacon Press, 2001).

121 Thanksgiving: Jean Boudin, interview.

121 how she'd championed the maids: Frustrated at the end of the year, Kathy and the student activists turned the problem of organizing the maids over to a professional union organizer from Philadelphia. Mary Thom, interview, 1994.

122 ideal mate: Victor Rabinowitz and Paul Mattick, interviews.
123 Kathy flew to Havana: Jean Boudin, interview.
123 close to hysteria: Jean Boudin, interview.
124 Kathy witnessed what few Americans had seen: Quirk, *Fidel Castro*.
   Che Guevara wrote:

> At the great public mass meetings, one can observe something like a counterpoint between two musical melodies whose vibrations provoke still newer notes. Fidel and the mass begin to vibrate together in a dialogue of growing intensity until they reach the climax in an abrupt conclusion culminating in our cry of struggle and victory. ("Man and Socialism in Cuba," p. 45; letter to Carlos Quijano, editor of *Marcho*, an independent radical weekly published in Uruguay, 1965, series 4b, no. 130)

124 illegal: Victor Rabinowitz, interview.
125 Karen Burstein: Unlike Kathy, Karen would follow in her father's footsteps in the law. Many believed she eventually lost the close race for New York state attorney in 1994 because she had spoken frankly about her homosexual life after the end of a long marriage.
126 Michael Meeropol: The Rosenberg and Coplon cases had their complex beginnings in the controversial Venona communiqués sent by anonymous Soviet agents in the United States to their anonymous bosses in the Soviet Union. The documents cast suspicion on Julius Rosenberg, but pseudonymously. Armed with the secret Venona communiqués in which Julius was code-named "Liberal," Hoover was determined to prosecute the Rosenbergs.
   But Hoover knew that an opposing lawyer such as Leonard might start asking tough questions if faced with the disguised Venona communiqués in court. The tapes were only partly decoded and Hoover did not know what other sensitive material they contained. Given the existence of the secret Venona tapes, it is possible to understand why the debate about the Rosenbergs' guilt raged in the United States. It is also possible to conclude, as does legal scholar Allen Dershowitz after vetting some of the Venona communiqués, that the two parents of Michael and Robert were probably illegally convicted. (Convinced of their guilt, but unable to use the Venona communiqués, Hoover quite likely framed them.)
   I also learned while researching this book that Leonard's firm had turned down Mike Meeropol's father as a client. The first time Julius Rosenberg had been asked to go in for questioning to FBI headquarters, he went without a lawyer. Before his second FBI interview, sometime in late 1948, he came to the Boudin office to ask for representation. It was in the midst of Judith Coplon's trials, and Victor recalled that he did not want the firm to become known as spy lawyers. So he turned down Julius Rosenberg, and recommended a trial lawyer named Emanuel Bloch. Victor and Leonard were highly critical of Bloch's handling of the case. When the government refused to show the court Julius's alleged diagram of the bomb, Bloch did not fight the issue. Victor and Leonard would have moved for, and odds are, gotten, a mistrial: the defendant was not being confronted with evidence against him—a cardinal lapse of justice in our system of law. In his oral history, Leonard disputes Victor's recollections of turning down Julius Rosenberg and recommending another lawyer. Leonard claimed that Julius Rosenberg had asked him—and only him—to be his lawyer. Like a supervising bureaucrat, perhaps, Leonard thought he owned Victor's thoughts and actions. All concerned, including Leonard and Victor, were stunned when the Rosenbergs were given

the death penalty. (Judge Irving Kauffman was prompted by the ambitious and ruthless young Roy Cohn. They scheduled Ethel's execution first, assuming her husband would crack and try to save her by confessing.) Victor said, "We figured Julie would get five or ten years; everybody was getting five or ten years. The FBI didn't see it as a capital case. We didn't see it as a capital case."

A few years after the trial, Leonard litigated for Michael's grandmother, who objected to Surrogate Court Judge William T. Collins naming an outside guardian for the two boys.

Critics say something more insidious was behind Victor and Leonard's rejection of Julius Rosenberg as a client. The Communist Party had, they say, ordered members to distance themselves from Julius Rosenberg. It was not until the Rosenbergs were convicted that the Party rallied; they needed a martyr, claim critics.

127 Leonard's speech: *Bryn Mawr College News*, winter 1961. Attacks on the current state of American democracy were in the air. Tom Hayden and other college students gathered in an old labor union camp on the shores of Lake Huron in Michigan to reactivate a college political group founded two generations earlier by members of LID (League for Industrial Democracy). "It was a holy time," recalled Casey Hayden. Tom Hayden, *Reunion: A Memoir* (New York: Random House, 1988).

The student group was SDS (Students for a Democratic Society). Members on hundreds of campuses would be the core of the loosely affiliated "student movement." (Louis Boudin and Jack London had been among those who had originally founded SDS on campuses at Yale and Columbia decades earlier as a junior forum for debates on socialism.)

After days of arguing, Tom Hayden, the principal author of the Port Huron Statement, rewrote his introductory sentence: "We are people of this generation, bred in at least modest comfort, housed now in universities looking uncomfortably at the world we inherit. . . ." The manifesto declared disillusionment about democracy, which was,, wrote Hayden, a far cry from the early years of town meetings. Poor people felt isolated and powerless because they had little or no connection to government. They tended not to vote.

Hayden contrasted the high-minded language of the Declaration of Independence to racist practices. He cited growing affluence of a few and the undernourishment of poor children. He accused the U.S. government of declaring peaceful intent while increasing military budgets.

The student intellectuals urged a participatory democracy, in which "the individual shares in those social decisions determining the quality and direction of his life." At Port Huron, young people were shocked by the ferocious debating style of old lefties from the parent group LID—who had witnessed disappointments with the Soviet Union. Michael Harrington also argued (per Karl Marx) that members of the labor movement, not students, made social changes. Two leaders, including Tom Hayden, were suspended from LID. Despite warnings that revolutionary leaders always become ruling Frankenstein monsters, Tom Hayden was confident. He said, "These horrors won't happen to us. We are too good."

Decades later, Tom Hayden wondered how he had been so confident. "We possessed the power to create through naïveté." Hayden, *Reunion*.

128 waylay Leonard: Leonard Boudin FBI files.

128 coop house: *Bryn Mawr College News* and Liz Bogen, interview, 1998.

129 "Second American Revolution": Professor Ariel Loewy, interview, 1994. The gross inequality of blacks in the southern United States had some forty years earlier scandal-

ized members of the old left, and had been seized as an issue by the American Communist Party. They had pinpointed it as a glaring flaw in the workings of the egalitarian and capitalist philosophies of the United States.

130 Paul Mattick: Mattick was popular with Bryn Mawr girls for his dry conversation, his unpretentious quick intellect, and the depth of his reading of literature and philosophers, his favorite being Karl Marx. What few knew besides Kathy was that Paul Mattick's mother taught Marxist economics. Paul's father was a Marxist intellectual whose writings were translated from his native German. Paul's perspective on politics was lofty—he held himself above the factional fights of Marxists in the United States. He felt they lacked historic sense. He was also a romantic and was in love with Kathy.

131 Kathy accosted a popular political science professor: Ellen Cantarow, "Kathy Boudin in Jail," *Mademoiselle* (Apr. 1984).

131 Cathlyn Wilkerson: Small, popular, peppery Cathlyn Wilkerson was a philosophy major with a stubborn streak. Her rich Quaker father owned the Greenwich Village town house that would explode in 1970 while his daughter Cathlyn and Kathy ran for their lives.

132 Kathy told Leonard: Jean Boudin, conversations.

132 She also filled spiral notebooks: Five years later Kathy published a stilted essay about her trip to the Soviet Union in the *Leviathan*. Revised drafts had become increasingly negative about the United States.

    Kathy wrote that disillusionment was rampant in the United States, because "no matter how passionate the speakers, no matter how free the press, or how distinguished or numerous the demonstrators, they have fallen far short of substantially altering a racist social structure or an imperialist economy."

133 harsh peasant life: Professor Thompson Bradley, interview, 1996.

133 "I'm not litigious": Thomas Powers, interview, 1995.

134 cataract: Victor Rabinowitz, interview.

135 Leonard flew to the Soviet Union: Jean Boudin, interview, 1993.

10: A Republican Just Wants to Get Rich

136 "passive technician": Jean Boudin, interview.

136 She wrote to Rockwell Kent: Archives of American Artists, Rockwell Kent papers.

137 "fiery swords": Tom Hayden, *Reunion* (New York: Random House, 1988).

137 rejection by Yale Law School: Jean Boudin, interview; Connie Brown, interview.

138 "holding other people's hands": Victor Rabinowitz, interview.

138 rarely returned Leonard's telephone calls: Jean Boudin, interview.

138 outrageous pink: Matthew Nimetz, interview.

139 Cleveland project SDS: Welfare Grievance Committee 1966; minutes, West Side Community Union Welfare Committee, Madison, Wisconsin, Historical Society.

139 communal living space: Charlotte Fein, interview, 1993.

140 seeds of the second wave of feminism: Sara Evans, *Personal Politics* (New York: Random House, 1979).

141 rat: Jean Boudin, interview.

142 "pool of freezing water": Leni Wildflower, interview, 1991.

142 women on welfare taking clothing in protest: *Plain Dealer* (Cleveland), August 20, 1966.

143 Dr. Spock comes to dinner: Roz Baxandall, interview, 1992.

144 "parlor liberal": Jean Boudin, interview.
144 Jimmy's bar: Sandy Katz, interview.
145 birthday party in Amagansett: Victor Rabinowitz, interview; John Simon, interview; Joanne Grant, interview.
146 Cleveland work too depressing: Jean Boudin, interview.
147 Madi Leof visited: Jean Boudin, interview.

11: Repenting Good Behavior

148 seduced Jennie Simon: Fred Gardner, interview.
148 gave Jennie one of Kathy's rings: Eleanor Brussel, interview.
149 sounds in the hotel hallway: Sandy Katz, interview, 1994.
149 Frances Waldman comes to dinner: Ann Waldman, letters and interview, 1993.
150 dinner with Julian Bond: Joanne Grant, interview, 1996.
150 Julian Bond: The stated reason why Julian Bond's peers refused to let him take his seat was the SNCC antiwar statement he'd signed. It was tough, and Izzy Stone wrote, "No mild murmur of disagreement."

   It declared the United States deceptive in its "concern for freedom of the Vietnamese people, just as the government had been deceptive in claiming concern for the freedom of colored people in such other countries as the Dominican Republic, the Congo, South Africa, Rhodesia and in the United States itself." The critique continued, "We recoil with horror at the inconsistency of a supposedly 'free' society where responsibility for freedom is equated with the responsibility to lend oneself to military agression."

   The legislature voted 184 to 12 that a man with Bond's views against U.S. participation in the war in Vietnam could not honestly take an oath to uphold the United States Constitution.
151 "rougher stuff": Jean Boudin, interview.
152 Michael won a second coveted clerkship: Matthew Nimetz, interview, 1997.
153 "boring life": Jean Boudin, interview.
153 Harlan: Michael Boudin, "Memoirs in a Classical Style," *University of Pennsylvania Law Review*, 1984.
153 Kathy was livid: Jean Boudin, interview.
156 "heavy" meetings with Das and Tom Hayden about the upcoming Democratic convention: Jean Boudin, interview; Norm Fruchter interview; Tom Hayden, *Reunion: A Memoir* (New York: Random House, 1988).

   The previous Democratic convention, held in Atlantic City in 1964, had been targeted by blacks from Mississippi. "They failed," Kathy told Jean, "because they were afraid to get down and dirty." They had played by the rules when they formally challenged the convention's legitimacy, citing the lack of a single black delegate from Mississippi, where blacks were too frightened to vote. But party bosses had turned away the citizens of Mississippi.
156 Das returned from Guatemala: Bill Ayers, *Fugitive Days* (Boston: Beacon Press, 2001).
156 "My name is Diana": Thomas Powers, interview, 1995.
156 twenty-five people could be killed in Chicago: Hayden, *Reunion*.

   Chicago had a history of being scarred by violence in the name of class struggle. Louis Adamic, *Dynamite: The Story of Class Violence in America* (New York: Viking, 1931–34). During economic depression in the 1880s, anarchist leaders spoke of "the revolution," "dynamite," "justice," "liberty," "misery," and "strikes." Jobless, hungry men waved black flags at rallies for the eight-hour workday. On May 3, 1886, workers locked out of McCormick factory attacked scabs with bricks. Shots were fired. Police fired into the crowd, killing several men. A pamphlet circulated throughout the city: "Revenge."

Three thousand men, women, and children assembled the next night in Haymarket Square. By ten o'clock fewer than five hundred people remained in the pouring rain. Police ordered the crowd to disperse. After exchanges of words, a cloud of foul-smelling gray smoke erupted. Someone had hurled a dynamite bomb at police. Police shot into the crowd and at one another; workers shot back. In three minutes, sixty-seven policemen were wounded, seven dead. The workers dragged away twice as many casualties. Eight men were indicted for murder in the famous Haymarket riot. When four were hanged, one of them declared: "This is the happiest moment of my life."

156 Spock telephoned Leonard: Jessica Mitford, *The Trial of Dr. Ben Spock* (New York: Alfred A. Knopf, 1969).

157 "expecting a call": Victor Rabinowitz, interview.

157 conspiring: Three months earlier, Dr. Spock and hundreds of male college students and professors had turned in and burned draft cards in Washington, D.C. Spock had gamely jumped police barriers. The hugely popular author and pediatrician hoped to embarrass the government—by getting himself arrested. But respectful National Guardsmen gently escorted him back.

157 Leonard grabbed his coat: Paul Mattick, interview, 1993.

158 conspiracy accusations were nearly impossible to counter: As Clarence Darrow said: If a boy steals a piece of candy, he has committed a misdemeanor. But if two boys talk about stealing candy and do not, they are guilty of conspiracy—a felony. Mitford, *The Trial of Dr. Ben Spock.*

Clarence Darrow wrote: "It is a serious reflection on America that this worn-out piece of tyranny, this dragnet for compassing the imprisonment and death of men whom the ruling class does not like, should find a home in our country."

Traditionally conspiracy has been used to convict perceived opponents of government, such as political dissenters, union organizers, and radicals like Ethel and Julius Rosenberg who were sentenced to death for "conspiracy to commit espionage."

158 pretrial hearings: Court transcript, *United States v. William Sloane Griffin Jr., Mitchell Goodman, Marcus Raskin, and Benjamin Spock.*

158 clean scent of English violet soap: Mitford, *The Trial of Dr. Ben Spock.*

158 successful appeal: Leonard revealed how ineptly the jury pool was selected. He desperately wanted women on the jury since they would tend to be sympathetic to the man whose books they relied upon to raise their children. But of the eighty-eight potential jurors in the jury pool, only five were women. He questioned, in court, the ex–assistant dean at Harvard Law School, who explained that he chose the jury pool by pointing a finger at random to a list. The man admitted that if he pointed to a woman's name, he immediately slid his finger away. The reason: women made too much paperwork, since they usually got themselves excused from jury duty. *U.S. v. Spock et al.*; Victor Rabinowitz interview.

160 Spock found guilty: Leonard went on to win the Spock case on appeal and he and Dr. Spock became good friends. They bicycled to Central Park and discussed legal cases such as the one against Spock's paperback publisher for putting product advertisements in his millions of books. A frequent guest, without Jean, on Spock's boat in the Caribbean, Leonard hid his seasickness. Letter, Mary Morgan Spock, Oct. 25, 1995.

160 Jean resisted her first impulse: Jean Boudin, interview.

161 two days before the convention: Hayden, *Reunion.*

162 SDS headquarters: Susan Stern, *With the Weathermen: The Personal Journey of a Revolutionary Woman* (Garden City, N.Y.: Doubleday, 1975).

162 Norm Fruchter: Norm Fruchter interview; anonymous interview, 1996.

163 "guerrilla" group: Connie Brown, interview.

163 "Why the hell": Anonymous interviews; David Gilbert, interviews Great Meadows Correctional Facility, 1993–94; David Gilbert, Columbia University Oral History Project.

163 while a student: David and other leaders of the antiwar movement romanticized the Vietnamese communists, noting that the Vietcong were nonmaterialistic and respected ancestors and the environment. Wrote Tom Hayden some twenty years later, in *Reunion: A Memoir:* "My tendency was to see [the Vietcong] as gentle, as lacking in hate, and as having insight. In my admiration, I turned the Vietnamese into caricatures of revolutionaries, a people who had provided me with an alternative to cynicism. So identified was I with their people's suffering and struggle that I lost objectivity; like an intoxicating spell their mythical stature served to heighten my apocalyptic intuition of the American future."

163 David tried hard to be fair: Professor Sam Gross, law; Professor Fred Bloch, sociology, Berkeley; Harriet Fraad and Naomi Jaffe, conversations and interviews.

163 Kathy was more hard-edged: Professor Lewis Cole, Columbia University, interview, 1997.

164 Praxis Axis: Martin Kenner, interview, 1995.

165 Boy Scout messages: David was disturbed—even scarred—by the way his parents, Bea and Sam, had sacrificed for David and his sister, Ruth, a Radcliffe graduate. If Sam and Bea had one belief, it was in the future of their children. Sam Gilbert commuted a total of nearly a thousand miles a week from their house on Plowshare Road near the synagogue in Brookline, Massachusetts, to Hasbro Toys in Rhode Island to work as an engineer. David was particularly embarrassed about the $400 G.I. Joe figurine with its green beret, bullets, gun, and battle fatigues that had earned over $17 million. His father had also been a leader of David's Scout troop, further emphasizing his uneasy sense of privilege.

165 expecting a government that would solve all problems: David Gilbert, interviews, Great Meadows Correctional Facility.

166 "pounded and gassed and beaten": Norman Mailer, "Miami and the Siege of Chicago," *New American Library* (Oct. 1968).

166 Seale urged "roasting pigs": Hayden, *Reunion.*

167 "convention hooker": Ayers, *Fugitive Days.*

167 Kathy writes with lipstick in Hilton ladies' room: Diana Oughton, conversation, 1969.

167 By the third day of the convention: Hayden, *Reunion.*

167 stink bombs: Connie Brown, interview; Bob Long, FBI Chicago Bureau, interview, 1996.

167 sharing cells with black lesbians: Stern, *With the Weathermen.*

169 Case Western Reserve: Arthur Austin, "The Revolution of Kathy Boudin," Case Western Reserve Law School *Daily Legal News* (July 19, 1996).

169 national SDS convention: Thomas Powers, *Diana: The Making of a Terrorist* (Boston: Houghton Mifflin, 1971).

170 contempt for the Rosenberg apartment: Powers, *Diana.*

170 changes in America: Many criticized the young radicals for not having a program for "after the revolution," to which Ted Gold responded: "An agency of the people of the world would be set up to run the United States after the defeat of U.S. imperialism abroad."

12: It Was Absolutely Up to Us

172 Bernardine and J.J.: Professor Lewis Cole, interview, 1998; Peter Collier and David Horowitz, *Destructive Generation: Second Thoughts About the Sixties* (New York: Summit Books, 1989); interview, Jeff Jones, 1993; "The Last Radical," *Vancouver Magazine*, November 1998.

173 J.J. as "a diabolical beauty": *With the Weathermen: The Personal Journey of a Revolutionary.*

174 "J.J. was frighteningly sane": Professor Lewis Cole, interview.

174 Ohrnstein to Dohrn: Collier and Horowitz, *Destructive Generation.*

176 Progressive Labor: Noel Ignatiev, interview, 1995.

176 frisked each time they entered the building: FBI files, Students for a Democratic Society.

177 Mad Dogs: Ray Bongartz, "Weathermen," *Esquire* (Aug. 1970), and extensive articles *The Rat* and *Liberation News Service*, 1968–1970

177 Wildflower wept: Leni Wildflower, interview, 1992.

177 "blown away": David Gilbert, interview.

177 Suddenly Kathy, Bernardine, and Das: Stern, *With the Weathermen.*

178 "Pussy power": Leni Wildflower, interview.

179 honored Jonah Raskin and Eleanor Stein by crashing with them: Jonah Raskin, *Out of the Whale: Growing Up in the American Left: An Autobiography* (New York: Links, 1974); Jonah Raskin, interview, 1993.

180 Kathy frightened Jean: Jean Boudin, interview.

180 *The Bust Book:* Victor Rabinowitz, conversation; Judge Gustin Reichbach, conversation. Reichbach, a coauthor of *The Bust Book* (as was Brian Glick), became a respected State Supreme Court judge in Brooklyn and was nicknamed by New York tabloids "the condom judge" for his courageous dispensing of condoms to prostitutes in his courtroom. He also recommended free AIDS testing. In 2003 he took a six-month leave to preside over war crimes tribunals of Kosovar Albanians convened by the United Nations in Kosovo.

181 Leonard took *The Bust Book* as a personal attack: Victor Rabinowitz, interview.

183 in Havana with the Vietcong: Kit Bakke, interview, 1998.

184 Kathy asked Jonah to work on Days of Rage shotgun: Raskin, *Out of the Whale.*

184 theft of Jeff Jones's wallet: The FBI knew all about problems with black children of all ages in the neighborhood. FBI files, June Mail, SDS:

> They have been robbed on the street; the children have invaded their office and stolen their money, and to complicate the problem the children are Negro, hence SDS cannot make a complaint even to their close associates in the Black Panther party.
>
> For example Jeff Jones [then main boyfriend of Bernardine Dohrn, and organizational secretary] apparently made an attempt to win these children over to his side and made a trip with them to their ghetto area. Upon return to the NO [National Office] at which point Jones felt he had been successful, the children proceeded to steal his wallet and disappear.

> The situation has gotten so bad that in addition to the steel door, Jeff Jones recently ordered sheet steel for the entire front of the building. He'd found one of the children using a crow bar in an attempt to gain entrance through one of the windows.

FBI agents cited the new steel door and walls to explain why they could not get inside the office. Hoover ordered agents to break in anyway, read documents, and plant bugs; but security was too tight.

Concluded an agent lamely defending his own inability to break in: "The premises is owned by John Rossen, former Communist Party member, and long-time activist in Communist front causes. Any work done in the building is done through Rossen. His anti-Bureau attitude is well-recorded. Thus no secure access to other offices adjoining the SDS office is available."

184 "If a kid tries to rob me": Martin Kenner, interview, 1997; Jonah Raskin, interview 1993; Raskin, *Out of the Whale*.

186 The Panthers were favorites of the white intelligentsia: Kirkpatrick Sale, *SDS: Ten Years Toward a Revolution* (New York: Random House, 1973).

Their program was a list of terse demands: freedom, full employment, decent housing, education about the black man's true history and position in society and in the world, exemption from military service defending a racist government that does not protect blacks, an end to police brutality and murder of blacks, release of black prisoners because they were not tried by peers, restitution for slavery as promised of forty acres and two mules, land, bread, housing, education, clothing, justice, and peace.

The Panthers declared war on the U.S. government. The reworded Panther Declaration of Independence ended with: "Under absolute despotism, it is [our] right, it is [our] duty, to throw off such government, and to provide new guards for their future security."

Leonard Bernstein had invited New York Panthers to a fund-raising gala at his sumptuous Manhattan apartment. Journalists dubbed Bernstein and his white guests "radical chic."

Panthers soon insulted and stole from Bernstein and others, quickly falling out of favor. But Kathy and her friends remained in their thrall.

186 Black Panthers: The Black Panther Party was a subject of increasing controversy. Eldridge Cleaver, the most famous Panther, was a convicted rapist who had written a stirring, best-selling autobiography called *Soul on Ice*. Cleaver was teaching a popular lecture course at the University of California at Berkeley.

Cleaver was also running for U.S. president on the ticket of the Peace and Freedom Party. Two days after Dr. Martin Luther King's murder, Oakland, California, police had shot a Panther named Robert Hutton to death while he was surrendering with Cleaver. Governor Ronald Reagan pressured the regents to cancel Cleaver's lecture course at Berkeley.

From that autumn to spring of 1969, in Berkeley alone, two thousand people would be arrested in twenty-two days of fighting in the streets. The small town was occupied for forty days by policemen from surrounding cities. Local police declared state-of-disaster conditions. Governor Reagan declared five months of extreme emergency. Students protested, occupied buildings, and then went on strike.

Finally in May, blood was shed when thousands of students fought police over the People's Park, a vacant lot owned by the university where hippies hung out. After the police put a barbed-wire fence around the park, they fought advancing students with tear gas and guns for seventeen days of street fighting. A hundred and fifty demonstrators were shot and wounded, many in the back. One was killed.

187   Kathy organizing Days of Rage: FBI telephone taps of SDS Chicago office.

187   SDS FBI transcripts: Reel JL 633 reveals that at 4 p.m., Kathy called her father at 202-OX7-8640, asking who in the East (U.S.) could help a friend of hers plan fund-raising events for SDS. "Father suggests EDITH TIGER (phonetic), CORA WEIS (phonetic), wife of playwright PETER WEIS, and DAVID SPAIN (phonetic) on Martha's Vineyard and also JOHN SIMON (phonetic) and MIKE STANDARD (phonetic)."

      Other calls include one from Bill Ayers on July 12, at 11 p.m., to Leonard Boudin's home in Manhattan, with no answer.

      Kathy's phone calls that summer for Days of Rage cost well over $1,000. The FBI surveillance of her telephone calls cost more than $3,000 a month.

187   Kathy flew to Seattle and expelled Susan Stern: Despite Kathy's disapproval, Susan Stern was reinstated by her local Weather group. She wrote with gusto:

> We weren't just a bunch of super violent kids out to destroy Chicago. Nor were we adolescents rebelling against our parent or adult authority. We were serious revolutionaries who felt the need to do something so earth-shattering in America that the American masses would finally take notice. Mr. and Mrs. America would really look at the news on television—would see our young bodies being blasted by shotguns, our terrified faces as we marched trembling but proud, to attack the armed might of this Nazi state of ours. Running blood, young white human blood spilling and splattering all over the streets of Chicago for NBC and CBS to pick up in glorious Technicolor, panning in close the gauged faces on TV for our racist parents to see, for the parents of all the helpless GIs killed in Vietnam to see, for the parents of all the lynched black sons in the Deep South to see, and for American children to see and hear and perhaps empathize with. But in order to make America really look and see, we had to do something so unholy, so strong and so deadly, that they would have no other recourse. [Stern, *With the Weathermen*].

188   Pittsburgh: Anonymous interviews; underground newspaper clippings; *The Pittsburgh Press*, Sept. 6, 18, 1969.

188   Days of Rage: Decades later, Victor Rabinowitz reconstructed Leonard's disapproval of the Days of Rage, diplomatically: "The Days of Rage protest was not Leonard's style, and he disliked it because it did not fit his public image. Leonard was temperamentally tied up with Kathy. Although he enjoyed the excitement, Leonard once said privately that Kathy's activities never accomplished anything. He pretty much disapproved of violence."

190   Kathy invaded Harvard Center for International Affairs: although Kathy's name is not mentioned in descriptions of the attack that appeared in the *New York Times*, Sept. 26, 1989; Jean Boudin, interview.

190   assault on Harvard: David Gilbert later explained that the Harvard incident was a symbolic attack on the CIA for its aggression against poor people around the world. They also chose Harvard because it impressed high-school students. "They eat it up to hear we are clobbering Harvard professors. They ask why, and soon we are explaining the whole movement to them."

190   David sent to Weather cadre in Brooklyn: David Gilbert, interview, 1993, Great Meadows Correctional Facility; James K. Glassman, "SDS at Chicago," *Atlantic Monthly*, Dec. 1969.

190 "I hear you want to kill me": Raskin, *Out of the Whale;* Jonah Raskin, interview.

191 inside Kathy's cadre: Paul Mattick, interview; Stern, *With the Weathermen.*

191 Das cooked and ate an alley cat: Diana Oughton, conversation, 1969; Thomas Powers, *Diana: The Making of a Terrorist* (Boston: Houghton Mifflin, 1971).

192 David was repeatedly criticized: David Gilbert, interview.

192 recruit poor white teenage boys: David Gilbert, interview.

192 a train was coming from Michigan: Stern, *With the Weathermen.*

192 war councils: Stern, *With the Weathermen.*

192 clubs made from banisters: Stern, *With the Weathermen.*

195 Kathy carried a large red Vietcong flag: Jean Boudin, interview; Stern, *With the Weathermen.*

196 Victor posted bail: Victor Rabinowitz, interview.

196 David Gilbert threw bottles and stones: John Castellucci, *The Big Dance: The Untold Story of Weatherman Kathy Boudin and the Terrorist Family That Committed the Brinks Robbery Murders* (New York: Dodd Mead, 1986).

197 David arrested in Denver: David Gilbert, interview; Columbia University Oral History Project.

197 Kathy helped to set bombs: Anonymous, Jean Boudin, interviews.

197 Kathy ran past Jonah waving a closed umbrella: Raskin, *Out of the Whale;* Jonah Raskin, interview.

197 wargasm: Ibid.; clippings from *The Rat, Liberation News Service,* and other underground newspapers.

199 Bobby Seale: During the trial of the Chicago Eight, the judge had ordered the only black defendant, Bobby Seale, who had nothing to do with the planning of the protest, to be chained and gagged in court. He had been speaking out of turn. Kathy had been appalled that the other defendants, including Abbie Hoffman and Rennie Davis, and their white liberal lawyers had simply sat and watched authorities shackle a black man without protesting. Dave Dellinger put his body between the sheriffs and Bobby Seale.

200 a venereal disease: *The New Yorker,* 2001; Jean Boudin, interview.

13: The "Little House on Heaven Street" Goes to Hell

201 cotton underwear for Kathy: Jean Boudin, interview.

201 homemade dynamite bomb on lawn of Judge John Murtagh: SDS FBI files.

202 "hurt the pigs materially": John Castellucci, *The Big Dance: The Untold Story of Weatherman Kathy Boudin and the Terrorist Family That Committed the Brinks Robbery Murders* (New York: Dodd Mead, 1986).

203 Panthers would establish community control: David Gilbert, interview.

203 Eleventh Street: Curt Gentry, *J. Edgar Hoover: The Man and the Secrets* (New York: W. W. Norton, 1991), 172; Nestor Michnyak, FBI, interview; Fugitive Publicity Department, FBI.

203 Russell Neufield and Teddy Gold: Mel Gussow, interview; Jean Boudin, interview; FBI files on SDS.

204 *The Chemistry of Powder and Explosives:* Pretrial transcript, Kathy Boudin; FBI files on SDS.

204 Leonard in Harrisburg: Although I could not verify this to my own complete satisfaction, I took Jean Boudin's word for it and checked dates in William O'Rourke, *The Harrisburg 7 and the New Catholic Left* (New York: Thomas Crowell, 1972).

205 bombs with nails in them: FBI files on SDS; Kit Bakke, interview.

205 Das mailed her ID cards and passport home: Thomas Powers: *Diana: The Making of a Terrorist* (Boston: Houghton Mifflin, 1971).

205 Das hung back: Powers, *Diana*.

205 at the Strand: Jean Boudin, interview.

206 FBI agent who had been part of surveillance team: FBI files on SDS. Another FBI agent, Larry Grathwohl, would attempt to take credit for the explosion, claiming he had tampered with the bomb's mechanisms.

207 Tiffany lamp: Mel Gussow, interview; Mel Gussow, "The House on West 11th Street," *New York Times*, Mar. 5, 2000.

208 burn medicine: *New York Times*, Mar. 12, 1970.

208 tired of outlaw games: Tom Hayden, *Reunion: A Memoir* (New York: Random House, 1988); anonymous interview.

208 Teddy Gold's frantic mother: FBI phone taps; SDS files.

209 Kathy answered, "Not sure": Jean Boudin, interview.

209 Izzy Stone on the town house explosion: I. F. Stone, *Polemics and Prophecies, 1967–70* (New York: Random House, 1970).

209 David was devastated: David Gilbert, interview.

210 Workmen digging: Dr. Elliot Gross, former medical examiner, interview.

210 unexploded dynamite: Jonah Raskin, *Out of the Whale: Growing Up in the American Left: An Autobiography* (New York: Links, 1974).

210 relished the cops-and-robbers aspect: Victor Rabinowitz, interview; Eleanor Brussel, interview.

210 Riverdale mansion: Eleanor Brussel described the Boudin visits in a stage whisper. Eleanor Brussel, interview, 1993.

Of all the Weathermen, Cathlyn Wilkerson faced the most serious charges, such as murder; she was an owner of the bomb factory. Her traumatized father never returned to live in the United States; he relocated with his second wife to Wales, where his daughter visits him regularly. Wilkerson did not speak of the explosion in public for thirty years, and then did so only to Mel Gussow, his neighbor.

211 "underground": In 1951, some Communist Party leaders jumped bail and went underground. The FBI combed the country. They also subpoenaed the few known leaders of a support group called the Civil Rights Congress who had forfeited the bail money they had posted. The FBI erroneously assumed that support people were angry because they lost money. The FBI was suprised by the support group's refusal to reveal the whereabouts of missing leaders.

The support group also refused to reveal identities of other people who had contributed money. Mystery writer Dashiell Hammett, for example, took the Fifth Amendment and served a jail term rather than discuss his bail contribution or those of others. In fact, all financial records quickly disappeared. (Victor Rabinowitz had burned them in his living-room fireplace, solemnly taciturn about the illegality of his action.) Despite the fact that Victor and Leonard disapproved of going underground, they defended the people who put up bail money.

A Communist Party official asked Victor to hide one or more of the four fugitive leaders in his attic. The Rabinowitz family had recently moved to New Rochelle, into a huge one-hundred-year-old cedar house with a wraparound shade porch and ample backyard. The attic contained four large rooms and a bathroom. It was empty except for chairs and a toy train track.

Victor refused to harbor the fugitives, saying that it would be impossible to prevent his children from talking about such visitors. He did not admit that he did not want to put his family at risk.

211 Kathy's wanted poster: Paul Wilkes, "The Left's Lawyers' Lawyer: A Profile of Leonard Boudin," *New York Times Magazine*, Nov. 17, 1971.

212 inflating the villainous stature of his enemy: Fred Cook, *The FBI Nobody Knows* (New York: Macmillan, 1964).

213 ambling man: Michelle Slung, interview, 1998.

213 Covington and Burling: Leonard was thrilled even though Covington had, for example, fought President Roosevelt's New Deal legislation because it threatened to fetter big business. Covington even fought rural electrification, a project by Roosevelt's Public Works Administration that brought electricity to backwater towns in the country.

Leonard knew Covington lawyers craftily protected the big commercial airlines in the 1930s by invoking consumer safety legislation and congressional connections to get laws passed that crushed upstarts in the new airlines industry. For three years, Covington's Howard Westwood used his government connections to draft and push legislation through Congress that transformed the brand-new airlines industry into a closed market. (Izzy said that a businessman's belief in free-market economy often shrinks as his share of the market expands.) Basically Covington's stealthy lobbying and other forms of hard work helped to keep the United States on course as a corporate state. Joseph Goulden, "Washingtonian: An Inside Look at Washington's Oldest and Biggest Law Firm, Covington and Burling," 1971.

213 courtroom histrionics "a cold bath": Roberts Owen, Covington and Burling historian.

213 Kathy was apoplectic: Rita Jensen, interview, 1994.

213 Weather summit meeting: FBI files on SDS.

214 Bernardine expelled J.J.: Kevin Gilles, "The Last Radical," *Vancouver Magazine*, Nov. 1998.

214 "a hippie period": Castellucci, *The Big Dance;* anonymous interviews.

215 Weather communiqué: The "New Morning" communiqué was signed by Bernardine Dohrn. Named after Bob Dylan's song about taking a deep, healing breath and enjoying simple pleasures of rural life, it promised a new "peaceful" beginning.

Something of a tour de force in lack of reference to pain or tenderness, the Weather essay admitted that they had been unsuccessful terrorists.

> The deaths of our friends ended our military conceptions of what we are doing. It took us weeks of careful talking to rediscover our roots, to remember that we had been turned on to the possibilities of revolution by denying the schools, jobs, the death relationships we were "educated" for. We went back to how we had begun living with groups of friends and found that this revolution could leave intact the enslavement of women if women did not fight to end and change it, together. And marijuana and LSD and little money and awakening to the black revolution, the people of the world. Unprogramming ourselves; relearning Amerikan history.

The essay scolds and uses words like "pig" for policemen and "dirty dick" for President Nixon. The admission of technical error was oblique: "Always install a safety switch so you can turn it off and on and a light to indicate if a short circuit exists."

215 heavily guarded Manhattan police headquarters: Anonymous interviews; Ron Jacobs, *The Way the Wind Blew: A History of Weather Underground* (London and New York: Verso, 1997).

215 second Weather Underground communiqué: June 9, 1970. Jacobs, *The Way the Wind Blew.*
216 eluding "the pigs": Peter Collier and David Horowitz, *Destructive Generation: Second Thoughts About the Sixties* (New York: Summit Books, 1989); anonymous interviews.
216 acts of highly public "revolutionary violence": Jacobs, *The Way the Wind Blew.*
217 David slouched in a chair: Raskin, *Out of the Whale.*
217 knowing her exact whereabouts: Kit Bakke, ex-Weatherman, interview, 1998; *Chicago Journalism Review,* Oct. 1969.
217 a young poet: Louise Bernikow, interview, 1995.
218 breaking Tim Leary out of prison: Timothy Leary, *Flashbacks: A Personal and Cultural History of an Era: An Autobiography* (Boston: Houghton Mifflin, 1983).
218 governor of California: Before sentencing Timothy Leary to ten years in prison, the judge had called him "the most dangerous man in the world."
218 From inside prison: Leary, *Flashbacks.*
219 Michael Standard: Although Michael Standard publicly denies involvement in the jail-break, friends say he has privately taken credit for putting Kathy's group in touch with Leary. Indeed, Victor Rabinowitz stated that sometimes, to hear Standard tell it, it sounds as if he broke Leary out of jail himself.
219 mastermind a jailbreak: Tim Leary, interview, 1992; Leary, *Flashbacks.*
220 his wife: Leary's death decades later would be utterly original. He arranged to die on the Internet, a frail cancer-wracked wraith as high as a kite.
220 flying on acid: Castellucci, *The Big Dance;* FBI files on SDS.
221 Angela Davis, also a fugitive: After a seven-week nationwide manhunt, Davis was cornered in autumn and captured at gunpoint by the FBI at Howard Johnson's Motor Lodge at Eighth Avenue and Fifty-first Street. Her towering afro was disguised by a short black wig, but nothing could dim the singular beauty of her face.
　　Angela was held at the Women's House of Detention, a few minutes' walk from Elisabeth Irwin High School. Her old friend Reverend Melish told the press that Angela was lucky to have been captured in Manhattan. "If she'd been picked up in Arkansas, she'd have been killed." Reginald Major, *Justice in the Round: The Trial of Angela Davis* (New York: The Third Press, 1973).
221 Food was frequently shoplifted: David Gilbert, interview.
221 an old Plymouth: FBI files, SDS.
222 started and broke off a sexual relationship: Jane Alpert, *Growing Up Underground: Autobiography of a Former Radical Fugitive* (New York: William Morrow, 1981).
222 little candy store: Jennie Simon, interview.

14: Changing the World

223 prideful prosperity: FBI file, Leonard Boudin; Michael Standard, interview.
223 charming old house at Gray Street: Jean Boudin, interview.
223 Boudin telephone was wiretapped: Jean Boudin, interview.
224 Leonard routinely escaped his FBI tail: Jean Boudin, interview.
224 Kathy understood: Jean Boudin, interview.
224 incident at an airport in Miami: Victor Rabinowitz, interview.
224 "sucks up water like a pig": Jean Boudin, correspondence.
226 within a hairsbreadth of forcing FBI Director J. Edgar Hoover out of his job: Partly based on Barry Denenberg, *The True Story of J. Edgar Hoover and the FBI* (New York: Scholastic, 1993).

226 twenty antiwar intellectuals: William Davidon, interview, 1996.

227 Davidon: When asked directly in 2003 about his involvement, retired professor Davidon answered, "You can say that I equivocated."

228 "had lost it": Cartha D. "Deke" Deloach, *Hoover's FBI: The Inside Story by Hoover's Trusted Lieutenant* (Washington, D.C.: Regnery Press, 1995).

228 Daniel Ellsberg: Leonard Boudin, Pentagon Papers legal papers case, courtesy Jean Boudin, and Daniel Ellsberg, *Secrets: A Memoir of Vietnam and the Pentagon Papers* (New York: Viking Penguin, 2002). I read Tom Wells's *Wild Man: The Life and Times of Daniel Ellsberg* for help with some of the narrative and also read Watergate Records, including Watergate Special Prosecution Force Records, National Archives, Dr. Lewis Fielding, boxes 2, 3, 18–23. I am also indebted to Anthony Russo and Daniel Ellsberg for interviews, 2001.

228 first met Ellsberg: Daniel Ellsberg, interviews, 2001; Peter and Cora Weiss, interview, 2001.

229 Ellsberg decided not to choose Leonard: Daniel Ellsberg, interview, 2001.

229 they ushered him to the door: Victor Rabinowitz, interview; Daniel Ellsberg, interview.

230 Dan said only: Daniel Ellsberg, interview.

231 dissuaded friends: Jim Peck, letter to Jean Boudin, University of Oregon at Eugene, Alexander Crosley letters.

232 The FBI agent was silent: Wells, *Wild Man*.

232 "decoy Ellsberg": Wells, *Wild Man*.

233 "a regular right-wing nut": Ted Szulc, *Compulsive Spy: The Strange Career of E. Howard Hunt* (New York: Viking, 1974).

233 militaristic conspiracy: Anthony Russo, interview, 2000.

234 Leonard opened the historic pretrial: Anthony Russo, interviews, 2001; and Mickeljohn Archive: The Pentagon Papers Trial of Daniel Ellsberg and Anthony Russo, University of California at Berkeley.

234 Leonard's long-windedness: Jean Boudin, interview.

234 Leonard was stretching out the pretrial: Victor Rabinowitz, interviews; Mickeljohn Archive: The Pentagon Papers Trial of Daniel Ellsberg and Anthony Russo.

235 Ellsberg began to demand: Anthony Russo, interview.

235 Bernie "Macho" Barker: Hunt's recruit and close friend Macho Barker—a man whose twists and turns could be an instant television movie—would surface in tawdry and illegal revelations of the Watergate investigation. Born in the United States, Macho had lived in Cuba until joining the U.S. Air Corps, where he was shot down. A survivor and a tough guy, after his release from a German prisoner-of-war camp he had been convinced to join the Cuban police as a member of the CIA. (He was Jewish and a wounded superpatriotic American: the covert spy mission in Castro's police force cost him his U.S. citizenship.)

236 the trial gained momentum: Leonard Boudin, Pentagon Papers case files.

237 a defiant Ellsberg: Jean Boudin, interview; Wells, *Wild Man*.

238 It smelled like a bribe: Victor Rabinowitz, interview.

238 Leonard . . . squeezed Russo's arm: Anthony Russo, interview.

238 Michael Boudin and Dow Chemical: The doctors, minority Dow stockholders, had asked Dow to allow a stockholder vote on limiting the sale of napalm to only those buyers who promised not to use it on humans. Dow Chemical had refused. After the case was argued before the Supreme Court but before a decision was reached, Dow Chemical hastily put the proposal up for vote. Stockholders voted it down, by some 97

percent. The Supreme Court then refused to rule, saying the stockholder vote mooted the case. Roberts Owen, interview, Covington and Burling.

239 legal mumbo jumbo: Jean Boudin, interview.

239 U.S. Capitol bombing: Harold Jacobs, *Weatherman: An Anthology* (New York: Ramparts Press, 1970).

239 Kathy and Bernardine settled on bombing: Emile De Antonio, *Underground* (documentary film).

239 feature on *Underground: Rolling Stone*, November 6, 1975.

239 "a monument to U.S. domination": Jonah Raskin, interview; anonymous interviews.

239 forty bombings: Cyril Payne, *Deep Cover: An FBI Agent Infiltrates the Radical Underground* (New York: Newsweek Books, 1979). In the cloak-and-dagger tradition, undercover FBI agents behaved like Weather fugitives. The agents were long-haired, dope-smoking young men who even gave impassioned TV interviews at protests about their opposition to the war in Vietnam. They also enjoyed sexual relationships with "hippie chicks." They copied the Weather fugitives' methods—including the use of designated pay phones and coded schedules to call the office. One agent was "radicalized" at the Republican national convention in Florida, when he refused to stop talking back and cursing angry cops who clubbed him "until he had to have his asshole rebuilt." On the basis of a rumor that Kathy or David or Bernardine had been sighted, undercover agents such as Cyril Payne drifted from communes to crash pads in California to Washington State and even to Canada. (An FBI agent exceeded his mandate by crossing the border into Canada.)

Agent Cyril Payne described a lonely, paranoid life; like Weather fugitives, he was unable to tell hippie bed partners the truth. He screwed up trying to remember the details of his "new identity" and to respond to a new name. Cyril posed as a drug dealer, which gave him an excuse to disappear from time to time—and for having ready cash. Unfortunately, it also put him at risk from local police.

239 twenty bombings: Kathy Boudin, SDS file.

240 Weather activities: FBI reports in Kathy's pretrial papers.

240 tourist map: De Antonio, *Underground*.

242 "heat in Leonard's life": Judy Pfeiffer, interview.

242 dress rehearsal: Anonymous interviews.

245 Michael responded calmly: Michele Slung, interview, 1996.

247 Mary Moylan: Jane Alpert, *Growing Up Underground: Autobiography of a Former Radical Fugitive* (New York: William Morrow, 1981).

247 lonely fugitive: Ibid.

249 Like Bernardine, Kathy's hair was: Ibid.; Jane Alpert, interview.

251 "omnipotence of the state": David Gilbert, interview.

15: The Devil's Party

252 partner at Covington and Burling: Roberts Owen, interview, Covington and Burling, 1998.

253 Michael protected: Although Michael's four-year term on the managerial board at Covington was coming to an end, he would continue to carry his heavy caseload, leading teams of lawyers to victory for AT&T. His cases on behalf of railroads continued to hammer at rate regulations, a holdover from eras when railroads were not struggling to compete with trucking companies.

253 liked Ronald Reagan: Stuart Taylor, interview.

253 he had many women friends: Michele Slung, interview.

253 Learned Hand: Michael Boudin, book review of Gerald Gunther's *Learned Hand,* *Stanford Law Review,* Jan. 1995.

254 Hugh Cox learned: Hugh Cox memorial book.

255 "What have you got?": Jean Boudin, interview.

256 Patty Hearst: *Chicago Tribune,* Feb. 20, 1976.

On August 13, 1975, the Symbionese Liberation Army bombed the Emoryville police station in California in the name of Clifford Glover, a black boy accidentally killed by police who saw a shiny object in his hand and mistook it for a gun. The Weather group also cited Glover as a reason for their bombing of the 103rd Police Precinct in Manhattan.

256 A radio announcer: Jean Boudin, "Jean Boudin Talks About Her Fugitive Daughter," *Ms.* magazine, Aug. 1976. "Sing a Battle Song," permission to reprint granted by Cheryl Rogers at *Ms.* magazine, 1996.

257 "Revolutionaries are often destroyed": Jean Boudin, interview.

258 Justice Marshall raised his palm: Herb Jordan, interview, 1998.

259 Kathy stalled: David Gilbert, interview.

260 Assata was known to thousands of blacks: Assata Shakur, *Assata: An Autobiography* (London: Zed Books, 1987).

260 Joanne Deborah Byron Chesimard a.k.a. Assata Shakur: Evelyn Williams, *Inadmissible Evidence: The Story of the African-American Trial Lawyer Who Defended the Black Liberation Army* (Chicago: Lawrence Hill Books, 1993). Ms. Williams is Joanne Chesimard's aunt and lawyer.

261 adept with guns: Curt Gentry, *J. Edgar Hoover: The Man and the Secrets* (New York: W. W. Norton, 1991), p. 172; Nestor Michnyak, FBI Fugitive Publicity Department, FBI, interview.

261 Black Liberation Army: Robert Daley, *Target Blue: An Insider's View of the N.Y.P.D.* (New York: Delacorte Press, 1973).

261 "revolutionary executions": Daley, *Target Blue.*

262 police were vulnerable targets: Daley, *Target Blue.*

262 shootout on the New Jersey Turnpike: Joanne Chesimard trial transcripts. The controversy over racial profiling in New Jersey made headlines again in 1999, when a middle-class black man complained of being poorly treated by police because he was driving an expensive car. It would also surface after the Middle East terrorist attacks on Manhattan and Washington.

263 In her autobiography: Shakur, *Assata: An Autobiography.*

264 Doc was the stepfather of the four-year-old Tupac Shakur: Tupac Shakur's early years were a tumultuous lesson in real and rhetorical street violence—and included talk of "retaliatory killing" of policemen and endless trials.

264 Lincoln Hospital Detox Center: The Lincoln Detox Center was a direct result of sit-ins and occupations at Lincoln Hospital (in which the author took part). It is the only public hospital in the South Bronx. Protests began on July 14, 1970, and were conducted by the Young Lords, Panthers, drug addicts, and hospital workers. The 346-bed hospital delivered appalling service to 400,000 residents a year, some of whom called it the "butcher shop." The leading cause of death in the South Bronx was called "Lincolnitis." Residents suffered from epidemics of heroin addiction, tuberculosis, malnutrition, and venereal disease, as well as high infant mortality rates. People died decades earlier

than their white counterparts, not just because of violence but because of delayed or insufficient treatment for cancer, drug abuse, stress, and cardiovascular diseases. It was common to find a man dying from inadequate treatment of illness. His legacy was unpaid bills and despairing children.

On July 14, 1970, South Bronx community activists occupied the nurses' residence for five hours to protest the fact, among others, that Lincoln Hospital had no serious drug detoxification program. The hospital administrator, Dr. Antero Lacot (installed because of activist demands for a Puerto Rican in the job), agreed with protesters. Authorities hastily promised to set up a detox program in the auditorium of the nurses' residence and to request city funding. University of Michigan School of Public Health lead researcher, Arlene Geronimus study published in *New England Journal of Medicine* (Dec. 1996); Bob Herbert, *New York Times,* Dec. 2, 1996; John Castellucci, *The Big Dance: The Untold Story of Weatherman Kathy Boudin and the Terrorist Family That Committed the Brinks Robbery Murders* (New York: Dodd Mead, 1986).

Doc Shakur had been born in 1950, in Baltimore, Maryland, his mother a serious Christian and his father, James MacMoore, a painter. By age eighteen, Doc had adopted an African name, joined the new Republic of New Africa—a radical black nationalist group—and was a convert to the Sunni Muslim religion.

Doc volunteered at Lincoln Detox in 1970, soon after the program began. He was hired as assistant director after he impressed administrators by researching ways other than methadone to help addicts.

Doc Shakur convinced the Lincoln Detox staff to adopt Malcolm X's "drug cure." He gave seven thousand drug addicts a year an eighty-six-page book called *The Opium Trail: Heroin and Imperialism.*

Doc's political education classes at Lincoln Detox taught that self-hatred as a black person was forced by whites. The recovering addict was to create a new name and identity for himself based on racial self-respect. Castellucci, *The Big Dance.*

264 recovering drug addict: Castellucci, *The Big Dance; U.S. v. Shakur* trial transcripts.

264 assisting Doc Shakur: Like the radical white women, David knew his would be a subordinate role. He knew sympathetic whites had been brokenhearted at being kicked out of SNCC. Weather had tried to support Black Panthers all over the country and had been rejected.

265 flattering letters from Emile De Antonio: *Rolling Stone,* Nov. 6, 1975.

266 David and Judith jeered: Castellucci, *The Big Dance.*

266 "Hard Times conference": David Gilbert, Columbia University Oral History Project.

267 living separately from David: Rita Jensen, interview.

267 subsequent meetings with De: *Rolling Stone,* Nov. 6, 1975.

267 Haskell Wexler: Wexler, one of the most respected cinematographers in the world, made *Medium Cool* and won an Academy Award for the film *Who's Afraid of Virginia Woolf?* Coincidentally, perhaps, Wexler had made films in the 1940s for the left-wing United Electrical Radio and Machine Workers Union, which was closely associated with Leonard's firm.

267 if he should get a gun for the filming: *Rolling Stone,* Nov. 6, 1975.

268 his "heavy" subjects: *Rolling Stone,* Nov. 6, 1975.

268 Bill Ayers opened: De Antonio, *Underground.*

268 Kathy began by introducing herself: De Antonio, *Underground.*

269 *Underground:* In the film Kathy lauded the end of the Vietnam War as their victory. The lesson was: "American imperialism was vulnerable, not loved by people of the world, and not satisfying the needs of the great majority of the American people." She called

the sixties a revelation: racism was exposed, women formulated independent identities, young people suddenly saw their government objectively. American imperialism was no longer just a term in history books.

269 "anonymous" poem: De Antonio, *Underground.*

269 Kathy did not mention: FBI files on SDS; Castellucci, *The Big Dance.*

270 To say good-bye: FBI files on SDS; Castellucci, *The Big Dance.*

271 Newspaper editorials: Editorials in the *Boston Globe* argued for De Antonio's right of free expression. A Georgia congressman denounced the filmmakers and Leonard ("their attorney, whose daughter is a Weather Underground fugitive last seen scrambling from the collapsing Greenwich Village town house blown up accidentally by her Weathermen comrades").

"Mr. Speaker, the Weather Underground Organization terrorists have taken responsibility for a whole series of bombings including one right here in the Capitol and one in the State Department earlier this year." He denounced signers of a petition protesting the subpoena of Wexler and Lampson. They are "members of 'the dishonor roll' " who were "a whole crew of Hollywood's radical chic colony . . . and left-wing crackpots" (*Congressional Record*, July 30, 1975).

Petition signers included Warren Beatty, Hal Ashby, Jack Nicholson, Ed Begley Jr., Harry Belafonte, Mel Brooks, Jeff Bridges, Sally Field, Shirley MacLaine, Michael Meeropol, and Dr. Alan Berkman, the doctor who treated Kathy and others and called himself a "white Panther."

271 Leonard agreed to be legal counsel: The case was close to Leonard's heart. Leonard was the man, after all, who in a particularly rancorous Wednesday staff meeting pretended to take seriously a letter from Winston Moseley, the young man who was sentenced to life in prison for the 1967 murder of a young woman returning to her home at 3 a.m. in Kew Gardens, Queens. The Kitty Genovese case was famous because none of her neighbors called police or helped her while she screamed for help for thirty minutes as she was stalked, stabbed repeatedly, and raped, first under a streetlight and then in the vestibule of her apartment building.

Kitty Genovese's murderer and rapist wrote to Leonard from prison complaining that all the felons he knew had been released from jail after serving five years or so. Thus his rights were being violated by his sentence of lifetime incarceration. He was, he wrote, now an asset to society, having earned a college degree in sociology. Leonard read the man's letter aloud in a staff meeting and pretended to be persuaded by shouting partners to forget it.

271 critical response to *Underground:* Stanley Kaufman wrote in the *New Republic,* "Sanctity and sagacity don't attach to political fugitives just because they're fugitives or constant to their beliefs, nor because the country is riddled with corruption. Those who are sacrificing themselves to a revolutionary cause need to convince more about the cause than the sacrifice. What we have here is only more political sentimentalizing and distortion." Kaufman disagreed with Bernardine who had said, "If you understand what happened in the Vietnamese War, and why the Vietnamese defeated the United States, it makes the possibility and the inevitablity of revolution in the United States very clear." *The New Republic*, May 29, 1976.

272 Bernardine quit Weather: Life had calmed for Bernardine. In 1978 she was a devoted mother and was working under an alias as a waitress at Teacher's Restaurant on Manhattan's Upper West Side. Respected by coworkers for her serious views, she was viewed as "a little intense." Her husband, Bill Ayers, was working long hours as a baker in Little Italy. Like David Gilbert, Bill had no outstanding infractions that made

it necessary to use an alias. He stayed underground in sympathy with his wife. He had taken a prominent role in the progressive day-care center at P.S. 9 that their son attended. Bill Ayers had also helped bring youngsters in cabs to protest the closing of Sydenham Hospital.

Bernardine was determined to begin an aboveground life of intellectual public service. After consulting Leonard, she hired the high-powered Michael Kennedy to negotiate her surrender. The government would agree—remarkably enough—not to investigate the forty instances of bombing that the FBI had overenthusiastically attributed to her group. With J. Edgar Hoover gone, the FBI was embarrassed by its former zeal. Thus, most charges had been dropped, including the federal fugitive warrant, because Chicago officials declared that they would not extradite Bernardine if she were found in another state regarding charges against her stemming from the Days of Rage. The only charges remaining from that period in Chicago were very minor misdemeanors. *New York Times,* 1979; Castellucci, *The Big Dance;* FBI files on SDS.

272 David angrily walked out: In 1977, a radical newspaper from Madison, Wisconsin, called *Take Over* wrote a brief notice. "David Gilbert, a federal fugitive on an arson and a conspiracy to commit arson charge, surfaced in Boulder, Colo., earlier this month, becoming the eighth Weather Underground member to [surface] seek the air." Nobody arrested David. The authorities were not interested in him.

272 collapse of the Weathermen: David Gilbert lamented the sorry dissolution of an unbeaten underground without mentioning the publicity blackout engineered by the U.S. government of Weather communiqués or the group's declining popularity. "By 1977, the Weather group fell apart, split," he recalled at Great Meadows prison, "and this was after [we spent] seven years underground where the FBI had never been able to break us . . . oh, they busted one or two people, but they never dented the organization. This was a major breakthrough in the history of the left."

16: The Secret Sits in the Middle and Knows

273 Rita Jensen and Kathy bonded: Rita Jensen, interview, 1996; and *People v. Katherine Boudin,* Rockland County, 1981.

274 "Is your roommate there?": Castellucci, *The Big Dance: The Untold Story of Weatherman Kathy Boudin and the Terrorist Family That Committed the Brinks Robbery Murders* (New York: Dodd Mead, 1986).

275 Kathy visited Doc Shakur: Jean Boudin, interview; letter to Chesa from Kathy, courtesy Jean Boudin.

275 Assata Shakur's poem: Assata Shakur, *Assata: An Autobiography* (London: Zed Books, 1987).

275 one morning in October: Castellucci, *The Big Dance.*

276 wagon keys to Sam Brown: Sam Brown trial transcript interviews: Sam Brown's "rap" included an astute analysis of black problems in the United States, a smattering of Eastern philosophy, a habit of blaming his keen interest in illegal drugs on white capitalists who allowed drugs to flourish in ghetto neighborhoods, and a vain belief in his own ability to change problems of blacks in the United States.

A friend of Kathy's was exasperated by her exaggerated respect for men like Brown. "The most lame street hustler and liar would be listened to with lots of eye contact, head nodding, and great respect—as long as he was black."

277 Leonard was showering: Jean Boudin, interview.

277 Leonard particularly hated: Jean Boudin, interview.

277 Authorities believe Bernardine helped with robberies: Bernardine had been working as manager of a store named Broadway Baby at Eighty-second Street and Broadway on the Upper West Side, selling high-quality children's toys, clothes, and accessories.

Authorities believed Bernardine's drill was simple: a customer would write a check for her purchases, and then show Bernardine her driver's license as ID. Bernardine then copied all the information from the driver's license onto the back of the check. The next day a woman, most likely Kathy or Judith Clark, applied for a duplicate driver's license using the customer's name, date of birth, height, weight, and motorist identification number. (Bernardine was never arrested for these actions.) Castellucci, *The Big Dance;* FBI files.

278 Leonard and Jean were delighted: Binnie Klein interview, Jan. 2003.

278 outdoor studio: Vacant due to the recent death of Crocket Johnson, author of *Harold and the Purple Crayon.*

279 letter to Madi Leof: Courtesy Nancy Carlen.

279 exhilarating brunches: Jean Boudin, interview.

280 perplexing invitation: Thomas Powers, interview; Thomas Powers, diary entry.

280 Bernardine was under the spell of the Boudin family: Bert Gross, interview, 1995.

281 station wagon, stolen with Kathy's assistance: Castellucci, *The Big Dance; People v. Katherine Boudin*, Rockland County, 1981; FBI files; Joanne Chesimard trial transcripts.

281 Marilyn Buck: Marilyn Buck wrote an evaluation of the Assata Shakur prison break, saying the gang should openly take credit. "The goal has been accomplished joyfully and shall be felt internationally in its time. The enemy was caught off-guard and the operation dictated the situation, despite the enemy's attempt to respond." John Castellucci, reporter's files.

282 Assata Shakur to Cuba: Evelyn Williams, *Inadmissible Evidence: The Story of the African-American Trial Lawyer Who Defended the Black Liberation Army* (Chicago: Lawrence Hill Books, 1993). Williams is Assata Shakur's aunt.

282 "two-bit": Castellucci, *The Big Dance.*

283 three levels of command: Castellucci, *The Big Dance.*

283 using robbery proceeds for cocaine: David Gilbert was one of several white men supporting the May 19 Communist collective. These were a fierce and suspicious bunch of women, and David spent a lot of time soothing and explaining his desire to treat women as equals.

David used at least four aliases to obtain fake driver's licenses in order to rent backup cars for five successful robberies and failed attempts that would take place between February 20, 1980, and October 20, 1981, starting with the audacious Assata Shakur breakout. His aliases would include Stephen F. Barranco, Ronald Hersh, and Michael Shatzkin. He created a paper trail for the FBI of driver's license and car rental applications with samples of his handwriting. The FBI also found his fingerprints on an application for a duplicate driver's license under the name Stephen F. Barranco dated November 28, 1979. David and the unidentified woman rented the blue backup van for the escape a few days before it was executed from Family Rental Center on Grand Avenue in Baldwin, Long Island, using a fake driver's license issued in the name of William Lichius of Turtle Creek, Pennsylvania. The signature on the fake driver's license was matched up to David Gilbert. Castellucci, *The Big Dance;* FBI files; anonymous interviews.

283 the real Anne Harriet Appelbaum: FBI files; Castellucci, *The Big Dance.*

285 traveled to Harlem for acupuncture: Papers courtesy Jean Boudin.

285 John Mwangi suggested: Castellucci, *The Big Dance.*

286 David wrote to his son: Papers courtesy Jean Boudin.

286 Again, the silver Brinks truck: FBI reports.

286 "my eensy beensy": Papers, courtesy Jean Boudin.

286 Chesa Jackson Boudin: As Kathy later wrote Chesa about the Black Panther for whom he was also named: "George Jackson was a beautiful human being who taught so many people about the struggle of black people for freedom and who fought for that freedom." After researching Chesa's birth date further, David also learned that it was also the birthday of Luis Martinez, a friend working for Puerto Rico's independence in Denver. Correspondence, Kathy and Jean Boudin, courtesy Jean Boudin.

287 Chesa was a year old: Letter from Kathy and David to Chesa, courtesy Jean Boudin.

288 revolutionary activities: Future "revolutionary" plans included planting a bomb in a Brooklyn police station. Local blacks abhorred police at the station for particularly cruel treatment, and Doc believed the bombing would galvanize community response. Some inside work had already been done by May 19 women, who had mapped a floor plan of the police station. Plans were also being formulated to bomb the Federal Court House and the Statue of Liberty. FBI files; Castellucci, *The Big Dance*.

288 Judith Clark and Susan Rosenberg: Castellucci, *The Big Dance*.

288 fifth robbery attempt: Castellucci, *The Big Dance;* FBI files.

289 Sekou was enraged: John Castellucci, *The Big Dance;* FBI reports; County Court of Rockland County, Surrogate Courthouse, Goshen, New York, Aug. 11, 1983, Indictment nos 81–285, 82–6, *The People of The State of New York against David Gilbert, Judith Clark and Kuwasi Balagoon, a.k.a. Donald Weems*.

290 David Gilbert did not want to surface: criticism–self-criticism by David Gilbert, courtesy John Castellucci.

290 could not stop quarreling: Psychiatrist Roger Gould later described Kathy's transformation to motherhood for the sake of her legal defense: "After Kathy became a mother this process of self-expansion and recovery of a fuller perspective leading to a wiser use of her strengths was accelerated. She became less of a group member and more of an individual moving away and out of the group." *People v. Katherine Boudin*, Rockland County, 1981.

290 Rockland robbery attempted again: *People v. Katherine Boudin*, Rockland County, 1981.

290 Kathy's fright was heightened: Castellucci, *The Big Dance;* FBI files.

291 now fourteen months old: Castellucci, *The Big Dance;* FBI file interviews.

292 Army had recently murdered a guard: FBI files; Castellucci, *The Big Dance;* Michael Daley, *New York Daily News*, Aug. 2001.

292 hung a burlap cloth: FBI files; James Stewart, interview.

293 James Kelly: *People v. Katherine Boudin*, Rockland County, 1981.

293 Balagoon watched: Katherine Boudin pretrial transcript.

294 broke three fingernails: Sam Brown, interviews; FBI, State of New York, *The People of the State of New York against Sam Brown*, May 24, 1984.

294 "I climbed in the back of the truck": *People v. Katherine Boudin*, Rockland County, 1981.

17: Murder in Nyack

295 David turned off the motor: *People v. Judith Clark, David Gilbert and Donald Weems*, August 11, 1983.

295 Standing behind the truck: Interviews about the robbery and roadblock with Chief Alan Colsey, Dr. Ronald Dreyer, Norma Hill, and James Stewart.

295 "a sexist arrogance": criticism–self-criticism by David Gilbert and given to me by John Castellucci.

296 the red Chevy van: *People v. Katherine Boudin,* Rockland County, 1981.

299 Norma Hill: Despite her traumatic reaction to the ordeal in Nyack, Norma had a peculiar memory for faces and would be the important eyewitness against Kathy, Judith Clark, Donald Weems (remembering his crooked front tooth), and Sam Brown. Norma Hill, interview, November 1999; trial transcript: *People of the State of New York against Sam Brown,* indictment # 0285 T-81, morning session, May 22, 1984, direct testimony, Norma Hill, Ken Gribetz.

300 David was far less frightened: David Gilbert, conversations.

300 "put the gun back": Although Kathy insists she never said this, after extensive readings of trial transcripts and conversations with police and Kathy's lawyers, I think she said and did several things that indicated her fear of the gun and her desire that O'Grady order his men to put the guns away.

300 O'Grady put his handgun in his holster: Diane O'Grady, conversation, 2003.
    Brian Lennon was disturbed by a telephone call about the case in 1999. After a sharp intake of breath he said, "That woman killed my partners."

301 "It's on": John Castellucci, interview.

302 Michael Koch braked his camper: *People v. Judith Clark et al.*

304 "Don't let them hurt me": Dr. Ronald Dreyer, interview, 1996.

305 a dozen Thanksgiving turkeys: John Castellucci, *The Big Dance: The Untold Story of Weatherman Kathy Boudin and the Terrorist Family That Committed the Brinks Robbery Murders* (New York: Dodd Mead, 1986)

305 massive bleeding: *People v. Shakur.*

305 the town's only black policeman: Chief Alan Colsey, interviews.

306 Driving by: Chief Alan Colsey, interviews, 1997.

306 Colsey was horrified: Chief Alan Colsey, interviews.

308 R.C. JAIL: Ellen Frankfort, *Kathy Boudin and the Dance of Death* (New York: Stein and Day, 1984).

308 "Give them the electric chair": *People v. Katherine Boudin.*

308 Judith Clark grinning: Victor Rabinowitz, interview.

309 radicals arrested throughout history: In 1918 Eugene V. Debs, the Socialist Party leader and five-time candidate for president, said in Canton, Ohio: "If it had not been for the men and women who, in the past, have had the moral courage to go to jail, we would still be in the jungles."

310 Kathy called William Kunstler: William Kunstler, interview, 1993. William Kunstler cultivated a high press profile. He was the most famous radical lawyer in the United States. He bragged of breaking laws in support of clients. He would, nonetheless, be hailed by *New York Times* columnist Tom Wicker as "a tireless voice for the voiceless."
    Kathy had a history of clandestine meetings with Kunstler at his home and at restaurants. He gave her small amounts of money. William Kunstler wrote in his memoir, *My Life as a Radical Lawyer* (New York: Citadel Press, 1994).

> On one occasion I received instructions to drive in a rented car to a Long Island diner, sit at the counter, and order a hamburger. I did so and within minutes there was a woman on either side of me. "Hello Bill, we are everywhere," murmured the one disguised in a shapeless dress and red wig [Bernardine]. All three of us [including Kathy] got into my car, and they directed me to a modest frame house.
> [Later] a go-between would contact me and direct me to a designated safe house where they would ask me eagerly for information about what was going

on in legal circles and with my clients and about the political scene in general. I enjoyed the cloak-and-dagger aspects of meeting clandestinely with people the government was eager to find and prosecute. The danger also appealed to me because I was always a little uncomfortable with the fact that lawyers took no risks, while our clients took many.

310 David and Judith were beaten: John Castellucci, interview.
311 Wisps of his longish white hair: Victor Rabinowitz, interview.
312 Other friends were horrified: Andrew Patner, interview; Alice Carlen, interview.

18: My Daughter Loves This Country Very Much

314 five graying intellectuals: Victor Rabinowitz, interview.
314 "ice princess": John Castellucci, *The Big Dance: The Untold Story of Weatherman Kathy Boudin and the Terrorist Family That Committed the Brinks Robbery Murders* (New York: Dodd Mead, 1986).
314 "Are you okay?": Victor Rabinowitz, interview.
315 Bill Kunstler felt proud: William Kunstler, memoir.
316 silently fired him: Victor Rabinowitz, interview.
316 Leonard mused about defense strategies: William Kunstler, interview.
317 Kathy's action immersed Leonard in feelings of failure: Jon Snow, interview.
317 terrorists poised to kill: Castellucci, *The Big Dance*.
317 bomb-making manuals: FBI reports.
318 self-important demeanor: Castellucci, *The Big Dance;* Ellen Frankfort, *Kathy Boudin and the Dance of Death* (New York: Stein and Day, 1983).
319 slave auction: Frankfort, *Kathy Boudin and the Dance of Death*.
319 broken Sam Brown's neck: David Gilbert, interview.
319 "Oh, really what a pity": Castellucci, *The Big Dance*.
319 he hugged her, kissed her: John Castellucci's notes on interview with Murray Kempton.
319 pretending she was invisible: John Castellucci, notes.
319 four defendants: Judith Clark's father, the former Moscow correspondent for the *Daily Worker,* was so mortified and angered by the robbery that he did not speak to her and refused to attend the trial. Jean Boudin, interview.
319 "I never thought of that": Robin Reisig, interview, 1994.
320 Kathy had initially refused to participate in a line-up: *People v. Katherine Boudin*. The prosecution was represented by the chief assistant district attorney of Rockland County, James Mellion.

> MR. MELLION: . . . the record should reflect that . . . we're in the Rockland County Courthouse for the purpose of a court-ordered corporeal lineup concerning the defendant Katherine Boudin—
>
> MR. LEONARD BOUDIN: —Kathy, there's no birth certificate or anything that has Katherine. . . .
>
> MR. MELLION [to Kathy]: Is it your intention to participate voluntarily in the lineup procedure this evening? . . .
>
> MS. BOUDIN: I object to the lineup because I feel the lineups have historically been used to unjustly frame and convict black people.
>
> MR. MELLION: And he's explained to you that given your position this evening, you would be carried into the lineup and placed in position?

Ms. Boudin: Yes.

Mr. Leonard Boudin: —What is the importance of use—this goes on the record?

Mr. Garbus: Should we talk for a moment?

(Mr. Garbus and Mr. Boudin have off-the-record discussion.)

Mr. Garbus: The decision to participate in the lineup is my decision. The decision to the use of force that I have indicated is Miss Boudin's decision. The decision to protest the lineup both for reasons that Miss Boudin stated are clearly Miss Boudin's decisions.

Mr. Mellion: Mr. Garbus, I would like to ask you and your client to be clear on the record. It is my understanding that once in the lineup room, your client, Miss Boudin, will cooperate and will look at the viewing window, is that correct?

Mr. Garbus: My understanding is that in the lineup room, my client, Miss Boudin, will be shackled in the way that she is shackled now, which is to say that she has shackles on her feet and shackles on her hands. It is my understanding that this is the normal way, if I can use the term "normal" that lineups are being conducted and that in the lineup room, Miss Boudin will be seated alongside other people and that the other people may or may not be shackled, but in any event, her shackles will be covered with the blanket or something else so that the viewing witnesses will not be able to tell that she is shackled. Given the fact that she is shackled, she has indicated to me that she will not make any attempt to draw attention to herself as different than the other people, the other witnesses who are being identified.

Again it is my understanding and it is also Miss Boudin's understanding that the people who were identified here today pursuant to Judge Stolarik's decision are both people who have previously picked her out in the photo identification and also people who identified her solely at the U-Haul stop site. Is that correct, Miss Boudin?

(Mr. Garbus and Ms. Boudin have an off-the-record conversation.) . . .

Ms. Boudin: What's the purpose of all this?

Mr. Garbus: What we're now doing?

Ms. Boudin: What's the purpose of all this?

(Mr. Garbus and Ms. Boudin have off-the-record discussion.)

Mr. Mellion: Furthermore, Mr. Garbus, pursuant to the understanding reached in conference when these matters were discussed, it is my understanding when you explain your client's position to us concerning the lineup tonight, so at any particular time when she is viewed by a particular witness, your client refuses to cooperate and call attention to herself, that any resulting prejudices will be waived concerning that particular witness?

Mr. Garbus: I agree.

Mr. Mellion: Mr. Garbus has explained this fact?

Ms. Boudin: That's correct.

Mr. Mellion: At this time also, Miss Boudin, the officers have explained to me they would like you to remove your glasses and your earrings. Will you be able to do that for the purpose of the line-up?

Ms. Boudin: No, I never have my glasses off and I never have my earrings off. I haven't had my earrings off for three years.

Mr. Mellion: Would you be willing to remove your glasses for the purposes of the lineup?

Ms. Boudin: Okay, I'll take them off.

Mr. Mellion: Very good. The time should be reflected as approximately 7:29 p.m. and we're about to proceed with the identification procedures.

Eyewitness Norma Hill quickly picked Kathy out of the lineup of six women. Hill's life, a policeman soon told her, was in danger from terrorist reprisals. She was given a round-the-clock police guard and suffered an acute nervous breakdown. Norma Hill, interview.

320 footsteps of Julius and Ethel Rosenberg: Rita Jensen, interview.

321 pressed into service: Ellen Winner, interview.

321 friends dropped out of their own lives: Leni Wildflower, interview.

321 Leonard berated Bernardine daily: Sherri Wertheimer, interview.

322 David Gilbert presented an ongoing problem: Sandy Katz, interview.

323 Leonard worried: Jean Boudin, interview.

323 guards sneered: Jean Boudin, personal papers.

326 Leonard's increased dependence: Letty Pogrebin, interview.

326 illustrious visitors: Dave Dellinger, the upper-class pacifist and humanitarian accustomed to going in and out of jail for his beliefs, publicly congratulated Kathy for her courage. The historian Howard Zinn visited on Jean's invitation. He saw the catastrophic robbery as part of a serious clandestine war, but deplored the deaths of the policemen and the Brinks guard. Dr. Ben Spock's visit was recorded in the *Washington Post* society column. He asked reporters why on earth Kathy was not allowed to touch her child. Kathy was, he said, worried sick that her child might forget her.

328 inside Chesa's diaper: Jean Boudin, personal papers.

328 Leonard engaged Brown in games of "telephonic" chess: Letters from Sam Brown to Leonard Boudin.

328 asked David to testify: Jean Boudin, papers.

19: A Safe Harbor

329 Michael astonished his friends: Michelle Slung, interview.

330 Marty was eccentric: Victor Rabinowitz and Jean Boudin, interviews.

331 Abe Fortas resigned: Abe Fortas, FBI file.

Abe Fortas had been President Lyndon Johnson's closest and most canny Mr. Fix-it and political adviser. Neighbors glimpsed the president's car parked outside Fortas's house on many nights. Fortas was a southern Jew who had been a protégé of Harold Ickes during the New Deal and a commuting professor at Yale Law School. He had bullied and cajoled the military when charged with the delicate operation of relocating interned Japanese Americans after World War II. During the McCarthy era he took on scores of loyalty cases without fee. His wife was also a brilliant lawyer. The couple was childless. As one of his last acts in office, President Johnson tried to promote Fortas to Chief Justice. Fortas had been against the promotion, which meant a fuller commitment of time to the Supreme Court and another FBI investigation into his life.

Newly elected President Richard Nixon's henchmen took public aim at Fortas for having briefly served (while on the Court) as the salaried head of a foundation set up by his former client, Louis Wolfson. This was not a major sin. It was therefore surprising that Fortas resigned abruptly, marking the downfall of the trailblazing liberal Warren court. (Chief Justice Earl Warren himself had retired.) It would be many years before a hint of more complicated factors leading to Fortas's resignation surfaced. According to a document from the FBI files, an FBI agent had visited Fortas and politely explained that on Director Hoover's orders, he was alerting Fortas to the dismaying fact that an informant had seen Fortas at a homosexual club. Abe Fortas thanked his visitor and resigned from the Supreme Court.

332 Jay Schulman: Schulman had surveyed 463 Middlesex County residents about Assata Shakur's second trial in New Jersey. Schulman had found that 90 percent of people had heard of her, and of them 71 percent thought she was guilty. He had concluded that she could not receive a fair trial there and recommended a change of venue, but the judge denied it. Castellucci, *The Big Dance*. Schulman was never paid for his work. Robin Reisig, interview, 1996.

333 "I think your long robe is silly": *People v. Katherine Boudin*, Rockland County, 1981.

333 Norma Hill fainted: Norma Hill, interview.

334 David had agreed to lie under oath: Leonard's request was not that outrageous. To my surprise, many men (including lawyers and legal reporters) answered in the affirmative when I asked if they would perjure themselves in court for the sake of their family. It is perhaps one of those rules of conventional morality that is unstated in conversation or in law books.

334 spellbinding: *People v. Katherine Boudin*, Rockland County, voire dire, 1981. Victor Rabinowitz had also defended his daughter, with Leonard's help.

334 Martin Garbus: Martin Garbus and Leonard Weinglass had been hired as Kathy's lawyers but would not be paid for all of their time. The legal team was superb. Leonard Weinglass had distinguished himself working with Leonard on the Ellsberg court case. He had been second to Bill Kunstler on the trial of the Chicago 7.

20: *The Barrel of a Gun*

335 David was awed: Jean Boudin, interview.

336 "only marginally tryable": This was something of an overstatement. Despite Kathy's decorum, in Rockland County local people were still furious and referred to Kathy for years to come as "the mastermind of the Brinks robbery and shootout." Anonymous, Rockland County interviews, 1993–2001.

338 Father and daughter each spoke: Leonard said:

> Thank you, your honor. It is not easy for a lawyer and impossible for a father to be objective. But since I am both in this courtroom, I want to say a few words for my wife and for myself about our daughter, Kathy, in the context of this case.
>
> They are appropriate because we, her father and mother—rather her mother and father, are responsible in a large sense for our daughter's views on

life—the prelude in this case to a long prison sentence. She's a first offender, but the felony murder rule, increasingly criticized as harsh by scholars and judges, makes her legally responsible for the death of Mr. Paige because of her involvement in the robbery, although Kathy was not present at the scene and was not armed.

People I respect in the community have written that Kathy's contributions to political action, educational activities, demonstrations, nonviolent civil disobedience, with a primary focus on the Indo-Chinese War, with other rights, civil rights issues, community organizing and so on, made a great impression on them and she brought compassion, understanding, perspicacious analysis, and a profound commitment to help people who were suffering and disadvantaged.

That her role was minor, that she was not armed then or ever in her forty years of life, is not an excuse under the law. As a lawyer, as a citizen, as a father, I recognize that. It is for that reason that she has pleaded guilty, a plea which with the acceptance of the District Attorney and the approval of the Court, has spared everyone, society, the Court, the defense lawyers, the prosecution, Kathy, a probable very difficult six months or so of contested trial, possible preliminary applications to the Appellate Division for various forms of relief and applications to Your Honor and, if necessary, at least two years in the light of my experience, two years is a small matter for appellate review.

Kathy has suffered two terrible years of isolation, a punishment that until this particular event, I do not recall has been suffered in the State of New York in recent years. Added to this, there is a tragic separation from her child who she now sees and will only see on prison visits. We have felt her pain; we have had equal pain. But the three of us, Kathy, Jean, and I, know that nothing compares to what Mr. Gribetz correctly referred to as the losses of Mrs. Paige, Mrs. O'Grady, Mrs. Brown, and their families.

There is a terrible irony in the death [of] Mr. Brown, in particular, although she isn't charged with that, because Kathy's whole life, unlike mine, by the way, has been governed by devotion to black people and more largely to what we call the Third World. Again, a term I don't normally use but I recognize many do.

I disagreed with her on many things, including her devotion to the black people of the world and to the Third World, but I have to recognize it was an honest feeling, deeply felt, and although it may seem strange in its context, the highest level of idealism. As I say, I recognize the context.

The public conception of Kathy as a "terrorist" which did dominate the courts, the prosecution, the public, the newspapers, everyone, however unjustified, is now changing. I think that even those who disagree with Kathy's views and are very angry about her involvement in this particular situation recognize her humanity. I'll be through in a second.

I have given to the Court today two statements that sort of reflect this new conception of her. One letter, from a former lawyer who opposed me, an Assistant United States Attorney, some forty years ago, quite a religious man, I see, says, "I want you to know, however, that I constantly pray for you and all your family including Kathy who behaved so nobly and courageously during the past few months. You can be proud of that." I haven't seen this man forty or fifty years. I think I remember him.

Another letter is from a friend who argued recently in the United States Supreme Court. We had a bitter argument in the Supreme Court but this is a nice ending. I don't want to indicate—well it's perfectly obvious it came from the court of the Solicitor General.

This brings me to the end. I am confident that when that time comes, Kathy will make the great contributions to society with the humanity that she has and with the kind of devotion that people have always shown to her and she to them.

I want to thank Your Honor for allowing me in this difficult situation, a father who happens to be a lawyer, to say these few words. Thank you." *People v. Katherine Boudin*, Rockland County, 1981.

Leonard also formally requested that it be stricken from the record that the Boudin family was dysfunctional—and that Leonard and Jean lived separate lives. John Castellucci, interview.

338   "pull every string" Leonard Boudin, papers.

340   Lordie: Anonymous guards, interviews.

The guards were initially hostile to Elaine Lord: they had been a law unto themselves. Some male guards had fathered babies both with a prisoner and with a female guard, whose jealousy endangered the safety of the prisoner. Sex was traded for cigarettes, drugs, and cosmetics. Under Elaine Lord's rules, serious relationships between prisoners and administrators were not illegal, as long as authorities were made aware of them. Anonymous guards, interviews.

340   Sister Elaine Roulet: She supported her innovative programs for children of Bedford mothers with a thrift shop and toil around the clock. In later years after the children's programs were rolling, she turned her unswerving attentions to women at Bedford Hills who were criminally insane.

340   Kathy arrived at Bedford Hills: Except for steam hissing from an exhaust pipe, a sentry, and a car backing out of the parking lot, there were no signs of life. Judith Clark was trapped somewhere behind the brick walls with more than five hundred unhappy women. Judith had reported life here a marginal improvement, despite solitary confinement and extra guards. One prisoner serving a short term later remonstrated with herself for cowardly self-pity every time she heard Judith laugh. Kathy and Judith would argue for hours such questions as whether or not they were political prisoners. It had to gall Kathy to argue with Judith and to defend herself as the least committed, least "heavy," least revolutionary member of the group.

340   Kathy's allotted prison clothes: sources: Anonymous guards, interviews; Jean Harris, *They Always Call Us Ladies: Stories from Prison* (New York: Scribner's, 1988).

342   Kathy heard a woman sobbing: Kathy Boudin, "An Approach to Literacy: A Study at Bedford Hills Prison for Women," Apr. 20, 1989. Submitted in partial fulfillment of the requirements for the degree of master of arts, Vermont College of Norwich University.

In her master's thesis (excerpted in the *Harvard Education Review*), Kathy wrote about the depressing state of literacy education in prison. The thesis is laden with dutiful academic phrases, such as "meaning-driven" and "implement an alternative model of adult literacy." A few personal words dot the text: the most striking is "depressing." It must have been a relief to admit sad feelings in formal prose, if only to recall her trajectory from teacher's aide to teaching star.

342   schedule visitors one after another: Kathy Boudin, conversation, 1996.

342   Bernardine was "pissed off": Leonard Boudin, papers.

343 "forgetting" Chesa's visits: Paul Mattick, interview.

343 "I hate you": Jean Harris, interview, 1997.

344 Chesa blamed himself: Chesa Boudin, speech to the Osborne Society, Times Square Hotel, July 14, 2003.

344 early signs of autism: Connie Brown, interview.

344 admission to the general population: Juanita Diaz-Cotto, *Latina and Latino Prison Politics* (New York: State University of New York Press, 1996).

344 an intimate relationship: Anonymous guards, interviews; Jonah Raskin, interview, 1995.

346 Kathy cut ties: Bryn Mawr College public relations office.

346 first day as teacher's aide: Boudin, *An Approach to Literacy.*

347 "Our Play": Boudin, *An Approach to literacy.*

348 Chesa asked his father: David Gilbert, "Imprisoned Fatherhood," Fortune Society newsletter #2, June 1994.

348 "Sunday, after our meeting": courtesy Jean Boudin, Leonard Boudin, files.

21: *Everything I Know About the Law*

351 unusual father-son relationship: Henry Sailer, interview; Roberts Owen, interview.

352 Eleanor Stein: Jeff Jones, Eleanor Stein conversations, 1992.

352 Bernardine had made the most visible transformation: Bernardine existed in a state of adroit denial: she gave no interviews about the excesses of the past such as her extolling of Charles Manson's murders and eating the entrails of his victims, which she told friends now "embarrassed her." A feature article in *Chicago Magazine* quoted her only about such issues as whether or not to have a midlife face-lift.

352 Bill Ayers said that raising three fine boys: Bill Ayers, speech, Manhattan, and conversation, 1994.

352 amnesia about violent actions: Harvey Klehr, interview, 2001.

354 high-school classmates' letters: Courtesy Jean Boudin, Leonard Boudin, papers.

355 "Life has become more meaningful": Eva Heyn, "Female Inmates Fight Stigma of AIDS," Gannett suburban newspapers.

355 abandoning Chesa: Leonard Boudin, papers.

356 *New York Times* obituary: The following day, a *New York Times* editorial praised a "teacher and meticulous craftsman buttressing unfashionable views (against the Vietnam War, for example) with relentless spade work into unread official documents."

The editorial concluded that in recent years Stone had "more harshly condemned abuses in Communist states than he did successive Republican Presidents—a fitting coda for a great dissident who disputed all the tidy dogmas about human behavior."

356 "He clapped three times": Paul Mattick, interview.

356 Leonard was forced to write: Leonard Boudin, papers.

357 Angolans were giggling: Sherri Wertheimer, interviews.

Leonard and Victor also represented Chile under the revolutionary Allende. They had represented the bank of Iran when "the good guys" took over. When they were kicked out, Leonard and Victor represented "the bad guys" for a brief time through the public nightmare of the hostage crisis. They represented Greece under Papandreou. They never quite landed China. Jules Lobell, interview.

357 Thanksgiving Day: Jean Boudin, interviews.

357 "Everything I know about the law": Bernardine Dohrn at Leonard Boudin memorial service.

357 "Ding, dong, the witch is dead": Judy Levine, conversation.

358 "Great Spirit": Corliss Lamont at Leonard Boudin memorial service.

358 Jean shared her bed: Helena Kennedy at Leonard Boudin Memorial service.

358 "the big player": Lucille Perlman.

360 uncashed check: Sherri Wertheimer, interview.

360 Kathy asked for a divorce: Leonard Boudin, papers.

362 circuit court judge: In July 1992, Michael wrote a judicial opinion siding with waiters at a restaurant in Puerto Rico. The owner of Tango was paying less than minimum wages because he was factoring tips into his wages. It was illegal, because the owner had not obtained waiters' consent.

On February 27, 1993, Michael sided with a big HMO company challenged for monopolistic practices by a smaller company. He began the story of the conflict:

> In simpler days, health care comprised a doctor, a patient, and sometimes a hospital, but the Norman Rockwell era of medicine has given way to a new world of diverse and complex insurance and provider arrangements. One of the more successful innovations is the HMO which acts as both the insurer and the provider. The specific conflict arose when the bigger HMO added an exclusivity cause (AND more pay) to contracts with its doctors. Michael decided the exclusivity clause was not monopolistic. He compared the doctors to "every distributor or retailer who agreed with a manufacturer to handle only one brand of television or bicycle."

363 campaign for Kathy's clemency: Roz Baxandall said it was a done deal. She had it from a sociology professor named Gilda Schwerner, who had it from Judith Clark, who was drawing closer to Kathy. Judith had written a letter to the Fortune Society newsletter favoring nonviolence.

363 Precious Bedell: Precious and Kathy were working for Ph.D.s, taking poetry classes, and running parenting classes for new mothers. Precious spoke in dramatic religious terms of the daughter she had murdered. "I pray and pray and I believe she forgives me." The actress Glenn Close, who lived near the prison, wrote a letter to authorities asking for Precious to be released. Glenn Close declared she would trust her own daughter to her friend Precious's care.

364 "Not hoping, expecting": Victor analyzed the politics of the situation. First, so far they had heard nothing from Governor Cuomo. Maybe because the governor had not wanted to give a negative Christmas present to the widows of policemen who had collected some five thousand signatures protesting clemency for Kathy. On the other hand, Victor said maybe Cuomo's silence was bad. To announce such a radical pardon at the end of Cuomo's term would make it very conspicuous.

On the plus side, the governor had not carried Westchester County and had no known plans to stay in politics.

367 slugged her in the face: *Vancouver* Magazine, Oct. 1998.

368 Chesa's junior year in Chile: Victor Rabinowitz, interview.

370 Kathy soon invited me to Bedford Hills: Kathy Boudin, Bedford Hills Prison, 1997.

370 one of Clinton's last acts: Friends of Susan Rosenberg were petitioning President Clinton to pardon her. She'd been captured in May 1985. Authorities believe that she had also been a participant in the jailbreak of Assata Shakur and that she had been in Nyack and escaped from the Brinks robbery.

Rosenberg had first been arrested in 1979 for assaulting a court officer during a melee at the trial of a Puerto Rican terrorist leader named William Morales.

After Brinks, she was sentenced by a federal judge to fifty-eight years in prison for possession of firearms and explosives. Rosenberg told supporters who rose when she entered the courtroom and raised clenched fists, "We were busted because we vacillated on our politics." John Castellucci, *The Big Dance: The Untold Story of Weatherman Kathy Boudin and the Terrorist Family That Committed the Brinks Robbery Murders* (New York: Dodd Mead, 1986); John Castellucci, interviews; Susan Rosenberg, trial transcripts.

371 a high-powered lawyer: Victor Rabinowitz, interview.

372 Senator Charles Schumer: Erica Spellman, conversation, 1998.

372 she looked stunned: Minutes of Parole Board Hearing, Initial Appearance of Kathy Boudin 84G0171, State of New York Executive Department Division of Parole.

377 Elaine Lord punished Kathy: Victor Rabinowitz, interview.

383 seemed likely to Chesa Boudin: speech to the Osborne Society, Times Square Hotel, July 14, 2003.

Select Bibliography

Books

Adamic, Louis. *The Story of Class Violence in America*. New York: Viking, 1931.

Alpert, Jane. *Growing Up Underground: Autobiography of a Former Radical Fugitive*. New York: William Morrow, 1981.

Aptheker, Bettina. *The Morning Breaks*. New York: International Publishers, 1974.

The Autobiography of Malcolm X. New York: Ballantine Books, 1973.

Ayers, Bill. *A Kind and Just Parent: The Children of Juvenile Court*. Boston: Beacon Press, 1997.

————. *Fugitive Days: A Memoir*. Boston: Beacon Press, 2001.

Bentley, Eric, ed. *Thirty Years of Treason: Excerpts from Hearings Before the House Committee on Un-American Activities*. New York: Viking, 1971.

Berrigan, Daniel, S.J. *They Call Us Dead Men: Reflections on Life and Conscience*. New York: Macmillan, 1966.

Boudin, Jean. *Some of the Parts: Poems*. Boston: Pomegranate Press, 1982.

Boudin, Jean, and Lillian Morrison. *Miranda's Music: Poems*. New York: Thomas Y. Crowell, 1968.

Boudin, Kathy. *Breaking the Walls of Silence: AIDS and Women in a New York State Maximum Security Prison*, by the members of the ACE Program, AIDS Counseling and Education of the Bedford Hills Correctional Facility (including Kathy Boudin) with a foreword by Whoopi Goldberg. Woodstock, N.Y.: Overlook Press, 1998.

Boudin, Kathy, Brian Glick, Eleanor Raskin, and Gustin Reichbach. *The Bust Book: What to Do Till the Lawyer Comes* (eds. 1–4). New York: Grove Press, 1970.

Boudin, Louis B. *Government by Judiciary*, vols. 1 and 2. New York: William Godwin, 1932.

Boudin, Sara. *The Unmarried Mother in Our Society: A Frank and Constructive Approach to an Age-Old Problem*. New York: Farrar, Straus, and Young, 1954.

Buhle, Paul, Mari-Jo Buhle, and Dan Georgokas. *Encyclopedia of the American Left*. New York: Garland Publishing, Inc., 1990.

Castellucci, John. *The Big Dance: The Untold Story of Weatherman Kathy Boudin and the Terrorist Family That Committed the Brinks Robbery Murders*. New York: Dodd Mead, 1986.

Collier, Peter, and David Horowitz. *Destructive Generation: Second Thoughts About the Sixties*. New York: Summit Books, 1989.

Cook, Fred. *The F.B.I. Nobody Knows*. New York: Macmillan, 1964.

Cottrell, Robert. *Izzy: A Biography of I. F. Stone*. New Brunswick, N.J.: Rutgers University Press, 1992.

Daley, Robert. *Target Blue: An Insider's View of the N.Y.P.D.* New York: Delacorte Press, 1973.

Davis, Angela. *Angela Davis: An Autobiography*. New York: Random House, 1974.

Deloach, Cartha D. "Deke." *Hoover's FBI: The Inside Story by Hoover's Trusted Lieutenant*. Washington, D.C.: Regnery Publishing, 1995.

Denenberg, Barry. *The True Story of J. Edgar Hoover and the FBI*. New York: Scholastic, 1993.

Du Bois, W. E. B. *The Souls of Black Folk*. New York: Blue Heron, 1953.

Ellsberg, Daniel. *Secrets: A Memoir of Vietnam and the Pentagon Papers*. New York: Viking Penguin, 2002.

Fariello, Griffin. *Red Scare: Memories of the American Inquisition—An Oral History*. New York: W. W. Norton, 1995.

FBI. The Venona Papers. Maryland.

Fettamen, Ann. *Thrashing*. San Francisco: Straight Arrow Books, 1970.

Foner, Phillip S., ed. *Paul Robeson Speaks*. New York: Citadel Press, 1978.

Frankfort, Ellen. *Kathy Boudin and the Dance of Death*. New York: Stein and Day, 1983.

Gentry, Curt. *J. Edgar Hoover: The Man and the Secrets*. New York: Penguin, 1991.

Goodman, Paul. *The Breakup of Our Camp: Stories 1932–35*. Introduction by Taylor Stoehr. San Francisco: Black Sparrow Press, 1978.

———. *Format and Anxiety*. Edited and introduction by Taylor Stoehr. Autonomedia, 1995.

Gunther, Gerald. *Learned Hand: The Man and the Judge*. New York: Alfred A. Knopf, 1994.

Harris, Jean. *Marking Time*. New York: Charles Scribner's Sons, 1991.

———. *Stranger in Two Worlds*. New York: Macmillan, 1986.

———. *They Always Call Us Ladies: Stories from Prison*. New York: Charles Scribner's Sons, 1988.

Hayden, Tom. *Reunion: A Memoir*. New York: Random House, 1988.

High Times Encyclopedia of Recreational Drugs. New York: Stonehill Publishing, 1978.

Horwitz, Morton J. *The Warren Court and the Pursuit of Justice*. New York: Farrar Strauss, 1998.

Jacobs, Harold. *Weatherman: An Anthology*. New York: Ramparts Press, 1970.

Jacobs, Ron. *The Way the Wind Blew: A History of the Weather Underground*. London and New York: Verso, 1997.

Kempton, Murray. *The Briar Patch: The People of the State of New York v. Lamumba Shakur et al.* New York: E. P. Dutton, 1973.

Kent, Rockwell. *This Is My Own*. New York: Duell, Sloan and Pearce, 1940.

Klehr, Harvey, John Earl Haynes, and Kyrill M. Anderson. *The Soviet World of American Communism*. New Haven, Conn.: Yale University Press, 1998.

Klehr, Harvey, John Earl Haynes, and Fridrikh Igorevich Firsov. *The Secret World of American Communism*. New Haven, Conn.: Yale University Press, 1995.

Knightley, Phillip. *The First Casualty from the Crimea to Vietnam: The War Correspondent as Hero, Propagandist, and Myth Maker*. New York: Harcourt Brace Jovanovich, 1975.

Kovel, Joel. *Red Hunting in the Promised Land: Anticommunism and the Making of America*. New York: Cassel, 1994.

Lamphere, Robert, with Tom Schachtman. *The FBI-KGB War: A Special Agent's Story*. New York: Random House, 1986.

Lazarus, Edward. *Closed Chambers: The First Eyewitness Account of the Epic Struggles Inside the Supreme Court*. New York: Times Books, 1988.

Leary, Timothy. *Flashbacks: A Personal and Cultural History of an Era: An Autobiography*. Boston: Houghton Mifflin, 1983.

McGilligan, Patrick, and Paul Buhle. *Tender Comrades: A Backstory of the Hollywood Blacklist*. New York: St. Martin's Press, 1977.

Mailer, Norman. *Miami and the Siege of Chicago: An Informal History of the Republican and Democratic Conventions of 1968.* New York: Signet Books, 1968.

Malkin, Maurice. *Return to My Father's House: A Memoir.* New York: Arlington House, 1972.

Medwick, Cathleen. *Teresa of Avila: The Progress of a Soul.* New York: Alfred A. Knopf, 1999.

Meeropol, Robert. *An Execution in the Family: One Son's Journey.* New York: St. Martin's Press, 2003.

Meeropol, Robert and Michael. *We Are Your Sons: The Legacy of Ethel and Julius Rosenberg.* Boston: Houghton Mifflin, 1975.

Miller, Alice. *The Drama of the Gifted Child: The Search for the True Self.* Originally published as *Prisoners of Childhood.* New York: Basic Books, 1981.

Mitford, Jessica. *The Trial of Dr. Spock.* New York: Alfred A. Knopf, 1969.

Molesworth, Charles. *Marianne Moore: A Literary Life.* New York: Atheneum, 1990.

Monroe, Kristen Renwick. *The Heart of Altruism: Perceptions of a Common Humanity.* Princeton, N.J.: Princeton University Press, 1996.

Morgan, Ted. *A Covert Life: Jay Lovestone: Communist, Anti-Communist, and Spymaster.* New York: Random House, 1999.

Navasky, Victor. *Naming Names.* New York: Viking, 1980.

Oppenheimer, Martin. *The Urban Guerrilla.* Chicago: Quadrangle Books, 1969.

O'Rourke, William. *The Harrisburg 7 and the New Catholic Left.* New York: Thomas Crowell, 1972.

Payne, Cyril. *Deep Cover: An FBI Agent Infiltrates the Radical Underground.* New York: Newsweek Books, 1979.

Powers, Thomas. *Diana: The Making of a Terrorist.* Boston: Houghton Mifflin, 1971.

Quirk, Robert. *Fidel Castro.* New York: W. W. Norton, 1993.

Rabinowitz, Victor. *An Unrepentant Leftist: A Memoir.* Ann Arbor: University of Michigan Press, 1996.

Raskin, Jonah. *Out of the Whale: Growing Up in the American Left: An Autobiography.* New York: Links, 1974.

Sale, Kirkpatrick. *SDS: Ten Years Toward a Revolution.* New York: Random House, 1973.

Shakur, Assata. *Assata: An Autobiography.* London: Zed Books, 1987.

Shanks, Hershel, ed. *The Art and Craft of Judging: The Decisions of Judge Learned Hand.* New York: Macmillan, 1968.

Skvorecky, Josef. *The Cowards.* New York: Grove Press, 1970.

Stein, Judith E. *I Tell My Heart: The Art of Horace Pippin.* Philadelphia: Pennsylvania Academy of Fine Arts, 1993.

Stern, Susan. *With the Weathermen: The Personal Journey of a Revolutionary Woman.* Garden City, N.Y.: Doubleday, 1975.

Stone, I. F. *The Hidden History of the Korean War.* New York: Monthly Review Press, 1952.

Wells, Tom. *Wild Man: The Life and Times of Daniel Ellsberg.* New York: St. Martin's Press, 2001.

Westwood, Howard C. *Covington and Burling, 1919–1984.* Washington, D.C.: Covington and Burling, 1986.

Whitman, Alden. *American Reformers.* New York: H. W. Wilson Company, 1985.

Williams, Evelyn A. *Inadmissible Evidence: The Story of the African-American Trial Lawyer Who Defended the Black Liberation Army.* Chicago: Lawrence Hill Books, 1993.

Yarbrough, Tinsley E. *John Marshall Harlan: Great Dissenter of the Warren Court.* Oxford: Oxford University Press, 1992.

Periodicals and Unpublished Manuscripts

Boudin, Jean. "Jean Boudin Talks About Her Fugitive Daughter." *Ms.* magazine, Aug. 1976.

Boudin, Kathy. "An Approach to Literacy: A Study at Bedford Hills Prison for Women," master's thesis, Vermont College of Norwich University, Apr. 20, 1989.

————. *Harvard Educational Review,* Guttman Library, excerpt from master's thesis, 1990.

————. "Sometimes It's the Small Things" (poem by Kathy Boudin). *Fortune Society News,* Feb. 4, 1994.

Boudin, Leonard. "History of Political Conspiracy Cases," 1971. Special Collections, Harvard Law School Library.

Boudin, Michael. "The Free Exercise of Religion Clause of the Constitution: A Study of Supreme Court Interpretation Since the Civil War." Senior honors thesis, Pusey Library, Harvard University, 1961.

————. "Memoirs in a Classical Style (of John Marshall Harlan)." *University of Pennsylvania Law Review,* 1984.

————. *Stanford Law Review,* Jan. 1995, book review of Learned Hand biography by Gerald Gunther (Alfred A. Knopf, 1994).

Cantarow, Ellen. "Kathy Boudin in Jail." *Mademoiselle,* Apr. 1984.

Castellucci, John. Reporter's notes including unpublished interviews with Murray Kempton, 1981–1985.

Collier, Peter, and David Horowitz. "Doing It: The Inside Story of the Rise and Fall of the Weather Underground." *Rolling Stone,* Sept. 30, 1982.

Eastman, Max. "The Chicago Conventions." *The Liberator,* 1919.

Fields, Adelaide, ed. Childrens' Better Health Institute, Indianapolis, Ind., *Child Life* magazine, 1954, 55.

Gilbert, David. "Anatomy of a Traitor." *Resistance* magazine, Apr. 1983.

————. Book reviews, *New York Press,* 1989–1992.

————. Self-criticism of the Brinks robbery in Nanuet. (It was seized from Silvia Baraldini when she was finally arrested thirteen months after the Rockland County robbery in November 1982. On it she wrote, "What a male chauvinist pig.")

————. *Fortune Society* newsletter #2. "Imprisoned Fatherhood," 1998.

Gussow, Mel. "The House on West 11th Street." *New York Times,* City Section, Mar. 5, 2000.

Ignatiev, Noel, Beth Henson, and John Garvey. *Race Traitor: Treason to Whiteness Is Loyalty to Humanity,* published by the New Abolitionist Inc., no. 10, winter 1999: "Renew the Legacy of John Brown, Dorchester, Massachusetts."

Lazarre, Jane. "Conversations with Kathy Boudin." *Village Voice,* Feb. 14, 1984.

Lincoln Detox pamphlet: "Dope Is Death," 1978.

Lowenthal, John, Venona and Alger Hiss. *Intelligence and National Security,* vol. 15, no. 5, autumn 2000.

Phillips, Charlotte, et al. Kathy Boudin newsletters 1981ff, by the Friends of Kathy Boudin Committee.

Phillips, Charlotte, et al. "On Trial: Kathy Boudin."

Wilkes, Paul. "Leonard Boudin: The Left's Lawyer's Lawyer." *New York Times Magazine,* Nov. 14, 1971.

Films

Leonard Boudin Memorial Service, videotape: Jan. 1990.

The Weather Underground, a documentary by Sam Green and Bill Segal, featuring Bill Ayers, Kathleen Cleaver, Bernardine Dohrn, Naomi Jaffe, David Gilbert, Mark Rudd, 2003.

Underground, a documentary by Emile De Antonio, featuring Kathy Boudin, Bernardine Dohrn, Cathlyn Wilkerson, Bill Ayers, and Jeff Jones, 1976, plus author conversations with De Antonio, 1980.

Archives

Federal Bureau of Investigation (FBI) Freedom of Information, Privacy Acts Section, Office of Public and Congressional Affairs, Files: Leonard Boudin, Students for a Democratic Society, Weather Underground, Black Panther Party, Jean Roisman Boudin, I. F. Stone, Diana Oughton, Victor Rabinowitz, Joni Rabinowitz, Ted Gold, Russell Neufield, Terry Robbins.

Madison, Wisconsin, State Historical Society: Carol McEldowney, Papers from Students for a Democratic Society (SDS) community organizing project in Cleveland, Ohio, 1964–1971.

Mickeljohn Archive: The Pentagon Papers Trial of Daniel Ellsberg and Anthony Russo, University of California at Berkeley, courtesy Ann Ginger.

National Lawyers Guild, courtesy Victor Rabinowitz.

New York Landmarks Society.

New York Public Library, I. F. Stone: *I. F. Stone's Weekly,* microfilms.

New York Public Library, Schomburg Center for Research in Black Culture.

Schlesinger Library, Harvard: Virginia Foster Durr papers.

Smithsonian, Archives of American Art: Rockwell Kent papers and Leon Berkowitz papers.

Tamiment Labor Library, New York University.

Temple University Urban Archives: the Leof and Roisman families.

University of Texas at Austin, Harry Ransom Humanities Research Center: Leonard Boudin/Jessica Mitford correspondence and Angus Cameron/Kathy Boudin correspondence.

FBI Tapes

Tyrone Rison testimony against the Black Liberation Army to lighten his own sentence, Sept.–Oct. 1982.

Surveillance tapes:

Black Liberation Army and Acupuncture headquarters, Manhattan, Jan. 1982.

SDS Chicago headquarters, 1968–1970.

Correspondence

Boudin, Jean, correspondence, 1932–1992, and photographs, courtesy Jean Boudin.

Boudin, Jean/Jim Peck correspondence, University of Oregon.

Boudin, Jean, letters, courtesy Robert Carlen Gallery Archives.

Boudin, Jean, letters, courtesy Binnie Klein.

Boudin, Jean/Frances Waldman correspondence, courtesy Ann Waldman.

Boudin, Jean, manuscripts and correspondence, Archives and Special Collections/Fiddlehead Cogswell Collection, Harriet Irving Library, University of New Brunswick.

Boudin, Kathy, correspondence, courtesy Jean Boudin and author's collection.

Boudin, Leonard, letter, courtesy Alan Lelchuk.

Boudin, Leonard, correspondence, case files, calendars: 1932–1989, courtesy Jean Boudin.

Boudin, Leonard, correspondence, files, 1952–1962, courtesy Edith Tiger.

Columbia University Archives: Louis Boudin papers; Emergency Civil Liberties Committee, papers.

Columbia University Oral History Project.

Interview files of: Victor Rabinowitz, Leonard Boudin, David Gilbert, Leni Wildflower.

Legal Proceedings, partial list

LOUIS BOUDIN, ATTORNEY

Supreme Court of the United States, January 31, 1940. *Amalgamated Utility Workers v. Con Ed*. The Supreme Court said that it was up to the National Labor Relations Board—not the courts—to make sure Con Edison was fair to unions.

LEONARD BOUDIN, ATTORNEY

Supreme Court of the United States, October 1957. *Rockwell Kent and Walter Briehl v. John Foster Dulles, Secretary of State*. Leonard won, arguing that the right to travel is a natural right.

United States v. Judith Coplon and *New York State v. Judith Coplon*. Leonard appealed Judith Coplon's two convictions for passing government documents and for stealing them; both convictions were reversed, 1952. The FBI cooked evidence against her.

United States v. Benjamin Spock, et al. Dr. Spock was one of several men accused of conspiring to help young men avoid the draft. Leonard won the case on appeal. The conspirators barely knew each other and they performed their actions in public, frequently at press conferences.

Transcripts of multiple trials of Joanne Chesimard a.k.a. Assata Shakur. The "soul of the Black Liberation Army" was accused of being at the scenes of crimes where policemen were killed. Technical arguments resulted in the dismissal of all charges except those stemming from a shoot-out on the New Jersey Turnpike.

MICHAEL BOUDIN, ATTORNEY AT COVINGTON AND BURLING, AND CIRCUIT COURT JUDGE

U.S. Supreme Court, February 1974. *Pernell v. Southall Realty*. Attorney Michael Boudin won pro bono the rights of a tenant to jury trial.

U.S. Supreme Court, January 1981. *Doe v. Delaware*. Michael Boudin wrote the brief pro bono citing parental rights.

U.S. Supreme Court, January 1972. *The S.E.C. v. Medical Committee for Human Rights*. Michael was one of two authors of the pro bono brief appeal on behalf of the doctors of the Medical Committee for Human Rights. The doctors had sued Dow Chemical to permit a shareholder's request to put to shareholder vote limits on customers' use of the deadly gas napalm.

At Covington and Burling, Michael Boudin was a chief lawyer for AT&T and railroads in many litigations against government regulation, such as U.S. Supreme Court, January 1986. *Louisiana et al. Public Service Commissions v. Federal Communications Commission*.

U.S. Supreme Court, 1983. *United States v. Ptasynski et al*. Michael argued for tax exemptions for Alaskan oil companies.

U.S. Court of Appeals, District of Columbia. *United States v. Baker Hughes et al*. As assistant attorney general, Michael argued for federal regulation of big businesses. For example, in 1990, he challenged the acquisition by an oil-drilling company of a similar company, arguing that it would lessen competition. The Court ruled against the government.

Wessman v. Gittens, 1998. As one of three judges on the powerful U.S. First Circuit Court of Appeals in Boston, Michael wrote his separate opinion, siding with the majority of the Court in the growing judicial clamor against affirmative action. As a result, a young white girl won admission to the prestigious Boston Latin public school.

In his written opinion, Michael dismissed the relevance of a study cited by the proponents of affirmative action, because the study was made in Kansas City, not Boston. He wrote that there was no reason to assume that teacher expectations of minority students would be raised if there were more minority students. He also maintained that affirmative action gives preference to Asian Americans and African-American graduates of private schools—and he believed that neither group was discriminated against or affected by lower teacher expectations. Most important, he wrote that the affirmative action plan failed to meet the "Supreme Court's narrow tailoring requirement."

KATHY BOUDIN (ERRONEOUSLY NAMED KATHERINE BOUDIN IN MANY JUDICIAL DOCUMENTS)
Hearing before commissioners of the New York State Parole Board, August 2001, Freedom of Information Act, New York State, courtesy Ann Crowell.

New York v. Katherine Boudin and Samuel Brown, defendants. Indictment #81-285, October 1981.

New York v. Katherine Boudin, Samuel Brown, Nathaniel Burns, Judith Clark, David Gilbert, Anthony LaBorde, and Donald Weems, defendants. Indictment #81-285, New York State Supreme Court, Rockland County.

New York v. Sekou Odinga, a/k/a Nathaniel Burns and Samuel Brown. Indictment #285/81.

Brown v. U.S. Manhattan Federal Court, March 1982, filed for Sam Brown by David Gilbert.

Jensen v. Times-Mirror Company. Connecticut Federal Court 1982.

Pretrial hearings, *People v. Katherine Boudin,* October 22, 1982.

Letter about Kathy from psychiatrist Roger Gould to Judge David Ritter, 1984.

U.S. v. Shakur. Manhattan Federal Court, May 1983.

Rockland County Probation report at sentencing of Kathy Boudin, April 1984.

Sam Brown's X rays and medical records, courtesy John Castellucci.

People v. Gilbert, Clark, and Weems. Goshen, N.Y., July 20, 1983.

AFFIDAVIT *Boudin v. Thomas.* Manhattan Federal Court, 1981 and March 1982.

Parole Board Hearing, Kathy Boudin, Transcript.

Division of Parole, August 2001; and Transcript, May 2002.

Partial List of Acknowledgments

Jane Alpert
Stanley Aronowitz
Bill Ayers
Richard Babcock
Kit Bakke
Mary Catherine
 Bateson
Roz Baxandall
Bernard Berkowitz
Louise Bernikow
Phil Berrigan

Gwenda Blair and the
 Dick Goldensohn Fund
Liz Bogen
Jean Boudin
Kathy Boudin
Thompson Bradley
David Brind
Connie Brown
Gregory Brown
Susan Brownmiller
Eleanor Brussel

Paul Buhle
Karen Burstein
Alice Carlen
Nancy Carlen
John Castellucci
Marion Castellucci
Alan Colsey, Chief, South
 Nyack-Grand View
 Police Department
Ed Copelan
William Davidon

Emile De Antonio
Eugene Dennis Jr.
Dr. Ronald Dreyer
Karen Durbin
John Ehrenreich
Ronnie Eldridge
Daniel Ellsberg
Joan Fairman
Judge Shirley Fingerhood
Phil Foner
Francine Fontaine
Leon Friedman
Martin Garbus
Fred Gardner
Jennie Simon Gardner
Barbara Garson
David Gilbert
Ruth Gilbert
Kristin Glenn
Sally Goodman
Joanne Grant
Sam Gross
Bertram Gross
Elliot Gross, M.D.
John Hancher
Nancy Hardin
Belle Harper
Jean Harris
Eleanor Harte
Leslie Hartley Gise, M.D.
Norma Hill
Noel Ignatiev
Rita Jensen
Jeff Jones
Susan Husserl Kapit
Sandy Katz
Martin Kenner
Harvey Klehr
Binnie Klein
Kenneth Koch
Andrew Kopkind
Richard Kostelanitz
Ron Kuby
William Kunstler

Doriane Kurtz
Robert Lamphere, FBI
Elinor Langer
Alan Lelchuk
Judy Levin
Jules Lobell
Ariel Loewy
Robert Long, FBI
Phil Lopate
Harriet Lyons
Carleton Mabee
Michael Macdonald
Eugene Malkin
Paul Mattick
Donna Mildvan, M.D.
Honor Moore
Frances Murphy
Gary B. Myers
Annie Navasky
Victor Navasky
Jack Newfield
Matthew Nimetz
Paul O'Dwyer
Diane O'Grady
Ed O'Grady Jr.
Wendy Raudenbush
   Omsted
Roberts B. Owen,
   Covington and Burling
Andrew Patner
Marge Piercy
Letty Cottin Pogrebin
Bert Pogrebin
Thomas Powers
Joni Rabinowitz
Marcia Rabinowitz
Victor Rabinowitz
Jonah Raskin
Marcus Raskin
Charley Reich
Judge Gustin Reichbach
Robin Reisig
Robert Riley
Paul Robeson Jr.

Lila Roisman
Richard Roisman
Anthony Russo
Henry Sailer
Elizabeth St. Clare
Steve Schlesinger
Diane Schulder
Hugh Seidman
John Simon
Michele Slung
Jon Snow
Mary Spock
Brian Stafford,
   Haddonfield Memorial
   High School
Michael Standard
Eleanor Stein
Detective Jim Stewart
Taylor Stoehr
Celia Stone
Esther Roisman Stone
Jeremy Stone
Judy Stone
Gertrude Goheen
   Swain
Stuart Taylor
Mary Thom
Edith Tiger
Milton Viorst
Ann Waldman
Jan Warren
Leonard Weinglass
Joe Weintraub
Cora Weiss
Peter Weiss
Sherry Wertheimer
Martha Ullman West
Joshua White Jr.
Frances Whyatt
Leni Zeigler
   Wildflower
Ellen Winner
Ethan Young
Andrew Zelman

Index

Italicized page numbers indicate photographs.

Photographic Credits

A Note on the Type

Pierre Simon Fournier (1712–1768), who designed the type used in this book, was both an originator and a collector of types. His services to the art of printing were his design of letters, his creation of ornaments and initials, and his standardization of type sizes. His types are old style in character and sharply cut. In 1764 and 1766 he published his *Manuel typographique*, a treatise on the history of French types and printing, on typefounding in all its details, and on what many consider his most important contribution to typography—the measurement of type by the point system.

Composed by North Market Street Graphics,
Lancaster, Pennsylvania
Printed and bound by Berryville Graphics,
Berryville, Virginia
Designed by Anthea Lingeman